Organizations: Theory and Analysis

Organizations: Theory and Analysis

Arthur G. Bedeian
Auburn University

The Dryden Press
Hinsdale, Illinois

lh 1-6

To Lynda,
Kathy, and Tab

Contents

Chapter 4   The Establishment of Organizational Goals   77

Chapter 5   The Nature and Measurement of Organizational Effectiveness   105

Chapter 6   The Organization and Its External Environment   127

Contents

Contents

Preface

Organizations, the dominant form of institution in our modern society, are a fundamental part of our existence, pervading all aspects of contemporary life. As the title indicates, this book is about organizations. To be more specific, the intent of the present undertaking is to provide a general survey of contemporary knowledge in the areas of "organization theory and analysis" in the hope of enhancing our current understanding of organizations and assisting in the development of the perspective necessary for meeting the demands of today's organizational world.

Although an awareness of the importance of organization dates to the beginning of written history, it has only been within the last two decades that the study of organizations has emerged as an independent field of investigation. Indeed, as will be noted in Chapter 1, thirty-five to forty years ago, the structure of formal organizations was little more than a peripheral interest of a small number of economists and social anthropologists. The emergence of self-designated "organization theorists" is a recent occurrence. Consequently, organization theory is largely an emerging discipline a field of research at the beginning of its scientific development.

Acknowledging the present growing interest in the study of organizations, the general impetus for undertaking this book was the realization that a major void existed in terms of teaching materials devoted exclusively to organization theory. In the past, instructors of organization theory have had few alternatives but to adapt to their own purposes course materials designed for other areas, ever striving to minimize the resulting overlap in coverage among courses. This has largely continued to be the case despite the fact that several texts have only recently been released under the general title "organization theory." With only minor exceptions, an examination of these works reveals that they are generally texts on organizational behavior and that frequently less than half of their contents deals with "pure" organization theory.

It is the explicit intent of this book to break from tradition and to deal exclusively with "pure" organization theory. A specific attempt has been made to combine both a theoretical and a practical perspective, in the belief that each, by itself, is insufficient. An effort has been made to analyze and integrate the major findings upon which current organization theory is based. To achieve this end, superficial "pronouncements of truth" have been purposefully avoided in favor of providing the reader with an informed understanding of the fragmented and often conflicting results of the available research in many of the topic areas to be discussed.

An undertaking such as that represented by this book inevitably involves the work of many people besides its author. This book is no exception. To my students who have taught *me* much by their reactions to my work (positive, negative, and occasionally indifferent), I express my sincere appreciation. Of this group, the comments of Billye Asherbranner, Emlen M. Bailey, Raymond A. Drogan, Dennis R. Langlois, Donald W. Phillips, Charles R. Schwarz, Dale P. Scruggs, Jan Crow Scruggs, and Victor E. Sower were especially helpful. Their assistance in the preparation of the Instructor's Manual that accompanies the book is gratefully acknowledged.

I am indebted to Achilles A. Armenakis and Hubert S. Feild, Jr., for the many long discussions we had over what began as a collaborative project. Of my other colleagues here at Auburn, I am particularly grateful to William H. Holley, Jr., and William F. Giles for contributing ideas and moral support and to Judith S. Meadows, my graduate assistant, whose help in the final stages of manuscript preparation was indispensable.

Elsewhere, special appreciation is due Jody W. Fry of Texas A&M University, Bernard C. Reimann of Cleveland State University, and Richard J. Ward of Bowling Green State University for their beneficial suggestions and criticisms. They each read the entire manuscript and were responsible for revisions in several places. The comments of Carl R. Anderson of the University of North Carolina at Chapel Hill, H. Kirk Downey of Oklahoma State University, Richard M. Steers of the University of Oregon, and Neil Snyder of the University of Virginia are also gratefully acknowledged.

At Dryden Press, Anne Boynton-Trigg and Anita A. Constant have guided me past pitfalls too numerous to list, and Madelyn Roesch has been a copy editor of rare skill and vigilance. I would like to thank Bernice Gordon, project editor, and Alan Wendt, designer, for their conscientiousness and support. I also greatly appreciate the work of Ann Congdon, indexer, and Flora Foss, Judy Lary, and Wanda Giles, proofreaders.

Finally, I am especially grateful to the staff of the Manuscript Preparation Center of the School of Business at Auburn University. Theresa P. Briscoe and Peggy A. St. John typed endless manuscripts and saw to it that numerous other details were superbly handled. Bess E. Yellen read every chapter as it was prepared and not only gave continued and much appreciated encouragement but provided invaluable editorial assistance.

Arthur G. Bedeian

Auburn University
January 1980

Introduction

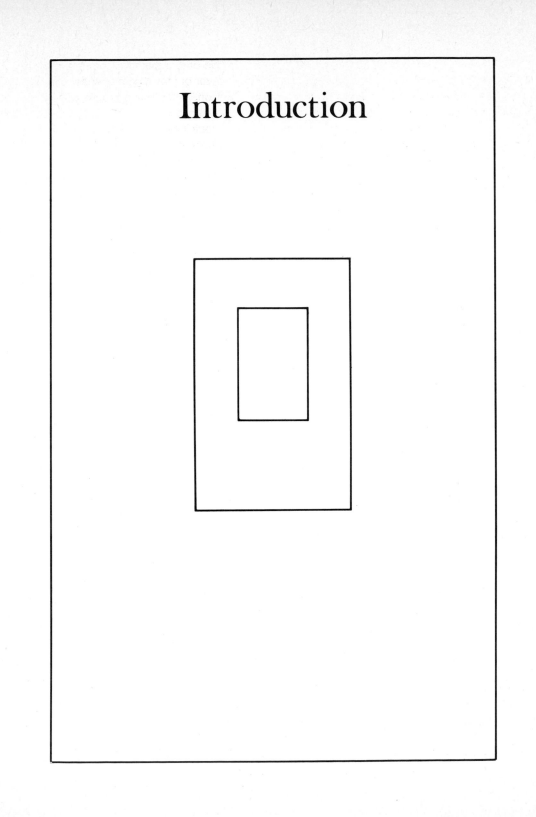

Introduction

Chapter 1

While much of recorded history chronicles changes in organizational forms (for example, nations, city states, governments, churches, and military empires), the systematic accumulation and analysis of knowledge of organization is largely an outgrowth of the late nineteenth and twentieth centuries. The dramatic growth in the number, size, and significance of organizations over that time period is a product of the development of an increasingly complex society that requires an equally increased understanding of complex organization phenomena.

As an applied science, the study of organization is an emerging discipline. It is a field of research at the beginning of its scientific development. Thirty-five to forty years ago, the structure of formal organizations was largely nothing more than a peripheral interest of a small number of economists and social anthropologists. The emergence of self-designated "organization theorists" has only occurred in the last two decades. Without question, the most important contributions of this group of theorists lie in the yet unexplored future. Indeed, as Caplow has so accurately noted, organization theory "still stands somewhere between folklore and science."[1] While this observation was made over fifteen years ago, it disappointingly still stands true today.

What Are Organizations?

Organizations have been viewed from many perspectives. Depending upon the background and interests of the investigators, the elements and characteristics of organizations that are emphasized vary greatly. There does, however, appear to be some agreement on the fact that organizations generally develop as instruments for attaining specific goals and are likely to emerge in situations where people recognize a common or complementary advantage that can best be served through collective, as opposed to individual, action. Thus, by its very nature, organization implies an integrating and structuring of activities directed toward goal accomplishment.

---

[1] T. E. Caplow, *Principles of Organization* (New York: Harcourt, Brace & World, 1964), p. 3.

Several features or attributes of organizations can therefore be recognized.

1. *Organizations are social institutions (entities) composed of sets of persons with established patterns of interaction.*
2. *Organizations develop to achieve specific goals.* Therefore, organizations are social creations that require order and cooperation.
3. *Organizations are consciously coordinated and deliberately structured.* Activities are differentiated according to some logical pattern. Coordination of these inter-dependent subtasks requires the assignment of authority and the communication of duties.
4. *Organizations are social instruments possessing relatively identifiable boundaries and existing on a relatively permanent basis.* While this final point is perhaps less clear than were those that precede it, the identification of fixed boundaries (for instance, the distinction between members and nonmembers) and continuity (that is, existence and identity over time) provide a conceptual framework for the study of organizational activity.

Thus, when we speak of organizations in this book, we refer to: (1) a consciously coordinated and deliberately structured social entity; (2) composed of sets of persons with established patterns of interaction; (3) possessing relatively identifiable boundaries and existing on a relatively continuous basis; (4) having been developed to achieve a specific goal or goals.

Organizations as Social Systems

In the preceding definition, organizations were variously referred to as "social institu-tions," "social entities," and "social instruments." Each of these phrases reflects the essential social character of human organization. As such, organizations are typically referred to under the broader rubric of "social systems." For our purposes, a *system* may be defined as "a set of *components* surrounded by a *boundary* which accepts *inputs* from some other system and discharges *outputs* into another system"[2] (see Figure 1–1). As living systems, organizations are by definition "open" systems. That is, they receive inputs from and discharge outputs into their surrounding environment. Inputs are those messages or stimuli that trigger the internal components of a system to perform those activities for which the system was designed. Such inputs may take the form of people, materials, money, and/or information. These inputs are then acted upon (that is, transformed) into a variety of outputs which are subsequently returned to the external environment in the form of products, goods, and services. Systems, and hence organizations, are thus involved in a never-ending exchange process with

[2]F. K. Berrien, "A General Systems Approach to Social Taxonomy, "in *People, Groups, and Organizations,* ed. B. P. Indik and F. K. Berrien (New York: Teachers College Press, Columbia University, 1968), p. 111.

Chapter 1

Figure 1–1 *Basic Systems Model*

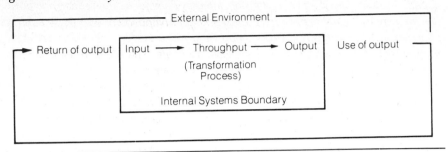

their environment. As Porter, Lawler, and Hackman note, the two most important aspects of this exchange process are:

1. *the fact that different characteristics or attributes of organizations do have a mutual interdependence with other attributes and cannot be regarded as completely separate and independent features and*
2. *the fact that organizations are in a constant exchange interaction with—receiving input from and discharging output into—an uncertain environment.*[3]

These two aspects serve to underline the important point that organizations are located in continuously changing and uncertain environments; they can survive only so long as they are capable of producing some output that can be exchanged for the necessary resources required both to obtain new inputs *and* to maintain themselves in operating order. While this will be a central theme of each of the chapters to follow, it will be discussed in depth in Chapter 6, "The Organization and Its External Environment."

Organization Character

As living systems, organizations exhibit a tendency to grow and change and, in short, to take on a momentum of their own. In so doing, organizations become "infused with value" and develop a unique self, a distinctive identity, that is referred to as *organization character.* According to Selznick, this special character is a historical, integrated, functional, dynamic product that is essential for the transformation of an organization from a mere technical arrangement into a social system capable of evolving and adapting to the demands of an uncertain and changing environment.[4] Selznick makes this point by stating that

---

[3]L. W. Porter, E. E. Lawler, and J. R. Hackman, *Behavior in Organizations* (New York: McGraw-Hill, 1975), p. 99.
[4]P. Selznick, *Leadership in Administration* (Evanston, Ill.: Row, Peterson, 1957), pp. 38–42.

the integrity of an enterprise goes beyond efficiency, beyond organization forms and procedures, even beyond group cohesion. Integrity combines organization and policy. It is the unity that emerges when a particular orientation becomes so firmly a part of group life that it colors and directs a wide variety of attitudes, decisions, and forms of organization, and does so at many levels of experience. The building of integrity is part of what we have called the "institutional embodiment of purpose" and its protection is a major function of leadership. [5]

The major issue evident in the above is that organizations are not just technical instruments but possess social properties (distinctive personalities and character traits) that provide them with unique identities and that serve to further define the overall organization process. Thus, General Electric is associated with "Progress is our most important product," United Airlines with "Friendly skies," and Avis with "We try harder." In each case, the social properties of the organizations in question are caught up in the character they are attempting to project, which serves to effectively relate the organization to the wider society of which it is a part.

The Emergence of Large-Scale Organizations

The emergence of large-scale organizations over the last century has hardly gone unnoticed. Their pervasiveness in present-day society is clearly responsible for several dominant social trends: in the United States the typical adult is an employee, rather than self-employed; the individual employee is a member of a large organization, be it industrial, governmental, educational, retail, communications, financial, or even agricultural, which in turn is administered by other employees. Similar patterns have been reported for other countries such as Great Britain and Australia.[6] The predominance of these trends in the United States is shown in Tables 1–1 and 1–2.

As can be seen in Table 1–1, in the United States there has been a steady trend away from self-employment almost without interruption for at least the last three-quarters of a century. In 1900, a full third of the civilian labor force was self-employed. In contrast, by 1977 the percentage of self-employed persons had decreased to roughly a quarter of this proportion. A large share of this decline can be explained by the corresponding drop in agricultural employment. In the same period (1900 to 1977) the proportion of farm employees in the civilian labor force dropped from almost 39 percent to just under 4 percent. It is, nevertheless, significant that fewer than 9 out of every 100 workers are self-employed, with those remaining being employees in organizations of one type or other.

---

[5]Ibid., pp. 138–139.

[6]S. J. Prais, *The Evolution of Giant Firms in Britain* (Cambridge: Cambridge University Press, 1976); and R. D. Lansbury and P. Gilmour, *Organisations: An Australian Perspective* (Melbourne: Longman Cheshire Pty. Ltd., 1977), p. 12.

Table 1-1 *Percentage of the U.S. Civilian Labor Force Self-Employed, 1900–1977*

Year	Labor Force (in thousands)	Total Self-Employed (in thousands)	Percentage Self-Employed
1900	29,073	9,679	33.3
1910	38,167	10,845	28.4
1920	41,614	10,919	26.2
1930	48,830	11,258	23.1
1940	53,011	10,870	20.5
1950	59,643	10,415	17.5
1960	69,877	9,169	13.1
1970	82,049	7,027	8.6
1977	90,546	7,576	8.4

Sources: Used by permisssion from S. Lebergott, *Manpower in Economic Growth: The American Record since 1900* (New York: McGraw-Hill, 1964), Table A–4, p. 513. Also from U.S. Department of Commerce, Bureau of the Census, *Historical Statistics of the United States: Colonial Times to 1970* (Washington, D.C.: U.S. Government Printing Office, 1975), p. 127, and *Statistical Abstract of the United States,* 99th ed. (Washington, D.C.: U.S. Government Printing Office, 1978), p. 407.

Table 1-2 *Percentage Breakdown of U.S. Workers by Size of Employing Organization, 1975*[a]

Size of Firm (number of employees)	Percentage of Total Work Force Employed	Percentage of Total Number of Employing Organizations
0–3	.04	.51
4–9	.09	.25
10–19	.09	.11
20–49	.13	.07
50–99	.10	.03
100–249	.13	.02
250–499	.10	.005
500–999	.09	.003
1,000 and over	.23	.002
Total Number of Workers	69,123,850	
Total Number of Employing Organizations		4,033,156

Source: U.S. Department of Labor, Bureau of Labor Statistics, *Employment and Wages, First Quarter, 1976* (Springfield, Va.: National Technical Information Service, 1979), pp. 548–549.

[a]Organizations here refers to units reporting employment and wage data for workers covered by state unemployment insurance laws and for federal civilian workers covered by the program of unemployment compensation for federal employees. This includes virtually all private nonagricultural employees, all federal employees, and almost 80 percent of all state employees. However, only 15 percent of local government employees and only 4 percent of workers engaged in agricultural production activities are included.

Introduction

Information on the influence of large-scale organizations on employment patterns is presented in Table 1–2. As is obvious, of the total number of employing organizations, a relatively small number of firms provide employment for most of the work force. Indeed, 3 percent of the employing organizations account for some 55 percent of worker employment. Or, to put it differently, the odds are greater than one out of two that an individual works for an organization that employs 100 or more people.

In sum, it is evident that large-scale enterprises have become the characteristic form of organization in an "employee society."[7] Their dominance has become so complete that, as Mason contends, "to suggest a drastic change in the scope or character of [their] activity is to suggest a drastic alteration in the structure of society."[8]

The Case of the Corporation

The extent to which large organizations pervade today's society can be further appreciated by looking at the historical development of the modern corporation. As has been noted by Caplow: "From the foundation in 1791 of the first U.S. manufacturing corporation, The Society for Useful Manufactures of New Jersey, the importance of corporations in this country has increased without interruption."[9] Shortly after the turn of the century (1909), 262,490 corporations existed in the United States. By 1975, their number had multiplied almost eight times to 2,024,000, and their reported income was well over $3 trillion. Today's corporations run the gamut from small, family-dominated enterprises to the world's largest, American Telephone and Telegraph (AT&T), with 660 million shares owned by almost 3 million people. Its $5.3 billion net income in 1978 was equivalent to $14.5 million dollars a day, or over $10,000 every minute. The wealthiest company in the world, AT&T has assets of over $103 billion, more than the combined assets of General Motors, Ford, General Electric, Chrysler, and International Business Machines. Given the nearly one million people on its payroll, managing AT&T is similar in many respects to governing a nation. Indeed, its 1978 operating revenues of $41 billion were greater than the gross domestic products of all but a dozen and a half countries in the world.

While it is true that organizations such as AT&T have not operated without being subjected to what many feel is legitimate criticism, the pervasiveness of their influence seems without question. As Roy has noted: "In human society almost everyone, save the few who live in hermitlike seclusion, belongs to more than one organi-

---

[7]C. Tausky, *Work Organizations: Major Theoretical Perspectives,* 2nd ed. (Itasca, Ill.: Peacock, 1978), p. 2.
[8]E. S. Mason, *The Corporation in Modern Society* (Cambridge, Mass.: Harvard University Press, 1966), p. 1. On this point, see also R. P. Mohan, "The Role of the Large Organization in the Contemporary World," in *Management and Complex Organizations in Comparative Perspective,* ed. R. P. Mohan (Westport, Conn.: Greenwood Press, 1979), pp. xvii–xxxix.
[9]Caplow, *Principles,* p. 229.

zation, and most belong to many. Organizations are as familiar and ubiquitous as people."[10]

Having attained a central position in modern society, large corporations serve as mirrors of the contemporary scene. Their far-ranging influence as powerful social institutions has been summed up well by Miller:

It is the big enterprises which occupy the strategic centers. Most small businessmen, independents, professionals and even farmers gain their livelihood largely as suppliers or as distributors for the large enterprises. It is the large enterprises which establish the price and wage policies of the nation. The pattern of union-management relations is set by the contracts drawn between big labor and big business. Governmental regulations grow up to harness and channel the economic power and practice of large enterprise. The personnel policies adopted by the large industry become the models for the entire industrial society.[11]

The Organizational Milieu

The movement toward large-scale organization is closely related to a variety of contemporary and historical trends. Each has contributed to the development of the social milieu in which today's organizational society exists. An understanding and appreciation of the implications of these trends has become increasingly important as the social environment in which organizations operate becomes increasingly complex.

Population Dynamics

Recent changes in population trends have greatly affected the social environment within which organizations operate. The most recent data available indicate that the world population reached 4.12 billion in 1977 and will double, increasing 1.9 percent a year, to 8.24 billion by 2014.[12] This increase is significant not only in terms of sheer numbers but also with regard to both the location and composition of the world's population. With respect to the United States, which in 1979 accounted for roughly 5.3 percent of the world's total population, or approximately 220 million people (see Table 1–3), the shift from a rural to an urban population has been virtually unceasing since census records were first compiled in 1790. As illustrated in Figure 1–2, almost three-quarters of the U.S. population now lives in large cities and their suburbs. This

---

[10]R. H. Roy, *The Cultures of Management* (Baltimore: Johns Hopkins University Press, 1977), p. 3.

[11]D. C. Miller, "Influence of Technology on Industry," in *Technology and Social Change,* ed. F. R. Allen et al. (New York: Appleton-Century-Crofts, 1957), p. 270.

[12]*Demographic Yearbook 1977,* 29th issue (New York: U.N. Department of International Economic and Social Affairs, 1978), p. 137.

Table 1-3   *The Growth of United States Population, 1790–1979*

Year	Population	Year	Population
1790	3,929,214	1890	62,947,714
1800	5,308,483	1900	75,994,575
1810	7,239,881	1910	91,972,266
1820	9,638,453	1920	105,710,620
1830	12,866,020	1930	122,775,046
1840	17,069,453	1940	131,669,275
1850	23,191,876	1950	150,697,361
1860	31,443,321	1960	178,464,236
1870	39,818,449	1970	203,235,298
1880	50,155,783	1979	220,000,000 (est.)

Sources: U.S. Department of Commerce, Bureau of the Census, *Stastical Abstract of the United States,* 99th ed. (Washington, D.C.: U.S. Government Printing Office, 1978), Table 1, p. 6; miscellaneous Bureau of the Census news releases.

shift in population patterns has contributed to crises evident in nearly all our large urban areas. Housing shortages, transit difficulties, crime, and air and water pollution are all environmental developments that further complicate organizational problems.[13]

Significant changes have also taken place in the composition of the U.S. population. Of particular relevance to the work sphere are Department of Labor employment figures showing that, in 1977, women comprised a record 41 percent of the 97.4 million member civilian labor force (see Figure 1–3). Thus, since 1970 women have accounted for 57 percent of the increase in the working population. In 1977, 48 percent of all adult women were in the labor force, an increase of 10 percent from 1960. In the same period, the proportion of working wives increased from 40 to 46 percent. By 1975, women held 19 percent of all management positions in the United States. The rapid increase in the number of women working (from 18.4 million in 1950 to over 22.5 million in 1960, and 39.3 million in 1977) has raised numerous questions about whether many of our traditional views of organizational governance are outdated. Without doubt, the result of this and similar trends, such as the extension of the mandatory retirement age to 70, carries serious implications for both the present and the future of organizational society.

Education

Increased levels of education among the working population have also resulted in a need for organizational adaptation (see Figure 1–4). At the turn of the century, less

---

[13]F. E. Kast and J. E. Rosenzweig, *Organization and Management: A Systems and Contingency Approach,* 3rd ed. (New York: McGraw-Hill, 1979), p. 14.

Chapter 1

Figure 1-2 *Urban and Rural Population of the U.S., 1790–1970 (in millions)*

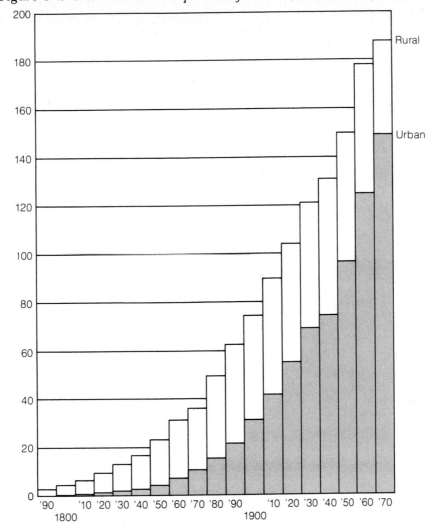

Source: U.S. Department of Commerce, Bureau of the Census, *Historical Statistics of the United States: Colonial Times to 1970,* bicentennial ed. (Washington, D.C.: U.S. Government Printing Office, 1975), Series A 57–72, pp. 11–12.

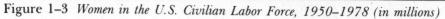

Figure 1–3 *Women in the U.S. Civilian Labor Force, 1950–1978 (in millions)*

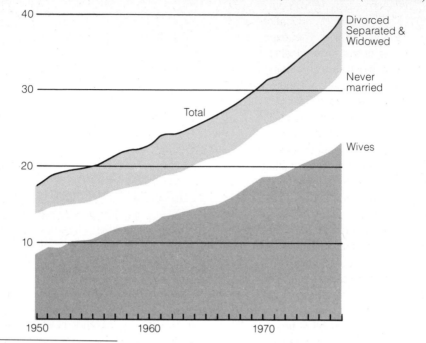

Sources: "Women in the Labor Force," *Road Maps of Industry,* no. 1800 (New York: The Conference Board, 1976); U.S. Department of Commerce, Bureau of the Census, *Statistical Abstract of the United States: 1978,* 99th ed. (Washington, D.C.: U.S. Government Printing Office, 1978), Table 655, p. 404. Used by permission of The Conference Board.

Chapter 1

than 1 out of every 20 persons of college age in the U.S. was enrolled in an institution of higher learning. By 1976, 3 out of every 10 persons of this age were enrolled. Much of today's emphasis on education can be traced to the rapid economic growth that followed World War II. This expansion led to a sharp increase in incomes accompanied by a desire for vertical mobility, necessitating increased levels of education. It also led to significant changes in our values and interests. Philosophically, the belief that a higher education should be available to all became widely accepted and resulted in increases in college enrollments. Further, the GI Bill of Rights provided many veterans with the financial means to obtain a college education. The Vietnam conflict also contributed to increases in enrollment since college deferments were for a time sought as a legal means of avoiding the military draft. More recently, the economic downturn has resulted in many high school graduates continuing their education rather than competing in a weak job market.

The results of this trend are becoming increasingly apparent. By 1970, virtually half of the civilian labor force (compared to 18 percent in 1900, and 31 percent in 1940) could be classified as white-collar workers. Fully half had completed a high school education. By 1972, median family income had far exceeded $10,000, and one out of every four U.S. citizens had completed some years of college and could be categorized as upper-middle class. While it is true that income and economic advantages are still to a degree unequally distributed, a greater percentage of U.S. families can now afford to look beyond the concerns of daily life to other less pressing concerns than at any other time in history. As Hays notes, "education was an especially important factor in changing the values of Americans and developing an interest in matters termed 'quality of life.' "[14] The organizational changes that have been wrought by these developments are still actively evolving. Without question, these are significant factors with which contemporary organizations must be concerned.

Technological Dynamics

The movement toward complex organizations has been made possible largely by increasing technological sophistication. As has been pointed out, "the Industrial Revolution transformed all of society by taking men away from the traditional agricultural pursuits which had formed their main occupation throughout history and introduced them to novel ways of working and living in factory and city."[15] As a process, the Industrial Revolution was not the result of a single stroke of genius but of advances in a variety of industrial fields. In the United States, the revolution in technology took place in the automobile industry.[16]

---

[14]S. Hays, "The Limits-to-Growth Issue: A Historical Perspective," in *Growth in America,* ed. C. L. Cooper (Westport, Conn.: Greenwood Press, 1976), p. 121.

[15]M. Kranzberg, "Prerequisites for Industrialization," in *Technology in Western Civilization,* vol. 1, ed. M. Kranzberg and C. W. Pursell (New York: Oxford University Press, 1967), p. 217.

[16]J. B. Rae, "The Rationalization of Production," in Kranzberg and Pursell, eds., *Technology in Western Civilization,* vol. 2, p. 43.

Figure 1–4 *Enrollment in U.S. Institutions of Higher Education,*
1899–1984 (in millions)

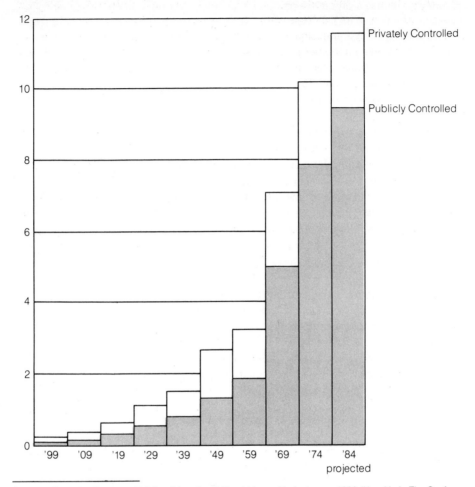

Source: "Changing Patterns of Higher Education," *Road Maps of Industry,* no. 1800 (New York: The Conference Board, 1977). Used by permission of The Conference Board.

Chapter 1

The Ford Motor Car Company, formed in 1903, epitomizes the rise of modern technology. Henry Ford's Highland Park, Michigan, plant, constructed in 1911, was the largest factory in the world and the first complete system of true mass production. Mass production, in turn, increased productivity and lowered prices. With urban population growing at an increasing rate, the cycle of modern capitalism was underway. The outcome was phenomenal. There were 24,000 automobiles sold in the United States in 1905 (2,000 were Fords); by 1912, one year after the opening of the Highland Park plant, over 170,000 Model T's, or "Tin Lizzies," alone were sold, and by 1920 every other motor vehicle in the world was a Model T Ford. Sales reached a million in 1924. In 1929, three years after the introduction of the Model A, Ford sold two million autos world-wide. As productivity went up, the price of a new Ford went down. By 1914, 1,000 vehicles were being produced daily. Output was doubled by 1916. Soon 60 percent of the cars on the road were Model T's. In 1925, a new Ford sold for an all-time low price of $260, down over 90 percent from the 1907 price of $2,800. The boom continued unabated until the beginning of the Depression in 1929. By 1930, sales of the Model A were down 50 percent.

In retrospect, it is clear that in addition to its technological repercussions, the Industrial Revolution also involved economic, political, social, cultural, and psychological changes.

A series of economic changes *which profoundly affected the technological changes and were affected by them involved a wider distribution of wealth, the transfer of the source of wealth from land to industrial production, the growth of large-scale international trade, and the advancement of capitalistic growth.* Political changes *reflected the economic shifts. New institutions were developed and novel governmental policies were employed, corresponding to the new needs developed by a society which was in the throes of industrialization. There were also sweeping* social changes, *including urbanization, the rise of working-class movements, and the emergence of new patterns of authority.* Cultural transformations *of a broad order also occurred. The worker, for example, acquired new and distinctive skills, and his relation to his work shifted: instead of being a handicraft worker with tools, he became a machine operator subjected to factory discipline. Finally, there was a deep-seated* psychological change *in man's view of his relations with Nature: the Industrial Revolution heightened man's confidence in his ability to use the resources of nature and to master her. [Emphasis added.]*[17]

The acceleration of advancements in technology has created problems of obsolescence in all professions. For example, it was estimated that by 1960 the "half life" of an engineering degree had been reduced to five years.[18] That is half of what was

[17]Kranzberg, "Prerequisites," p. 219.

[18]S. B. Zelikoff, "On the Obsolescence and Retraining of Engineering Personnel," *Training and Development Journal* 23, no. 5 (1969): 3–15. A similar estimate places the half-life of today's managers at 5–10 years, with variations depending on function. See: C.L. Cooper "Executive Half-Life," *Employee Relations* 1, no. 3 (1979): 7, 12.

learned in 1960 was technically obsolete five years after graduation. This is a sobering fact when coupled with the knowledge that the number of engineers and scientists in the United States per million persons has quintupled over the last 50 years.[19] Indeed, it has been estimated that over nine out of ten of all engineers and scientists who ever lived are alive today. Perhaps the most succinct summary of the situation has been provided by Drucker, who incisively concludes a comprehensive review of the relationship between technology and society by simply stating that the "explosion of technology has created the first worldwide civilization; and it is a technological civilization."[20]

In sum, an appreciation of the influence of recent changes in population patterns, increasing education levels, and growing technological sophistication is of great importance in understanding the social environment in which today's organizational society exists. As will become apparent in forthcoming chapters, organizations, in order to survive, have been forced to keep pace with these as well as other contemporary and historical trends.

Why Formally Study Organizations?

As previously noted, organizations are the dominant form of institution in our modern society. As such, they are a fundamental part of our existence, pervading all aspects of contemporary life. Most of us belong to many organizations and will undoubtedly join others in the future. While it is true that we all have common sense notions of how organizations function, it is only by studying them that we can gain the perspective necessary to improve our understanding of the ways in which they operate. As Corwin and Edelfelt note:

Each of us has ideas about how organizations operate based on the "street knowledge" of personal experiences. We have tried to cash a check on an out-of-town bank, or tried to register at a hotel when the clerk has no record of the reservation, or tried to locate a medical specialist familiar with a unique medical problem. When we confront these kinds of problems, we are forced to use some "theory" about how the organization operates in order to deal with it. So the question is not whether theories of organization are useful; we use them every day. The question is whether we can improve our theories by studying and thinking about organizations.[21]

Thus, as the preceding comments indicate, there are several reasons for formally studying organizations.

---

[19]C. Starr and R. Rudman, "Parameters of Technological Growth," *Science* 182 (1973): 358–364.

[20]P. F. Drucker, "Technology and Society in the Twentieth Century," in Kranzberg and Pursell, eds., *Technology in Western Civilization,* vol. 2, p. 23.

[21]R. G. Corwin and R. A. Edelfelt, *Perspectives on Organizations* (Washington, D.C.: American Association of Colleges for Teacher Education, 1976), p. 14.

Chapter 1

1. They are a basic part of our existence, pervading all aspects of today's society. The complexities of modern life make all of us, for good and ill, dependent on organizations. No matter where we turn, we are subject to their influence. This alone is justification for their study.

2. By studying organizations we will be better able to improve our understanding of how they operate and the many ways in which they can be structured. Such knowledge is, of course, indispensable if we are to meet the challenge of designing improved organizations.

3. The study of organizations has great practical value for both present and future managers.[22] As the data in Table 1–2 suggests, most of us work, or will work, in large organizations. Knowledge of how organizations function increases our ability to anticipate the kinds of problems we may encounter at work and, at the same time, serves to increase the probability of our success in such situations. For those readers preparing for a specific vocation, whether in business, government, education, or health care, the study of formal organizations offers an important opportunity to learn certain skills that will doubtlessly prove a vital supplement to the experience that will be gained in working.

Purpose of the Book

As suggested, the general purpose of this book is to increase understanding of organizations. More specifically, our aim has been to provide a general survey of contemporary knowledge in the areas of "organization theory and analysis." In doing so, we do not purport to have presented an exhaustive review of the organization literature; rather we have attempted to explain and integrate the major findings upon which current organization theory and analysis are based. It is our belief that an appreciation of the basic knowledge upon which our understanding of organization is grounded will greatly assist in developing the perspective necessary to meet the demands of today's organizational world.

Focus of the Book

The study of organizations can be conducted at either of two levels: the "macro," or general organization level, and the "micro," or interpersonal/intergroup level. Stated differently, "organizations can be viewed either in terms of their structure ('anatomy') or their processes ('physiology')."[23] While the system of personal interactions (micro

---

[22]K. Roberts, L. Hulin, and D. Rousseau, *Developing an Interdisciplinary Science of Organizations* (San Francisco: Jossey-Bass, 1978), p. 3.

[23]H. Simon, foreword to A. J. Melcher, *Structure and Process of Organizations: A Systems Approach* (Englewood Cliffs, N.J.: Prentice-Hall, 1976), p. xi.

level) comprises what may be considered the "fabric" of an organization, the intent of this book is to specifically deal with the "action field" (macro level) within which these interactions take place. Therefore, its focus is primarily upon the organization as a unit, not upon individuals or groups. This is not to say, however, that the behavior of individuals and groups will not be discussed. On the contrary, the extent to which individual and group behavior affects, or in turn is affected by, the structure of an organization is a legitimate concern of all organization theorists and will be specifically addressed throughout the chapters that follow.

Plan of the Book

The preceding sections have provided a general introduction for the discussion in the following chapters of this book. Given our aim to provide a general survey of contemporary knowledge in the areas of "organization theory and analysis," Chapter 2 is designed to provide the reader with a general framework for evaluating the theoretical and methodological issues that will be encountered in the remainder of the book. Numerous approaches to studying organizations are examined, and the role of theory in developing a general model of organizations is explained.

Chapter 3 provides the reader with an introductory overview of the major functions and dimensions of organization design. In addition, the origins of the so-called "traditional concepts" of organization are discussed and critically examined. In that the purpose of organization design is to create conditions that are conducive to the optimum accomplishment of enterprise effectiveness, Chapter 4 is concerned with the operation of the goal systems that exist within an organization, and Chapter 5 with the various approaches that have been developed to measure this effectiveness. As previously noted, organizations, as open systems, are constantly involved in an exchange process with their external environment. Organizational effectiveness is thus partially a function of environmental constraints. The close connection between organization and environmental conditions is discussed in Chapter 6. Given the ability to successfully adapt to their environment, organizations not only endure, but also grow and otherwise develop. In Chapter 7, we consider organizational growth as a process and examine the changes in organization composition and structure that typically result.

Chapter 8 is an analysis of the relationship between technology and structure. The nature of technology and its influence on organization design is critically examined from both an internal and external perspective. Next, in Chapter 9, we turn our attention to a discussion of organizational communication. Because a well-developed communication system is the prime mechanism available to an organization for sensing external conditions and, as necessary, effecting modifications in its operations, Chapter 10 is devoted to a brief treatment of organizational change. Finally, in closing, we undertake to provide the reader with a summary perspective on organizations and organization theory.

Chapter 1

Summary

The purpose of this chapter has been to present a general overview of the concept of organizations and to provide the reader with a brief indication of the material to be covered in the chapters to follow. After first answering the question "What are organizations?" the essential nature of organizations as "open" systems was discussed. We then briefly touched upon the concept of "organization character" and subsequently turned to a consideration of the pervasive influence of large-scale organizations on present-day society. Building on this background, we then considered the impact of recent changes in population trends, increasing education levels, and growing technological sophistication on the development of the social milieu in which today's organizational society exists.

Finally, after responding to the question "Why formally study organizations?" the purpose and the focus of the present text were discussed, and the plan of analysis to be followed in the remaining chapters was outlined.

Review and Discussion Questions

1. Depending upon the background and interests of the investigators involved, the elements and characteristics of organizations that are emphasized vary greatly. Certain features of organizations, however, are widely accepted by virtually all organization theorists. Identify these features.
2. Describe and discuss the basic characteristics of an open system.
3. Briefly comment on the major changes wrought by the Industrial Revolution in the United States.
4. Explain the effect on organizations of recent changes in population trends, increasing levels of education, and growing technological sophistication.
5. What is meant by the term "employee society"? How is the evolution of such a society related to the growth of organizations?

References

Berrien, F. K. "A General Systems Approach to Social Taxonomy." In *People, Groups, and Organizations,* edited by B. P. Indik and F. K. Berrien. New York: Teachers College Press, Columbia University, 1968.

Caplow, T. E. *Principles of Organization.* New York: Harcourt, Brace & World, 1964.

"Changing Patterns of Higher Education." *Road Maps of Industry,* no. 1800. New York: The Conference Board, 1977.

Cooper, C. L. "Executive Half-Life." *Employee Relations* 1, no. 3 (1979); 7, 12.

Corwin, R. G., and Edelfelt, R. A. *Perspectives on Organizations.* Washington, D.C.: American Association of Colleges for Teacher Education, 1976.

Demographic Yearbook 1977. 29th issue. New York: United Nations Department of International Economic and Social Affairs, 1978.

Drucker, P. F. "Technology and Society in the Twentieth Century." In *Technology in Western Civilization,* vol. 2, edited by M. Kranzberg and C. W. Pursell. New York: Oxford University Press, 1967.

Hays, S. "The Limits-to-Growth Issue: A Historical Perspective." In *Growth in America,* edited by C. L. Cooper. Westport, Conn.: Greenwood Press, 1976.

Kast, F. E., and Rosenzweig, J. E. *Organization and Management: A Systems and Contingency Approach.* 3rd ed. New York: McGraw-Hill, 1979.

Kranzberg, M. "Prerequisites for Industrialization." In *Technology in Western Civilization,* vol. 1, edited by M. Kranzberg and C. W. Pursell. New York: Oxford University Press, 1967.

Lansbury, R. D., and Gilmour, P. *Organisations: An Australian Perspective.* Melbourne: Longman Cheshire Pty. Ltd., 1977.

Lebergott, S. *Manpower in Economic Growth: The American Record since 1800.* New York: McGraw-Hill, 1964.

Mason, E. S. *The Corporation in Modern Society.* Cambridge, Mass.: Harvard University Press, 1966.

Miller, D. C. "Influence of Technology on Industry." In *Technology and Social Change,* edited by F. R. Allen et al. New York: Appleton-Century-Crofts, 1957.

Mohan, R. P. "The Role of the Large Organization in the Contemporary World." In *Management and Complex Organizations in Comparative Perspective,* edited by R. P. Mohan. Westport, Conn.: Greenwood Press, 1979.

Porter, L. W., Lawler, E. E., and Hackman, J. R. *Behavior in Organizations.* New York: McGraw-Hill, 1975.

Prais, S. J. *The Evolution of Giant Firms in Britain.* Cambridge: Cambridge University Press, 1976.

Rae, J. B. "The Rationalization of Production." In *Technology in Western Civilization,* vol. 2, edited by M. Kranzberg and C. W. Pursell. New York: Oxford University Press, 1967.

Roberts, K., Hulin, L. and Rousseau, D. *Developing an Interdisciplinary Science of Organizations.* San Francisco: Jossey-Bass, 1978.

Roy, R. H. *The Cultures of Management.* Baltimore: Johns Hopkins University Press, 1977.

Selznick, P. *Leadership in Administration.* Evanston, Ill.: Row, Peterson, 1957.

Simon, H. Foreword to *Structure and Process of Organizations: A Systems Approach,* by A. J. Melcher. Englewood Cliffs, N.J.: Prentice-Hall, 1976.

Starr, C., and Rudman, R. "Parameters of Technological Growth." *Science* 182 (1973): 358–364.

Tausky, C. *Work Organizations: Major Theoretical Perspectives.* 2nd ed. Itasca, Ill.: Peacock, 1978.

U.S. Department of Commerce, Bureau of the Census. *Historical Statistics of the United States: Colonial Times to 1970.* Bicentennial edition. Part 1. Washington, D.C.: U.S. Government Printing Office, 1975.

U.S. Department of Commerce, Bureau of the Census. *Statistical Abstract of the United States.* 99th ed. Washington, D.C.: U.S. Government Printing Office, 1978.

U.S. Department of Labor, Bureau of Labor Statistics. *Employment and Wages, First Quarter, 1976.* Springfield, Va.: National Technical Information Service, 1979.

"Women in the Labor Force." *Road Maps of Industry,* no. 1794. New York: The Conference Board, 1976.

Zelikoff, S. B. "On the Obsolescence and Retraining of Engineering Personnel." *Training and Development Journal,* 23, no. 5 (1969): 3–15.

Chapter 1

Strategies for Studying Organizations

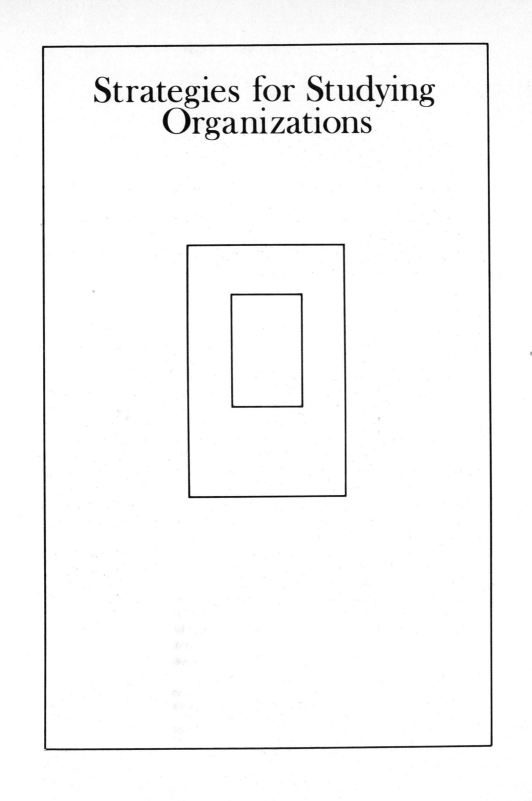

Strategies for Studying Organizations

Chapter 2

Over the past half century, researchers from a wide variety of disciplines have developed various strategies for studying organizations. Historically as well as inherently an interdisciplinary field, organization theory has been particularly influenced by its sister social sciences, especially sociology, psychology, anthropology, and economics. As a consequence, diversity has long been a dominant feature of research on organizations.

This diversity, however, has had both positive and negative effects on the development of organization theory as an established field of study.[1] On the plus side, it has contributed greatly to the dynamic and pluralistic growth of organization research. Moreover, the cross-fertilization of ideas among disciplines has served as a substantial safeguard against academic isolationism and conceptual stagnation. On the other hand, such diversity has also produced substantial differences in concepts, terminology, and methods of study. Needless to say, such disparities have naturally led to substantial and frequent disagreements. Confusion and controversy are nevertheless traditionally characteristic of a new and growing area of study. In this regard, organization theory has been no exception.

Our aim in this chapter, then, is to present the reader with the knowledge necessary to benefit from the often conflicting theory and research that will be encountered in the following pages, and to assess the interpretations drawn from the supporting data presented. At the same time, it is specifically not our intention to instruct the readers of this chapter in the mechanics of how to actually conduct organization research. Rather we wish to familiarize them with the more common methods of organization analysis so that they will be able to more critically appraise the results of such investigations. For, as will soon be apparent, each of the methods to be discussed has certain limitations as well as certain strong points. Hence, as recognized by Hamner and Organ, if the readers of this book are to act intelligently as consumers of knowledge about organizations, they "must be able to qualify that knowledge on the basis of the shortcomings that produced it."[2]

---

[1] J. E. McGrath, "Toward a 'Theory of Method' for Research on Organizations," in *New Perspectives in Organization Research*, ed. W. W. Cooper et al. (New York: John Wiley & Sons, 1964), p. 534.

[2] W. C. Hamner and D. W. Organ, *Organizational Behavior: An Applied Psychological Approach* (Dallas: Business Publications, 1978), p. 18.

The Relationship between Theory and Research

Before beginning our discussion of the various strategies for studying organizations, it may prove helpful to briefly comment on the relationship between theory and research.[3] It should be realized that our ability to analyze phenomena of various kinds depends on the adequacy of the theoretical schemes we employ.[4] Such theoretical schemes not only guide our search for significant relationships among the limitless facts that exist in an organizational setting but also make the important difference between simply knowing a fact and understanding its meaning.[5]

As a consequence, research efforts in any field are greatly aided by the development of a substantive body of theory. In this regard, as suggested in the preceding paragraph, theory serves both as a tool and as a goal. The tool function of theory "is evident in the generally accepted proposition that theories guide research by generating *new* predictions not otherwise likely to occur."[6] As a goal, theory is often an end in itself, providing "an economical and efficient means of abstracting, codifying, summarizing, integrating, and storing information."[7] Although the field of organization study is still in an early stage of development, both the tool and the goal functions of its theory will become increasingly evident with each of the chapters that follow.

Methods of Research in Organization Theory

As noted in Chapter 1, each of us has common sense notions of how organizations operate. That is, we all have ideas about how organizations function based on the "street knowledge" of personal experience. However, knowledge based solely upon such informal sources is limited. To overcome this limitation, methods of research (or methodologies) used in studies of organizations range from broad and sweeping surveys of large numbers of organizations to carefully delimited and tightly controlled laboratory experiments. Research studies include case analyses of single organizations, surveys employing highly-structured, self-administered questionnaires on which respondents simply check off appropriate answers, anecdotal accounts of organizational experiences, intensive in-depth interviews, systematic forms of direct observation, and more. At first glance, it would seem that the only feature all these approaches have in common is that they are, or are meant to be, of value in the study of organizations.[8]

---

[3]Portions of the following discussion have been taken from A. G. Bedeian, "Management Theory: A Pediatric Note," *Business Perspectives* 9, no. 4 (1973): 2–5.

[4]J. D. Thompson, *Organizations in Action* (New York: McGraw-Hill, 1967), p. 2.

[5]J. F. Scott and R. P. Lynton, *Three Studies in Management* (London: Routledge & Kegan Paul, 1952), p. 201.

[6]M. H. Marx, "The General Nature of Theory Construction," in *Theories in Contemporary Psychology,* ed. M. H. Marx (New York: MacMillan, 1963), p. 6.

[7]Ibid.

[8]McGrath, "Toward a 'Theory of Method,' " p. 536.

Given additional thought, however, certain common elements do emerge. This is particularly so if, following McGrath's suggestion, "we consider each of them in terms of the nature of the setting within which data-collection takes place and in terms of the extent to which activities of the investigator intrude upon, or are responsible for, the nature of the setting."[9] Viewed from this perspective, four major strategies for studying organizations can be identified: (1) case studies, (2) interviews and questionnaire surveys, (3) laboratory experiments, and (4) use of secondary source materials.

In evaluating these strategies we will attempt to show that their characteristic differences account for differences in research results. As we have previously noted, theory serves to guide our choice and evaluation of research findings. It should also serve to guide our selection of methods by which data are collected. In this regard, a most significant point to continually bear in mind when reading the following chapters is that "when we choose one methodology over others in a study of organization, we are thereby affecting the kinds and amount of information which we can obtain from results of that study."[10] In other words, differences in methodology do make a difference both in research yield *and* in interpretation.

Internal and External Validity

Before entering into a discussion of each of the strategies for studying organizations, it would seem wise to touch upon two fundamental questions that are of paramount concern *regardless* of the research approach taken. These questions relate to the concepts of internal and external validity.[11] *Internal validity* is *the* basic minimum without which a research effort is uninterpretable. It asks the question, "Has the research strategy in question controlled the influence of extraneous variables that could serve as alternative explanations for why the results of a study turned out the way they did?" This underlines the necessity, central to any research, of making certain that the influence of all variables that might account for observed changes be taken into consideration both in the design of a study and in the interpretation of its findings. If, when compared to the reported findings, there are no other equally likely interpretations of a study's results, it is said to possess internal validity. Any inferences advanced on the basis of the study in question would thus seem warranted.[12]

External validity concerns the representativeness or generalizability of an investigation's results. It asks the question, "To what extent can a study's findings be generalized?" That is, are the findings applicable to, or across, persons, settings, and times not represented in its sample? The problem of external validity is whether the

---

[9]Ibid.

[10]Ibid., p. 534.

[11]D. T. Campbell, "Factors Relevant to the Validity of Experiments in Social Settings," *Psychological Bulletin* 47 (1957): 297–312.

[12]W. G. Scott and T. R. Mitchell, *Organization Theory: A Structural and Behavioral Analysis,* 3rd ed. (Homewood, Ill.: Richard D. Irwin, 1976), p. 397.

results of a study are specific to factors such as the nature of the setting in which the study was conducted and the nature of the persons participating. If not, and the results of a study can be shown to hold for or be representative of other realms (populations, situations, and times), it is said to possess external validity.

Our attention now turns to a discussion of the four major research strategies identified earlier as being among the most commonly used by organization theorists.

Case Studies

Long the traditional approach to the study of organizations, the case study method was pioneered in the early 1950s by organization investigators who, taking an almost anthropological approach, literally lived and worked in the organizations they studied. When utilizing this strategy, one or more researchers or their agents enter an organization, either openly in the role of investigators or covertly in some disguised role, for the express purpose of learning more about its activities. Data are collected through the use of *field notes* describing those organizational events which seem to have meaning, checklists of specific activities, coding schemes for detailing daily experiences, and ratings of organizational properties judged to be of importance on the basis of the meaning attributed to the events and activities observed.

The case study method is particularly valuable for exploratory analyses of organizations or groups that are not yet well enough known for an investigator to be precise and systematic about the variables he or she wishes to investigate.[13] In such circumstances, the case method is useful for generating hypotheses that can subsequently be tested. This flexibility is of particular value in allowing a researcher to modify his or her data collection techniques when new insights emerge as a study progresses. Furthermore, case analysis is well suited for obtaining an overall picture of a social unit. The depth of penetration, and thus understanding, that it allows the researcher is unmatched by any other approach; it often leads to the discovery of significant facts that a researcher from "outside" would not ordinarily look for or that might be purposefully hidden. Indeed, some of the richest and most descriptive data on the nature of organizations has come through studies utilizing the case method.[14] Many of these studies are considered classics in the organization theory field and will be discussed at various points in later chapters.

An outstanding example of the case study method is Dalton's investigation of conflict between line and staff officials in four firms, which took over a decade to complete.[15] Dalton was in the unique position of being both a concealed observer (gathering information for his Ph.D. dissertation at the Universtiy of Chicago) and a legitimate employee (working his way through school) in two of the firms analyzed in his study. In one, a steel mill, Dalton served as a checker, measuring work output and

---

[13]W. F. Whyte, *Organizational Behavior: Theory and Application* (Homewood, Ill.: Richard D. Irwin, 1969), p. 41.

[14]W. F. Whyte, "On Making the Most of Participant Observation," *American Sociologist* 14 (1979): 56–66.

[15]M. Dalton, *Men Who Manage: Fusions of Feeling and Theory in Administration* (New York: John Wiley & Sons, 1959).

Chapter 2

computing the pay of over 100 employees in a large maintenance department. Of particular significance was the fact that this role allowed him to circulate freely and at times to have access to personnel files. On occasion he even had the opportunity to interview various members of the mill's management staff. The specific conclusions of Dalton's study, as they relate to line-staff communication, will be part of our discussion in Chapter 9.

Despite its many virtues, the limitations of the case study method must also be recognized. Ironically, its major strength, intimacy and detail of input, is also one of its principal weaknesses. There is a very real possibility that a researcher who lives and works in an organization over an extended period of time lose his or her objectivity. In such circumstances, the role of case researcher requires both detachment *and* personal involvement. Because the internal validity of this type of study depends entirely on the special talents and observational accuracy of the case analyst, the necessity of maintaining a proper perspective cannot be minimized. A researcher's relationships with an organization and its members may well influence his or her observations and any inferences derived. In the instance of the known observer, this is even further complicated by the well-known tendency (known as *reactivity*) for the presence of a researcher to alter the behavior of those being studied, which further biases the validity of any findings. Such difficulties, of course, make replication of the study virtually impossible.

Case studies have also been criticized on the basis of lack of measurability. Because the data gathered are generally based on the perceptions and subjective interpretations of individual researchers, quantification and the manageable summary of findings is often very difficult.[16] Since they are presented in narrative form, case studies generally require a great deal of time and space for results to be adequately dealt with. Quantification, where used, is primarily an illustration of patterns of worker interaction. Information pertaining to such factors as an organization's structural properties is usually presented in an almost entirely descriptive fashion.[17]

There is also substance in the criticism that "generalizations about organizations . . . [can]not be justified on the basis of one or a handful of cases."[18] Having each been conducted by different researchers, in unique social situations, and during specific periods of time, case studies can rarely be duplicated. Hence, generalizations are difficult to make and apply, and external validity virtually impossible to establish. Perhaps Lijphart says it simplest and best: "A single case can constitute neither the basis for a valid generalization nor the ground for disproving an established generalization."[19]

Another shortcoming of the case method is that such studies are often both very time consuming and very expensive. As previously mentioned, case analyses involve

[16]E. M. Glaser and T. E. Backer, "A Look at Participant Observation," *Evaluation* 1, no. 3 (1973): 46–49.

[17]M. W. Meyer, "Recent Developments in Organizational Research and Theory," in *Environments and Organizations,* ed. M. W. Meyer (San Francisco: Jossey-Bass, 1978), p. 3.

[18]M.W. Meyer, *Theory of Organizational Structure* (Indianapolis: Bobbs-Merrill, 1977), p. 70.

[19]A. Lijphart, "Comparative Politics and the Comparative Method," *American Political Science Review* 65 (1971): 691.

the tedious collection of specific data and careful observation over a considerable period of time. Such activities require a trained researcher and, simply put, are hard work. Additionally, an important limitation exists with respect to the concealed observer role. Namely, "the role can only be assumed when the researcher possesses or can acquire the attributes of a subject group member."[20] As an extreme, for one study a researcher underwent surgery to prepare him for his role as an undercover observer.[21]

Given the extremes that some researchers are apparently willing to go to in order to gain access to data, a final problem emerges—the question of ethics. Cases involving covert entry into a firm and deception by a researcher regarding his or her true role are especially open to charges of ethical impropriety.[22] In commenting specifically on this issue, that is, the researcher who is in a situation under false pretenses and claiming to be something he or she is not, Scott points out that "most groups take a dim view of people who tell lies to insiders and reveal secrets to outsiders."[23]

Interviews/Questionnaire Surveys

Given its various limitations, the case study method is often combined with other research strategies such as the surveying or interviewing of persons whom the case researcher cannot observe directly. The interview and what has been called its "stepbrother," the questionnaire, capitalize on language, our most powerful form of communication.[24] Both are especially suited for gathering data on the values, attitudes, and beliefs of members as well as information pertaining to the characteristics of the organizations of which they are a part. Moreover, both methods have several special advantages. Most notably, they each allow researchers to exercise considerable control over the selection of their subjects. They may choose to study an entire population, or simply some portion of it deemed to be representative of the whole.[25] In the case of the questionnaire, great quantities of comparable data can be collected from large numbers of people (by mail or through group administrations) in a relatively short time and at a minimal cost. Interviews, by comparison, are typically more time consuming and more costly. The collection of comparable data in either case gives the questionnaire/interview approach its chief advantage: the restatement of findings in quantitative terms so that they can be aggregated and subsequently analyzed using computerized statistical techniques.

Although it employed few statistical analyses, an outstanding example of the

---

[20]W. R. Scott, "Field Methods in the Study of Organizations," in *Handbook of Organizations*, ed. J. G. March (Chicago: Rand McNally, 1965), p. 272.

[21]M. A. Sullivan, A. S. Queen, and R. C. Patrick, "Participant Observation as Employed in the Study of a Military Training Program," *American Sociological Review* 23 (1958): 660–667.

[22]K. T. Erikson, "A Comment on Disguised Observation in Sociology," *Social Problems* 14 (1967): 366–373.

[23]Scott, "Field Methods," p. 274.

[24]T. J. Bouchard, "Field Research Methods: Interviewing, Questionnaires, Participant Observation, Systematic Observation, Unobtrusive Measures," in *Handbook of Industrial and Organizational Pschology,* ed. M. D. Dunnette (Chicago: Rand McNally 1976), p. 368.

[25]Scott, "Field Methods," p. 294.

interview approach to organization research is Gouldner's three-year investigation of a gypsum factory that employed 225 people.[26] As will be discussed in Chapter 3, Gouldner, in one of the first studies of its kind, described in extensive detail the process of bureaucratization, its causes and its consequences. Of particular interest to our present topic is that the data which formed the basis for his study were largely obtained through 174 formal interviews, each lasting an average of an hour-and-a-half to two hours. Of this total, 132 interviewees were drawn from a representative cross-section of employees stratified to take into account seniority, rank, and departmental affiliation. This data base was then supplemented with information gathered through simple observation (for example, walks around the plant) and thousands of pages of documentary material (for example, company reports, memoranda, private corre-spondence, and newspaper clippings).

A good illustration of the questionnaire approach is Lawrence and Lorsch's investigation of the relationship between environmental differences and effective organization design.[27] Utilizing data from questionnaires, augmented on occasion by interviews, Lawrence and Lorsch surveyed key personnel representing the middle- and upper-level management of ten firms in three divergent industrial environments. Data were collected on the assumption that such organizational incumbents have special knowledge, as well as access to certain types of information, by virtue of their position in an organization. Lawrence and Lorsch's questionnaire measuring environ-mental certainty is reproduced here in Table 2–1 as a sample of this kind of instru-ment. A more complete discussion of Lawrence and Lorsch's findings will be presented in Chapter 6.

Before proceeding further, it is important to raise a troublesome issue suggested by both the Gouldner and the Lawrence and Lorsch studies. This concerns the *reliability* (that is, accuracy) of data received from respondents. The very nature of self-reported data is somewhat suspect because, when individuals talk or write about themselves, events they took part in, or the actions of others, their statements have often been shown to more accurately reflect their own wishes and their relationship to those inquiring than the actual reality of a situation. All too often this type of error goes unacknowledged, and, as suggested by Rubenstein and Haberstroh, it is implic-itly assumed "that reports of events by informants or subjects correspond closely or exactly with the actual way in which the events occurred."[28] Rubenstein and Haber-stroh give insight into the sources of error that may contaminate a researcher's data and thus prevent a determination of what "really happened." The following is taken from their discussion:

1.   *One general source of error is the informant's perceptual slant—his einstellung or perceptual set. The effect of perceptual set or slant has been investigated by many students of intergroup prejudice by such means as attitude tests. Percep-*

[26]A. W. Gouldner, *Patterns of Industrial Bureaucracy* (New York: Free Press, 1954).

[27]P. R. Lawrence and J. W. Lorsch, *Organizations and Environment: Managing Differentiation and Integration* (Boston: Division of Research, Graduate School of Business Administration, Harvard University, 1967).

[28]A. H. Rubenstein and C. J. Haberstroh, *Some Theories of Organization,* rev. ed. (Homewood, Ill.: Richard D. Irwin, 1966), p. 699.

Strategies for Studying Organizations

Table 2-1 *Lawrence and Lorsch's Questionnaire Measuring Environmental Certainty*

Due to rapid change in an industry, or the state of development in the technology used by the industry, or vast differences in customer requirements, etc., company executives often have varying degrees of certainty concerning what their departmental job requirements are and the kinds of activities their departments *must* engage in to achieve these requirements. The following series of questions is an effort to obtain data concerning this aspect of your industry. Please answer each question for each functional area.

Please circle the point on the scale provided which most nearly describes the degree to which present job requirements in each functional department are clearly stated or known in your company for the:

Research Department

| Job requirements are very clear in most instances | 1 2 3 4 5 6 7 | Job requirements are not at all clear in most instances |

Manufacturing Department

| Job requirements are not at all clear in most instances | 1 2 3 4 5 6 7 | Job requirements are very clear in most instances |

Marketing Department

| Job requirements are very clear in most instances | 1 2 3 4 5 6 7 | Job requirements are not at all clear in most instances |

Please circle the point on the scale provided which most nearly describes the degree of difficulty each functional department has in accomplishing its assigned job, given the limitation of the technical and economic resources which are available to it:

Degree of Difficulty in:

Developing a product which can be manufactured and sold profitably

1 2 3 4 5 6 7
Little   Extremely
difficulty   difficult

Manufacturing economically a product which can be designed and sold

1 2 3 4 5 6 7
Extremely   Little
difficult   difficulty

Selling a product which can be developed and manufactured economically

1 2 3 4 5 6 7
Little   Extremely
difficulty   difficult

Chapter 2

Table 2–1 *continued*

Please check the alternative which most nearly describes the typical length of time involved before feedback is available to each functional area concerning the success of its job performance. For example: the sales department manager may be able to determine at the end of each day how successful the selling effort was by examining the total sales reported by his salesmen for that day. In contrast, the production manager may not know whether production meets required specifications until the results of several performance tests are available, often a period of several days from the time his department completes its processing.

Research Department

____ one day
____ one week
____ one month
____ six months
____ one year
____ three years or more

Manufacturing Department

____ one day
____ one week
____ one month
____ six months
____ one year
____ three years or more

Marketing Department

____ one day
____ one week
____ one month
____ six months
____ one year
____ three years or more

Source: P. R. Lawrence and J. W. Lorsch, *Organization and Environment: Managing Differentiation and Integration* (Boston: Division of Research, Graduate School of Business Administration, Harvard University, 1967). pp. 248–250. Copyright © 1967 by the President and Fellows of Harvard College; all rights reserved. Reprinted by permission.

tual ability is also known to vary and much has been said about it. Reports of a given event from several witnesses without training in careful observation have often been found to bear little resemblance to each other.

2. *A second general source of error is the informant's failure to remember just what did happen. Assuming that he received a fairly reliable impression of an event at the time that it happened, it has been indicated by experiments in recall and by the experience of all of us that it generally becomes more difficult with passage of time to describe the details of an event as we originally perceived it. A great deal has been said on this matter in relation to the reliability of witness reports weeks or months after the occurrence of the event.*

3. *A third general source of error may be the reluctance of the subject, for whatever reason, to report his "true" impression of what occurred. This condition has been*

encountered often in organizational studies where subjects may distort descriptions of events or interpersonal relationships for fear of retaliation, desire not to upset others, or a general reluctance to verbalize a particular type of situation or event.

4. *Assuming that all of these sources of error have been acknowledged and accounted for, there is a fourth and overriding source of error which is usually explicit in rigorously designed and executed investigations—the inability of the subject to communicate his report; or conversely, the inability of the investigator to get from the subject through whatever techniques (interview, questionnaire, observation) the information that the subject is willing and able to give.*[29]

One last difficulty involves the true representativeness of samples included in interviews and questionnaire surveys. As Meyer has noted, "It is hard to know what constitutes a representative sample of organizations . . . and we can never be sure that any sample is representative of all extant organizations, as in public opinion polls."[30] Whereas conventional interview/questionnaire research primarily relies on the use of probability samples drawn from a defined population to minimize the likely margin of error, organizational studies seldom draw random samples and no claim of representativeness can be made. The external validity of results under such circumstances is, of course, quite suspect.[31]

As these comments suggest, both the development of a list of items for a questionnaire and the development of a line of questioning to be pursued in an interview require a great deal of work and, in some instances, are part art and part science.[32]

Laboratory Experiments

The problems associated with the interview and questionnaire approaches have led to the development of a third research strategy: laboratory experiments. Within the context of organization theory, the term *laboratory* refers to *any* setting that allows an investigator to rigorously control the conditions under which observations are made.[33] It is thus simply an analytic concept and does not necessarily denote cameras, white coats, one-way mirrors, or any other paraphernalia typical of many experimental settings. An office, a factory, or a government bureau may function as a laboratory.

The most important feature of laboratory experiments is the possibility of control and experimental manipulation. "In a laboratory experiment, the conditions under which an event occurs are manipulated so that the effects of . . . experimental vari-

---

[29]Ibid., pp. 699–700.

[30]Meyer, *Theory,* pp. 66, 75.

[31]Meyer, "Recent Developments," p. 36.

[32]Bouchard, "Field Research Methods," p. 380.

[33]M. Zelditch and T. K. Hopkins, "Laboratory Experiments with Organizations," in *Complex Organizations: A Sociological Reader,* ed. A. Etzioni (New York: Holt, Rinehart and Winston, 1961), p. 465.

ables and . . . antecedent conditions can be contrasted. The intention is to isolate theoretically relevant variables, and to measure the response of dependent variables when either independent or intervening variables are manipulated."[34] This, of course, requires the establishment of highly controlled conditions so that the influence of potentially confounding variables can be minimized.

Such control allows the systematic variation of dependent-variable measures, as well as the systematic modification of the independent or intervening variables whose influence is being investigated. As a result of this greater control, conclusive answers can often be obtained and relatively precise and subtle theoretical points tested.[35] Laboratory experiments are thus excellent when honing concepts and refining measurement techniques. This is even more true when the conditions necessary to test a hypothesis are uneconomical, difficult, or even impossible to obtain in a field situation.[36]

The prime criticism of the laboratory approach concerns the issue of realism versus artificiality—that is, whether laboratory experiments truly reflect the realities of organizational life. Both sides in this debate have their vocal advocates, and at times their exchange of views has become quite heated. Barnes, for one, argues that laboratory experiments are seldom representative of real organizational conditions. In pursuing this point, he offers the following observations:

The laboratory involves a temporary system; the organization is a quasi-permanent system that exists beyond the lives of its members. The laboratory sets up temporary human relationships which all too often have a pretend-like quality. Organizations require relationships that are, so the slang expression goes, "for real." The laboratory builds an ambiguous hierarchy in which subjects report to an experimenter most often as volunteer or nonvolunteer enrollees taking his college course. An organization has several complex hierarchical systems which depend upon both formal authority and colleague influence over a period of time.[37]

To this Barnes adds, "To change and study a single variable in a laboratory may be relatively easy compared with isolating, changing, and studying the variable within an organization."[38]

In response to such criticisms, defenders of the laboratory approach turn the argument around and reply that this is precisely the purpose of taking an issue into the laboratory: "to see the phenomenon for what it actually is, not as we ordinarily find it camouflaged in the natural elements. In the laboratory, the only reality that

---

[34] R. J. House, "Scientific Investigation in Management," *Management International Review* 10, nos. 4–5 (1970): 145.

[35] L. Festinger, "Laboratory Experiments," in *Research Methods in the Behavioral Sciences,* ed. L. Festinger and D. Katz (New York: Holt, Rinehart and Winston, 1953), pp. 140–141.

[36] Zelditch and Hopkins, "Laboratory Experiments," p.. 466.

[37] L. B. Barnes, "Organizational Change and Field Experiment Methods," in *Methods of Organizational Research,* ed. V. H. Vroom (Pittsburgh: University of Pittsburgh Press, 1967), p. 77.

[38] Ibid.

counts is the reality of the variable we are looking at, and it is just as real there as it is anywhere else."[39]

In further defense of the laboratory experiment, Weick contends that "one of the ironies of laboratory experimentation is that presumed liabilities turn out to be conceptual assets for organizational researchers."[40] To support his contention, he notes numerous similarities (as opposed to Barnes' contrasts) between laboratory experiments and the conditions that prevail in many organizations.

To illustrate, research participants are apprehensive about being evaluated, but so are ambitious employees. Laboratory tasks require limited skills, ignoring the "rest" of what the person brings to the laboratory, but the same holds true with a division of labor and partial inclusion. Relationships between experimenter and respondent involve asymmetrical power, but the same holds true for superiors and subordinates. Participants seldom know why they are doing the things they do in laboratories but employees often operate under similar conditions of ignorance and faith. Participants in laboratory groups seldom know one another intimately, but the same is true in organizations where personnel transfers are common, where temporary problem solving units are the rule, and where impression management is abundant. People participate in experiments for a variety of reasons, but the decision to participate in an organization is similarly over-determined. Finally, people are suspicious of what happens to them in laboratories but so are employees suspicious as they become . . . [alerted] to the reality of hidden agendas and internal politics.[41]

The significance of these competing views leads us directly to an additional consideration. This is the degree or extent to which the results of laboratory experiments may be generalized to real life organizational settings. This, of course, bears directly on the preceding discussion and involves the crucial question of external validity. If, indeed, the purpose of taking an issue into the laboratory is to avoid dealing with the "camouflage" common to field conditions, it should be clearly realized that, when conditions in an experiment are hard to find in everyday life, external validity (that is, the generalizability of results) is severely restricted.[42]

As one might suspect, given the controversy surrounding the laboratory approach, it is the least frequently used of the research strategies employed by organization theorists. One example, however, that will be discussed in a coming section (in Chapter 6) is Huber, O'Connell, and Cummings's [43] study of the effects of environmental information and group structure (independent variables) on an individual's judgment of perceived uncertainty (dependent variable). To tightly control the objec-

[39]Hamner and Organ, *Organizational Behavior,* p. 29.

[40]K. E. Weick, "Laboratory Experimentation with Organizations: A Reappraisal," *Academy of Management Review* 2 (1977): 124.

[41]Ibid.

[42]K. E. Weick, "Organizations in the Laboratory," in Vroom, ed., *Methods,* p. 44.

[43]G. P. Huber, M. J. O'Connell, and L. L. Cummings, "Perceived Environmental Uncertainty: Effects of Information and Structure," *Academy of Management Journal* 18 (1975): 725–740.

tive environment and test the hypotheses in question, a laboratory simulation, in which three-person decision-making teams (students) played a military game, was employed. Information concerning the state of the objective environment was varied on two dimensions, load (low, medium, or high number of messages) and specificity (low or high content). Team structure was controlled at two levels, loose and tight. Significant relationships were found between perceived environmental uncertainty and both information load (amount) and team structure.

Secondary Source Materials

A fourth and final major strategy for studying organizations is the use of data that others have compiled; these constitute a secondary source. An important and generally inexpensive source of information about organizations, secondary information is especially useful for obtaining background material that is frequently unavailable for a study otherwise. The sources of secondary data are virtually unlimited. The materials included in this category vary from raw files, such as transcripts of meetings, correspondence, organization charts, personnel files, and policy manuals, to already prepared statistics, such as departmental budgets and operating costs. Some organizations even publish employee-directed newsletters, newspapers, and periodicals. In many cases, data can also be found in directories like the *Encyclopedia of Associations* or in reports compiled by various government agencies.

A great many of the studies that will be cited in the following chapters made use of secondary source materials. Some relied upon them almost exclusively, while others used them as supplementary aids to gain additional insight into various facets of a research problem. For instance, Akers and Campbell, using information collected solely from the *Encyclopedia of Associations* and *National Associations of the United States* (a government publication), were able to analyze the relationship between membership size and the total and relative size of the administrative components of 197 occupational associations.[44] Their results will be discussed in more detail in Chapter 7. In contrast, Selznick, in his study of the efforts of the Tennessee Valley Authority to gain the political support of local agencies, principally relied upon personal interviews conducted both in Washington, D.C., and in the Tennessee Valley states, but also made use of the authority's files, some of which were confidential.[45] The findings of this study will be discussed in Chapters 3 and 4.

While in some instances secondary source material may be more reliable (that is, accurate) than data obtained by other means, this is not always so. If data come from a much earlier time period, they may be based on incomplete records and thus lead to findings and conclusions that are misleading, if not incorrect. There are other limitations, as well:

[44]R. Akers and F. L. Campbell, "Size and the Administrative Component in Occupational Associations," *Pacific Sociological Review* 13 (1970): 241–251.
[45]P. Selznick, *TVA and the Grass Roots: A Study in the Sociology of Formal Organizations* (Berkeley, Calif.: University of California Press, 1949).

1. Available secondary information is often unsuitable for the specific purpose of a research problem.
2. Different units of measurement may have been used by different organizations or sources.
3. Documents and records can seldom be taken at face value. They must always be carefully evaluated in terms of their *measurement validity* (degree to which they actually reflect the phenomenon that they are intended to measure).

Summary

It has been the sole purpose of this chapter to familiarize readers with the more common methods used in organization research so that they will be better able to more critically appreciate the results of such investigations. Plainly put, the important point to bear in mind is that the results of a research study can only be as good as the methods used to obtain them.

Furthermore, given the foregoing, it should be apparent that each of the research strategies identified has its own strengths and weaknesses. These are summarized in Table 2–2. As we have shown, there is no "one best research strategy"; the four methodologies discussed—case studies, interviews and questionnaire surveys, laboratory experiments, and the use of secondary materials—should be looked upon as complementary approaches to be used jointly whenever possible. The choice of the approach or approaches most suitable for a given problem in large part depends on the nature of the problem, how much is known about the variables involved, the extent to which these variables can be manipulated and observed, and the quality and accessibility of additional information relating to the problem.[46]

Bearing this in mind throughout the coming chapters, the reader should continually question whether the particular research strategy employed was the most appropriate for the problem(s) being studied and whether, in fact, it permits the conclusions that have been drawn.

Review and Discussion Questions

1. Why is it important to be familiar with research methodologies before studying research results?
2. Explain what is meant by internal and external validity. Why are they known as "twin" concepts?
3. Comment on the various ironies involved when a researcher enters an organization to study its activities more closely.
4. Why are case studies often accused of violating accepted ethics?
5. How are questionnaires and interviews related?

---

[46]House, "Scientific Investigation," p. 139.

Table 2–2 *Summary of the Strengths and Weaknesses of the Most Common Strategies for Studying Organizations*

Strengths	Weaknesses

Case Studies

1. Useful for exploratory analyses	1. Based on the perceptions and subjective interpretations of the researcher
2. Useful for gaining insights and generating propositions	2. Problem of reactivity
3. Flexibility to capitalize on new insights that emerge as a study develops	3. Lack of measurability
4. Depth of penetration and understanding	4. Require a great deal of time and space for presentation of results
	5. Difficult to draw generalizations—to establish external validity
	6. Time consuming and expensive
	7. Require careful observation and tedious collection of specific details
	8. Limits to the concealed observer rule

Interview/Questionnaire Studies

1. Especially suited for the collection of data describing employee values, attitudes, and beliefs, as well as organizational characteristics	1. Reliability of data collected, i.e., self-report bias
2. Control over the selection of subjects	2. Problem of perceptual slant
3. Capable of generating large amounts of comparable data	3. Subject's failure to remember what happened
4. Relatively fast and inexpensive	4. Reluctance of subjects to tell the truth
5. Suited to the quantification of findings	5. Inability of subject/researcher to communicate
6. Allow the statistical analysis of data	6. Questionable representativeness of samples and questionable external validity of results
	7. Difficulty of establishing external validity

Laboratory Experiments

1. Possibility of control and manipulation of variables	1. Artificiality—questionable realism
2. Allow for the creation of conditions that may be uneconomical, difficult, or even impossible to establish in the field	2. Require highly controlled conditions
3. Excellent for sharpening concepts and refining measurements	3. Difficult to generalize results to real life situations—to establish external validity
4. Allow a researcher to examine phenomena in an "uncamouflaged" state	

Secondary Source Materials

1. Economical	1. Reliability of data unknown
2. Plentiful	2. Often fail to fit specific purpose of a research problem
3. Helpful in providing background material	3. Units of measurement may not be comparable between sources
	4. Problems of measurement validity

Strategies for Studying Organizations

6. Why do questionnaires have a statistical advantage over case studies?
7. Discuss the impact of recall on self-report data.
8. What is the impact of manipulating a single variable in laboratory experiments?
9. What is meant by the statement, "Laboratory studies sacrifice external validity for internal validity"?
10. What are some possible causes of a lack of measurement validity in secondary sources?

References

Akers, R., and Campbell, F. L. "Size and the Administrative Component in Occupational Associations." *Pacific Sociological Review* 13 (1970): 241–251.

Barnes, L. B. "Organizational Change and Field Experiment Methods." In *Methods of Organizational Research,* edited by V. H. Vroom. Pittsburgh: University of Pittsburgh Press, 1967.

Bedeian, A. G. "Management Theory: A Pediatric Note." *Business Perspectives* 9, no. 4 (1973): 2–5.

Bouchard, T. J. "Field Research Methods: Interviewing, Questionnaires, Participant Observation, Systematic Observation, Unobtrusive Measures." In *Handbook of Industrial and Organizational Psychology,* edited by M. D. Dunnette. Chicago: Rand McNally, 1976.

Campbell, D. T. "Factors Relevant to the Validity of Experiments in Social Settings." *Psychological Bulletin* 47 (1957): 297–312.

Dalton, M. *Men Who Manage: Fusions of Feeling and Theory in Administration.* New York: John Wiley & Sons, 1959.

Erikson, K. T. "A Comment on Disguised Observation in Sociology." *Social Problems* 14 (1967): 366–373.

Festinger, L. "Laboratory Experiments." In *Research Methods in the Behavioral Sciences,* edited by L. Festinger and D. Katz. New York: Holt, Rinehart and Winston, 1953.

Glaser, E. M., and Backer, T. E. "A Look at Participant-Observation." *Evaluation* 1, no. 3 (1973): 46–49.

Gouldner, A. W. *Patterns of Industrial Bureaucracy.* New York: Free Press of Glencoe, 1954.

Hamner, W. C., and Organ, D. W. *Organizational Behavior: An Applied Psychological Approach.* Dallas: Business Publications, 1978.

House, R. J. "Scientific Investigation in Management." *Management International Review* 10, nos. 4–5 (1970): 139–150.

Huber, G. P., O'Connell, M. J., and Cummings, L. L. "Perceived Environmental Uncertainty: Effects of Information and Structure." *Academy of Management Journal* 18 (1975): 725–740.

Lawrence, P. R., and Lorsch, J. W. *Organization and Environment: Managing Differentiation and Integration.* Boston: Division of Research, Graduate School of Business Administration, Harvard University, 1967.

Lijphart, A. "Comparative Politics and the Comparative Method." *American Political Science Review* 65 (1971): 682–693.

Marx, M. H. "The General Nature of Theory Construction." In *Theories in Contemporary Psychology,* edited by M. H. Marx. New York: Macmillan, 1963.

McGrath, J. E. "Toward a 'Theory of Method' for Research on Organizations." In *New Perspectives in Organization Research,* edited by W. W. Cooper, H. J. Leavitt, and M. W. Shelly. New York: John Wiley & Sons, 1964.

Meyer, M. W. "Recent Developments in Organizational Research and Theory." In *Environments and Organizations,* edited by M. W. Meyer. San Francisco: Jossey-Bass, 1978.

Meyer, M. W. *Theory of Organizational Structure.* Indianapolis: Bobbs-Merrill, 1977.

Rubenstein, A. H., and Haberstroh, C. J. *Some Theories of Organization.* Rev. ed. Homewood, Ill.: Richard D. Irwin, 1966.

Scott, J. F., and Lynton, R. P. *Three Studies in Management.* London: Routledge & Kegan Paul, 1952.

Scott, W. G., and Mitchell, T. R. *Organization Theory: A Structural and Behavioral Analysis.* 3rd ed. Homewood, Ill.: Richard D. Irwin, 1976.

Scott, W. R. "Field Methods in the Study of Organizations." In *Handbook of Organizations,* edited by J. G. March. Chicago: Rand McNally, 1965.

Selznick, P. *TVA and the Grass Roots: A Study in the Sociology of Formal Organization.* Berkeley, Calif.: University of California Press, 1949.

Chapter 2

Sullivan, M. A., Queen, S. A., and Patrick, R. C. "Participant Observation as Employed in the Study of a Military Training Program." *American Sociological Review* 23 (1958): 660–667.

Thompson, J. D. *Organizations in Action.* New York: McGraw-Hill, 1967.

Weick, K. E. "Laboratory Experimentation with Organizations: A Reappraisal." *Academy of Management Review* 2 (1977): 123–128.

Weick, K. E. "Organizations in the Laboratory." In *Methods of Organizational Research,* edited by V. H. Vroom. Pittsburgh: University of Pittsburgh Press, 1967.

Whyte, W. F. "On Making the Most of Participant Observation." *American Sociologist* 14 (1979): 56–66.

Whyte, W. F. *Organizational Behavior: Theory and Application.* Homewood, Ill.: Richard D. Irwin, 1969.

Zelditch, M., and Hopkins, T. K. "Laboratory Experiments with Organizations." In *Complex Organizations: A Sociological Reader,* edited by A. Etzioni. New York: Holt, Rinehart and Winston, 1961.

Dimensions of Organization Design

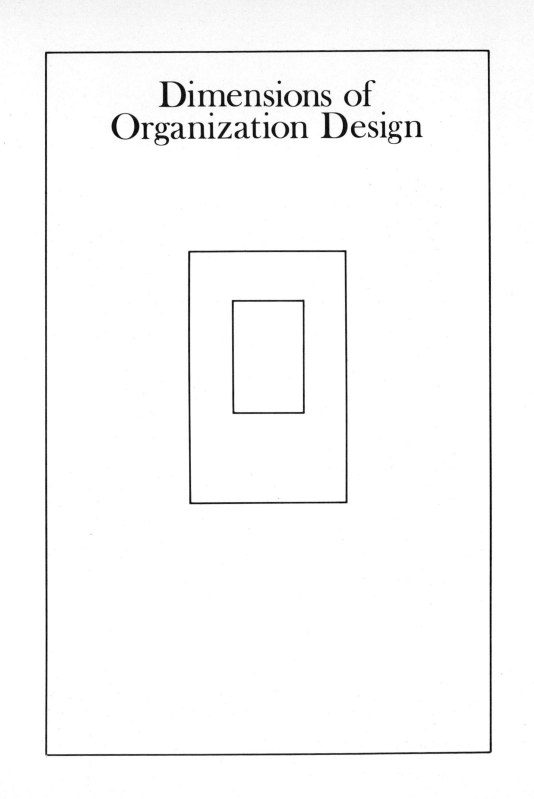

Dimensions of
Organization Design

Chapter 3

An awareness of the importance of organization design dates back beyond the beginning of written history.[1] Most historians, however, generally date the first recognized attempts at systematically studying the development and design of organization structures to the last two decades of the nineteenth century. The growth of an interest in organization paralleled the growing economic and industrial development of the United States and Western Europe. The forces of expanding technology and commerce, paired with new advances in transportation and communication, dramatically increased the scope and complexity of business undertakings. An unprecedented increase in the size of factories resulted in previously unexperienced problems of waste and inefficiency. These changes necessitated the formulation and investigation of new concepts for the design of organizations.

Organization design refers to the particular arangement or composition of an organization's structure. As suggested by Leavitt, design implies creation, that is, the purposive formulation and deliberate establishment of relationships among the components of an organization.[2] As such, "design is essentially the activity of constructing and changing organization structure to achieve optimum effectiveness."[3] In this respect, the structural features of an organization may be conceived of as a set of complex variables whose design is shaped by a considerable range of managerial choice.

The primary purpose of the present chapter is to provide the reader with a succinct review of the structural ("skeletal") characteristics of formal organizations. We begin with a historical overview of approaches to the study of organization design, briefly commenting on the contributions of the so-called "classicists," and then turn attention to Weber's theory of bureaucratic organization. Following a critical evaluation of Weber's work, we present an analysis of the basic dimensions of formal organization structure. Building on this background, we then describe the

---

[1] Parts of the following discussion have been taken from A. G. Bedeian, "Historical Development of Management," in *Encyclopedia of Professional Management,* ed. L. R. Bittel (New York: McGraw-Hill, 1978), pp. 645–650.

[2] H. J. Leavitt,"On the Design Part of Organization Design," in *The Management of Organization Design,* vol. 1, ed. R. H. Kilmann, L. R. Pondy, and D. P. Slevin (New York: Elsevier North-Holland, 1976), p. 17.

[3] B. J. Calder, K. M. Rowland, and H. Leblebici, "The Use of Scaling and Cluster Techniques in Investigating the Social Structure of Organizations," in Kilmann, Pondy, and Slevin, *Management of Organization Design,* vol. 2, p. 121.

basic structural arrangements that have been traditionally followed in the design of organizations. In this regard, it should perhaps be reemphasized that our general focus at this point is on structural patterns that managers can design and that are thus formal ("official") by definition. While it is realized, as has been pointed out by Child, that "unofficial practices have to be recognized as part of the context of organizational design, . . . organizational designers do not implement unofficial structures."[4]

The Early Development of Organization Theory

As indicated in the introduction to this chapter, the origins of organization theory may be traced to the application of technological principles to manual work. Interest in organizations and organizing was a natural outgrowth of an increasing world-wide trend towards industrialization. Expanding technology and commerce, paired with new advances in transportation and communication, increased the scope and complexity of business enterprises. The economic and industrial growth that ensued fostered the development of the factory system, as manufacturing progressed from unit to mass production methods. The resulting emergence of large factories in basic industries such as iron, steel, and petroleum necessitated significant changes in the design of organizations. In the words of one historian, "The technical achievements and the development of the factory system started a trend that changed the empirical and 'rule of thumb' approach of typical owner-managers of industry. Problems developed which could not be solved without planning systematic relationships of work methods and effective organization."[5]

By the turn of the century, the United States had become a major manufacturing center requiring new and efficient methods for dealing with the problems of organizational complexity. Between 1880 and 1910 alone, the number of businesses of sufficient size and stability to be listed with Dun & Bradstreet doubled to total over 1,500,000.[6] During this same period, manufacturing output for the first time increased at a rate surpassing population growth, expanding from 32 per cent of the nation's total commodity output in 1860, to 53 percent in 1900. This burst of industrialization was reflected in several areas: the number of miles of railroad track operated jumped from 30,626 in 1860, to 266,185 in 1910, an increase of 769 percent; pig iron production rose from 821 long tons in 1860, to 27,304 long tons in 1910; and the number of wage earners employed in manufacturing increased over fivefold, from 1,300,000 in 1860, to slightly above 7,000,000 in 1914. At the same time, this expansion increased the need for improved communication. The number of miles of telegraph wiring soared from 50,000 miles of wire in 1860, to over 1,600,000 miles in 1915. By

---

[4]J. Child, *Organization: A Guide to Problems and Practices* (London: Harper & Row, 1977), p. 9.

[5]J. F. Mee, "A History of Twentieth Century Management Thought" (Ph.D. diss., Ohio State University, Columbus, Ohio, 1959), p. 17.

[6]T. C. Cochran, *Business in American Life: A History* (New York: McGraw-Hill, 1972), p. 146.

Chapter 3

1879, three years after Alexander Graham Bell patented the telephone, telephone exchanges had been established in virtually every state and territory. In 1886 transatlantic cable service was inaugurated, and by 1901 introduction of the "wireless" made it possible to communicate with areas halfway around the world.[7] In short, the decades after 1860 marked the United States' transition from an agricultural and commercial-mercantile to an industrial-capitalistic economy.[8] Concomitantly, cultural and economic conditions had created an unprecedented need for an increased understanding of the nature and character of organizations.

A Beginning

Improvements in the prevailing methods of work and organization during this era were principally initiated by men actively engaged in industrial enterprises. The person most often referred to as the first to propose a rational and systematic science of management (and hence organization) was Henry R. Towne (1844–1924), president of the Yale and Towne Manufacturing Company, who, in 1886, presented a paper titled "The Engineer as Economist." His comments, delivered at a meeting of the American Society of Mechanical Engineers (ASME), stressed the importance of management as a field of independent study, equal to that of engineering. Noting the almost complete lack of management literature, the virtual absence of a medium for the exchange of administrative ideas and experience, and the total absence of management associations, Towne urged that ASME serve as a center for the development and study of industrial management. Such a suggestion was considered nothing less than revolutionary. For, indeed, as described by Urwick, at the time and for many years afterwards, "a large and influential section of the [ASME] membership continued vehemently to deny that there could be a science of management or, if there could, that it was any concern of an engineering society."[9] Towne's presentation was, above all, an appeal for the acknowledgment and nurturing of such a science.

Frederick W. Taylor: The Birth of Scientific Management

While Towne's presentation is recognized as marking the beginning of the search for a science of management, the birth of scientific management is generally accredited to Frederick W. Taylor (1856–1915). His book, *The Principles of Scientific Management,* published in 1911, seriously questioned the traditional role of management.

---

[7]Mee, "A History," p. 17.

[8]A. R. Pred, *The Spatial Dynamics of U.S. Urban-Industrial Growth, 1800–1914* (Cambridge, Mass.: M.I.T. Press, 1966), pp. 16–22.

[9]L. F. Urwick, *The Golden Book of Management* (London: Newman Neame, 1956), p. 25.

Synthesizing and refining the ideas and concepts developed in his earlier writings and experiments, Taylor envisioned a "mental revolution" in which the concerns both of management and of the worker would be based on a philosophy of "mutuality of interests." He conceived of management's new duties as involving: (1) the development of a true science of managing, complete with clearly stated laws, rules, and principles that would replace the old rule-of-thumb methods; (2) the scientific selection, training, and development of workers (in the past workers were randomly chosen and often untrained); (3) an enthusiastic cooperation with workers to ensure that all work performed is done in accordance with scientific principles; and (4) the equal division of tasks and responsibilities between the worker and management. Taylor was resolutely committed to eliminating the inefficient and wasteful practices of the past and to transcending what, at the time, appeared to be insolvable conflicts of interest between labor and management, believing that the interests of employers and employees could be made to coincide.[10] According to Taylor's doctrine, the increased productivity and expansion of output resulting from improved methods of organization were to be shared so that there would be both an increase in wages for labor and an increase in profits for investors. As Maier, borrowing from the language of game theory, has so aptly put it, "Taylorism promised an escape from zero-sum conflict, in which the gain of one party could be extracted only from the equal sacrifice of the other."[11]

The work of numerous other pioneers, such as Lyndall F. Urwick, Luther H. Gulick, and James D. Mooney and Alan C. Reiley, paralleled that of Taylor, contributing to the emergence and growth of organization theory.[12] While it is not our intent to completely review the historical development of this movement, two other authors, Henri Fayol and Max Weber, merit mention not only because of the special character of their contributions, but because of the lasting significance of their work.[13]

Criticisms of the Classicists

Before proceeding further, however, it would perhaps be best to first comment on the extensive criticism that has been directed at the work of the early (often called "classical") organization theorists. In addition to other criticisms, their work has been attacked as being too simplistic, as advancing "principles" that are really nothing more than "proverbs," and as reflecting a promanagement bias.[14] While in certain

---

[10]C. R. Littler, "Understanding Taylorism," *British Journal of Sociology* 29 (1978): 185–202; S. Klaw, "Frederick Winslow Taylor: The Messiah of Time and Motion Study," *American Heritage* 30, no. 5 (1979): 26–39.

[11]C. S. Maier, "Between Taylorism and Technocracy: European Ideologies and the Vision of Industrial Productivity in the 1920s," *Journal of Contemporary History* 5, no. 2 (1970): 27–61.

[12]L. F. Urwick, *The Elements of Administration* (New York: Harper & Row, 1943); L. H. Gulick and L. E. Urwick, eds., *Papers on the Science of Administration* (New York: Institute of Public Administration, Columbia University, 1937); J. D. Mooney and A. C. Reiley, *Onward Industry!* (New York: Harper & Bros., 1931).

[13]This development is well summarized in D. A. Wren, *The Evolution of Management Thought,* 2nd ed. (New York: John Wiley & Sons, 1979).

[14]See L. F. Urwick, "Why the So-called 'Classicists' Endure," *Management International Review* 11, no. 1 (1971): 3–14.

instances these criticisms are undeniably true, it should be realized that much of what we take for granted today was new a half-century ago and far from obvious. As a result, these early writers had very little alternative but to rely upon their past experience as a basis for the logic of their statements. Organization research as we know it today was nonexistent. Evaluated from this perspective, there is no question that the views of these early contributors were remarkably accurate and, in many instances, are still valid today. In this respect, the accomplishments of these early theorists are not to be minimized. Indeed, as noted by Perrow, a great many management consulting firms continue to make a "handsome living" by pointing out the simple proverbs first formulated by the so-called classicists.[15]

Henri Fayol: The Emergence of Administrative Theory

Like those of Taylor, the ideas of Henri Fayol (1841–1925) have had a lasting impact on the development of organization theory as a science. His views remain important not only because of his enormous influence on succeeding generations of organization theorists but also because of the continuing validity of much of his analysis. Although aware of Taylor's theories, Fayol worked independently in France during the same period that scientific management was developing in the United States. Whereas Taylor approached the study of organization from the workshop level, Fayol approached the subject from the viewpoint of upper-level administration. Writing in 1916, Fayol, in his classic work "Administration Industrielle et Générale" (not translated and made available in the United States until 1930), was the first author to classify the study of management according to functional areas (that is, planning, organizing, commanding, coordinating, and controlling). It is perhaps most notable that this system of classification is still used today as the foundation for a host of introductory management texts and as a framework for innumerable company and university development programs. Of particular relevance to the present discussion is Fayol's stress on the importance of organizing, defining it to include all activities associated with creating a business and with those human and material resources necessary for successful functioning. While this definition is certainly broader than that most commonly used today and contains many elements typically considered to be part of personnel or human resource administration, it reflects an appreciation of the significance of proper organization in accomplishing the goals of a business.

An industrialist with an outstanding record as General Director of the Commentry-Fourchambault Collieries, Fayol was also among the first authors to advance a set of general management principles. Arguing that the task of management should be approached in a spirit of scientific inquiry, Fayol was of the opinion that these principles could be distilled from experience by reason. Many of the principles Fayol developed, such as "division of work," "unity of command," "span of control," and

---

[15]C. Perrow, *Organizational Analysis: A Sociological View* (Monterey, Calif.: Belmont/Cole, 1970), p.15.

the "scalar chain," are, as the following sections will indicate, more than just principles of management; they are principles of organization.

In retrospect, the concepts and ideas developed by Fayol have clearly had an
impact on current thinking. The enduring nature of his contributions to management
and organization theory, in general, is perhaps best indicated by the fact that debate
still continues on questions that were first formally addressed by Fayol some sixty
years ago.[16]

Max Weber: Bureaucracy as the Ideal

Whereas Taylor's and Fayol's primary attention had been directed toward the practical problems of organizing for effective goal accomplishment, the concern of Max
Weber (1864–1920) was with the more fundamental issues of how organizations are
elaborated and sanctioned.[17] Although Weber, a German sociologist, published most
of his work at the turn of the century, his ideas remained virtually unknown to English-
speaking theorists until they were translated beginning in the late 1920s. Primarily
descriptive (normative) in nature, Weber's writings strike an interesting contrast with
the practitioner-oriented recommendations offered by Taylor and Fayol. The general
thrust, and lasting contribution, of Weber's work was an outline of the systematic
requirements (characteristics) of rational organization (bureaucracy).

In reviewing Weber's work it is important to emphasize three points:

1. Weber did not use the term bureaucracy in the disparaging, emotionally-tinged
    sense of red tape, endless lines, and rule-encumbered inefficiency. Rather, he
    used it as a descriptive, noncritical label referring to what he regarded as the
    most modern and efficient organization yet developed. In Weber's words,

    *Experience tends universally to show that the purely bureaucratic type of admin-
    istrative organization—that is, the monocratic variety of bureaucracy—is, from a
    purely technical point of view, capable of attaining the highest degree of effi-
    ciency and is in this sense formally the most rational known means of carrying
    out imperative control over human beings. It is superior to any other form in
    precision, in stability, in the stringency of its discipline, and in its reliability. It thus
    makes possible a particularly high degree of calculability of results for the heads
    of the organization and for those acting in relation to it. It is finally superior both
    in intensive efficiency and in the scope of its operations, and is formally capable
    of application to all kinds of administrative tasks.[18]*

---

[16]M. B. Brodie, *Fayol on Administration* (London: Lyon, Grant and Green, 1967), p. 5. See, for example, M.
J. Gannon and F. T. Paine, "Unity of Command and Job Attitudes of Managers in a Bureaucratic Organization,"
Journal of Applied Psychology 59 (1974): 392–394.

[17]D. Katz and R. L. Kahn, *The Social Psychology of Organizations* (New York: John Wiley & Sons, 1966),
p. 71.

[18]M. Weber, *Max Weber: The Theory of Social and Economic Organization,* ed. and trans. A. M. Henderson
and T. Parsons (New York: Oxford University Press, 1947), p. 337.

2. To Weber, bureaucracy was a mental construct, an idealized type of organization that did not exist in reality.[19] Bureaucracy was a standard or model to be used not only in constructing organizations but in assessing (through comparison) their relative performance. In this regard it should be noted that Weber's basic model is hypothetical in nature rather than factual.

3. Weber's idealized type of organization is based on "legal" authority as contrasted with that which rests on either "tradition" (custom) or "charisma" ("the gift of grace").[20] As explained by Blau and Scott, legal authority "assumes the existence of a formally established body of social norms designed to organize conduct for the rational pursuit of specific goals."[21] In the purest type of exercise of legal authority, obedience is not owed to a person such as a traditional chief or a charismatic leader, but to the impersonal authority of an office. Thus, in such systems, the prerogatives of authority adhere to specific positions rather than to individual persons. Familiar examples of legal authority structures are the military, the governmental bureau, the college or university, and the business firm (especially those above a certain size).

Characteristics of Bureaucracy

At several points in his writings, Weber identified the distinctive characteristics of his idealized bureaucracy.[22] It is the acceptance of these characteristics that determines the effectiveness of this type of organization. These essential characteristics have been summarized nicely by Wren:

1. Labor is divided so that the authority and responsibility of each member are clearly defined and are legitimatized as official duties.
2. The offices or positions are organized in a hierarchy of authority resulting in a chain of command (the scalar principle).
3. All organization members are to be selected on the basis of technical qualifications through formal examinations or by virtue of training or education.
4. Officials are appointed, not elected (with the exception, in some cases, of the chief of the whole unit—for example, an elected public official).
5. Administrative officials work for fixed salaries and are "career" officials.
6. The administrative official is not an owner of the unit being administered.
7. The administrator is subject to strict rules, discipline, and controls regarding the

---

[19]M. Weber, *The Methodology of the Social Sciences,* ed. and trans. E. A. Shils and H. H. Finch (New York: Free Press, 1949), p. 90.

[20]Weber, *Max Weber,* p. 328.

[21]P. M. Blau and W. R. Scott, *Formal Organization: A Comparative Approach* (San Francisco: Chandler, 1962), p. 31.

[22]M. Weber, *From Max Weber: Essays in Sociology,* ed. and trans. H. H. Gerth and C. W. Mills (New York: Oxford University Press, 1946), pp. 196–204; Weber, *Max Weber,* pp. 329–336.

conduct of his official duties. These rules and controls are impersonal and uniformly applied in all cases.[23]

It should be emphasized again that Weber described an idealized, hypothetical structure. The extent to which Weber's ideal type adequately describes real organizations has been the subject of a wealth of research. The results of these studies have underscored both functional and dysfunctional consequences of bureaucracy.

Functional and Dysfunctional Consequences of Bureaucracy

As noted, Weber considered bureaucracy to be the most efficient and rational means of organization because of its stability and reliability, the calculability of results that it permits, and its wide applicability. Subsequent research, however, has shown that the accomplishment of these functions is often not without certain undesirable effects or dysfunctions. Thompson has termed the study of the consequences of these dysfunctions "bureaupathology," and has suggested that such negative outcomes result from what may be called "bureaupathic behavior."[24] Examples of this malady have been reported in several studies.

Merton, for instance, has noted that, while bureaucratic rules and impersonality produce a high degree of reliability and calculability of results, over the long run such conformity can be detrimental.[25] Specifically, Merton suggests that over time: (1) rules and regulations often take on a symbolic significance of their own and, as a consequence, become ends rather than means to ends; and (2) such devotion to rules often leads to situations in which past decisions are blindly repeated with no appreciation or concern for changed conditions, and no provisions made for alternatives not previously defined. As a result, excessive inflexibility leads to the fostering of ineffectiveness and the likelihood of more or less serious maladjustments. As an example of the tendency to make ends of means, Merton cites the requirement, in the early stages of World War II, that naval officers carry calling cards, even when destined for combat in the South Pacific. And Bernt Balchen, Admiral Byrd's pilot on his famous flight over the South Pole, was denied citizenship by the Bureau of Naturalization on the grounds that he violated the requirement of five years' continuous residence in the United States, even though he was on a ship flying the U.S. flag and serving as an invaluable member of a U.S. expedition. A more recent, and somewhat more humorous, example of this same phenomenon is an incident involving a high-ranking Brazilian government official and a group of native Brazilian Indians. Appearing at the time scheduled for their appointment with the official, the Indians were refused entry

---

[23]Adapted from Wren, *The Evolution,* pp. 251–252.
[24]V. A. Thompson, *Modern Organizations* (New York: Alfred A. Knopf, 1961), pp. 23–24.
[25]R. K. Merton, "Bureaucratic Structure and Personality," *Social Forces* 18 (1940): 560–568.

Chapter 3

because they wore no neckties. Huddling for a moment and pondering the situation, the Indians announced that no government representative would be allowed in their village without feathered headdress and body paint.

Selznick, in his study of the Tennessee Valley Authority, has provided evidence to indicate that delegation of authority, while necessary for the growth of an organization beyond a certain size, also results in certain unintended consequences.[26] More specifically, while the delegation of authority is intended to increase operational effectiveness by providing for the exercise of specialized competencies, it also stimulates a divergence of interests and the internalization of specific subunit goals rather than overall organizational goals. Consequently, this divergence, or *bifurcation* of interests, is often the basis for conflict among organizational subunits. Obviously, such differences in orientation are not conducive to the accomplishment of the primary goals of an organization as a whole. Unfortunately, such subunit rivalries (based upon vested interests) seem to be a common element in a great many organizations. A typical example can be found in many, if not most, universities where conflicts over which department is going to offer what courses often result in unnecessary duplication of subject offerings, as well as the unnecessary expenditure of resources.

Gouldner, in his classic study of "General Gypsum Corporation" (a pseudonym), has suggested that, although bureaucratic rules are intended to counter work apathy, they actually contribute to it.[27] This seeming paradox occurs because rules not only define unacceptable behavior, they also serve to specify a *minimum* level of acceptable performance. Thus, to paraphrase Gouldner, it is possible, once rules have been defined, for workers to *remain* apathetic, for they now know just how *little* they can do and still remain secure.[28] Within an educational setting, statements such as "all students must attend at least 50 percent of the classes during a term to pass" or "the minimum requirement for graduation is a C average on all course work undertaken" are excellent illustrations of this phenomenon in that they clearly define minimum levels of acceptable behavior. Rules therefore may be functional in one sense, but in another (unintended) sense they permit participant involvement without requiring an emotional commitment. Unfortunately, a typical administrative response in such circumstances is to enact additional bureaucratic rules (such as mandatory class attendance) and, in turn, further aggravate an already poor situation.

There have been numerous other criticisms of Weber's work. As is the case with the classicists, the validity of much of this criticism can hardly be questioned. This should not, however, overshadow the fact that Weber's pioneering work, like that of Taylor and Fayol, has stimulated a wealth of further analysis and research into the nature and intricacies of organization. In this respect, the early works of Weber, Taylor, Fayol, and the other so-called classicists, although technically unsophis-

---

[26]P. Selznick, *TVA and the Grass Roots: A Study in the Sociology of Formal Organizations* (Berkeley: University of California Press, 1949), pp. 155–179.

[27]A. W. Gouldner, *Patterns of Industrial Bureacracy* (New York: Free Press, 1954), pp. 174–175.

[28]Ibid.

ticated by contemporary standards, remain landmarks in the study of organization theory and analysis.

Basic Dimensions of Organization Structure
Division of Labor: The Primordial Act

As suggested earlier, organization design essentially involves the structuring of an enterprise to achieve optimum effectiveness. Under norms of rationality (efficiency), as an enterprise grows, achieving a level of complexity such that the efforts of more than one person are needed, it is confronted by two primary concerns: (1) the subdivision of the work to be performed, and (2) the necessity of determining an appropriate basis for grouping the efforts of the resulting subunits efficiently and for the benefit of the whole. With respect to the former, the successive subdivision or decomposition of the overall task into smaller and smaller elements is termed "horizontal differentiation" or, more frequently, "division of labor." As noted by Sexton, the rationale behind this process is simple.

For one individual to perform all of the tasks required to complete a project would be extremely complex and demanding, probably impossible in most cases. However, each of these tasks alone likely demands little more than a unique set of arm and hand motions or, at best, a moderate degree of skill which could be mastered quickly. This preoccupation with a relatively uncomplicated activity is the source of benefits. There is time saved in training, due to the simplicity of the assignment, and in operation, since the worker need not change tasks nor [sic] equipment. In addition, it provides the opportunity for utilizing the dominant talents of each individual worker. Naturally, the consequent repetition leads to a degree of expertise which produces efficiency.[29]

More briefly stated, the division of labor has as its intended effect the establishment of a continuous, reliable, and predictable level of performance by minimizing dependence upon particular individuals or special skills.[30] While these benefits are obviously attractive, it should be hurriedly pointed out that over the last several years the costs associated with such high levels of specialization have elicited increasing concern. It has become more and more evident that the price of task specialization is reduced job satisfaction, lower levels of employee commitment, increased employee alienation, and decreased worker involvement. The general ramifications of this dilemma have been discussed elsewhere.[31] No attempt will be made here to summarize this

---

[29]W. P. Sexton, ed., *Organization Theories* (Columbus, Ohio: Merrill, 1970), p. 3.

[30]J. E. T. Eldridge and A. D. Crombie, *A Sociology of Organisation* (London: George Allen & Unwin, 1974), p. 115.

[31]See, for example, R. N. Kanungo, "The Concepts of Alienation and Involvement Revisited," *Psychological Bulletin* 86 (1979): 119–138.

literature. At this juncture, however, it should be made clear that, while task specialization is an organizational process, the specialization of people is clearly a social process.[32]

With respect to the second primary concern identified above, once the total task of an organization has been divided, it becomes necessary for reasons of efficiency (for example, economies of scale and overheads) to aggregate related tasks into groups. This process is called "departmentalization," and the individual groups of related jobs are typically labeled "departments."

Organization Charts: A Primer

The most common method of depicting the structure of an enterprise is through the use of an "organization chart." Occasionally referred to as a "table of organization" or "organization tree," an organization chart is merely a graphic representation or blueprint of all the positions in an organization and the formal relations by which they are connected. "In its commonest form it also shows the hierarchical structure which is typical of most complex organizations, the vertical dimensions representing the several levels of authority within the structure and the connecting lines showing the relationships between these levels and the channels by which communication takes place within the organization."[a] Figure 3–1 is an example of such a chart for a manufacturing company. The immediate value of this method of presentation is that it illustrates the overall shape or configuration of an enterprise in a readily comprehensible form. The familiar hollow squares or rectangles of these charts show the manner in which the principal subunits and positions within an organization are arranged. Distance from the top or the bottom, as pictured on the chart, is generally viewed as a measure of status. Horizontal lines between positions stand for the interaction of equals. Vertical connecting lines note prescribed relations between superiors and subordinates. In this regard, it has often been noted that "at best, organization charts . . . are static representations of what is in reality the dynamic process of organizational life."[b] Their inaccuracy primarily lies in the fact that no organization chart, if it is to be readable, can ever totally reflect the empirical entity that it is meant to depict. Typically, "among the omitted details are most of the relationships between people who have no authority or reporting responsibility with respect to each other, but must coordinate their activities anyway. Also omitted—by definition—are the informal norms which, in every organization, concentrate more authority in certain positions than the table of organization anticipates; and all the personal preferences, alliances, and coalitions, exchanges of favors, interferences by outsiders, and customary breaches of the rules that develop in any well-established organization."[c] All the

---

[32]Thompson, *Modern Organizations,* p. 28.
[a]F. Glen, *The Social Psychology of Organizations* (London: Methuen, 1975), pp. 50, 52.
[b]T. Caplow, *How to Run an Organization: A Manual of Practical Sociology* (Hinsdale, Ill.: Dryden Press, 1976), p. 18.
[c]H. G. Hicks and C. R. Gullett, *Organizations: Theory and Behavior* (New York: McGraw-Hill, 1975), p. 65.

same, the information an organization chart does include is a vital prerequisite to the accurate development and maintenance of an effective enterprise.

Basic Patterns of Departmentalization

Drawing upon both traditional theory and current operational practices, three *primary* bases for grouping specialized tasks into large specialized units or departments can be identified:

1. *Functional:* a grouping based on job activities such as purchasing, manufacturing, sales, finance, and personnel.
2. *Product:* a grouping based on differentiation of goods and/or of services according to distinctions in their manufacture and/or their end use.
3. *Area:* a grouping based on geographical locations with boundaries determined by distance, natural, legal, political, and/or cultural considerations.[33]

Functional Departmentalization

The most widely used basis for grouping activities, functional departmentalization evolved around the turn of this century as a response to the increasing size and complexity of business undertakings. Popular in the United States and abroad, "the basic organizing principle is to group similar logistic activities under major functional managers who, in turn, report to a central headquarters."[34] Departmentalization by function is structurally shown in Figure 3–2, in which the activities of the North American Automotive Operations of Ford Motor Company are grouped into such primary functions as purchasing, manufacturing, engineering, and sales. The functional form has as its principal advantages the maximizing of specialized interest within departmental units and, in the case of smaller enterprises, relatively simple communication and decision networks. The major shortcomings of this arrangement emerge, however, as coordination across functional areas (specializations) becomes more difficult and, as suggested by Selznick, departmental interests begin to take precedence over organizational goals.[35] This process has been documented by Price who, in a study of the impact of different forms of departmentalization on organizational performance, found that functional departmentalization not only hampered cooperation because it provides for no interoccupational contact, but fostered a parochial emphasis on functional objectives, with a minimum appreciation of or concern for broader organizational goals.[36]

[33]Adapted from S. M. Davis, "Two Models of Organization: Unity of Command versus Balance of Power," *Sloan Management Review* 16, no. 1 (1974): 29.

[34]H. I. Ansoff and R. G. Brandenburg, "A Language for Organization Design: Part II," *Management Science* 17 (1971): B 717–B 731.

[35]Selznick, *TVA and the Grass Roots,* pp. 155–179.

[36]J. L. Price, "The Impact of Departmentalization on Interoccupational Cooperation," *Human Organization* 27 (1968): 362–368.

Chapter 3

Product Departmentalization

The grouping of activities on the basis of related product-markets was pioneered by E. I. du Pont de Nemours & Company and General Motors in the 1920s. It evolved in response to the disadvantages of functional departmentalization mentioned above. "Both General Motors and DuPont had grown to large size, and both [had] multiplied their products to a point where [their] operational responsiveness was not adequate to the demands of their markets."[37] A majority of the world's largest corporations at their upper levels are structured according to one of the numerous variations on the product departmentalization pattern. In addition to General Motors, Kimberly-Clark, RCA, and du Pont, Westinghouse Electric is a prime example of this arrangement. As shown in Figure 3–3, Westinghouse's industry products company has as many as four layers of grouping by product, descending from "company" through an "executive vice-president" level, a "vice-president–divisions" level, and, finally, to a "division" level. The major disadvantage associated with this type of departmentalization is highlighted in this example; problems of coordination (for example, lack of clarity of responsibilities, decrease in professional communication) are likely to occur between specialized product areas as an organization increases complexity. As suggested by Kover's analysis of the reorganization of an advertising agency along product lines, coordination problems typically occur as a consequence of communication difficulties arising between units separated into specialized product departments.[38]

Area Departmentalization

Also known as *location* or *territorial* departmentalization, this form of grouping is especially appropriate for large firms or enterprises whose organizational activities are physically or geographically dispersed. Its principal advantage is that it allows units operating in a given environment to adapt to the particular local circumstances with which they are confronted. For this reason, territorial departmentalization is particularly popular not only among organizations that are geographically dispersed but also among those which operate in a variety of geographic areas with different legal, political, or cultural environments. Examples of organizations that are territorially departmentalized to overcome the difficulties of coordinating their activities over wide geographic areas include most regional sales offices, American Telephone & Telegraph, and such government agencies as the Federal Reserve Board, Internal Revenue Service, and Postal Service. This basis of departmentalization is also particularly suited for multinational business corporations. Such internationally based firms as Massey-Ferguson, Singer, Chase Manhattan Bank, and Kaiser Aluminum & Chemical (International Division) are structured on this basis. As an example, the organization structure of the International Banking Department of Chase Manhattan Bank is illustrated in Figure 3–4.

---

[37]Ansoff and Brandenburg, "A Language," p. B720.
[38]A. J. Kover, "Reorganization in an Advertising Agency: A Case Study of a Decrease in Integration," *Human Organization* 22 (1963–64): 252–259.

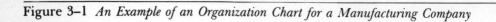

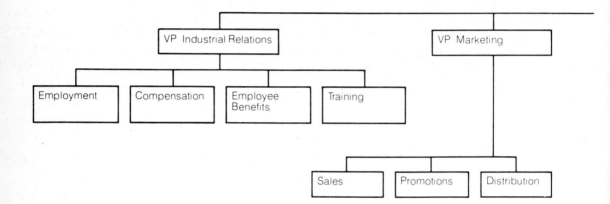

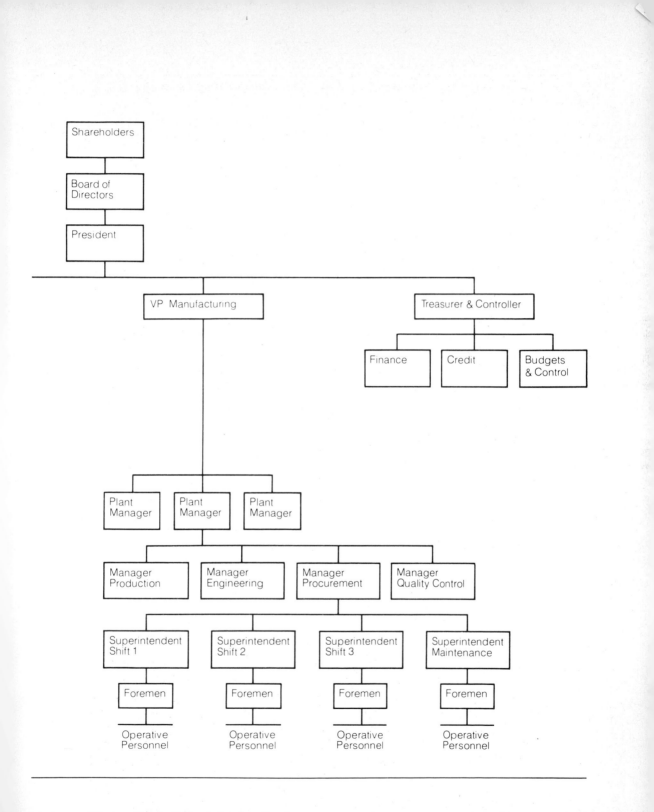

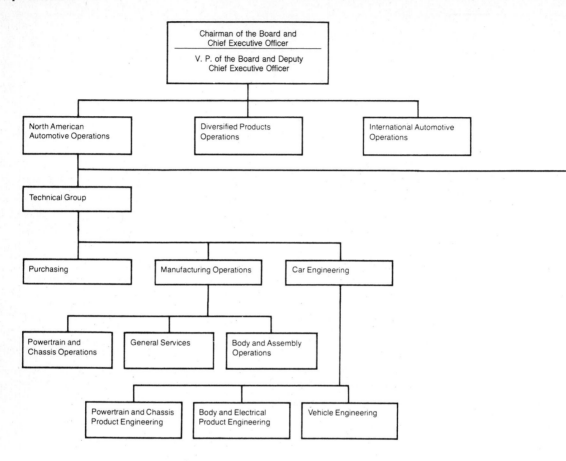

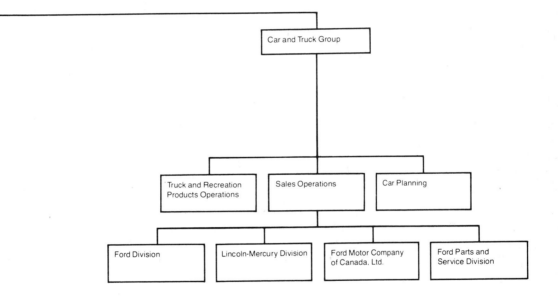

```
                          ┌─────────────────────┐
                          │  Car and Truck Group │
                          └─────────────────────┘
                                     │
         ┌───────────────────────────┼───────────────────────────┐
┌─────────────────────┐  ┌─────────────────────┐  ┌─────────────────────┐
│ Truck and Recreation │  │  Sales Operations   │  │    Car Planning     │
│ Products Operations  │  │                     │  │                     │
└─────────────────────┘  └─────────────────────┘  └─────────────────────┘
```

Truck and Recreation Products Operations

Sales Operations

Car Planning

Ford Division

Lincoln-Mercury Division

Ford Motor Company of Canada, Ltd.

Ford Parts and Service Division

Effective: June 8, 1978.
Source: Courtesy of Ford Motor Company.

Figure 3–3 *Product Departmentalization, Westinghouse Electric Corporation, 1978*

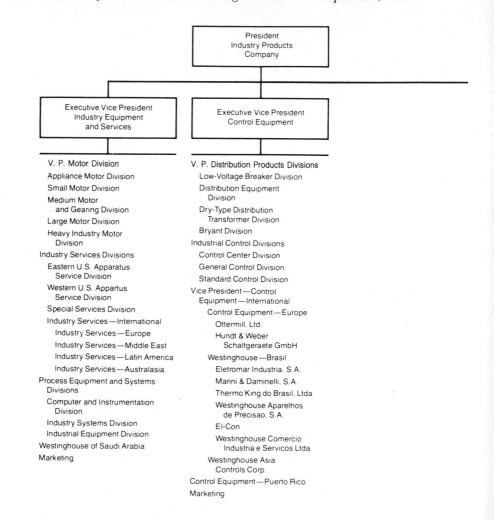

Chapter 3

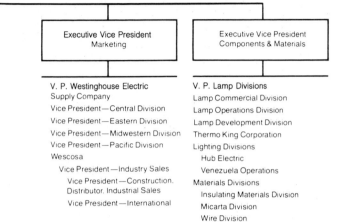

Executive Vice President Marketing	Executive Vice President Components & Materials

V. P. Westinghouse Electric
Supply Company
Vice President—Central Division
Vice President—Eastern Division
Vice President—Midwestern Division
Vice President—Pacific Division
Wescosa
   Vice President—Industry Sales
      Vice President—Construction.
      Distributor. Industrial Sales
         Vice President—International

V. P. Lamp Divisions
Lamp Commercial Division
Lamp Operations Division
Lamp Development Division
Thermo King Corporation
Lighting Divisions
  Hub Electric
  Venezuela Operations
Materials Divisions
  Insulating Materials Division
  Micarta Division
  Wire Division
Electronic Components Divisions
  Industrial & Government
    Tube Division
  Semiconductor Division
  K-W Battery Division
  Compagnie des Dispositifs
    Semiconducteurs Westinghouse
Marketing

Effective: July 1, 1978.
Source: Courtesy of Westinghouse Electric Corporation.

Mixed Departmentalization

Before leaving this topic, it is important to point out that departments organized according to any of these basic patterns may also contain subgroupings formed on the basis of other types of departmentalization. Indeed, in larger organizations, multiple or mixed patterns of departmentalization are quite common. For example, while General Motors has been cited as an example of an organization structured along product lines (that is, Buick, Cadillac, Chevrolet, Oldsmobile, and Pontiac Motor Divisions), within each of these divisions, departmental groupings strictly follow function: engineering, production, manufacturing, distribution, finance, etc. Further, within such functional areas as distribution, departmental groupings are structured according to geographical sales regions (for example, Southeast), then zones (for example, Birmingham), and, finally, zone districts (for example, central east Alabama).

Scalar Chain of Authority

With jobs specialized and responsibility divided among departments, coordination becomes necessary. As briefly put by Pfeffer: "Because the total task is subdivided, the differentiated roles in the organization are interdependent. Interdependence requires coordination."[39] Thus, just as the "total task" of the North American Automotive Operations of Ford Motor Company shown in Figure 3–2 is subdivided and grouped according to such functions as purchasing, manufacturing, engineering, and sales, the resulting differentiated roles, because of their interdependence, must be integrated. Integration, and, subsequently, coordination, are most commonly achieved through "vertical differentiation,"—that is, a systematic ordering of positions and duties which defines a hierarchy, or what is commonly termed a "scalar chain of authority" or, even more frequently, a "chain of command". Immediately derived from the division of labor, the scalar chain of authority relates to the number of levels in an organization and automatically exists whenever an individual is made the subordinate of a superior. More specifically, the scalar chain defines the differing levels of authority, or scales or grades of duties, that exist within an organization; the higher the level, the greater the authority. Further, as expressed by Katz and Kahn, place in the scalar chain "differentiates people according to the power, privilege, prestige, and rewards of their organizational positions."[40]

Unity of Command

Implicit in the scalar chain is another basic aspect of organization structure: one man, one boss. As described by Litterer, "If subordinates are to have their efforts coordi-

---

[39]J. Pfeffer, *Organizational Design* (Arlington Heights, Ill.: AHM Publishing, 1978), p. 24.
[40]Katz and Kahn, *The Social Psychology,* 2nd ed., p. 76.

Figure 3–4 *Area Departmentalization, Chase Manhattan Bank, N.A.,*
International Banking Department

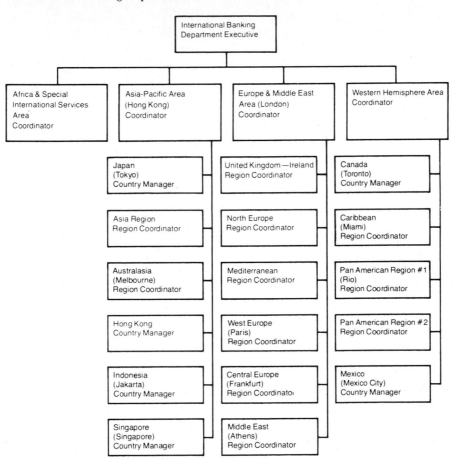

Effective: March 1978.
Source: Courtesy of The Chase Manhattan Bank.

Dimensions of Organization Design

nated, it seems necessary that they receive instructions from a single source."[41] In this respect, unity of command clearly facilitates coordination "because it charges one official with an area of responsibility and establishes a chain of command whereby every organization member knows to whom he reports and who reports to him. There is no confusion over who is responsible for organizational activities and over who gives orders and who carries them out."[42] However, to quote Litterer once again: "The difficulty is that this requirement is violated in varying degrees in almost every organization."[43] In particular, the emergence of specialized support units with extended authority and newer forms of departmentalization such as matrix organization (to be discussed later in this chapter) have undermined the principle of unity of command.

Span of Control

While the scalar chain and unity of command relate to the vertical composition of an organization, span of control relates to its horizontal arrangement. Just as the business of a firm grows to the point at which it is impossible for one person to handle all the work, there is a limit to the number of subordinates that a manager can effectively supervise. The actual number of subordinates under the *direct* authority of a given manager is termed span of control (also called span of management, span of authority, span of supervision, span of responsibility).

It is not our intent to discuss in detail the span of control concept or to rehash the various academic debates over it. Such information is readily available elsewhere.[44] What is particularly relevant to the present discussion is that span of control is a major element determining the shape of an organization. Perhaps more fundamentally, other things being equal, an inverse relationship can be said to prevail between the average span of control and the number of levels in an organizational hierarchy. That is, if an organization is structured with wide or broad spans of control, it will generally be flat in appearance, with few levels in relation to its overall size. Conversely, if an organization is structured with short or narrow spans of control, it will generally be tall or steep in appearance, with many levels in relation to its overall size. The operational nature of this fundamental point is schematically diagrammed in Figure 3–5, utilizing a hypothetical organization of 64 workers with alternative average spans of 64:1, 8:1, 4:1, and 2:1. Reducing the average span from 64:1 to 2:1 increases the number of organizational levels threefold, from two to six. Perhaps more importantly, this same progression increases the number of supervisors required from 1 to 63. The financial

---

[41]J. A. Litterer, *The Analysis of Organizations,* 2nd ed. (New York: John Wiley & Sons, 1973), p. 559.

[42]R. C. Carzo and J. N. Yanouzas, *Formal Organization: A Systems Approach* (Homewood, Ill.: Richard D. Irwin, 1967), p. 45.

[43]Litterer, *Analysis of Organizations,* p. 559.

[44]See, for example, D. D. Van Fleet and A. G. Bedeian, "A History of the Span of Management," *Academy of Management Review* 2 (1977): 356–372.

Figure 3–5 *Alternative Ratios of Span of Control*

A Ratio, 64:1

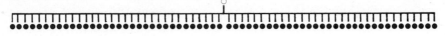

B Ratio, 8:1

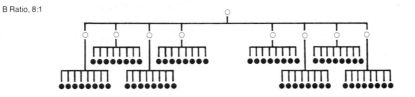

C Ratio, 4:1

D Ratio, 2:1

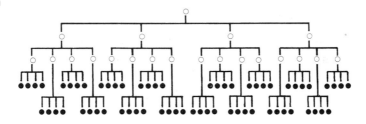

Legend: ○ One Supervisor
● One Worker

Source: Rocco Carzo, Jr., and John Yanouzas, *Formal Organizations: A Systems Approach* (Homewood, Ill.: Richard D. Irwin, 1967), p. 45. © 1967 by Richard D. Irwin, Inc. Reprinted by permission.

Dimensions of Organization Design

consequences of such a difference in terms of payroll costs are obvious and become even more so as an organization increases in size (that is, number of employees). For example, the difference between an average span of five and one of twenty in an organization comprised of 10,000 nonmanagerial personnel can make a difference of three levels of management and nearly 2,000 managers.[45] Seldom, of course, is span of control uniform across all supervisory levels, as it is in the hypothetical organizations in Figure 3–5. Nevertheless, despite structural differences among various departments and hierarchical levels, the basic effect is substantially the same.

In reflecting on this result, the question naturally arises as to whether an optimum span of control can be said to exist. Research relating to this issue clearly suggests that, while a finite limit exists relative to the number of subordinates any given manager can effectively supervise, it is equally clear that this limit varies depending upon characteristics of the manager, members of the work group involved, and the situation at hand.[46] Of particular pertinence to our future discussion (Chapter 8) are research findings which indicate that both span of control and number of hierarchical levels in an organization are related to the nature and complexity of its core technology (that is, its central throughput processes).[47] Furthermore, it should be noted that recent research suggests that it may be inappropriate to speak of *a* single optimum organization design, when in reality several equally efficient structural variations may exist.[48]

Line and Staff

One final aspect of basic organization structure should be mentioned. This is the distinction that is typically made between line and staff. As this topic is generally covered rather extensively in most introductory management texts, it will not be treated at length in the present discussion.[49] Briefly then, *line personnel* are typically defined as those organization members whose activities contribute *directly* to the accomplishment of an organization's primary objective(s). In contrast, *staff personnel* are generally classified as those individuals whose task it is to facilitate the work of the line by serving in an advisory or auxiliary function. Examples include the quality control and materials procurement departments in a manufacturing firm or the personnel and maintenance departments in a retail store.

---

[45]A. Easton, *Managing for Negative Growth* (Reston, Va.: Reston Publishing, 1976), p. 113.

[46]D. D. Van Fleet and A. G. Bedeian, "Conceptual Developments in the Span of Management," *Akron Business and Economic Review* 9, no. 1 (1978): 25–30.

[47]In, for example, J. Woodward, *Industrial Organization: Theory and Practice* (London: Oxford University Press, 1965); D. Hickson, D. Pugh, and D. Pheysey, "Operations Technology and Organization Structure: An Empirical Reappraisal," *Administrative Science Quarterly* 14 (1969): 378–397.

[48]See, for example, B. C. Reimann, "On the Dimensions of Bureaucratic Structure: An Empirical Reappraisal," *Administrative Science Quarterly* 18 (1973): 462–476.; A. A. Van de Ven, "Equally Efficient Structural Variations within Organizations," in Kilmann, Pondy, and Slevin, eds., *Management of Organizations,* vol. 2, pp. 155–170.

[49]See, for example, A. C. Filley, R. J. House, and S. Kerr, *Managerial Process and Organizational Behavior,* 2nd ed. (Glenview, Ill.: Scott, Foresman, 1976), chap. 17.

The emergence of the staff functions is ancient in origin, being primarily associated with early military organizations. As described by pioneer writers such as Fayol, as organizations grow in scope and complexity, a stage is generally reached at which it becomes necessary to seek the assistance of a specialized support staff.[50] As was true even in Fayol's day, very rare is the executive who is able to deal at one and the same time with the many demands of a large corporation. The emergence of staff personnel thus represents another facet of a seemingly irresistible trend toward a greater and greater division of labor in a society becoming ever more complex.

Matrix Organization

In recent years, especially since the early 1960s, an additional form of organization has emerged that in many ways runs counter to the basic and more traditional structural design discussed so far. Rather than being bound by the constraints of a vertical chain of command, span of control, and distinct line-staff activities, it represents an attempt to balance the need to allocate tasks to specialized departments and, at the same time, to be structurally adaptable.[51] More specifically, this form of organization "evolved in response to [the] need for structural responsiveness in firms whose product mix changed frequently, whose products were relatively short-lived, and which had to be both strategically and operationally responsive." [52] First popularized by the aerospace industry, current practitioners of this form include a wide range of firms like National Cash Register, International Telephone & Telegraph, Dow-Corning, Lockheed Aircraft, and Monsanto Chemical. Although a variety of titles, such as "program management" and "matrix organization," are used, the latter term is perhaps the most descriptive and will be employed in the present discussion.

While there seems to be general agreement on the basic characteristics of the matrix type of design, as might be expected, there are many variations in its practical application. "In the typical matrix organization, individuals are members of functional departments but they are also assigned on a full- or part-time basis to projects. Such individuals have two bosses, one in a functional department and the other the leader of the project." [53] This arrangement is depicted in Figure 3–6. As indicated, Universal Products Company (a hypothetical organization) is divided into functional support groups (such as production, engineering, and materials), as well as into specific work projects, namely, Venus Project, Mars Project, and Saturn Project. New projects are added as contracts are secured. As ongoing projects are completed, they are simply dropped, and project members return to their respective functional areas for reassign-

---

[50]H. Fayol, "Administration industrielle et générale," *Bulletin de la Société de l'Industrie Minerale,* 5th ser., 10 (1916): 89–90.
[51]D. C. Wilemon and J. P. Cicero, "The Project Manager—Anomalies and Ambiguities," *Academy of Management Journal* 13 (1970): 269.
[52]Ansoff and Brandenburg, "A Language," p. B722.
[53]Filley, House, and Kerr, *Managerial Process,* p. 361.

Figure 3–6 *Matrix Organization Form, Universal Products Company, Aerospace Division*

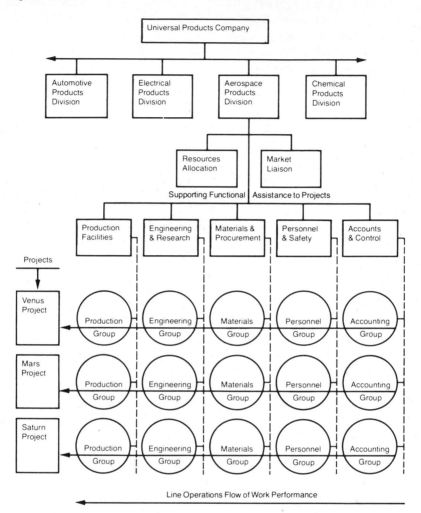

Source: John F. Mee, "Matrix Organization," *Business Horizons* 7 (Summer 1964): 71. Copyright, 1964, by the Foundation for the School of Business at Indiana University. Reprinted by permission.

ment. The result is an especially flexible and responsive approach to organization design, one that is particularly adaptable to fluctuating work loads.

While it is true that the matrix approach does allow a fluid structure, it should be realized that it also has certain drawbacks. Most notably, the existence of two separate operating systems (project-oriented control flowing horizontally and functionally-oriented control flowing vertically) within a single organization introduces the serious possibility of command conflict, particularly where authority intersects.[54] While, in theory, matrix forms of structure call for the appointment of one person, a project manager, to act as a central coordinator for all work related to a specific project, in reality, the authority of project-managers often amounts to little more than mere persuasiveness.[55] The potentially detrimental effects of such a situation are understandably great. Based on a detailed analysis of a wide variety of organizations employing the matrix design, Davis and Lawrence report that the matrix form of dual command is more vulnerable not only to what they term "anarchy" but also to such "pathologies" as power struggles, indecision, excessive overhead, and collapse during economic decline.[56]

Because it is not our intention in the current discussion to do more than simply provide a brief survey of existing information, no attempt will be made to provide a full-scale evaluation of matrix organizations. While their popularity is undeniably growing worldwide,[57] a recent evaluation, perhaps the most thorough undertaken to date, of the available information suggests that "their success and effectiveness has been extremely varied, ranging from structures which are viewed as flexible, efficient and motivating, to ones perceived as bureaucratic, conflict-ridden and stressful."[58] Given these inconsistencies, it is clear that the sooner we ascertain the situations in which matrix structures are most appropriate, the better we will be able to fully realize their benefits and avoid their associated pitfalls.

Summary

As suggested earlier, the principal intent of the present chapter has been to touch briefly upon the contributions of the so-called classical theorists and to provide a

---

[54]A. G. Butler, "Project Management: A Study in Organizational Conflict," *Academy of Management Journal* 16 (1973): 84–101.

[55]G. R. Gemmill and H. J. Thamhain, "Influence Styles of Project Managers: Some Project Performance Correlates," *Academy of Management Journal* 17 (1974): 216–224; E. J. Dunne, M. J. Stahl, and L. J. Melhart, "Influence Scores of Project and Functional Managers in Matrix Organizations," *Academy of Management Journal* 21 (1978): 135–140.

[56]S. M. Davis and P. R. Lawrence, *Matrix* (Reading, Mass.: Addison-Wesley, 1977), pp. 129–144; S. M. Davis and P. R. Lawrence, "Problems of Matrix Organization," *Harvard Business Review* 56, no. 3 (1978): 131–142.

[57]See, for example, M. K. Chandler, "Project Management in the Socialist Bloc," *Columbia Journal of World Business* 13, no. 2 (1978): 71–86; P. R. Lawrence, H. F. Kolodny, and S. M. Davis, "The Human Side of the Matrix," *Organizational Dynamics* 6, no. 1 (1977): 43–61; S. M. Davis and P. R. Lawrence, "The Matrix Diamond," *Wharton Magazine* 2, no. 2 (1978): 19–27; A. R. Janger, *Matrix Organization of Complex Businesses,* Report 763 (New York: The Conference Board, 1979).

[58]K. Knight, "Matrix Organization: A Review," *Journal of Management Studies* 13 (1976): 130.

succinct overview of the basic structural characteristics of formal organizations. In doing so, the importance of developing improved methods for designing organizations that are capable of obtaining optimum effectiveness has been stressed. Viewed in this light, organization design is, as termed by Selznick, the "structural expression of rational action."[59] To this end, the large-scale mobilization of human and technical resources requires the subdivison of the work to be performed and the determination of an appropriate (efficient) basis for grouping the efforts of the resulting subunits. Further, with jobs specialized and divided among departments, administrative integration and coordination of specialized functions, via the systematic ordering of positions and duties defining a hierarchy of authority, is a necessity. In this context, unity of command and span of control are further results of an attempt to coordinate organizational resources. Unity of command facilitates coordination by delineating clear lines of responsibility and authority; span of control facilitates coordination by postulating a limit to the number of subordinates that a manager can effectively supervise and, by implication, the range of activities that he or she can coordinate. Likewise, the development of a support staff also facilitates operational coordination by making available specialized expertise to assist in the efficient and effective integration of organizational activities.

With respect to the basic dimensions of organization structure, the horizontal differentiation of activities into departments (along functional, product, area, or matrix lines) and the vertical differentiation of levels of authority or grades of duties together serve to define the skeletal configuration, or what might even be called the "topology" (shape and structure), of an organization. In this sense, horizontal and vertical differentiation are universal phenomena, occurring in organizations of all types and sizes—governmental, educational, industrial; big, medium, and small. Bearing this point in mind, the primary message of the preceding discussion may be perhaps best summarized by again simply stating that to the degree that design implies creation —that is, the purposive formulation and deliberate establishment of relationships among the horizontal and vertical components of an organization—the specific structural features of an enterprise may be conceived of as a set of complex variables whose shape is subject to considerable managerial choice. The extent of this choice, as circumscribed by an organization's interaction with its surrounding environment, will be explored in Chapter 6. First, however, we turn, in Chapter 4, to a discussion of the nature and functioning of organizational goals and, in Chapter 5, to a consideration of the meaning and measurement of organizational effectiveness.

Review and Discussion Questions

1. Explain how Taylor's doctrine of scientific management was intended to alleviate zero-sum conflict where the gain of one party would be at the expense of another.
2. As identified in the text, what three fundamental points stand out in Weber's discussion of bureaucracy?

---

[59]P. Selznick, "Foundations of the Theory of Organization," *American Sociological Review* 13 (1948): 25.

3. Comment on the dysfunctional consequences frequently associated with bureaucracy.
4. How does the delegation of authority facilitate, and at the same time frequently hinder, the operational effectiveness of an organization?
5. Explain the paradox that occurs when bureaucratic rules are implemented to counter worker apathy.
6. With respect to the division of labor, what are some of the negative costs associated with increased levels of specialization?
7. Explain, in general terms, the relationship between the blocks and lines that make up an organization chart.
8. List some of the major relationships which are usually not found on an organization chart but significantly influence goal accomplishment.
9. Explain how the unity of command concept is implicit in the scalar chain of authority.
10. Comment on the unique structural characteristics of matrix organizations. Why did matrix organizations evolve?

References

Ansoff, H. I., and Brandenburg, R. G. "A Language for Organization Design: Part II." *Management Science* 17 (1971): B717–B731.

Bedeian, A. G. "Historical Development of Management." In *Encyclopedia of Professional Management,* edited by L. R. Bittel. New York: McGraw-Hill, 1978.

Blau, P. M., and Scott, W. R. *Formal Organization: A Comparative Approach.* San Francisco: Chandler, 1962.

Brodie, M. B. *Fayol on Administration.* London: Lyon, Grant and Green, 1967.

Butler, A. G. "Project Management: A Study in Organizational Conflict." *Academy of Management Journal* 16 (1973): 84–101.

Calder, B. J., Rowland, K. M., and Leblebici, H. "The Use of Scaling and Cluster Techniques in Investigating the Social Structure of Organizations." In *The Management of Organization Design,* vol. 2, edited by R. H. Kilmann, L. R. Pondy, and D. P. Selvin. New York: Elsevier North-Holland, 1976.

Caplow, T. *How to Run an Organization: A Manual of Practical Sociology.* Hinsdale, Ill.: Dryden Press, 1976.

Carzo, R. C., and Yanouzas, J. N. *Formal Organization: A Systems Approach.* Homewood, Ill.: Richard D. Irwin, 1967.

Chandler, M. K. "Project Management in the Socialist Bloc." *Columbia Journal of World Business,* 13, no. 2 (1978): 71–86.

Child, J. *Organization: A Guide to Problems and Practices.* London: Harper & Row, 1977.

Cochran, T. C. *Business in American Life: A History.* New York: McGraw-Hill, 1972.

Davis, S. M. "Two Models of Organization: Unity of Command versus Balance of Power." *Sloan Management Review* 16, no. 1 (1974): 29–40.

Davis, S. M., and Lawrence, P. R. *Matrix.* Reading, Mass.: Addison-Wesley, 1977.

Davis, S. M., and Lawrence, P. R. "The Matrix Diamond." *Wharton Magazine* 2, no. 2 (1978): 19–27.

Davis, S. M., and Lawrence, P. R. "Problems of Matrix Organizations." *Harvard Business Review* 56, no. 3 (1978): 131–142.

Dunne, E. J., Stahl, M. J., and Melhart, L. J. "Influence Scores of Project and Functional Managers in Matrix Organizations." *Academy of Management Journal* 21 (1978): 135–140.

Easton, A. *Managing for Negative Growth.* Reston, Va.: Reston Publishing, 1976.

Eldridge, J. E. T., and Crombie, A. D. *A Sociology of Organisation.* London: George Allen & Unwin, 1974.

Fayol, H. "Administration industrielle et générale." *Bulletin de la Société de l'Industrie Minerale,* 5th series, 10 (1916): 1–162.

Fayol, H. *Industrial and General Administration.* Translated by J. A. Coubrough. Geneva: International Management Institute, 1930. (Originally published in 1916.)

Filley, A. C., House, R. J., and Kerr, S. *Managerial Process and Organizational Behavior.* 2nd ed. Glenview, Ill.: Scott, Foresman, 1976.

Gannon, M. J., and Paine, F. T. "Unity of Command and Job Attitudes of Managers in a Bureaucratic Organization." *Journal of Applied Psychology* 59 (1974): 392–394.

Gemmill, G. R., and Thamhain, H. J. "Influence Styles of Project Managers: Some Project Performance Correlates." *Academy of Management Journal* 17 (1974): 216–224.

Glen, F. *The Social Psychology of Organizations.* London: Methuen, 1975.

Gouldner, A. W. *Patterns of Industrial Bureaucracy.* New York: Free Press of Glencoe, 1954.

Gulick, L. H., and Urwick, L. F., eds. *Papers on the Science of Administration.* New York: Institute of Public Administration, Columbia University, 1937.

Hicks, H. G., and Gullett, C. R. *Organizations: Theory and Behavior.* New York: McGraw-Hill, 1975.

Hickson, D., Pugh, D., and Pheysey, D. "Operations Technology and Organization Structure: An Empirical Reappraisal." *Administrative Science Quarterly* 14 (1969): 378–397.

Janger, A. R. *Matrix Organization of Complex Businesses.* Report 763. New York: The Conference Board, 1979.

Kanungo, R. N. "The Concepts of Alienation and Involvement Revisited." *Psychological Bulletin* 86 (1979): 119–138.

Katz, D., and Kahn, R. L. *The Social Psychology of Organizations.* New York: John Wiley & Sons, 1966.

Katz, D., and Kahn, R. L. *The Social Psychology of Organizations.* 2nd ed. New York: John Wiley & Sons, 1978.

Klaw, S. "Frederick Winslow Taylor: The Messiah of Time and Motion Study." *American Heritage* 30, no. 5 (1979): 26–39.

Knight, K. "Matrix Organization: A Review." *Journal of Management Studies* 13 (1976): 111–130.

Kover, A. J. "Reorganization in an Advertising Agency: A Case Study of a Decrease in Integration." *Human Organization* 22 (1963–64): 252–259.

Lawrence, P. R., Kolodny, H. F., and Davis, S. M. "The Human Side of the Matrix." *Organizational Dynamics* 6, no. 1 (1977): 43–61.

Leavitt, H. J. "On the Design Part of Organization Design." In *The Management of Organization Design,* vol. 1, edited by B. H. Kilmann, L. R. Pondy, and D. P. Slevin. New York: Elsevier North-Holland, 1976.

Litterer, J. A. *The Analysis of Organizations.* 2nd ed. New York: John Wiley & Sons, 1973.

Littler, C. R. "Understanding Taylorism." *British Journal of Sociology* 29 (1978): 185–202.

Maier, C. S. "Between Taylorism and Technocracy: European Ideologies and the Vision of Industrial Productivity in the 1920s." *Journal of Contemporary History* 5, no. 2 (1970): 27–61.

Mee, J. F. "A History of Twentieth Century Management Thought." Ph.D. dissertation, Ohio State University, Columbus, Ohio, 1959.

Mee, J. F. "Matrix Organization." *Business Horizons* 7, no. 2 (1964): 70–72.

Merton, R. K. "Bureaucratic Structure and Personality." *Social Forces* 18 (1940): 560–568.

Mooney, J. D., and Reiley, A. C. *Onward Industry!* New York: Harper & Bros., 1931. 2nd edition, 1939, retitled *The Principles of Organization.*

Perrow, C. *Organizational Analysis: A Sociological View.* Monterey, Calif.: Belmont/Cole, 1970.

Pfeffer, J. *Organizational Design.* Arlington Heights, Ill.: AHM Publishing, 1978.

Pred, A. R. *The Spatial Dynamics of U.S. Urban-Industrial Growth, 1800–1914.* Cambridge, Mass.: M.I.T. Press, 1966.

Price, J. L. "The Impact of Departmentalization on Interoccupational Cooperation." *Human Organization* 27 (1968): 362–368.

Reimann, B. C. "On the Dimensions of Bureaucratic Structure: An Empirical Reappraisal." *Administrative Science Quarterly* 18 (1973): 462–476.

Selznick, P. "Foundations of the Theory of Organization." *American Sociological Review* 13 (1948): 25–35.

Selznick, P. *TVA and the Grass Roots: A Study in the Sociology of Formal Organization.* Berkeley: University of California Press, 1949.

Sexton, W. P., ed. *Organization Theories.* Columbus, Ohio: Merrill, 1970.

Taylor, F. W. *The Principles of Scientific Management.* New York: Harper & Bros., 1911.

Thompson, V. A. *Modern Organization.* New York: Alfred A. Knopf, 1961.

Chapter 3

Towne, H. R. "The Engineer as Economist." *Transactions of the American Society of Mechanical Engineers* 7 (1886): 428–432.

Urwick, L. F. *The Elements of Administration.* New York: Harper & Row, 1943.

Urwick, L. F. *The Golden Book of Management.* London: Newman Neame, 1956.

Urwick, L. F. "Why the So-called 'Classicists' Endure." *Management International Review* 11, no. 1 (1971): 3–14.

Van De Ven, A. H. "Equally Efficient Structural Variations within Organizations." In *The Management of Organization Design,* vol. 2, edited by R. H. Kilmann, L. R. Pondy, and D. P. Slevin. New York: Elsevier North-Holland, 1976.

Van Fleet, D. D., and Bedeian, A. G. "Conceptual Developments in the Span of Management." *Akron Business and Economic Review* 9, no. 1 (1978): 25–30.

Van Fleet, D. D., and Bedeian, A. G. "A History of the Span of Management." *Academy of Management Review* 2 (1977): 356–372.

Weber, M. *From Max Weber: Essays in Sociology,* edited and translated by H. H. Gerth and C. W. Mills. New York: Oxford University Press, 1946. (Originally published 1906–1924.)

Weber, M. *Max Weber: The Theory of Social and Economic Organization,* edited and translated by A. M. Henderson and T. Parsons. New York: Oxford University Press, 1947. (Originally published in 1922.)

Weber, M. *The Methodology of the Social Sciences,* edited and translated by E. A. Shils and H. H. Finch. Glencoe, Ill.: Free Press, 1949. (Originally published 1904–1917).

Wilemon, D. C., and Cicero, J. P. "The Project Manager—Anomalies and Ambiguities." *Academy of Management Journal* 13 (1970): 269–282.

Woodward, J. *Industrial Organization: Theory and Practice.* London: Oxford University Press, 1965.

Wren, D. A. *The Evolution of Management Thought.* 2nd ed. New York: John Wiley & Sons, 1979.

The Establishment of Organizational Goals

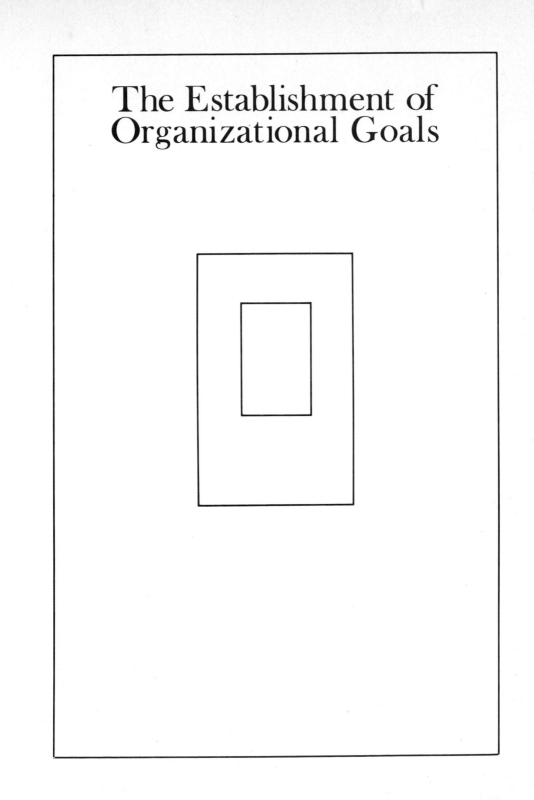

The Establishment of
Organizational Goals

Chapter 4

As stressed in Chapter 1, organizations are instruments for attaining specific goals and are likely to be created in situations where people recognize a common or complementary advantage that can be best served through collective, as opposed to individual, action. In this regard, Gross suggests that organizational goals are the *central factor in the study of organizations and that it is the presence of common goals and the subsequent organization of effort to maximize the probability of goal attainment that characterize modern organizations.[1] Interest in goal accomplishment may be easily traced to the work of such turn-of-the-century theorists as Taylor, Fayol, and Weber. Built upon this legacy, and on the work of more recent students of organization, the position taken in this chapter is that organizations are structural devices for the accomplishment of specific goals and that to understand them fully one must understand the goals that they pursue.*

The primary purpose of the present chapter is to explore the multidimensional nature of the goal systems within complex organizations. After first defining the term "goal" in the present context, and differentiating between "official" and "operative" goals, the numerous functions of organizational goals will be identified. A scheme for the classification of organizational goals will then be presented. Subsequently, after distinguishing between "individual" and "organizational" goals, our attention will turn to a discussion of the various forces that play on the actual determination of the goals an organization selects. Next, after questioning the fundamental assumptions of classical economic analysis concerning decision making, we introduce the alternate concept of "bounded rationality." Following this, we will consider the structural process whereby organizational goals are made operational, and finally, we will examine several ways in which organizational goals are modified, and even occasionally changed, as a result of various internal and external pressures.

Goals Defined

In spite of the fact that the goal concept is central to the study of organizations, few serious attempts have been made to develop a clear definition of the term *organiza-*

---

[1]E. Gross "The Definition of Organizational Goals," *British Journal of Sociology* 20 (1969): 277–294.

tional goal. Etzioni, probably the most frequently quoted authority on this point, defines an organizational goal as "a desired state of affairs which the organization attempts to realize" and as "that future state of affairs which the organization as a collectivity is trying to bring about."[2] Warner, in another often quoted definition, suggests that an organizational goal is "a state of affairs or situation which does not exist at present but is intended to be brought into existence in the future by the activities of the organization."[3] In each of these definitions, two elements emerge. Goals describe (1) *future* desired end results to which (2) *present* efforts are directed.

Official and Operative Goals

Closely associated with attempts to develop a clear definition of "goal" is the often troublesome distinction between what have been termed the *official* and *operative* goals of organizations, between what organizations say their goals are and what they actually are. "Official goals," according to Perrow, "are the general purposes of the organization as put forth in the charter, annual reports, public statements by key executives, and other authoritative pronouncements."[4] Operative goals, on the other hand, are "the ends sought through the actual operating policies of the organization; they tell us what the organization actually is trying to do, regardless of what the official goals say are the aims."[5] This distinction between the professed and the actual goals of an organization has long been a major problem in the study of organizations and has been noted by numerous investigators working in a variety of settings. For example, in his study of a state employment agency, Blau found that the official or declared goal of providing the best service possible to "workers seeking employment and employers seeking workers" was secondary to the goal of maximizing the proportion of interviews resulting in referrals, because the performance of agency interviewers was primarily measured by this and similar quantitative, rather than qualitative, indices.[6] Similarly, Cressey, in a study of prisons, and Zald, in a study of correctional institutions for delinquents, found that despite the fact that the announced aim of such organizations is to rehabilitate, in reality they spend very little time or effort in this area, instead providing primarily custodial care.[7] This would suggest that the real, or operative, goal of the institutions investigated was custodial care and not rehabilitation, as

---

[2]A. Etzioni, *Modern Organizations* (Englewood Cliffs, N.J.: Prentice-Hall, 1964), p. 6.

[3]W. K. Warner, "Problems in Measuring the Goal Attainment of Voluntary Organizations," *Adult Education* 19 (1967): 4.

[4]C. Perrow, "The Analysis of Goals in Complex Organizations," *American Sociological Review* 26 (1961): 855.

[5]Ibid.

[6]P. M. Blau, *The Dynamics of Bureaucracy* (Chicago: University of Chicago Press, 1955).

[7]D. Cressey, "Achievement of an Unstated Goal," *Pacific Sociological Review* 1, no. 2 (1958): 43–49; M. N. Zald, "Comparative Analysis and Measurement of Goals: The Case of Correctional Institutions for Delinquents," *Sociological Quarterly* 4 (1963): 206–230.

formally stated. As a final example, Warriner, in a study of a group of community service clubs, reports that community service is often an "incidental" part of the activities of such groups (as measured in terms of time and money spent) and that generating funds for club benefit via community service projects, such as the sale of products made by the handicapped, is often their operative, or true, goal.[8]

In assessing the role of an organization's official goals, one should not be led to believe that they do not perform a necessary role. By giving an organization a favorable self-image, official goals often provide a source of legitimacy, justifying its activities. (This point will be further developed in the following section.) However, it should be noted that operative goals may differ from official goals because organization members lack knowledge of what the actual goals of an organization are; because perceptions about how best to accomplish official goals differ; and because stated goals cannot be achieved for financial or other reasons. Furthermore, as we will discuss in a later section, the operative goals of an organization are the outcome of complex exchanges between individuals and groups pursuing a diversity of aims. As a result, while the official or publicly stated goals of an organization may remain unchanged over time, the operational goals of an organization at different points in time may well vary substantially as a consequence of such exchanges.

Functions of Organizational Goals

As the reader may begin to suspect, "the concept of organizational goal is among the most slippery and treacherous of all those employed by the analyst of organizations."[9] The primary source of this difficulty derives from the fact that organizational goals serve a variety of functions. Consequently, the goals an organization stresses in one instance (social and employee welfare) may not be the same as those that are emphasized in another (organizational productivity and profit maximization) *and* may, in fact, actually conflict. Viewed in broad perspective, organizational goals do, however, serve several important functions which vary according to time and circumstance.[10] Among other things, goals serve as:

1. *Guidelines for action:* By describing future desired end results, goals serve as guidelines for action directing and channeling the efforts and activities of organizational participants. In this regard, goals function to provide focus and direction for organizational activity by prescribing what "should be" and what "should not be" done.

---

[8]C. K. Warriner, "The Problem of Organizational Purpose," *Sociological Quarterly* 6 (1965): 139–146.

[9]S. M. Dornbusch and W. R. Scott, *Evaluation and the Exercise of Authority: A Theory of Control Applied to Diverse Organizations* (San Francisco: Jossey-Bass, 1975), p. 65.

[10]A. Etzioni, "Two Approaches to Organizational Analysis: A Critique and a Suggestion," *Administrative Science Quarterly* 5 (1960): 257–277; L. W. Porter, E. E. Lawler, and J. R. Hackman, *Behavior in Organizations* (New York: McGraw-Hill, 1975), pp. 78–79; R. M. Steers, *Organizational Effectiveness: A Behavioral View* (Santa Monica, Calif.: Goodyear, 1977), pp. 20–22.

2. *A source of legitimacy:* Goals also provide a source of legitimacy for an organization by justifying its activities, and, indeed, its very existence, to such groups as customers, politicians, employees, stockholders, and society at large. Prominent examples of organizations and the stated (official) goals that provide legitimacy for their existence include: hospitals (provision of medical services aimed at the cure, amelioration, and prevention of disease); prisons and mental hospitals (therapy and rehabilitation); churches (divine worship and spiritual salvation); and universities (teaching, research, and public service). Perhaps most importantly, recognition of legitimacy greatly enchances an organization's ability to obtain resources and support from its surrounding environment. This largely explains the fund-raising success of such organizations as the Girl Scouts, the Salvation Army, and the United Way. Each has achieved acceptance through the recognized legitimacy of its goals.

3. *Standards of performance:* To the extent that goals are clearly stated and understood, they offer direct standards for evaluating an organization's performance. That is, once an organization establishes goals in such quantifiable areas as sales, market standing, or profit, the degree to which it has succeeded in their attainment should be easily verifiable.

4. *A source of motivation:* The goals of an organization can serve as an important source of employee motivation and identification. In a very real sense, the goals of an organization often give incentives to members. This phenomenon is perhaps clearest in organizations that offer their top executives bonuses for achieving specified levels of sales, or whose pay schemes (stock options, deferred income credits, etc.) are tied directly to annual profit. Professional (or even amateur) sports organizations provide an additional example. The status and prestige of being identified with a championship team is almost always a strong source of motivation.

5. *A rationale for organizing:* Stated simply, organizational goals provide a basis for organization design. Organizational goals and organization structure interact in that the actions necessary for goal accomplishment may impose unavoidable restrictions on employee activities and resource utilization patterns, necessitating implementation of a variety of organization design elements: communication patterns, control mechanisms, departmental structures, and so on.

In summary, goals perform several useful functions. In addition to serving as (1) guidelines for action; they provide (2) a source of legitimacy by justifying an organization's activities; serve (3) as standards or criteria against which an organization can evaluate its performance; and thus (4) motivate participants toward greater goal accomplishment. Finally, (5) goals provide an important basis for organization design.

Types of Goals

As noted in the introduction to this chapter, an interest in the goal-seeking behavior of organizations may be traced to the writings of a variety of early management theorists. It has only been within the last few decades, however, that attempts have been made in the literature to categorize the types or classes of goals sought by organizations.[11] Perhaps the most broadly applicable and widely accepted of these attempts is that by Perrow. Directed toward organizations in general, his classification scheme distinguishes among five types of goals according to "whose point of view is being recognized": that of society, the customer, the investor, the top executive, or others.

1. Societal goals. Referent: *society in general. Examples: produce goods and services; maintain order; generate and maintain cultural values. . . . This category deals with large classes of organizations that fulfill societal needs. . . .*

2. Output goals. Referent: *the public in contact with the organization. This category deals with types of output defined in terms of consumer functions. Examples: consumer goods; business services; health care; education. . . .*

3. System goals. Referent: *the state or manner of functioning of the organization, independent of the goods or services it produces or its derived goals. Examples: the emphasis upon growth, stability, profits, or upon modes of functioning, such as being tightly or loosely controlled or structured. Organizations have options in these respects, and the way the system functions and what it generates irrespective of products can become goals for the members.*

4. Product goals *(or, more exactly, product-characteristic goals)*. Referent: *the characteristics of the goods or services produced. Examples: an emphasis upon quality or quantity, variety, styling, availability, uniqueness, or innovativeness of the products. Organizations may vary widely and deliberately in this respect.*

5. Derived goals. Referent: *the uses to which the organization puts the power it generates in pursuit of other goals. Examples: political aims; community services; employee development; investment and plant-location policies which affect the state of the economy and the future of specific communities. . . .*[12]

In addition to emphasizing that virtually all organizations have multiple goals that are often competing (that is, have trade-off value) and are sometimes even incompatible (negatively correlated), Perrow's listing also suggests that the goals of an organiza-

---

[11]See, for example, P. Drucker, *The Practice of Management* (New York: Harper & Row, 1954), chap. 7; B. M. Gross, "What Are Your Organization's Objectives?" *Human Relations* 18 (1965): 195–216; Gross, "The Definition."

[12]C. Perrow, *Organizational Analysis: A Sociological View* (Monterey, Calif.: Brooks/Cole, 1970), pp. 135–136.

tion are not mutually exclusive. That is, what is viewed by one group of referents as an output goal, may well be seen by another as a product goal. Affirmative action guidelines are a case in point. For many people, increasing the number of women and minority group members in higher level administrative positions is undoubtedly a societal goal. For some it likely represents a system goal. For still others, it may be a derived goal.[13]

The Formulation of Goals
Individual Preferences and Organizational Goals

Having discussed the function and nature of organizational goals, we now turn our attention to the more specific topic of how goals are selected. In our opening dialogue, organizations were defined as goal-seeking social systems. It is extremely important to realize, however, that organizations as such cannot have goals except in a purely metaphorical or figurative sense.[14] Attributing such things as goals and needs to organizations places us in a position of *reifying* the concept of organization, that is, treating an abstraction—an organization—as if it were a concrete reality capable of having an existence and behavior independent of the behavior of its members.[15] In short, people have goals; organizations do not. At the same time, the opposite extreme of equating the goals of an organization with the sum total of the purposes and needs of its individual members is also unacceptable. The personal goals and motives of an organization's members may or may not be the goals of the formal structure. As Barnard points out,

we have clearly to distinguish between organization purpose and individual motive. It is frequently assumed in reasoning about organizations that common purpose and individual motive are or should be identical. With the exception noted below, this is never the case; and under modern conditions it rarely even appears to be the case. Individual motive is necessarily an internal, personal, subjective thing; common purpose is necessarily an external, impersonal, objective thing even though the individual interpretation of it is subjective. The one exception to this general rule, an important one, is that the accomplishment of an organization purpose becomes itself a source of personal satisfaction and a motive for many individuals in many organizations. It is rare, however, if ever, and then I think only in connection with family, patriotic, and

---

[13]F. S. Hall, "Organizational Goals: The Status of Theory and Research," in *Managerial Accounting: The Behavioral Foundations,* ed. J. L. Livingstone (Columbus, Ohio: Grid, 1975), p, 13.

[14]A. W. Gouldner, "Organizational Analysis," in *Sociology Today: Problems and Prospects,* ed. R. K. Merton, L. Broom, and L. S. Cottrell (New York: Basic Books, 1959), p. 420; L. Haworth, "Do Organizations Act?" *Ethics* 70 (1959): 59–63.

[15]H. A. Simon, "On the Concept of Organizational Goal," *Administrative Science Quarterly* 9 (1964): 1–22.

religious organizations under special conditions, that organization purpose becomes or can become the only or even the major individual motive.[16]

The issue being taken up here is thus much more complex than might initially be assumed. If organizations per se cannot be said to set and pursue goals, and if the goals of an organization are more than the simple sum of the personal goals of all the individuals in the organization, how then are the goals of an organization formulated? Fortunately, an answer to this question is provided by the work of Cyert and March.[17]

Coalitions and Organizational Goals

In an effort to explicitly deal with this apparent goal-setting dilemma, Cyert and March proposed an alternative conceptualization of organizations and organizational goal setting. Rather than viewing organizations as integrated entities, they are seen as being comprised of interacting interest groups, or coalitions, that make competing claims on an organization's resources. As traditionally defined, a coalition "is any group within an organization whose members have identified common interests that they try to promote. Such a constituency can be delineated by departmental or hierarchical boundaries, or more generally, by clusters of members that share distinct values and interests."[18]

This more sophisticated conception has gained widespread support as organizations have increasingly been shown to be comprised of sets of subgroups that have divergent interests and views regarding what organizations are and what they should be.[19] According to this model, organizational goals are determined by continued *bargaining* among various coalitions attempting to ensure that their differing interests are represented. Thus, for example, stockholders bargain with employees over the relative division of profits, and departmental units bargain with one another for increased prestige and status. As a consequence of such exchanges, organizational goals represent compromises reflecting the relative power of various organizational coalitions. Power, and thus influence, is achieved through control over critical events and essential resources.[20]

---

[16]C. I. Barnard, *The Functions of the Executive* (Cambridge, Mass.: Harvard University Press, 1938), pp. 88–89.

[17]R. M. Cyert and J. G. March, *A Behavioral Theory of the Firm* (Englewood Cliffs, N.J.: Prentice-Hall, 1963).

[18]J. M. Pennings and P. S. Goodman, "Toward a Workable Framework," in *New Perspectives on Organizational Effectiveness,* ed. P. S. Goodman and J. M. Pennings (San Francisco: Jossey-Bass, 1977), p. 148.

[19]W. R. Scott, et al., "Organizational Effectiveness and the Quality of Surgical Care in Hospitals," in *Environments and Organizations*, ed. M. W. Meyer (San Francisco: Jossey-Bass, 1978), p. 295.

[20]For examples, see E. E. Carter, "The Behavioral Theory of the Firm and Top-Level Corporate Decision," *Administrative Science Quarterly* 16 (1970): 413–429; F. S. Hills and T. A. Mahoney, "University Budgets and Organization Decision Making," *Administrative Science Quarterly* 23 (1978): 454–465; G. R. Salancik and J. Pfeffer, "The Bases and Use of Power in Organization Decision Making: The Case of a University," *Administrative Science Quarterly* 19 (1974): 453–473; R. Stagner, "Corporate Decision Making: An Empirical Study," *Journal of Applied Psychology* 53 (1969): 1–13.

Side Payments

A fundamental part of the Cyert and March concept of coalition formation centers around the idea of *side payments.* Throughout the bargaining process, side payments are employed by coalitions to induce other individuals or interest groups in the organization to join with them in the pursuit of certain goals. These inducements to participate can take any of numerous forms: money payments, perquisites, privileged personal treatment, private commitments, grants of authority, position, and so on. Side payments are, in a sense, the price in return for which individuals adopt organizational goals. Thus, in exchange for decent wages and favorable working conditions, employees produce. Similarly, in exchange for increased dividends, shareholders continue to invest. The concept of side payments may also be expanded to incorporate significant outsiders or special interest groups who influence the goals of an organization and who attempt to see that their interests are represented.[21] In this way, consumers, tax collectors, regulatory agencies, political parties, and other nonmembers may seek lower prices, tax code revisions, safer products, donations, etc., in return for their support and approval.

In effect, the essentially reciprocal nature of coalition formation can perhaps be best appreciated through a simple example. Consider an organization composed of an entrepreneur, one employee, and one customer. The system of inducements (side payments) and return contributions may be represented as follows:

Participant	Inducements	Contributions
Entrepreneur	Revenue from Sales	Costs of Production
Employee	Wage	Labor
Customer	Goods	Purchase Price

As indicated, each *participant* (interest group) is offered an *inducement* to adopt the organization's goals, and it is through this participation that they make a *contribution* to the organization. "The customer's contribution of the purchase price is used to provide inducements to the entrepreneur in the form of revenue. The entrepreneur's contribution provides the employee's wages. The employee's contribution is transformed into goods that provide the customer's inducement."[22]

While this example is obviously an oversimplification, including only the most tangible inducements and contributions, it does illustrate the fundamental symmetrical nature of coalition bargaining. Briefly put, the contributions made by the various participants are transformed by the organization into inducements, which it then reapportions. Even more fundamental, however, is the fact that an organization can survive and grow only so long as it is able to distribute enough inducements, produced out of the contributions it receives, to maintain the flow of contributions. That is, the organization must receive enough revenue from customer sales to pay its employees' wages; it must receive enough labor from its employees to produce goods ade-

---

[21]J. D. Thompson, *Organizations in Action* (New York: McGraw-Hill, 1967), p. 127.
[22]H. A. Simon, "A Comparison of Organisation Theories," *Review of Economic Studies* 20 (1952–53): 42.

quate to maintain a steady stream of money from customers; and, finally, on balance there must be enough revenue remaining (over and above any remaining residual costs of production) to meet the entrepreneur's demand for an acceptable level of revenue.[23]

Organizational Slack

As argued by Cyert and March, an organization will continue to be viable as long as the payments made to its various internal interest groups (coalitions) are sufficient to induce them to remain in the organization, or, stated differently, if the utility the coalitions derive from the net balance of inducements over contributions is greater than that they could obtain elsewhere.[24] Cyert and March further suggest that under favorable conditions, organizations often accumulate resources in excess of those necessary to meet their required side payments (that is, inducements). The resulting difference between the total resources thus available to an organization and the total payments necessary to maintain the contributions of coalition members comprises what has been termed *organizational slack*.[25] Slack consists of payments to coalition members beyond those necessary to keep them in the organization. Organizational slack exists in many forms: dividends are declared in excess of those required to ensure continued shareholder investment; wages are paid at a level above that necessary to attract an acceptable labor force; executives are provided perquisites and personal treatments in excess of those necessary to keep them; subunits are allowed to grow in size and expense without real concern for maintaining an acceptable relation between marginal costs and marginal revenues; and so on.

With respect to the present discussion, organizational slack is of direct significance to what may be called the *coalition process of goal formation.* The structuring of coalitions and the intensity of their conflict is directly related to the availability of resources. March and Simon underscore this point by stating that

when resources are relatively unlimited, organizations need not resolve the relative merits of subgroup claims. Thus these claims and the rationalizations for them tend not to be challenged; substantial differentiation of goals occurs within the organization. . . . When resources are restricted and this slack is taken up, the relations among individual members and subgroups in the organization become more nearly a strictly competitive game. From this we predict that as resources are reduced (e.g., in a business recession for a business organization; after a legislative economy move in a governmental organization), intergroup conflict tends to increase.[26]

---

[23]H. A. Simon, "Administrative Behavior," in *International Encyclopedia of the Social Sciences,* rev. ed., ed. D. L. Sills (New York: Macmillan and Free Press, 1968), p. 76.

[24]Cyert and March, *Behavioral Theory,* p. 36.

[25]R. M. Cyert and J. G. March, "Organizational Factors in the Theory of Oligopoly," *Quarterly Journal of Economics* 70 (1956): 44–64.

[26]J. G. March and H. A. Simon, *Organizations* (New York: John Wiley & Sons, 1958), p. 126.

In summary, the Cyert-March model essentially views organizations as political systems in which goals are formulated through a complex process of bargaining among various coalitions with different, and possibly competing, expectations. This view clearly contrasts with the notion expressed earlier that organizations are concrete objects capable of independently establishing their own objectives. Furthermore, this model takes into account that the goals of an organization cannot be determined by simply totaling the preferences of all members. Rather, as Cyert and March have suggested, the goals of an organization are established through a process of bargaining involving interdependent individuals who, to borrow Thompson's phrase, "collectively have sufficient control of organizational resources to commit them in certain directions and to withold them from others."[27]

Organizational Decision Making

Given a set of goals to pursue, the preceding discussion naturally leads to a consideration of how specific courses of action are selected for the accomplishment of intended outcomes. Classical economic theory for the most part portrays organizational decision makers as maximizing intended outcomes based on complete information. This representation flows largely from the two fundamental assumptions upon which classical economic analysis rests. The first assumption is that organizations seek to maximize expected utility or profits above all else. The second assumption is that human beings are substantively rational. Combining these two assumptions, and given a particular economic environment (for example, monopoly, oligarchy, and so on), a standard economic analysis can generally be conducted using such traditional techniques as calculus or linear programming.[28]

The realism and applicability of these assumptions (utility or profit maximization on the one hand and substantive rationality on the other) were first seriously questioned by Herbert A. Simon in two classic papers[29] which have since become the basis for over two decades of research in the area of *organizational decision making,* or what is often called the *theory of organizational choice.*[30] Initially focusing on the process by which organizations develop and evaluate alternative courses of action for achieving organizational goals, Simon advanced the view that the actual choice or decision, far from being substantively rational, is limited by the finite cognitive capacity and affective attributes of the individuals involved, as well as by environmental constraints over which there is virtually no control. This situation is described by

---

[27]Thompson, *Organizations in Action,* p. 128.

[28]H. A. Simon, "From Substantive to Procedural Rationality," in *Method and Appraisals in Economics*, ed. S. J. Latsis (Cambridge: Cambridge University Press, 1976), p. 131.

[29]H. A. Simon, "A Behavioral Model of Rational Choice," *Quarterly Journal of Economics* 69 (1955): 99–118; "Rational Choice and the Structure of the Environment," *Psychological Review* 63 (1956): 129–138.

[30]J. G. March, "Bounded Rationality, Ambiguity, and the Engineering of Choice," *Bell Journal of Economics* 9 (1978): 587–608.

Simon as one of *limited* or *bounded rationality.*[31] Such circumstances are seen as not only reflecting the limited capability of the human mind to grasp the full complexity of organizational problems, but also as reflecting the uncertainty of future events with which organizations must deal. Given that organizations exist in environments that do not fully disclose the alternative courses of action available, or the consequences of those alternatives, all intendedly rational behavior is, by definition, behavior that is inherently bounded.

As such a condition would suggest, optimum decisions are almost never made (except by chance). Even if it were possible to acquire complete knowledge about all the factors affecting a decision and to predict their outcomes, it is doubtful, given the limitations of human beings as processors of information, that an adequate evaluation could be made. In response to this dilemma, Simon suggests that humans typically reduce the complexity they confront by constructing a simplified personal model of the real situation. As a result of this procedure, only a limited number of factors (usually those most closely connected with the decision in terms of cause and time) and a limited range of consequences are taken into consideration.

Simon argues further that once decision makers have isolated a limited set of variables (by constructing a simplified personal model of the real situation), they typically again deviate from the demands of rationality by selecting the first course of action deemed "satisfactory" or "good enough," rather than searching further for the optimum choice. That is, rather than examine all possible alternatives and attempt to order them according to a well-organized and stable hierarchy of preferences, they settle for the first satisfactory alternative that presents itself. As a shorthand label for such a decision process, Simon revived the Scottish word *satisficing* (= satisfying) to distinguish it from maximizing behavior. Examples of satisficing criteria include "share of market," "adequate profit," and "fair price." On a more personal level, satisficing can be seen in the common dilemma of a man seeking a new job. As suggested by Carzo and Yanouzas, "In order to make a rational choice, that is select the best job, he needs to know of every available job in the universe." To this they appropriately add, "Even if this information were attainable, it would be practically impossible to assemble, classify, and analyze according to the values sought in the job."[32]

In reflecting on the above situation and others of a similar nature (for example, the purchase of a car, the acquisition of a source of raw materials to ensure an uninterrupted supply), it is important that the making of such decisions not be mistaken for examples of irrationality. Indeed, as noted by March: "Bounded rationality has come to be recognized widely . . . as a normatively sensible adjustment to the

[31]H. A. Simon, *Administrative Behavior: A Study of Decision Making Processes in Administrative Organizations* (New York: Macmillan, 1947), pp. 39–41.
[32]R. Carzo and J. N. Yanouzas, *Formal Organizations: A Systems Approach* (Homewood, Ill.: Richard D. Irwin, 1967), p. 326.

costs and character of information gathering and processing by human beings."[33] Simply stated, the cost of searching for additional decision alternatives may, past a point, exceed their likely benefit. Thus, as March goes on to note, given the constraints associated with limited human information-processing capabilities and the uncertainty of future events, the decision procedures human beings employ are basically sensible, "even though they might not be sensible if the constraints were removed."[34]

On balance, the work of Simon rejects the basic assumptions of classical economic analysis. Whereas economists have traditionally focused on how organizations *ought to* or *should* rationally behave, the primary focus of Simon's research has been on how they *do* behave. Human beings are not mere opportunists who simply seek to maximize gains, nor are they substantively rational. The Simon concept of bounded rationality negates the myth of the so-called "economic man" and replaces it with a more realistic model of human decision making.

Means-Ends Chain

As we have thus far indicated: (1) an organization's goals reflect the resolution reached through a process of bargaining among various coalitions attempting to ensure that their differing views are represented; and (2) it is only after organizational goals have been agreed upon, and working relationships have been established, that the feasibility of alternative courses of action for their achievement can be evaluated. A major consequence of this process, and the topic of this section, is that, once specific courses of action are chosen for attaining agreed upon goals, subsequent decisions must be made to complete what is called the *means-ends chain.* That is, given the limited or bounded rationality of individual decision makers, and the fact that both goals and means at the highest level of an organization are often both complex and abstract, it becomes necessary to divide "ultimate" goals into subgoals for participants at lower organizational levels. Thus, as described by Meyer: "What are means intended to contribute to the accomplishment of ends articulated at the highest level become ends in themselves for individuals at the second level of organizations. These ends, in turn, are translated into specific means and are parcelled out to people at the third level who treat what are means for the second level as ends for themselves. Through the elaboration of successive ends-means chains, nonoperational organizational goals are eventually transformed into very specific routines of behavior for people at the lowest level."[35]

A logical interrelationship should exist between the goals and subgoals within an organization, the accomplishment of each subgoal serving as a means for the attain-

---

[33]March, "Bounded Rationality," p. 589.
[34]Ibid., p. 590.
[35]M. W. Meyer, *Theory of Organizational Structure* (Indianapolis, Ind.: Bobbs-Merrill, 1977), p. 20.

Chapter 4

ment of a more general goal. Hence, except for the broadest, most encompassing objective, each goal within an organization can be considered to be an end in itself as well as a means for achieving a higher level goal. Accordingly, an organization's primary or overall goals can be viewed as being divided into second-, third-, and *N* th-order goals, and as forming a hierarchy of means and ends. An example of such a means-ends structure is illustrated in Figure 4–1.

Looking at Figure 4–1, we can see that the ultimate or overall organizational goal has been simply stated as "organizational survival." As depicted, the organization can choose either or both of two *means* (at the vice-presidential level) to ensure its overall *goal* of survival: one would be to raise revenues; a second would be to cut costs. Each of these *means* can then be considered *subgoals*. Following the first alternative, we see that at the middle management level in the diagram there are two (not incompatible) *means* indicated for raising revenues: increase sales of X and develop product Y. If increasing sales of X is selected as the *means* for raising revenues, it becomes a *goal* itself and in turn can be pursued at the operative level by such *means* as putting the organization's best sales personnel on product X and changing the organization's production schedule to ensure adequate availability of product X.

This analysis could easily be extended to include goals that are more and more specific in nature, each being an appropriate means for fulfilling a more general goal. In this manner we would eventually come to include all the *means* necessary for ensuring the accomplishment of the organization's ultimate goal—continued survival.

Empirical Support

Empirical studies of the means-ends hierarchy are virtually nonexistent. With the exception of Wallroth's investigation of the means-ends structure of a Swedish hospital, no other research-based analyses have been performed.[36] Utilizing interview data drawn from representatives of various departments within each hierarchical level of the hospital he studied, Wallroth was able to develop a conceptual scheme for analyzing the various characteristics of the hospital's means-ends structure. Of particular interest, the results of his investigation disclosed a direct negative relationship between goal attainment and the extent to which different decision makers at various hierarchical levels had contradictory conceptions of the hospital's goals. Three patterns, or types of goal conflict, were identified: incongruence, inconsistence, and inconsonance.

The Incongruence of Goals

Clearly defined and agreed upon goals are a fundamental aspect of job performance. Organizations employ a variety of means such as training programs, apprenticeships,

---

[36]C. Wallroth, "An Analysis of Means-End Structures," *Acta Sociologica* 11 (1968): 110–118.

Figure 4–1 *A Means-Ends Hierarchy*

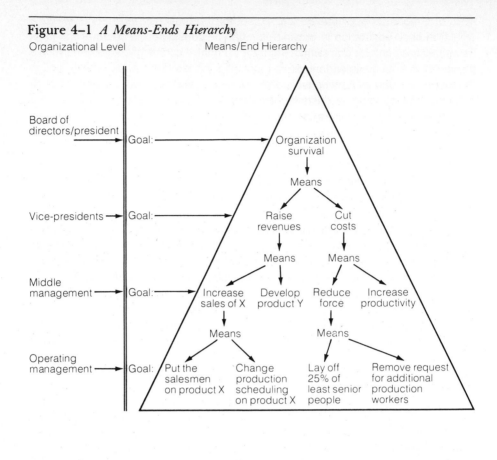

and other modes of socialization to ensure that organizational objectives are understood. Further assistance is provided by rules, budgets, memoranda, and similar administrative devices. Nevertheless, organization members often have a limited appreciation of the dependencies and complicated connections existing between departments or tasks. As a consequence, individual organization members' conceptions of goals tend to be greatly influenced by the nature of their particular task assignments and their knowledge of other units. Moreover, it should be realized that an individual's conception of an organization's goals and the means of attaining them may, to a large extent, be a function of his or her personal goals. The existence of such differences were termed by Wallroth *incongruence in the means-ends structure*.[37] Such differences reduce the probability of an organization attaining its goal because the likelihood of conflicts and non-cooperation is increased. Incongruent goal conception is particularly noticeable among areas of activity that are highly dependent upon one another. As an example of this type of goal conflict, Wallroth cites an instance in a clinic of the hospital he studied where the resident staff nurses felt that, to ensure patient survival, there should be more contact with patients and less time spent on instrument treatment procedures. As shown in Figure 4–2, this was the exact opposite of the view held by the clinic superintendent, who perceived that the best way to ensure patient survival was to increase treatment with instruments. Thus, while both the nurses and the clinic superintendent agreed on a common goal, they disagreed on the most appropriate means of achieving it.

The Inconsistence of Goals

As we have already noted, the rationality of decision makers is constrained by the finite cognitive capacity and limited information-processing capabilities of the human

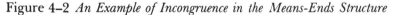

Figure 4–2 *An Example of Incongruence in the Means-Ends Structure*

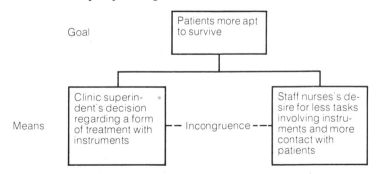

Source: Adapted from C. Wallroth, "An Analysis of Means-End Structures," *Acta Sociologica* 11 (1968): 114. Reprinted by permission of Universitetsforloget, Oslo, publishers.

[37]Ibid., p. 113.

The Establishment of Organizational Goals

mind. The possibility thus arises that organization members may occasionally choose an alternative course of action that is incompatible with the achievement of an intended higher-level goal. Wallroth labels this situation *inconsistence in the means-ends structure* and states that "an inconsistence is said to exist when a means cannot lead to the intended goal."[38] Thus, by definition, an inconsistence in its means-ends structure reduces an organization's degree of goal attainment.

In providing an illustration of such a situation, Wallroth notes that it is often difficult to determine whether a particular means leads to the accomplishment of a particular goal. The ambiguities associated with measuring the effects of advertising or the benefits of research and development departments are cases in point. At the hospital in which Wallroth conducted his study, a simple form of inconsistence was found to exist between the desire (goal) of one employee to personally prepare operating reports and compute payrolls, while at the same time seeking to reduce the amount of time he devoted to paperwork. (See Figure 4–3.)

The Inconsonance of Goals

A third and final type of goal conflict identified by Wallroth was found to exist when goals on the same level in the means-ends hierarchy produced conflicting demands. Such situations were found to be particularly prevalent among units representing different subgoals. This type of conflict has been designated as *inconsonance of goals* and is diagrammed in Figure 4–4.

As depicted, inconsonance exists between the hospital administration's demands for an organization run at low costs and the doctors' demand for expensive, first-rate equipment. In commenting on the resulting dilemma, Wallroth suggests that goal conflicts of this type may be solved in one of three ways:

Figure 4–3 *An Example of Inconsistence in the Means-Ends Structure*

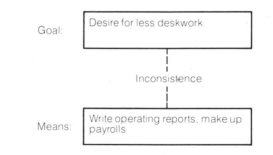

Source: Adapted from C. Wallroth, "An Analysis of Means-End Structures," *Acta Sociologica* 11 (1968): 115. Reprinted by permission of Universitetsforloget, Oslo, publishers.

---

[38]Ibid., p.114

Figure 4-4 *An Example of Inconsonance in the Means-Ends Structure*

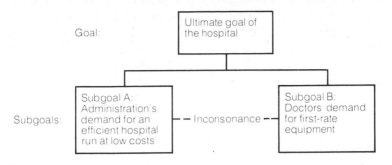

Source: Adapted from C. Wallroth, "An Analysis of Means-End Structures," *Acta Sociologica* 11 (1968): 116. Reprinted by permission of Universitetsforloget, Oslo, publishers.

1. *In different decisions, consideration is given to only one of the goals. Every separate decision, however, determines which goal is most pertinent.*
2. *In each decision efforts are made to reach a compromise.*
3. *Various members or units of the organization may represent different goals. This type of solution is for example, reflected by the conflict situation prevailing between the administrative personnel, defenders of economic effectiveness and the doctors, defenders of professional values.* [39]

Wallroth's analysis is of significance for at least two major reasons. First, and most obviously, it clearly suggests the importance of minimizing incongruence, inconsistence, and inconsonance for effective goal attainment. Second, at a more theoretical level, it also suggests that organizational goals differ in the degree to which they are *operational,* that is, the extent to which there are "agreed-upon criteria for determining the extent to which particular activities or programs of activity contribute to these goals."[40] Thus, to use examples other than those already provided, a philanthropic foundation's goal of "contributing to the general welfare of mankind" is non-operational insofar as its attainment cannot be evaluated objectively and insofar as the connection between specific actions and attainment cannot be determined. On the other hand, for a fire department, a residential inspection program directed toward the goal of reducing home fires is, to a much greater degree, operational insofar as it can be observed and its results clearly measured. In sum, Wallroth's analysis thus implies that to the extent that the connection between actions (means) and goal attainment can be objectively determined, it is much more likely that subgoals will not only be in harmony, but will also be in line with the ultimate or overall goal(s) that they

---

[39]Ibid., pp. 115-116.
[40]March and Simon, *Organizations,* p. 194.

The Establishment of Organizational Goals

theoretically support, thereby reducing inconsistence, incongruence, and inconsonance in an organization's means-ends structure.

Goal Change and Adaptation

In concluding our discussion of the nature of goals and goal structure, it is essential to realize that the goals of an organization should not be thought of as invariant. Goal change and adaptation occur more or less continuously as the general aims of an organization are redefined and recast in light of changes in its surrounding environment and in its internal state. For instance, as the set of members within an organization changes, and the character of its surrounding environment fluctuates, organizational goals appropriate at one point in time may become either irrelevant or impractical. In this respect, it is possible to distinguish two basic forms of goal change —*goal succession* and *goal transformation*—with the latter including two subtypes: *goal diversion* and *goal displacement*.

Goal Succession

As a basic form of goal change, goal succession refers to the conscious, intentional replacement of an organization's primary goal, once it has been achieved, with a new goal.[41] Goal succession takes on special significance when it is realized that goal achievement and survival are often inimical. As Hannan and Freeman have pointed out, "Being too successful may result in a loss of mission, which results in survival failure."[42]

Perhaps the best known example of this paradox is that cited by Sills in a case study of the National Foundation for Infantile Paralysis, which is widely known for its annual March of Dimes Campaign.[43] Established in 1938, the foundation was initially formed to gather public support for medical research into the prevention and treatment of polio. The foundation had always reflected the fundamental belief that infantile paralysis was a disease that could be brought under control. However, it was not until the successful development of the foundation-sponsored Salk vaccine (1952–54) that it became clear that its primary purpose was about to be realized and that the foundation would no longer have a meaningful goal. Thus, the foundation's success threatened its very survival. The organization was consequently faced with the choice of either disbanding or developing a new goal or goals. It chose the latter alternative, selecting as its new goal combating arthritis and birth defects, and subsequently changed its name to simply the National Foundation. This case provides an

---

[41]Blau, *Dynamics of Bureaucracy,* p.195.

[42]M. T. Hannan and J. Freeman, "Obstacles to Comparative Studies," in Goodman and Penning, eds., *New Perspectives,* p. 128.

[43]D. L. Sills, *The Volunteers: Means and Ends in a National Organization* (Glencoe, Ill.: Free Press, 1957).

explicit example of goal succession in that, had the foundation not consciously and intentionally replaced its primary goal with a new goal after its original purpose had been realized, it would have ceased to exist as a meaningful and viable organization.

Goal Transformation

Goal Diversion

One of the two basic types of goal transformation, goal diversion refers to instances in which an organization's original goals are *not* realized but are supplanted by alternative ones. As such, goal diversion involves the deliberate diverting of an organization from its original course. Numerous illustrations of this process can be cited. The Townsend Organization, for instance, was founded in 1933 by Dr. Francis E. Townsend, who proposed that Congress end the depression by retiring all U.S. citizens at age 60 with a pension of $200 a month. Within three years the organization had over 2¼ million members. In 1935, however, with the passage of the Social Security Act, the organization was deprived of much of its original purpose. Between 1936 and 1951, as provisions of Social Security were expanded and as private pension plans became more widespread, the organization's membership dropped almost 98 percent to less than 57,000. Faced with a severe challenge to its continued existence, the organization underwent a transformation (goal diversion) from a political movement to a social club, supporting itself through the sale of vitamins, health foods, and other consumer goods.[44] As such, the Townsend Organization continues to survive even today, but in doing so has all but abandoned its original goal for more pragmatic concerns.

The Women's Christian Temperance Union (WCTU) also provides an interesting example of goal diversion. Founded over 175 years ago, the WCTU undertook as its major goal, "the changing of American drinking habits." Primarily devoted to moral reform, the zenith of the WCTU movement was reached in 1919 with the passage of the Eighteenth Amendment to the Constitution, outlawing the sale of alcohol in the United States. Its success, however, was shortlived, reaching a dramatic downturn with the repeal of Prohibition in 1933. In an interesting analysis of the circumstances leading up to and following these two events, Gusfield has shown how the WCTU's refusal to adapt to the reality of changing drinking norms has resulted in its original goal of "active" moral reform being slowly eroded (diverted) and, over time, being supplanted by the occasional expression of what he terms "moral indignation" directed toward upper-middle-class life.[45]

A third and somewhat different example of goal diversion can be found in Zald and Denton's analysis of the successful transformation of the Young Men's Christian

---

[44]S. L. Messinger, "Organizational Transformation: A Case Study of a Declining Social Movement," *American Sociological Review* 20 (1955): 3–10.

[45]J. S. Gusfield, "Social Structure and Moral Reform: A Study of the Women's Christian Temperance Union," *American Journal of Sociology* 61 (1955): 221–232.

Association (YMCA) from an evangelistic social movement to a general, all-purpose service organization.[46] Founded in London in 1844, the YMCA spread to Boston shortly thereafter. Zald and Denton explain the YMCA's transformation over the intervening years in terms of its ability to successfully adapt to a changing society and to meet the consequent new demands placed upon it by a changing clientele. Originally restricted to young men of Protestant upbringing, it has long since expanded its membership criteria to include all religions and ages and both sexes, and at the same time changed its basic goal from evangelism to a secular commitment to develop the "whole man." The YMCA's successful transformation in the face of changing social conditions stands in stark contrast to the decline experienced by both the WCTU, as a result of its strict insistence on ideological purity, and the Townsend Organization, as a result of its failure to adapt to changing political conditions.

A final, and more recent, example of goal diversion is Jenkins' analysis of the transformation of the National Council of Churches (NCC) over the period 1951 to 1975.[47] A successor to the Federal Council of Churches and several other inter-denominational agencies that merged in 1951, the primary function of the NCC was to serve as a coordinating body for the activities of some thirty Protestant denominations. As described by Jenkins, up until the late 1950s, the goals of the NCC could clearly be labeled "social gospel" in nature, with the professed aim to "Christianize the social order." In fulfilling this calling, church agencies were directed to preserve a uniform separation between church and state. The methods the NCC employed in accomplishing its goals were those associated with traditional missionary activity: Christian education directed at individuals and the provision of welfare services for those in need. In short, the NCC's primary activities were aimed at changing individuals, not institutions.

By the early 1960s, all this began to change. Rather than focusing on the provision of "Christian services," agencies of the NCC, such as The National Migrant Ministry, became increasingly involved in various forms of social action directed at institutional rather than individual change. Lobbying for reform legislation, community organization, and political advocacy became popular activities. The NCC, for instance, was a major supporter of civil rights reform and sponsored the 1963 March on Washington led by Dr. Martin Luther King, Jr. As analyzed by Jenkins, this "radical" transformation of NCC goals was the result of changing power relations within the NCC, which in turn were the consequence of the underlying growth and affluence of organized Protestantism. Whereas the case of the NCC is another clear illustration of goal divergence, much like that which took place within the Townsend Organization, the WCTU, and the YMCA, it does differ with respect to the fact that the transformation of NCC goals was primarily an outgrowth of internal forces rather than a response to pressures deriving from the surrounding social environment.

---

[46]M. N. Zald and P. Denton, "From Evangelism to General Service: The Transformation of the YMCA," *Administrative Science Quarterly* 8 (1963): 214–234.

[47]J. C. Jenkins, "Radical Transformation of Organizational Goals," *Administrative Science Quarterly* 22 (1977): 587–608.

Goal Displacement

The second basic type of goal transformation, goal displacement, "arises when an organization displaces its goal—that is, substitutes for its legitimate goal some other goal for which it was not created, for which resources were not allocated to it, and which it is not known to serve."[48] Goal displacement is particularly characteristic of organizations such as research and development laboratories and social service agencies that seek goals that are abstract and intangible.[49] The less concrete and visible an organization's goals, the less they provide a workable basis for achieving goal consensus and subsequent group action, and the more likely there is to be disagreement over goal interpretation. In this regard, tangibility of goals is a function of: (1) the precision with which goals can be described; (2) the clarity with which they can be identified; and (3) the extent to which they can be made operational (that is, be observed and measured).

In addition to goal intangibility, there are several other causes of goal displacement. Perhaps the most frequently mentioned is the substitution of means (the methods of doing work) for ends (output), or what is frequently referred to as *means-ends inversion*. As Cyert and MacCrimmon explain, "At any point in the organization's means-ends chain, the activities performed may become divorced from the higher-level goals they were directed toward. . . . Under such circumstances means may easily become ends in themselves."[50] This is essentially the same phenomenon that Merton noted (as mentioned in Chapter 3) to be a dysfunctional consequence of bureaucratic rules and regulations.[51] Renault Robinson, a Chicago policeman, interviewed in Studs Terkel's book *Working*, in which "people talk about what they do all day and how they feel about what they do," cites a classic example of means-ends inversion.[52] In the excerpt that follows, note how the behavior ordered by Officer Robinson's supervisor (originally intended as a means to an end—the reduction of vice) becomes transformed into an end in itself, shifting or displacing effort away from the original goal.

My supervisor would say, "We need two policy arrests, so we can be equal with the other areas." So we go out and hunt for a policy operator. . . .

A vice officer spends quite a bit of time in court. You learn the judges, the things they look for. You become proficient in testifying. You change your testimony, you change the facts. You switch things around 'cause you're trying to get convictions. . . .

Certain units in the task force have developed a science around stopping your

[48]Etzioni, *Modern Organizations,* p. 10.

[49]W. K. Warner and A. E. Havens, "Goal Displacement and the Intangibility of Organizational Goals," *Administrative Science Quarterly* 12 (1968): 539–555.

[50]R. M. Cyert and K. R. MacCrimmon, "Organizations," in *Handbook of Social Psychology,* 2nd ed., vol. 1, ed. G. Lindzey and E. Aronson (Reading, Mass.: Addison-Wesley, 1968), p. 575.

[51]R. K. Merton, "Bureaucratic Structure and Personality," *Social Forces* 18 (1940): 560–568.

[52]S. Terkel, *Working* (New York: Pantheon, 1974), pp. 137–143.

The Establishment of Organizational Goals

automobile. These men know it's impossible to drive three blocks without committing a traffic violation. We've got so many rules on the books. These police officers use these things to get points and also hustle for money. The traffic law is a fat book. He knows if you don't have two lights on your license plate, that's a violation. If you have a crack in your windshield, that's a violation. If your muffler's dragging, that's a violation. He knows all these little things. . . .

So many points for a robbery, so many points for a man having a gun. When they go to the scene and the man with the gun has gone, they'll lock up somebody anyway, knowing he's not the one. The record says, "Locked up two people for UUW"—unlawful use of weapons. The report will say, "When we got there, we saw these guys and they looked suspicious." They'll get a point even if the case is thrown out of court. The arrest is all that counts.[53]

Another common reason for goal displacement is associated with what Etzioni calls *over-measurement* and Gross labels *number magic.*[54] Both terms refer to the tendency of organizations to attach an artificial importance to goals that are easy to quantify and hence readily measureable. Such distortion can result in the overemphasis of quantitative and measureable goals at the expense of nonquantitative goals. As a consequence, the more qualitative a goal, the more likely it is to become displaced. Familiar examples of this phenomenon include emphasizing production output with little regard for product quality; compensating university faculty on the basis of number of courses taught rather than on the quality of their classroom performance; looking at profit rather than customer goodwill; and determining promotions on the basis of seniority rather than job knowledge.

Still another reason for the displacement of goals is the tendency within many, if not most, complex organizations to *suboptimize,* or to function at less than an optimum level because subunit goals take on an importance greater than that of overall organizational goals. As Mintzburg notes, "Units are naturally inclined to pursue narrow goals that pertain to their own function at the expense of the broad or formal goals that pertain to the overall organization."[55] We noted this same problem in our earlier discussion (Chapter 3) of the dysfunctions associated with bureaucracy when we indicated that the *bifurcation* of interests is often the basis for conflict among organizational subunits. Available research suggests that such suboptimization and resulting goal displacement is most likely to occur in *loosely coupled,* decentralized organizations that permit their various subunits to operate in partial independence of their larger supporting systems.[56] Loose coupling exists when the activities of the various subunits of an organization are only weakly related and

---

[53]Ibid., pp. 137–140.

[54]Etzioni, *Modern Organizations,* p. 8; B. M. Gross, *Organizations and Their Managing* (New York: Free Press, 1968), p. 293.

[55]H. Mintzburg, "Organizational Power and Goals: A Skeletal Theory," in *Strategic Management: A New View of Business and Policy Planning,* ed. D. E. Schendel and C. W. Hofer (Boston: Little, Brown, 1979), p. 71.

[56]H. A. Simon, "The Organization of Complex Systems," in *Hierarchy Theory: The Challenge of Complex Systems,* ed. H. H. Patee (New York: Braziller, 1973), pp. 3–27.

Chapter 4

therefore are free to vary independently. In such circumstances, the degree of coupling, or interaction, among subunits depends solely on the activity of the elements they share.[57] As a consequence, it would not be surprising to find two loosely coupled units within the same organization pursuing dissimilar or even opposing goals. It is precisely this type of situation that seems to largely explain the contradictory actions of the Department of Agriculture in supporting tobacco allotments and the Department of Health, Education, and Welfare in discouraging smoking by the general public. The pursuit by each department of its own narrow goals without regard for the relevance of its actions to the overall benefit of the nation is an example of goal displacement in what would indeed appear to be an extremely loosely coupled organization.

In summary, the primary intent of this final section has been to address the topic of "organizational goal change and adaptation." It has hopefully made the point that organizations exhibit adaptive behavior over time, redefining and recasting their goals in response both to changes in their surrounding environment and to the relevancy and practicality of their objectives. Beyond this rather general statement, very little specific information is available with which to answer the crucial question, "What determines whether goal succession or goal transformation predominates in an organization?" In one of the few efforts to address this issue, Blau suggests the existence of at least two partially determining factors: (1) "structural constraints in the organization," such as member interest and willingness to provide continuing financial support, and (2) community acceptance. "When the community permits an organization . . . to become established and attain at least some of its first objectives in a relatively short period, it will probably find new fields to conquer in the course of its development."[58] These factors seem to be particularly applicable when considering the rather remarkable development of the National Foundation as compared to the present state of either the Townsend Organization or the WCTU.

Summary

In this chapter we have been concerned with the multidimensional nature of the goal systems that operate within complex organizations. After first defining the term *goal* and differentiating between "official" and "operative" goals, the numerous functions of organizational goals were identified and a scheme for the classification of organizational goals was presented. Next, after distinguishing between "individual" and "organizational" goals, our attention turned to a consideration of the role of competing coalitions or interest groups in determining organizational goals. Questioning the fundamental assumptions of classical economic analysis, we then introduced the

---

[57]R. B. Glassman, "Persistence and Loose Coupling in Living Systems," *Behavioral Science* 18 (1973): 83–98.
[58]P. M. Blau, *Bureaucracy in a Modern Society* (New York: Random House, 1956), p. 96.

concept of "bounded rationality." We subsequently pointed out that organizational goals are differentiated into a means-ends hierarchy and that goals cannot be separated from the means of their accomplishments. Moreover, it was stressed that the ability of an organization to attain its goals depends on its capacity to "operationalize" its aims and objectives. Finally, we examined the several ways in which organizational goals change and adapt as a result of various internal and external pressures.

Taken together, the material presented in this chapter points to at least two relevant implications: (1) the setting of organizational goals is a dynamic rather than a static process, and (2) organizations do not possess unlimited goal-setting discretion; factors from without and interest groups from within each impose conflicting and competing priorities. In this respect, goals appear to be a function of interaction, both within an organization and between an organization and its external environment. It is the latter interaction that will be the focus of Chapter 6. First, however, we turn our attention to a discussion of the various approaches that have been developed to measure an organization's ability to successfully survive in a turbulent environment —that is, to be effective.

Review and Discussion Questions

1. Distinguish between "operative" and "official" goals. Cite examples of each.
2. Discuss the major functions of organizational goals.
3. Cite an example of an instance where the multiple goals of an organization might possibly conflict.
4. Comment on the essentially reciprocal nature of coalition formation.
5. What is organizational slack? Of what significance is organizational slack to the so-called "coalition process of goal formation"?
6. What is meant by the term "bounded rationality"? Cite several examples from your own experience of this phenomenon.
7. Is "satisficing" an irrational process? Explain.
8. Why is the "means-ends chain" an important part of the goal implementation process?
9. Distinguish between the two basic forms of goal change: goal succession and goal transformation.
10. What determines whether goal succession or goal transformation predominates in an organization?

References

Barnard, C. I. *The Functions of the Executive.* Cambridge, Mass.: Harvard University Press, 1938.

Blau, P. M. *Bureaucracy in Modern Society.* New York: Random House, 1956.

Blau, P. M. *The Dynamics of Bureaucracy.* Chicago: University of Chicago Press, 1955.

Carter, E. E. "The Behavioral Theory of the Firm and Top-Level Corporate Decision." *Administrative Science Quarterly* 16 (1971): 413–429.

Carzo, R., and Yanouzas, J. N. *Formal Organization: A Systems Approach.* Homewood, Ill.: Richard D. Irwin, 1967.

Cressey, D. "Achievement of an Unstated Organizational Goal." *Pacific Sociological Review* 1, no. 2 (1958): 43–49.

Cyert, R. M., and MacCrimmon, K. R. "Organizations." In *Handbook of Social Psychology,* 2nd ed., vol. 1, edited by G. Lindzey and E. Aronson. Reading, Mass.: Addison-Wesley, 1968.

Cyert, R. M., and March, J. G. *A Behavioral Theory of the Firm.* Englewood Cliffs, N.J.: Prentice-Hall, 1963.

Cyert, R. M., and March, J. G. "Organizational Factors in the Theory of Oliogopoly." *Quarterly Journal of Economics* 70 (1956): 44–64.

Dornbusch, S. M., and Scott, W. R. *Evaluation and the Exercise of Authority: A Theory of Control Applied to Diverse Organizations.* San Francisco: Jossey-Bass, 1975.

Drucker, P. *The Practice of Management.* New York: Harper & Row, 1954.

Etzioni, A. *Modern Organizations.* Englewood Cliffs, N.J.: Prentice-Hall, 1964.

Etzioni, A. "Two Approaches to Organizational Analysis: A Critique and a Suggestion." *Administrative Science Quarterly* 5 (1960): 257–277.

Glassman, R. B. "Persistence and Loose Coupling in Living Systems. " *Behavioral Science* 18 (1973):83–98.

Gouldner, A. W. "Organizational Analysis." In *Sociology Today: Problems and Prospects,* edited by R. K. Merton, L. Broom, and L. S. Cottrell. New York: Basic Books, 1959.

Gross, B. M. *Organizations and Their Managing.* New York: Free Press, 1968.

Gross, B. M. "What Are Your Organization's Objectives?" *Human Relations* 18 (1965): 195–216.

Gross, E. "The Definition of Organizational Goals." *British Journal of Sociology* 20 (1969): 277–294.

Gusfield, J. S. "Social Structure and Moral Reform: A Study of the Women's Christian Temperance Union." *American Journal of Sociology* 61 (1955): 221–232.

Hall, F. S. "Organizational Goals: The Status of Theory and Research." In *Managerial Accounting: The Behavioral Foundations,* edited by J. L. Livingstone. Columbus, Ohio: Grid, 1975.

Hannan, M. T., and Freeman, J. "Obstacles to Comparative Studies." In *New Perspectives on Organizational Effectiveness,* edited by P. S. Goodman and J. M. Pennings. San Francisco: Jossey-Bass, 1977.

Haworth, L. "Do Organizations Act?" *Ethics* 70 (1959): 59–63.

Hills, F. S., and Mahoney, T. A. "University Budgets and Organization Decision Making." *Administrative Science Quarterly* 23 (1978): 454–465.

Jackson, J. H., and Morgan, C. P. *Organization Theory: A Macro Perspective for Management.* Englewood Cliffs, N.J.: Prentice-Hall, 1978.

Jenkins, J. C. "Radical Transformation of Organizational Goals." *Administrative Science Quarterly* 22 (1977): 568–586.

March, J. G. "Bounded Rationality, Ambiguity, and the Engineering of Choice." *Bell Journal of Economics* 9 (1978): 587–608.

March, J. G., and Simon, H. A. *Organizations.* New York: John Wiley & Sons, 1958.

Merton, R. K. "Bureaucratic Structure and Personality." *Social Forces* 18 (1940): 560–568.

Messinger, S. L. "Organizational Transformation: A Case Study of a Declining Social Movement." *American Sociological Review* 20 (1955): 3–10.

Meyer, M. W. *Theory of Organizational Structure.* Indianapolis, Ind.: Bobbs-Merrill, 1977.

Mintzberg, H. "Organizational Power and Goals: A Skeletal Theory." In *Strategic Management: A New View of Business Policy and Planning,* edited by D. E. Schendel and C. W. Hofer. Boston: Little, Brown, 1979.

Pennings, J. M., and Goodman, P. S. "Toward a Workable Framework." In *New Perspectives on Organizational Effectiveness,* edited by P. S. Goodman and J. M. Pennings. San Francisco: Jossey-Bass, 1977.

Perrow, C. "The Analysis of Goals in Complex Organizations." *American Sociological Review* 26 (1961): 854–865.

Perrow, C. *Organizational Analysis: A Sociological View.* Monterey, Calif.: Brooks/Cole, 1970.

Porter, L. W., Lawler, E. E., and Hackman, J. R. *Behavior in Organizations.* New York: McGraw-Hill, 1975.

Salancik, G. R., and Pfeffer, J. "The Bases and Use of Power in Organizational Decision Making: The Case of a University." *Administrative Science Quarterly* 19 (1974): 453–473.

Scott, W. R., Flood, A. B., Ewy, W., and Forrest, W. H. "Organizational Effectiveness and the Quality of Surgical Care in Hospitals." In *Environments and Organizations,* edited by M. W. Meyer. San Francisco: Jossey-Bass, 1978.

Sills, D. L. *The Volunteers: Means and Ends in a National Organization.* Glencoe, Ill.: Free Press, 1957.

The Establishment of Organizational Goals

Simon, H. A. *Administrative Behavior: A Study of Decision Making Processes in Administrative Organization.* New York: Macmillan, 1947.

Simon, H. A. "A Comparison of Organisation Theories." *Review of Economic Studies* 20 (1952–53): 40–48.

Simon, H. A. "A Behavioral Model of Rational Choice." *Quarterly Journal of Economics* 69 (1955): 99–118.

Simon, H. A. "Rational Choice and the Structure of the Environment." *Psychological Review* 63 (1956): 129–138.

Simon, H. A. "On the Concept of Organizational Goal." *Administrative Science Quarterly* 9 (1964): 1–22.

Simon, H. A. "Administrative Behavior." In *International Encyclopedia of the Social Sciences,* rev. ed., edited by D. L. Sills. New York: Macmillan and Free Press, 1968.

Simon, H. A. "The Organization of Complex Systems." In *Hierarchy Theory: The Challenge of Complex Systems,* edited by H. H. Pattee. New York: Braziller, 1973.

Simon, H. A. "From Substantive to Procedural Rationality." In *Method and Appraisal in Economics,* edited by S. J. Latsis. Cambridge: Cambridge University Press, 1976.

Stagner, R. "Corporate Decision Making: An Empirical Study." *Journal of Applied Psychology* 53 (1969): 1–13.

Steers, R. M. *Organizational Effectiveness: A Behavioral View.* Santa Monica, Calif.: Goodyear, 1977.

Terkel, S. *Working.* New York: Pantheon, 1974.

Thompson, J. D. *Organizations in Action.* New York: McGraw-Hill, 1967.

Wallroth, C. "An Analysis of Means-End Structures." *Acta Sociologica* 11 (1968): 110–118.

Warner, W. K. "Problems in Measuring the Goal Attainment of Voluntary Organizations." *Adult Education* 19 (1967): 3–14.

Warner, W. K., and Havens, A. E. "Goal Displacement and the Intangibility of Organizational Goals." *Administrative Science Quarterly* 12 (1968): 539–555.

Warriner, C. K. "The Problem of Organizational Purpose." *Sociological Quarterly* 6 (1965): 139–146.

Zald, M. N. "Comparative Analysis and Measurement of Goals: The Case of Correctional Institutions for Delinquents." *Sociological Quarterly* 4 (1963): 206–230.

Zald, M. N., and Denton, P. "From Evangelism to General Service: The Transformation of the YMCA." *Administrative Science Quarterly* 8 (1963): 214–234.

Chapter 4

The Nature and Measurement of Organizational Effectiveness

The Nature and Measurement of Organizational Effectiveness

Chapter 5

Effectiveness, a central theme in the study of organizations, is one of the most frequently referenced yet least understood concepts in organization theory. Indeed, much of the literature about organizations has been a by-product of the quest for improved organizational effectiveness. Disappointingly, however, this search has not as yet led to the development of a universally accepted theory or methodology for assessing the overall effectiveness of an organization. This fact is reflected in divergent definitions of "effectiveness," the identification of different sets of explanatory variables, and the adherence of researchers to equally diverse schemes for measuring effectiveness.

Early management theorists defined effectiveness as the meeting or surpassing of organizational goals. Barnard, for example, viewed effectiveness in terms of goal attainment. "When a specific desired end is attained we shall say that the action is 'effective.'"[1] This perspective has been labeled the goal model approach to the study of organizational effectiveness, since it is a view of organizations as principally concerned with the attainment of certain end "products" or goals.

More recently, however, a second view of organizational effectiveness has emerged. This is an approach to organizations as social systems operating in environments of scarce resources. Incorporating an open-systems viewpoint, the so-called system resource model approach defines effectiveness as the degree to which an organization is successful in acquiring and utilizing scarce and valued resources. Thus, considering the whole of an organization and not just its ends, effectiveness, according to this approach, relates to the nature of the interaction between an organization and its surrounding environment.

As indicated by the title, the purpose of the present chapter is to explore the nature and measurement of organizational effectiveness. In doing so, our discussion naturally builds on that of the previous chapter, in which we dealt with the nature and establishment of organizational goals. Given that an organization can clearly define and establish agreed upon goals, the extent to which its performance may be judged effective in reaching these goals is a fundamental managerial concern. As stated earlier, a great deal of controversy, as well as numerous perplexing

---

[1]C. I. Barnard, *The Functions of the Executive* (Cambridge, Mass.: Harvard University Press, 1938), p. 19.

methodological problems, surrounds the measurement of organizational effectiveness. Consequently, after pausing briefly to comment on the relationship of effectiveness to its companion concept, efficiency, we will analyze more completely the goal and system resource models as the two dominant underlying approaches to the study of organizational effectiveness. In addition to providing a further explanation of the operation of these models, the discussion will stress their complementary natures, and an attempt will be made to at least partially reconcile their differences. The balance of the chapter will then be devoted to a discussion of several of the major unresolved problems associated with the actual measurement of organizational effectiveness.

Effectiveness versus Efficiency

Before beginning our discussion of organizational effectiveness models, it is important to establish a distinction between *organizational effectiveness* and *organizational efficiency.* The usefulness of this distinction can perhaps be best appreciated when it is noted that virtually all organizations must strive to achieve their goals within the constraints of limited resources. Consequently, the concept of efficiency, the ratio of an organization's outputs to its inputs, must be introduced. An organization is judged efficient if, when compared to similar organizations, its outputs (or benefits received) are relatively high in comparison to its inputs (or costs). Thus, as Steers observes: "If two companies making the same product finish the fiscal year with equal production levels but one attained the level with fewer invested resources than the other, that company [other things being equal] would be described as being more efficient. It achieved the same level of output with fewer inputs."[2]

The important point to note is that, while effectiveness and efficiency are closely related, they are not interchangeable.[3] That is, an organization could easily be judged effective without being efficient, just as it could be judged efficient without being effective. Neither condition is a necessary prerequisite for the other.

The Goal Model of Organizational Effectiveness

Originating in traditional measures of performance used in accounting, the goal model is unquestionably the most commonly used and widely discussed approach for assessing organizational effectiveness. As noted earlier, its distinctive feature is that it defines effectiveness in terms of goal attainment. That is, the greater the extent to which an organization's goals are met or surpassed, the greater its effectiveness.

---

[2]R. M. Steers, *Organizational Effectiveness: A Behavioral View* (Santa Monica, Calif.: Goodyear, 1977), p. 51.
[3]T. Caplow, *How to Run Any Organization: A Manual of Practical Sociology* (Hinsdale, Ill.: Dryden Press, 1976), p. 91.

The goal model primarily rests on the implicit assumption that the goals of an organization can be neatly established and that the necessary human and material resources can be dutifully manipulated for the attainment of given goals.[4] It follows (according to this approach) that the way to assess an organization's effectiveness is to establish criterion measures to evaluate how well its goals are being achieved.[5] Such evaluative criteria (for example, turnover, productivity, quality of output, and so on) would thus be directly derived from the goals the organization is attempting to achieve (morale, return on investment, cost performance, and so on). A typical statement of this position is offered by Reddin, who argues that "there is only one realistic and unambiguous definition of managerial effectiveness. Effectiveness is the extent to which a manager achieves the output requirements of his job."[6]

The work of Mahoney and Weitzel provides an excellent illustration of the goal-oriented view of organizational effectiveness.[7] Eighty-four managers representing thirteen general business organizations were asked to respond to a questionnaire, rating 283 subordinate departments on 114 items frequently mentioned in the literature as indicators of organizational effectiveness. The 283 descriptions were then subjected to factor analysis, a mathematical procedure used to group those items that are most alike. This analysis resulted in the identification of twenty-four separate criteria—or factors, as they are generally called—of organizational effectiveness. Further data analysis resulted in the identification of four factors (see Figure 5–1) of particular importance.

1. *Productivity-Support-Utilization.* Efficient performance; mutual support and respect of supervisors and subordinates; utilization of personnel skills and abilities.

2. *Planning.* Operations planned and scheduled to avoid lost time; little time spent on minor crises.

3. *Reliability.* Meets objectives without necessity of follow-up and checking.

4. *Initiative.* Initiates improvements in work methods and operations.[8]

While additional analyses presented in their study revealed that the factors differ in applicability to various subgroups (for example, production versus research and development) within the organizations studied, Mahoney and Weitzel interpreted their results to suggest that judgments of organizational effectiveness can be reduced to a small number of basic factors. This conclusion thus provides support for the goal model viewpoint that organizational effectiveness is largely a function of the successful attainment of specific desired end states.

---

[4]R. J. Webb, "Organizational Effectiveness and the Voluntary Organization,"*Academy of Management Journal* 17 (1974): 663–677.

[5]J. P. Campbell, "Contributions Research Can Make in Understanding Organization Effectiveness," *Organization and Administrative Sciences* 7, no. 1 (1976): 29–45.

[6]W. J. Reddin, *Managerial Effectiveness* (New York: McGraw-Hill, 1970), p. 3.

[7]T. A. Mahoney and W. Weitzel, "Managerial Models of Organizational Effectiveness," *Administrative Science Quarterly* 14 (1969): 357–365; T. A. Mahoney, "Managerial Perceptions of Organizational Effectiveness," *Management Science* 14 (1967): 1376–1391.

[8]Adapted from Mahoney and Weitzel, "Managerial Models," p. 358.

Figure 5–1 *Diagram of Relationships of Criteria for Organizational Effectiveness to Overall Effectiveness Following a Goal Model Approach*

Source: Adapted from "Managerial Models of Organizational Effectiveness" by T. A. Mahoney and W. Weitzel, published in *Administrative Science Quarterly* 14 (1969), p. 359, by permission of *Administrative Science Quarterly*. Copyright © 1969 by *Administrative Science Quarterly*.

On the surface, the goal model appears to be a valid and reliable approach to the measurement of organizational effectiveness. Closer inspection, however, suggests that it carries with it several methodological as well as theoretical shortcomings. Etzioni, for example, contends that it is unrealistic to use goals as the single standard of organizational effectiveness.[9] Goals, as norms or targets, are ideal states. Organizations, as systems of coordinated activity, are social systems. Goals represent targets established at a certain point in time. In actual performance, organizations tend to be less consistent and less perfect than anticipated. Etzioni thus argues that some discrepancy between goals (an ideal state) and performance (a real state) is almost inevitable, and that to judge effectiveness solely in terms of complete, or even substantial, goal attainment is to virtually foredoom any investigation to a disappointing conclusion.

Another shortcoming of the goal model is associated with the fact that most organizations are multifunctional. That is, they generally seek to accomplish several different goals at the same time. The realization of one of these goals, however, may inhibit the attainment of another. For example, a high rate of return on investment may well be achieved at the expense of long-term organization growth or long-term research and development. As suggested by Reimann, the goal model of effectiveness therefore "raises the possibility that an organization really cannot be effective if it means attainment of all or even most of its goals."[10]

A further difficulty with the goal model is the establishment of unambiguous criteria for measuring effectiveness. While sales, number of units of production, turnover, absenteeism, and the like are readily identifiable outputs, many organizations

[9]A. Etzioni, "Two Approaches to Organizational Analysis: A Critique and a Suggestion," *Administrative Science Quarterly* 5 (1960): 257–277.

[10]B. C. Reimann, "Organizational Effectiveness and Management's Public Values: A Canonical Analysis," *Academy of Management Journal* 8 (1975): 225.

Chapter 5

do not have such outputs. Service organizations (such as social welfare programs and voluntary associations) cannot be evaluated in this way.[11] Do, for example, youth groups reduce the threat of neighborhood delinquency? Do consumer education classes result in increased buying skills? The intangibility of such criteria thus serves to highlight the difficulty encountered in establishing what exactly constitutes goal attainment in many situations.

The System Resource Model

As an alternative to the goal approach, the system resource model has been attracting increasing attention. Defining effectiveness as the degree to which an organization is successful in acquiring and utilizing scarce and valued resources, the system resource approach focuses on the interaction between an organization and its environment. Organizations are viewed as being involved in a bargaining relationship with their surroundings, importing various scarce resources (for example, physical facilities, ideas, raw materials, personnel, funds, and so on) to be returned as valued outputs (products or services). Clearly, an organization will only survive through time if it can maintain a greater intake than is required to produce its output. That is, an organization's long-run success hinges upon its ability to establish and maintain a favorable input-output ratio.[12] It is thus the procurement and transformation of inputs and their subsequent distribution that serve as the focal frame of reference for the system resource model. Accordingly, the system resource approach proposes that an organization is most effective when it "maximizes its bargaining position and optimizes its resource procurement."[13]

This last consideration serves to emphasize an important aspect of the system resource model—that is, the interdependence of an organization and its environment. The system resource approach explicitly recognizes the dangers inherent in an organization maximizing the exploitation of its supporting environment. A careful distinction is made between an organization's capability to totally exploit its surroundings and the attainment of an *optimum* balance in organization-environment transactions. This distinction is made with the realization that, by drawing too heavily upon its supporting environment, an organization endangers its effectiveness, not only by potentially depleting its resource base, but also by running the risk of stimulating countervailing forces (such as legislation) within its environment.[14]

---

[11]See, for example, P. Levinson, "Evaluation of Social Welfare Programs," *Welfare in Review* 4, no. 9 (1966): 5–12; W. K. Warner, "Problems in Measuring the Goal Attainment of Voluntary Organizations," *Adult Education* 19 (1967): 3–14.

[12]J. Ghorpade, "Toward a Methodology for the Study of Organizational Effectiveness," in *Assessment of Organizational Effectiveness,* ed. J. Ghorpade (Pacific Palisades, Calif.: Goodyear, 1971), p. 211–240.

[13]E. Yuchtman and S. E. Seashore, "A System Resource Approach to Organization Effectiveness," *American Sociological Review* 32 (1967): 898.

[14]J. M. Pennings and P. S. Goodman, "Toward a Workable Framework," in *New Perspectives on Organizational Effectiveness,* ed. P. S. Goodman and J. M. Pennings (San Francisco: Jossey-Bass, 1977), p. 159.

A frequently cited example of the system resource approach is Georgopoulos and Tannenbaum's analysis of the effectiveness of thirty-two operating units (or stations, as they were called) representing five plants of a nation-wide service organization specializing in the delivery, on a contract basis, of retail merchandise for department stores. Organizational effectiveness was defined as "the extent to which an organization as a social system, given certain resources and means, fulfills its objectives without incapacitating its means and resources and without placing undue strain upon its members."[15] Rather than concentrating on the goals of the organizational units under study, the researchers constructed three indices, each meant to measure a basic means-ends dimension of the overall system. These were: (1) station productivity; (2) absence of intraorganizational strain or conflict as indicated by conflict among subgroups; and (3) organizational flexibility, conceptualized as the ability to adapt to internal or external change. Overall effectiveness ratings for the various stations were calculated by averaging the "expert" judgments of six to nine key employees in each of the five company plants. The resulting evaluations were then correlated with the criterion variables previously described. Comparing the stations to one another, rather than to an idealized notion of what a delivery station should be, revealed that effective stations were more productive, lower in intergroup strain, and somewhat more flexible than less effective stations. Following additional analysis, Georgopoulos and Tannenbaum concluded that the criteria identified represented important aspects of organizational effectiveness, being commonly accepted as generally applicable across organizations.

While the system resource approach, like the goal model, appears on the surface to be a valid and reliable approach to the measurement of organizational effectiveness, it too has a number of recognized shortcomings. Principal among these is that, while the system resource model takes into account that organizations are dependent on their surrounding environment for maintenance, making "optimum" a key word in achieving a balance in organization-environment transactions, it provides little guidance as to what constitutes this optimum exploitation.[16] We are thus left with an unanswered question: "How does one know when the system has or has not reached a point of optimal input or exploitation?"[17]

A second drawback of the system resource model concerns its failure to provide guidance in determining *which* scarce and valued resources are relevant as a basis for the absolute or comparative assessment of an organization's effectiveness.[18] Although advocates of the system resource approach have long recognized the need for general measures of resource effectiveness, they have seldom been used.

---

[15]B. S. Georgopoulos and A. S. Tannenbaum, "A Study of Organizational Effectiveness," *American Sociological Review* 22 (1957): 535–536.

[16]R. H. Kilmann and R. P. Herden, "Towards a Systematic Methodology for Evaluating the Impact of Interventions on Organizational Effectiveness," *Academy of Management Review* 1, no. 3 (1976): 87–98.

[17]F. K. Berrien, "A General Systems Approach to Organizations," in *Handbook of Industrial and Organizational Psychology,* ed. M. D. Dunnette (Chicago: Rand McNally, 1976), p. 57.

[18]L. B. Mohr, "The Concept of Organizational Goal," *American Political Science Review* 67 (1973): 470–481.

A final shortcoming of the system resource model deals with what Price refers to as the *rule of mutual exclusiveness*. Price argues that many system-oriented researchers have failed to adequately delineate the constructs they employ and have thus violated a basic rule of classification. "Effectiveness, for example, should not refer to the same phenomenon as efficiency."[19] Note, for instance, in the Georgopoulos and Tannenbaum study described earlier, how one of the three criterion variables used to predict effectiveness is station productivity, a measure that also refers to unit efficiency. In this context, the terms are almost interchangeable.

Reconciling the Two Approaches to Effectiveness

As the preceding discussion suggests, the differences between the goal approach and system resource approach to organizational effectiveness are meaningful, reflecting not only divergent definitions but also diverse schemes for evaluating organizational performance. While each model has a certain appeal, both have identifiable weaknesses. It would be an error, however, to assume that they are mutually exclusive. Campbell and his associates, for instance, argue that both views have to be taken into account simultaneously and that, far from being in conflict, both can be used to advantage. They explain, "For an organization to understand or seek to change its effectiveness it must be able to specify both the tasks it is trying to accomplish and the processes that are involved in accomplishing them."[20] This implies that, to be effective in the long run, organizations need to be concerned not only with the attainment of internally established objectives (the emphasis of the goal approach) but also with the manner in which objectives are achieved (the emphasis of the system resource approach). A combination of perspectives would thus contribute both to a more complete understanding of how effectiveness is achieved and to a greater appreciation of the specific means by which that achievement is facilitated.

The Measurement of Organizational Effectiveness

Now that we have introduced and reviewed the goal and system resource models as the two dominant underlying approaches to the study of organizational effectiveness, our attention turns to a discussion of several of the major unresolved problems associated with the actual measurement of organizational effectiveness. Not too

---

[19]J. L. Price, "The Study of Organizational Effectiveness," *Sociological Quarterly* 13 (1972): 10.
[20]J. P. Campbell et al., *The Measurement of Organizational Effectiveness: A Review of Relevant Research and Opinion* (San Diego, Calif.: Navy Personnel Research and Development Center, 1974), p. 223.

surprisingly, given the differences between the goal and system resource approaches, there is a similar divergence in the criteria used by researchers when studying organizational effectiveness.[21] In a recent evaluation of previous attempts to assess organizational effectiveness, Steers was able to distinguish between two models, or approaches, to the measurement of effectiveness and to identify several problem areas associated with each.[22] The following discussion depends heavily on his analysis, as well as that of Campbell and of Cameron.[23]

Univariate Effectiveness Models

As was pointed out earlier, initial attempts to study and measure organizational effectiveness generally followed the goal approach. Thorndike was one of the first to note the tendency of researchers to equate effectiveness with the attainment of some "ultimate criterion."[24] He found that "productivity," "net profits," and the "extent to which the organization accomplishes its missions" were the most common measures or indices of effectiveness.[25] Campbell's more recent survey of studies that focused on a single (univariate) property to assess effectiveness identified an amazing total of thirty different variables that have been used as indicators of effectiveness.[26] They are listed in Table 5–1.

An evaluation of the various properties listed leads to several observations.[27] First, given the diversity of the properties listed, it would seem difficult to argue that any *one* of the variables identified (for example, absenteeism) would by itself be a comprehensive or adequate (that is, valid) measure of organizational effectiveness. Second, several of the entries in the list (for example, job satisfaction and morale) seem to describe normative value judgments made by researchers of qualities effective organizations "should have," rather than objective measures of the capability of an organization to accomplish its goals. Third, one may question the independence of the variables listed. Few attempts have been made to weed out the overlap and identify a set of core variables which are consistent, complete, and parsimonious. As already noted, defining effectiveness in terms of a single variable such as "profit" or "productivity" contributes little to a more complete understanding of how effective-

[21]W. R. Scott, "Effectiveness of Organizational Effectiveness Studies," in Goodman and Pennings, eds., *New Perspectives,* p. 72.

[22]R. M. Steers, "Problems in the Measurement of Organizational Effectiveness," *Administrative Science Quarterly* 20 (1975): 546–558.

[23]J. P. Campbell, "On the Nature of Organizational Effectiveness," in Goodman and Pennings, eds., *New Perspectives,* pp. 13–55; K. Cameron, "Measuring Organizational Effectiveness in Institutions of Higher Education," *Administrative Science Quarterly* 23 (1978): 604–632.

[24]R. L. Thorndike, *Personnel Selection: Test and Measurement Techniques* (New York: John Wiley & Sons, 1949), pp. 121–124.

[25]J. W. Hunt, *The Restless Organization* (Sidney, Australia: John Wiley & Sons Australasia Ltd., 1972), p. 313.

[26]Campbell, "On the Nature of Organizational Effectiveness," pp. 36–39.

[27]Ibid., pp. 39–41; Steers, *Organizational Effectiveness,* pp. 39–42.

ness is achieved or of the specific means by which this achievement is facilitated. Katz and Kahn have assessed the consequence of this incomplete development in rather disappointing, yet predictable, terms. Noting the wide range of criteria that have been offered to assess organizational effectiveness, and the many ways in which effectiveness has been defined, they conclude that most of what has been written, although presented otherwise, is largely judgmental and open to question, offering advice that is not only frequently faulty in logic, but often inconsistent as well.

There is no lack of material on criteria of organizational success. The literature is studded with references to efficiency, productivity, absence, turnover, and profitability —all of these offered implicitly or explicitly, separately or in combination, as definitions of organizational effectiveness. Most of what has been written on the meaning of these criteria and on their interrelatedness, however, is judgmental and open to question. What is worse, it is filled with advice that seems sagacious but is tautological and contradictory.[28]

Unfortunately, the numerous univariate studies of organizational effectiveness that have been published since this appraisal by Katz and Kahn have done little to rectify this situation.[29]

Multivariate Effectiveness Models

Recent efforts to measure organizational effectiveness have focused not on a single property to assess effectiveness but on more sophisticated models that employ multiple (multivariate) properties. "These models have a distinct advantage over univariate techniques in that they generally represent attempts to study in a more comprehensive fashion the major sets of variables involved in the effectiveness construct and to demonstrate or at least suggest how such variables fit together."[30]

The basic dilemma, of course, with multivariate models is identifying a reliable and valid set of variables which can be used to measure effectiveness. The current lack of consensus in this regard is highlighted in Steers' survey of seventeen studies that used multiple criteria of effectiveness.[31] A summary of his findings is provided in Table 5–2. Of the fifteen criteria that were proposed as indices of effectiveness, only one (adaptability-flexibility) was mentioned in a majority of the studies. Further, only a third (5) of the criteria were even mentioned more than once or twice. Clearly, there is very little agreement in the multivariate literature on what constitutes (or contributes to) organizational effectiveness. While this lack of consensus may in part

---

[28]D. Katz and R. L. Kahn, *The Social Psychology of Organizations* (New York: John Wiley & Sons, 1966), p. 149.
[29]Steers, *Organizational Effectiveness*, p. 42.
[30]Ibid.
[31]Steers, "Problems in Measurement."

Table 5–1 *A Listing of Univariate Measures of Organizational Effectiveness*

Overall Effectiveness. The general evaluation that takes into account as many criteria facets as possible. It is visually measured by combining archival performance records or by obtaining overall ratings or judgments from persons thought to be knowledgeable about the organization.

Productivity. Usually defined as the quantity or volume of the major product or service that the organization provides. It can be measured at three levels: individual, group, and total organization via either archival records or ratings, or both.

Efficiency. A ratio that reflects a comparison of some aspect of unit performance to the costs incurred for that performance.

Profit. The amount of revenue from sales left after all costs and obligations are met. Percent return on investment or percent return on total sales are sometimes used as alternative definitions.

Quality. The quality of the primary service or product provided by the organization may take many operational forms, which are largely determined by the kind of product or service provided by the organization. They are too numerous to mention here.

Accidents. The frequency of on-the-job accidents resulting in lost time.

Growth. Represented by an increase in such variables as total manpower, plant capacity, assets, sales, profits, market share, and number of innovations. It implies a comparison of an organization's present state with its own past state.

Absenteeism. The usual definition stipulates unexcused absences, but even within this constraint there are a number of alternative definitions (for example, total time absence versus frequency of occurrence).

Turnover. Some measure of the relative number of voluntary terminations, which is almost always assessed via archival records. They yield a surprising number of variations and few studies use directly comparable measures.

Job Satisfaction. Has been conceptualized in many ways...but the modal view might define it as the individual's satisfaction with the amount of various job outcomes he or she is receiving. Whether a particular amount of some outcome (for example, promotional opportunities) is "satisfying" is in time a function of the importance of that outcome to the individual and the equity comparisons the individual makes with others.

Motivation. In general, the strength of the predisposition of an individual to engage in goal-directed action or activity on the job. It is not a feeling of relative satisfaction with various job outcomes but is more akin to a readiness or willingness to work at accomplishing the job's goals. As an organizational index, it must be summed across people.

Morale. It is often difficult to define or even understand how organizational theorists and researchers are using this concept. The modal definition seems to view morale as a group phenomenon involving extra effort, goal communality, commitment, and feelings of belonging. Groups have some degree of morale, whereas individuals have some degree of motivation (and satisfaction).

Control. The degree of, and distribution of, management control that exists within an organization for influencing and directing the behavior of organization members.

Conflict/Cohesion. Defined at the cohesion end by an organization in which the members like one another, work well together, communicate fully and openly, and coordinate their work efforts. At the other end lies the organization with verbal and physical clashes, poor coordination, and ineffective communication.

Flexibility/Adaptation (Adaptation/Innovation). Refers to the ability of an organization to change its standard operating procedures in response to environmental changes. Many people have written about this dimension, but relatively few have made attempts to measure it.

Planning and Goal Setting. The degree to which an organization systematically plans its future steps and engages in explicit goal-setting behavior.

Goal Consensus. Distinct from actual commitment to the organization's goals, consensus refers to the degree to which all individuals perceive the same goals for the organization.

Internalization of Organizational Goals. Refers to the acceptance of the organization's goals. It includes their belief that the organization's goals are right and proper. It is *not* the extent to which goals are clear or agreed upon by the organization members (goal clarity and goal consensus, respectively).

Role and Norm Congruence. The degree to which the members of an organization are in agreement on such things as desirable supervisory attitudes, performance expectations, morale, role requirements, and so on.

Managerial Interpersonal Skills. The level of skill with which managers deal with superiors, subordinates, and peers in terms of giving support, facilitating constructive interaction, and generating enthusiasm for meeting goals and achieving excellent performance. It includes such things as consideration, employee centeredness, and so on.

Managerial Task Skills. The overall level of skills with which the organization's managers, commanding officers, or group leaders perform work-centered tasks, tasks centered on work to be done, and not the skills employed when interacting with other organizational members.

Information Management and Communication. Completeness, efficiency, and accuracy in analysis and distribution of information critical to organizational effectiveness.

Readiness. An overall judgment concerning the probability that the organization could successfully perform some specified task if asked to do so. Work on measuring this variable has been largely confined to military settings.

Utilization of Environment. The extent to which the organization successfully interacts with its environment and acquires scarce and valued resources necessary to its effective operation.

Evaluations by External Entities. Evaluations of the organization, or unit, by the individuals and organizations in its environment with which it interacts. Loyalty to, confidence in, and support given the organization by such groups as suppliers, customers, stockholders, enforcement agencies, and the general public would fall under this label.

Stability. The maintenance of structure, function, and resources through time, and more particularly, through periods of stress.

Value of Human Resources. A composite criterion that refers to the total value or total worth of the individual members, in an accounting or balance sheet sense, to the organization.

Participation and Shared Influence. The degree to which individuals in the organization participate in making the decisions that directly affect them.

Training and Development Emphasis. The amount of effort the organization devotes to developing its human resources.

Achievement Emphasis. An analog to the individual need for achievement referring to the degree to which the organization appears to place a high value on achieving major new goals.

Source: J. P. Campbell, "On the Nature of Organizational Effectiveness," in *New Perspectives on Organizational Effectiveness,* ed. P. S. Goodman and J. M. Pennings (San Francisco: Jossey-Bass, 1977), pp. 36–39. Reprinted by permission.

Table 5–2 *Frequency of Occurrence of Evaluation Criteria in 17 Multivariate Models of Organizational Effectiveness*

Evaluation Criteria	No. of Times Mentioned ($N = 17$)
Adaptability — Flexibility	10
Productivity	6
Satisfaction	5
Profitability	3
Resource acquisition	3
Absence of strain	2
Control over environment	2
Development	2
Efficiency	2
Employee retention	2
Growth	2
Integration	2
Open communications	2
Survival	2
All other criteria	1

Source: From "Problems in the Measurement of Organizational Effectiveness" by R. M. Steers, published in *Administrative Science Quarterly* 20 (December 1975), by permission of *Administrative Science Quarterly*. Copyright © 1975 by *Administrative Science Quarterly*.

be due to the different frames of reference with which various effectiveness models have been constructed, it also suggests the possibility (to be more fully discussed in the next section) that "organizational uniqueness, based on different environments, different technologies, different objectives, or other contingencies, may require different effectiveness criteria and/or different criteria weightings between organizations."[32]

Highlighting Some Problem Areas

Certain of the shortcomings associated with the goal and system resource models are in actuality problems of measurement. For example, with the goal model it is difficult to establish unambiguous criteria for measuring effectiveness. While many organizations have readily identifiable outputs, some do not, making it difficult to judge what exactly constitutes goal attainment. A basic measurement difficulty of the system resource model is the failure of many researchers to adequately delineate the constructs they employ, resulting in the violation of the rule of mutual exclusiveness: two constructs (such as effectiveness and efficiency) should not refer to the same phenomenon. In addition to these difficulties, several other problems more generally associated with the measurement of effectiveness should be briefly mentioned. These are problems that affect the measurement of effectiveness regardless of the approach adopted.

[32]M. A. Hitt and R. D. Middlemist, "A Methodology to Develop the Criteria and Criteria Weightings for Assessing Subunit Effectiveness in Organizations," *Academy of Management Journal* 22 (1979): 357.

Effectiveness over Time

A major unresolved problem in measuring effectiveness is the assessment of organizational performance over time. Although most studies have examined effectiveness at one point in time (using static measures of inputs, processes, or outcomes), organizations are undeniably dynamic over time, reflecting environmental as well as organizational changes. As a result of such static views, the effectiveness of an organization has generally been judged in absolute terms—high, medium, or low effectiveness. In truth, the few longitudinal studies that have monitored effectiveness dynamically over time have shown that effectiveness is entirely relative and best described as stable, increasing, or decreasing.[33] The contrasting nature of these views is depicted in Figure 5–2, which shows the relationship of level of effectiveness to changes in effectiveness at four points lying along the same diagonal. Note how, when viewed statically, solely with respect to "level of effectiveness," Organization B is judged in absolute terms as being more effective than Organization A. However, when viewed dynamically, with respect to both "level of effectiveness" and "changes in effectiveness," Organization A is seen as experiencing an increase in effectiveness, while Organization B is shown to be decreasing in effectiveness.

This example underscores two important points. First, "movement toward goals does not necessarily occur in regular increments which are uniformly distributed over

Figure 5–2 *Relationship of Level of Effectiveness to Changes in Effectiveness*

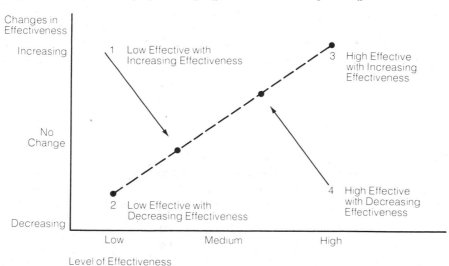

Source: R. M. Atherton, "The Assessment of Organization Effectiveness," in *Managing the Changing Organization,* ed. D. F. Ray and T. B. Green (Mississippi State, Miss.: Southern Management Association, 1974), p. 157. Used by permission.

[33]R. M. Atherton, "The Assessment of Organization Effectiveness," in *Managing the Changing Organization,* ed. D. F. Ray and T. B. Green (Mississippi State, Miss.: Southern Management Association, 1974), pp. 155–162.

The Nature and Measurement of Organizational Effectiveness

all time periods.''[34] Thus, the actual time frame—short-run versus long-run—used in assessing an organization's effectiveness is important. The real problem, as suggested by Steers, is "how best to balance short-run considerations with long-run interests in an effort to maximize stability and growth over time.''[35] Attempts have only recently been made to deal with this problem.[36]

Second, related to an issue we will discuss more fully in Chapter 7, is the relevance of different effectiveness criteria over the life cycle of an organization. Organizations are at different stages (birth, maturity, decline) in their life cycle, and criteria appropriate at one stage may not be suitable at another.[37] To paraphrase Katz and Kahn, the meaning of growth for the health, survival, and overall effectiveness of an organization may very well be different at different stages in an organization's life cycle.[38] As a consequence, failure to appropriately identify the stage of development an organization is at could conceivably lead to the specification of unsuitable effectiveness criteria.

In sum, the arguments presented suggest that static assessments—one-time evaluations of organizational performance—do not provide a reliable and valid indication of an organization's effectiveness. They also suggest that research strategies need to be designed to take into consideration both the necessity of balancing short- and long-run goal attainment and the implications of an organization's life stage for determining suitable effectiveness criteria.

Constituent Perspectives

Another measurement problem arises as a result of the fact that perceptions of an organization's effectiveness have been shown to depend largely upon an individual's frame of reference or perspective. Any judgment about effectiveness hinges on a given set of ranked goals and on a given evaluation of alternative means of reaching them. With the varied interests and values of the diverse groups comprising most complex organizations, sharp differences concerning the state of an organization's effectiveness could (and frequently do) develop. Thus, as Hall and Clark note, "It is possible to conceive of effectiveness on a particular goal or set of goals from the standpoint of the organization itself and its professional staff, from the standpoint of the community-at-large, and from the standpoint of the individuals being served or processed by the organizations." They go on to add, however, that "effectiveness

---

[34]Warner, "Problems in Measuring," pp. 9–10.

[35]Steers, "Problems in Measurement," p. 553.

[36]See, for example, R. H. Miles and K. Cameron, "Coffin Nails and Corporate Strategy: A Quarter Century View of Organizational Adaptation to Environment in the U.S. Tobacco Industry," *Business-Government Relations Series, Paper No. 3* (New Haven, Conn.: Yale University, 1977); P. S. Goodman and J. M. Pennings, "Critical Issues in Assessing Organizational Effectiveness," in *Organizational Assessment: Perspectives on the Measurement of Organizational Behavior and the Quality of Working Life,* ed. E. E. Lawler, D. A. Nadler, and C. Cammann (New York: Wiley-Interscience, in press).

[37]Scott, "Effectiveness of Studies," p. 74.

[38]Katz and Kahn, *Social Psychology,* p. 149.

from one of these standpoints could well be gross ineffectiveness from another standpoint."[39]

Hall and Clark's own work as well as several additional studies lend credence to this observation.[40] The implications of this rather uncomfortable dilemma have direct significance for the establishment of criteria for measuring organizational effectiveness. To begin with, any criteria that are proposed will be viewed in terms of self-interest by each of the groups involved.[41] Employees, for example, will seek higher wages and increased fringe benefits, and owners will prefer higher profits and lower costs. As suggested in the last chapter's discussion of dominant coalitions, however, the relative power of each participant group to pursue its own interest will vary widely. Second, despite claims otherwise, "no criteria are disinterested," to use a phrase of Scott's.[42] Each criterion will benefit some groups more than others. Third, given the first two conditions, and a situation in which resources are scarce (limited or no organizational slack), we would have every reason to expect a wide divergence and some conflict in the criteria proposed by each group for assessing an organization's effectiveness. This suggests that organizational effectiveness depends upon who we ask to define it and that in partial support of the multivariate model, measuring effectiveness requires dealing with many criteria rather than just one.

Level of Analysis

A third but related measurement problem is the translation of effectiveness criteria across units of analysis. While there are those who advocate evaluating effectiveness criteria on an organization-wide basis, such an approach neglects the critical relationships between an organization and its various parts.[43] Effectiveness not only relates to the goals and processes of an organization as a unit but is also dependent upon the successful performance of both departmental subunits and individual employees. To date, there have been very few attempts to link these differing aspects in the evaluation of effectiveness. Needless to say, however, as Steers has pointed out, "If we are to increase our understanding of organizational processes—and, indeed, if we are to make meaningful recommendations to managers about effectiveness—models of organizational effectiveness must be developed which attempt to specify

[39]R. H. Hall and J. P. Clark, "Organizational Effectiveness: Some Conceptual, Methodological and Moral Issues," paper presented at the annual meeting of the American Sociological Convention, September 1977, Chicago, p. 17.

[40]See, for example, F. Friedlander and H. Pickle, "Components of Effectiveness in Small Organizations," *Administrative Science Quarterly* 13 (1968): 289–304; D. P. Leitch, "A Study of Judgments of Organizational Effectiveness," in *Proceedings of the Executive Study Conference*, Spring 1968 (Princeton, N.J.: Educational Testing Service, 1969); J. J. Molnar and D. L. Rogers, "Organizational Effectiveness: An Empirical Comparison of the Goal and System Resources Approaches," *Sociological Quarterly* 17 (1976): 401–413; S. M. Schmidt, "Client-Oriented Evaluation of Public Agency Effectiveness," *Administration and Society* 8 (1977): 403–422.

[41]Scott, "Effectiveness of Studies," p. 71.

[42]Ibid.

[43]R. M. Steers, "When Is an Organization Effective? A Process Approach to Understanding Effectiveness," *Organizational Dynamics* 5, no. 2 (1976): 53.

The Nature and Measurement of Organizational Effectiveness

or at least account for the relationships between individual processes and organizational behavior."[44]

Universality of Criteria

A final measurement problem is the appropriateness of criteria across organizations. Given that different kinds of organizations have different characteristics, goals, and constituencies, it would seem reasonable that particular criteria of effectiveness should be applied to different types of organizations.[45] Research does, in fact, support this view. Webb, for instance, has shown that the criteria typically applicable to measuring effectiveness in business organizations, government organizations, and religious organizations generally differ.[46] Similarly, Rushing has shown that profit and nonprofit hospitals differ in their determinants of effectiveness.[47] In explaining this finding, he argues that it is largely a result of the contrasting orientations (one type being primarily economically-oriented and the other not) of profit and nonprofit organizations. The upshot of this is simply that while certain criteria (for example, profitability and market share) may be relevant for certain types of organizations (business firms and other profit-oriented undertakings), they may have little applicability for others (voluntary associations such as churches, and service organizations such as juvenile courts and social welfare programs). This realization is further complicated by the fact that even though similar organizations (for example, two nonprofit hospitals) may appear to be comparable, they may have entirely different priorities (for example, research versus patient care), resulting in contrasting goal structures.[48] Hence, a researcher must take special care in selecting a set of effectiveness criteria which accurately reflect the goals of the organization under study. If inappropriate evaluation criteria are employed, subsequent judgments may well be erroneous.

Summary

The major purpose of this chapter has been to examine the nature and measurement of organizational effectiveness. In doing so, the two dominant underlying approaches to the study of organizational effectiveness—goal model and system resource model —were analyzed. Each model was evaluated and its principal drawbacks identified and discussed. It was pointed out that, with respect to the goal model, many feel it

---

[44]Steers,"Problems in Measurement," pp. 554–555.

[45]Cameron, "Measuring Organizational Effectiveness," p. 605.

[46]Webb, "Organizational Effectiveness and the Voluntary Organization."

[47]W. A. Rushing, "Differences in Profit and Nonprofit Organizations: A Study of Effectiveness and Efficiency in General Short-Stay Hospitals," *Administrative Science Quarterly* 19 (1974): 474–484; Rushing, "Profit and Nonprofit Orientations in the Differentiation-Coordination Hypothesis for Organizations: A Study of Small General Hospitals," *American Sociological Review* 41 (1976): 676–691.

[48]P. S. Goodman, D. Schoorman, and R. Atkin, "Organizational Effectiveness as a Decision Making Process," paper presented at the annual meeting of the National Academy of Management, August 1979, Atlanta, Georgia, p. 7.

Chapter 5

is unrealistic to use goals as a single standard of organizational effectiveness. This feeling is based on the beliefs that: (1) since organizations are social systems they will almost always be less perfect than they anticipate being; (2) organizations are multifunctional and thus must seek to accomplish several different goals at the same time; and (3) the output of certain types of organizations defies the establishment of unambiguous criteria for measuring effectiveness. With respect to the system resource model, it was indicated that it, too, has received its share of criticism for: (1) providing little guidance as to what constitutes optimum environmental exploitation, a key concept in the approach; (2) failing to develop general measures of resource effectiveness to be used in determining which "scarce and valued resources" are relevant as a basis for the absolute or comparative assessment of an organization's effectiveness; and (3) violating the rule of mutual exclusiveness, a basic rule of classification requiring that no construct refer to more than one phenomenon.

Following this discussion, an attempt was made to reconcile the differences between the goal approach and system resource approach by suggesting that, to be effective in the long run, organizations need to be concerned not only with the attainment of internally established aims (the emphasis of the goal approach), but also with the circumstances under which those aims are achieved (the emphasis of the system resource approach). It was thus suggested that a combination of perspectives would contribute to a more complete understanding of how effectiveness is achieved, as well as to a greater appreciation of the specific means by which this achievement is facilitated.

Our attention then turned to a discussion of two approaches to the measurement of effectiveness—univariate and multivariate—and a consideration of several of the major unresolved problems associated with effectiveness measures. These problems included the following: (1) effectiveness criteria are dynamic over time, so different criteria may be appropriate not only at different times (short- versus long-run) but at different stages in an organization's life cycle; (2) different groups have different perceptions of effectiveness; (3) the concept of effectiveness varies at different levels of analysis; and (4) different sets of effectiveness criteria are required for different types of organizations.

From the preceding discussion, it becomes obvious that effectiveness is not a simple issue. Evaluating the performance of an organization is one of the greatest challenges in organization theory. This challenge becomes even more engaging when one considers the role of an organization's surrounding environment in influencing both the establishment of its goals (Chapter 4) and the extent of its success or effectiveness in meeting these goals. The importance of an organization being able to adapt to the external environment in which it functions and to the changes that take place within it is the topic of our next chapter.

Review and Discussion Questions

1. Contrast the goal model and system resource model approaches to measuring organizational effectiveness.

The Nature and Measurement of Organizational Effectiveness

2. Distinguish between the concepts of organizational effectiveness and organizational efficiency.
3. What are the shortcomings of the goal model of effectiveness?
4. What are the shortcomings of the system resource model of effectiveness?
5. Reconcile the goal model and the system resource model approaches to effectiveness.
6. Briefly explain the two most common approaches to the measurement of effectiveness.
7. Comment on the shortcomings associated with both univariate and multivariate models of measuring effectiveness.
8. Discuss several common problems that pertain to the measurement of effectiveness.

References

Atherton, R. M. "The Assessment of Organization Effectiveness." In *Managing the Changing Organization,* edited by D. E. Ray and T. B. Green. Mississippi State, Miss.: Southern Management Association, 1974.

Barnard, C. I. *The Functions of the Executive.* Cambridge, Mass.: Harvard University Press, 1938.

Berrien, F. K. "A General Systems Approach to Organizations." In *Handbook of Industrial and Organizational Psychology,* edited by M. D. Dunnette. Chicago: Rand McNally, 1976.

Cameron, K. "Measuring Organizational Effectiveness in Institutions of Higher Education." *Administrative Science Quarterly* 23 (1978): 604–632.

Campbell, J. P. "Contributions Research Can Make in Understanding Organizational Effectiveness." *Organization and Administrative Sciences* 7, no. 1 (1976): 29–45.

Campbell, J. P. "On the Nature of Organizational Effectiveness." In *New Perspectives on Organizational Effectiveness,* edited by P. S. Goodman and J. M. Pennings. San Francisco: Jossey-Bass, 1977.

Campbell, J. P., Bownas, D. A., Peterson, N. G., and Dunnette, M. D. *The Measurement of Organizational Effectiveness: A Review of Relevant Research and Opinion.* San Diego, Calif.: Navy Personnel Research and Development Center, 1974.

Caplow, T. *How to Run Any Organization: A Manual of Practical Sociology.* Hinsdale, Ill.: Dryden Press, 1976.

Etzioni, A. "Two Approaches to Organizational Analysis: A Critique and a Suggestion." *Administrative Science Quarterly* 5 (1960): 257–277.

Friedlander, F., and Pickle, H. "Components of Effectiveness in Small Organizations." *Administrative Science Quarterly* 13 (1968): 289–304.

Georgopoulos, B. S., and Tannenbaum, A. S. "A Study of Organizational Effectiveness." *American Sociological Review* 22 (1957): 534–540.

Ghorpade, J. "Toward a Methodology for the Study of Organizational Effectiveness." In *Assessment of Organizational Effectiveness,* edited by J. Ghorpade. Pacific Palisades, Calif.: Goodyear, 1971.

Goodman, P. S., and Pennings, J. M. "Critical Issues in Assessing Organizational Effectiveness." In *Organizational Assessment: Perspectives on the Measurement of Organizational Behavior and the Quality of Working Life,* edited by E. E. Lawler, D. A. Nadler, and C. Cammann (New York: Wiley-Interscience, in press).

Hall, R. H., and Clark, J. P. "Organizational Effectiveness: Some Conceptual, Methodological and Moral Issues." Paper presented at the annual meeting of the American Sociological Association, September 1977, Chicago, Ill.

Hitt, M. A., and Middlemist, R. D. "A Methodology to Develop the Criteria and Criteria Weightings for Assessing Subunit Effectiveness in Organizations." *Academy of Management Journal* 22 (1979): 356–374.

Hunt, J. W. *The Restless Organization.* Sydney, Australia: John Wiley & Sons Australasia, Ltd., 1972.

Katz, D., and Kahn, R. L. *The Social Psychology of Organizations.* New York: John Wiley & Sons, 1966.

Kilmann, R. H., and Herden, R. P. "Towards a Systemic Methodology for Evaluating the Impact of Interventions on Organizational Effectiveness." *Academy of Management Review* 1, no. 3 (1976): 87–98.

Leitch, D. P. "A Study of Judgments of Organizational Effectiveness." In *Proceedings of the Executive Study Conference,* Spring 1968. Princeton, N.J.: Educational Testing Service, 1969.

Levinson, P. "Evaluation of Social Welfare Programs." *Welfare in Review* 4, no. 9 (1966): 5–12.

Mahoney, T. A. "Managerial Perceptions of Organizational Effectiveness." *Management Science* 14 (1967): 1376–1391.

Mahoney, T. A., and Weitzel, W. "Managerial Models of Organizational Effectiveness." *Administrative Science Quarterly* 14 (1969): 357–365.

Miles, R. H., and Cameron, K. "Coffin Nails and Corporate Strategies: A Quarter Century View of Organizational Adaptation to Environment in the U.S. Tobacco Industry." *Business-Government Relations Series, Paper No. 3.* New Haven, Conn.: Yale University, 1977.

Mohr, L. B. "The Concept of Organizational Goal." *American Political Science Review* 67 (1973): 470–481.

Molnar, J. J., and Rogers, D. L. "Organizational Effectiveness: An Empirical Comparison of the Goal and System Resources Approaches." *Sociological Quarterly* 17 (1976): 401–413.

Pennings, J. M., and Goodman, P. S. "Toward a Workable Framework." In *New Perspectives on Organizational Effectiveness,* edited by P. S. Goodman and J. M. Pennings. San Francisco: Jossey-Bass, 1977.

Price, J. L. "The Study of Organizational Effectiveness." *Sociological Quarterly* 13 (1972): 3–15.

Reddin, W. J. *Managerial Effectiveness.* New York: McGraw-Hill, 1970.

Reimann, B. C. "Organizational Effectiveness and Management's Public Values: A Canonical Analysis." *Academy of Management Journal* 18 (1975): 224–241.

Rushing, W. A. "Differences in Profit and Nonprofit Organizations: A Study of Effectiveness and Efficiency in General Short-Stay Hospitals." *Administrative Science Quarterly* 19 (1974): 474–484.

Rushing, W. A. "Profit and Nonprofit Orientations and the Differentiation-Coordination Hypothesis for Organizations: A Study of Small General Hospitals." *American Sociological Review* 41 (1976): 676–691.

Schmidt, S. M. "Client-Oriented Evaluation of Public Agency Effectiveness." *Administration & Society* 8 (1977): 403–422.

Scott, W. R. "Effectiveness of Organizational Effectiveness Studies." In *New Perspectives on Organizational Effectiveness,* edited by P. S. Goodman and J. M. Pennings. San Francisco: Jossey-Bass, 1977.

Steers, R. M. "Problems in the Measurement of Organizational Effectiveness." *Administrative Science Quarterly* 20 (1975): 546–558.

Steers, R. M. "When Is an Organization Effective? A Process Approach to Understanding Effectiveness." *Organizational Dynamics* 5, no. 2 (1976): 50–63.

Steers, R. M. *Organizational Effectiveness: A Behavioral View.* Santa Monica, Calif.: Goodyear, 1977.

Thorndike, R. L. *Personnel Selection: Test and Measurement Techniques.* New York: John Wiley & Sons, 1949.

Warner, W. K. "Problems in Measuring the Goal Attainment of Voluntary Organizations." *Adult Education* 19 (1967): 3–14.

Webb, R. J. "Organizational Effectiveness and the Voluntary Organization." *Academy of Management Journal* 17 (1974): 663–677.

Yuchtman, E., and Seashore, S. E. "A System Resource Approach to Organizational Effectiveness." *American Sociological Review* 32 (1967): 891–903.

The Nature and Measurement of Organizational Effectiveness

The Organization and Its External Environment

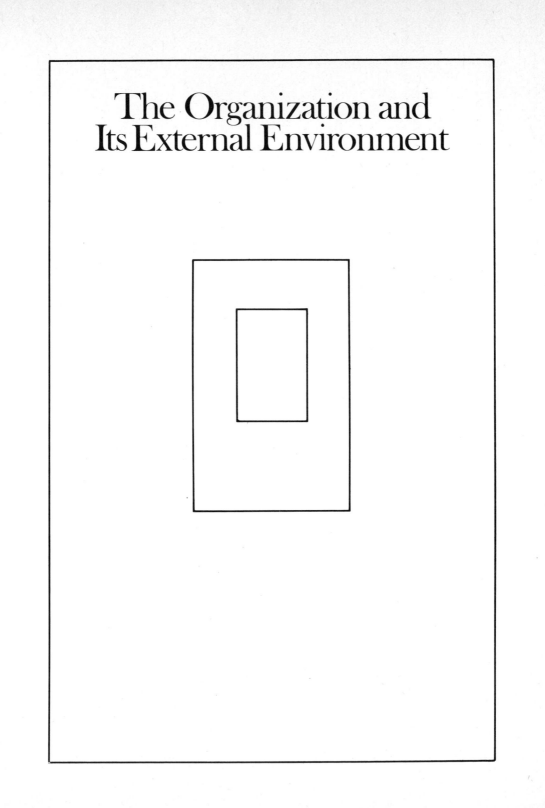

The Organization and Its External Environment

Chapter 6

In this chapter, the importance of an organization being able to adapt to changes in its external environment is discussed. Organizations do not exist in isolation. As open systems, they are greatly influenced by the properties of their associated surroundings. The degree to which an organization thrives depends largely upon how well it adapts or "fits" into its surrounding environment. As we shall relate below, certain organizational forms have been found to correlate strongly with the occurrence of specific environmental conditions.

Throughout this chapter, the continual interaction between organizations and their external environment will be explored from several perspectives. First, after establishing what is meant by environment, the effect of social structure on the rate at which organizations are founded will be briefly discussed. The focus here will be on how environmental conditions affect the formation rate of new organizations. Next, we will review various approaches to the description of the dimensions and characteristics of the external environment in which organizations occur. Following this, we will examine the more important studies exploring the relationship between an organization and its environment. At this point, we will introduce the concepts of enacted environment and strategic choice. Finally, we will consider interorganizational relationships and discuss specific strategies used by organizations to minimize the uncertainties associated with their external environment.

Before proceeding further, it should again be emphasized that organizations continually interact with their external environment. The importance of this point is expressed by Eldridge and Crombie, who stress that "we should appreciate that neither the organisation nor its environment may be fully understood apart from an understanding of the constant processes of interchange between them. The organisation itself is no more than a crystallization of formerly scattered elements of the environment—a regrouping of energies, and its maintenance entails the more or less constant ingestion of further parts of the environment—men, materials, information—and its subsequent enrichment with new or transformed products."[1]

---

[1] J. E. T. Eldridge and A. D. Crombie, *A Sociology of Organisations* (London: George Allen & Unwin, 1975), pp. 72–73.

The Organization and Its External Environment

The Nature of the Environment
Task Environment

The impact of environmental factors on organizational functioning has drawn the attention of researchers for the greater part of the last two decades. Not unlike other areas of organization theory, the literature on organization-environment relations reflects numerous fundamental differences. Indeed, Starbuck has identified some twenty different uses of the word environment.[2] Relevant to our present discussion, the term *task environment* was coined by Dill to refer to those parts of an organization's external environment that are relevant or "potentially relevant to goal setting and goal attainment."[3] The value of this concept lies in the distinction between the general environment in which all organizations function and the more immediate environment of customers, suppliers, employees, competitors, and regulatory agencies in which individual organizations operate.[4]

Organizational Domain

The concept of *organizational domain* is closely related to the idea of task environment.[5] Stated simply, the domain of an organization is the claim that it "stakes out for itself" with respect to: (a) range of products offered, (b) markets served, and (c) services rendered. Thus, hospitals are hospitals, but only to a degree. Some offer rehabilitative services; others do not. Some provide physical therapy to patients confined to their beds; others treat only those who are ambulatory. Two universities may be alike in some respects, but quite different in others. Some offer vocational courses, recruit faculty and students locally, and only offer courses at the undergraduate level; others offer only "professional" courses of study, recruit faculty and students nationally or even internationally, and primarily offer a graduate education. Similarly, certain business organizations only sell wholesale, while others trade strictly at the retail level.

The concept of domain thus locates an organization in terms of its role or niche within the larger environment. The establishment of domain, however, is not a unilateral action. Only if the claims an organization stakes out for itself are acknowledged by those who can furnish the required support—by the task environment—can a

---

[2]W. H. Starbuck, "Organizations and Their Environments," in *Handbook of Industrial and Organizational Psychology*, ed. M. D. Dunnette (Chicago: Rand McNally, 1976), pp. 1069–1123.

[3]W. R. Dill, "Environment as an Influence on Managerial Autonomy," *Administrative Science Quarterly* 2 (1958): 410; W. R. Dill, "The Impact of Environment on Organizational Development," in *Concepts and Issues in Administrative Behavior,* ed. S. Mailick and E. H. Van Ness (Englewood Cliffs, N.J.: Prentice-Hall, 1962), pp. 29–48.

[4]P. M. Hirsch, "Organizational Effectiveness and the Institutional Environment," *Administrative Science Quarterly* 20 (1975): 327–343.

[5]S. Levine and P. E. White, "Exchange as a Conceptual Framework for the Study of Interorganizational Relationships," *Administrative Science Quarterly* 5 (1961): 395–420.

domain be operational. To the extent that there is general agreement on an organization's claims to domain, *domain consensus* may be said to exist. Domain consensus serves to define "a set of expectations both for members of an organization and for others with whom they interact, about what the organization will and will not do."[6]

The important point here is that the domain of an organization determines the points at which it is dependent upon its task environment. For example, an organization may find it necessary to use a certain combination of resources in the manufacture of a desired range of products for the rendering of certain services to a specific market (the three basic components of domain). The feasibility of such an undertaking, however, will not only depend upon the availability of the appropriate resources, but upon recognition of and agreement upon the organization's role within its larger environment. A classic example of domain conflict in the social services sector centers around the self-claimed versus the medically recognized role of chiropractors. Although the chiropractic profession is concerned with determining the relationship between health problems and spinal misalignments, chiropractors, despite the American Chiropractic Association's years of protest, are prevented in many states from administering drugs, employing surgical techniques, and writing prescriptions. At present, the domain claims of chiropractors, particularly with respect to diseases covered and services rendered, have yet to be recognized.

Societal Development and Environmental Conditions

Since the relationship between an organization and its environment can only be accurately examined in terms of the larger order in which they both occur, a brief consideration of the nature and stages of the development of society may be helpful. Stinchcombe has examined the association between organizations and the kind of environmental conditions to which they must adapt at various stages in the development of a society.[7] Especially relevant to the present discussion is the conclusion that a large number of organizations tend to be created in post-industrial societies. In particular, Stinchcombe contends that the number of organizations increases in societies where the population is (a) highly literate, (b) urbanized, (c) accustomed to monetary transactions, (d) used to political change, and (e) has an active social life. These conditions are important because they create an environment where, as Silverman suggests, "the potential founders of organisations are more likely to have the necessary financial and intellectual resources and to be aware that they and their groups can gain by organizing. At the same time, the replacement of traditional with rational-legal types of legitimate authority means that the actors are likely to be aware

---

[6]J. D. Thompson, *Organizations in Action* (New York: McGraw-Hill, 1967), p. 29.
[7]A. L. Stinchcombe, "Social Structure and Organizations," in *Handbook of Organization,* ed. J. G. March (Chicago: Rand McNally, 1965), pp. 142–193.

of more alternative courses of action, to perceive that they are less likely to be defeated by vested interests, and to make use of a calculable system of laws and taxation in predicting the chances of success of a new organisation."[8] Thus, Stinchcombe argues that neither the "railroad age" nor the automobile industry could be "invented" until society had developed the necessary social structure, appropriate organizational forms, necessary administrative expertise, and, most importantly, a means by which new forms of authority could be legitimated.[9] While Stinchcombe's propositions have yet to be documented conclusively,[10] their central message seems clear: a two-way relationship exists between the societal development of an environment and the emergence of various types of organizations.

Specific Environmental Components

There are, in general, two basic approaches to describing the nature of an organization's environment. Perhaps the most popular is that of theorists and researchers who view environment as composed of specific components or factors. For example, Sethi conceptualizes the environment as being comprised of the following elements:

1. physical structure
2. social structure
3. ecological structure
4. legal structure
5. cultural structure
6. political structure
7. economic structure
8. psychological structure
9. international structure[11]

Similarly, as presented in Table 6–1, Kast and Rosenzweig describe the general environment in terms of cultural, technological, educational, political, legal, natural resource, demographic, sociological, and economic characteristics. When evaluated, this approach presents the environment as a constraining phenomenon that surrounds an organization but within which it must function.

Environmental Dimensions

A *second* and somewhat broader approach to describing the environment is more abstract but also more useful in comparing the properties of organizational environ-

---

[8]D. Silverman, *The Theory of Organisations* (New York: Basic Books, 1971), p. 148.
[9]Stinchcombe, "Social Structures," pp. 153–169.
[10]See Starbuck, "Organizations and Their Environment," p. 1076n, on this point.
[11]N. S. Sethi, "A Research Model to Study the Environmental Factors in Management," *Management International Review* 10, no. 6 (1970): 75–81.

Table 6–1   *General Environmental Characteristics for Organizations*

Cultural. Including the historical background, ideologies, values, and norms of the society. Views on authority relationships, leadership patterns, interpersonal relationships, rationalism, science, and technology define the nature of social institutions.

Technological. The level of scientific and technological advancement in society. Including the physical base (plant, equipment, facilities) and the knowledge base of technology. Degree to which the scientific and technological community is able to develop new knowledge and apply it.

Educational. The general literacy level of the population. The degree of sophistication and specialization in the educational system. The proportion of the people with a high level of professional and/or specialized training.

Political. The general political climate of society. The degree of concentration of political power. The nature of political organization (degrees of decentralization, diversity of functions, etc.). The political party system.

Legal. Constitutional considerations, nature of legal system, jurisdictions of various governmental units. Specific laws concerning formation, taxation, and control of organizations.

Natural Resources. The nature, quantity, and availability of natural resources, including climatic and other conditions.

Demographic. The nature of human resources available to the society; their number, distribution, age, and sex. Concentration or urbanization of population is a characteristic of industrialized societies.

Sociological. Class structure and mobility. Definition of social roles. Nature of the social organization and development of social institutions.

Economic. General economic framework, including the type of economic organization–private versus public ownership; the centralization or decentralization of economic planning; the banking system; and fiscal policies. The level of the investment in physical resources and consumption characteristics.

Source: F. E. Kast and J. E. Rosenzweig, *Organization and Management: A Systems and Contingency Approach,* 3rd ed. (New York: McGraw-Hill, 1979), p. 131. Reprinted by permission.

ments on a general level.[12] Rather than viewing the environment as a collection of external constraints, this approach identifies major dimensions that relate to the nature and distribution of an environment's resources. Each dimension is conceptualized as a continuum. As an example, Aldrich has specified six dimensions along which organizational environments may vary:

1. *Environmental Capacity* in terms of the relative level (rich/lean) of resources available to an organization within its domain.

2. *Homogeneity-Heterogeneity* in terms of the degree of similarity between the elements of the population dealt with, including organizations as well as individuals.

---

[12]R. M. Steers, *Organizational Effectiveness: A Behavioral View* (Santa Monica, Calif.: Goodyear, 1977), p. 86.

The Organization and Its External Environment

3. *Stability-Instability* in terms of the degree of turnover in the task environment, with respect to either persons or organizations.

4. *Concentration-Dispersion* in terms of the degree to which the population dealt with is evenly distributed over the range of an organization's domain.

5. *Domain Consensus-Dissensus* in terms of the degree to which an organization's claim to a specific domain is disputed or recognized by other organizations.

6. *Environmental Turbulence* in terms of the extent to which the environments of the focal organizations are being distributed or changed by other external activities.[13]

To summarize, this second approach presents a number of continua against which the nature and distribution of an environment's resources are measured. Its focus is on the major dimensions of an organization's *task* environment, rather than on specific constraining factors associated with its *general* environment.

A Synthesis

In reviewing these two approaches for describing the nature of an organization's environment, it becomes apparent that they have a great deal in common. In an empirical analysis of the characteristics of organizational environments, Duncan has proposed a model that provides a synthesis of these approaches.[14] Built on the work of earlier theorists, the model identifies two primary environmental components under which much of the previous discussion can be subsumed. These interrelated components are identified as *simple-complex* and *static-dynamic. Simple-complex* refers to the degree to which a decision unit (an individual or organization) must deal with few or many, similar or dissimilar elements. Thus, a simple environment would be one in which an organization deals with few elements that are, for the most part, homogeneous. As an example, the needs served by dry cleaners or barber shops are fairly uniform and similar. In contrast, a complex environment would be said to exist when an organization must deal with a wide diversity of elements that are heterogeneous —for example, hospital emergency rooms or rescue units.

The *static-dynamic* component refers to the degree to which elements of an individual's or an organization's surrounding environment remain the same or are marked by change. The basic issue here is one of stability versus turbulence. "When," as Litterer observes, "an organization faces a regular set of demands from the same environment, such as producing the same product or the same service for the same or very similar clients, the organization faces stable conditions."[15] He offers

[13]H. E. Aldrich, *Organizations and Environments* (Englewood Cliffs, N.J.: Prentice-Hall, 1979): pp. 63–70.

[14]R. B. Duncan, "Characteristics of Organizational Environments and Perceived Environmental Uncertainty," *Administrative Science Quarterly* 17 (1972): 3l3–327.

[15]J. A. Litterer, *The Analysis of Organizations,* 2nd ed. (New York: John Wiley & Sons, 1973), pp. 335–336.

as an example public utilities that produce a standard product, such as electricity, at a limited range of voltages and at a single frequency. The only variation is in the amount of electricity a client will demand, and even this is restricted. The opposite, of course, is the turbulent environment in which new products and operating innovations are common. Examples include the environments of the electronics and aerospace industries. It should be emphasized that an organization may experience stability in one of its subenvironments (for example, production) and dynamic change in another (for example, programming and planning).

According to Duncan, understanding the environment is important because it facilitates identification of characteristics that contribute to uncertainty in organizational decision making.[16] Such uncertainty is thought to be comprised of three components: (1) a lack of information concerning the environmental factors associated with particular decision-making situations; (2) an inability to accurately assess the probabilities of environmental factors affecting the success or failure of an organization performing its function(s); (3) lack of knowledge regarding the costs associated with an incorrect decision.

Duncan's proposed model is presented in Table 6–2. It suggests that organizations operating in "static-simple" environments (Cell 1) experience the least amount of perceived uncertainty in decision making, whereas organizations in "dynamic-complex" environments (Cell 4) experience the greatest amount of perceived uncertainty. Analyses of environmental characteristics that contribute to perceived uncertainty in twenty-two decision-making groups in three manufacturing and three research and development organizations not only provided support for the model, but further revealed that the "static-dynamic" component of the environment makes a more significant contribution to perceived uncertainty than the "simple-complex" component does.[17] In summarizing his findings, Duncan has concluded that

decision units with dynamic environments always experience significantly more uncertainty in decision making regardless of whether their environment is simple or complex. The difference in perceived uncertainty between decision units with simple and complex environments is not significant, unless the decision unit's environment is also dynamic.[18]

Duncan's conceptual framework is useful because it emphasizes that perceived uncertainty and the degree of complexity and dynamics of an organization's environment must be considered as dominant features in its decision making. It should also be helpful in achieving an understanding of the results presented in the following

---

[16]Duncan, "Characteristics of Organizational Environments."

[17]Ibid.; R. B. Duncan, "Multiple Decision Making Structures in Adapting to Environmental Uncertainty: The Impact of Organizational Effectiveness," *Human Relations* 26 (1973): 273–291; R. B. Duncan, "Modifications in Decision Structure in Adapting to the Environment: Some Implications for Organizational Learning," *Decision Sciences* 5 (1974): 705–725.

[18]Duncan, "Characteristics of Organizational Environments," p. 325.

Table 6–2 *Characteristics of Various Environmental States*

	Simple	Complex
Static	**1** *low perceived uncertainty* Small number of factors and components in the environment Factors and components are somewhat similar to one another Factors and components remain basically the same and are not changing *Example: Soft drink industry*	**2** *moderately low perceived uncertainty* Large number of factors and components in the environment Factors and components are not similar to one another Factors and components remain basically the same *Example: Food products*
Dynamic	**3** *moderately high perceived uncertainty* Small number of factors and components in the environment Factors and components are somewhat similar to one another Factors and components of the environment are in continual process of change *Example: Fast food industry*	**4** *high perceived uncertainty* Large number of factors and components in the environment Factors and components are not similar to one another Factors and components of environment are in a continual process of change *Example: Commercial airline industry*

Source: Reprinted by permission of the publisher from "What Is the Right Organization Structure? Decision Tree Analysis Provides the Answer," by R. B. Duncan, *Organizational Dynamics* 7 (Winter 1979). © by AMACOM, a division of American Management Associations, p. 63. All rights reserved.

Note: *Simple-complex* refers to the degree to which a decision unit (an individual or organization) must deal with few or many elements that are similar or dissimilar to one another. *Static-dynamic* refers to the degree to which elements of a decision unit's surrounding environment remain the same or are marked by change. *Perceived uncertainty* is seen as resulting from an interaction of the simple-complex and static-dynamic components and as comprised of: (1) a lack of information concerning environmental factors; (2) an inability to accurately assess environmental probabilities; and (3) lack of knowledge regarding the costs associated with an incorrect decision.

Chapter 6

review of the pioneer studies of Burns and Stalker and Lawrence and Lorsch dealing with the nature of organization-environment relations.

The Nature of Organization-Environment Relations
Burns and Stalker Study

While numerous studies have dealt with the nature of organization-environment relations, the first major attempt to identify the types of organizational structure and managerial practice that are appropriate for different environmental conditions was conducted by Burns and Stalker, who studied twenty manufacturing firms in England and Scotland.[19] Of these, fifteen were in the electronics industry, four were in research and development, and one was a major manufacturer. The particular environmental conditions examined were the rates of change in the scientific technology and the relevant product markets of the selected firms. Data were collected through unstructured interviews with managers and supervisors and through observation. No systematic quantitative measuring devices were employed, however, and consequently the reliability and external validity of the study's findings must be judged accordingly. Nevertheless, through a descriptive analysis, Burns and Stalker were able to identify "two divergent systems of management practice," which they named *organic* and *mechanistic.* As shown in Table 6–3, the characteristics of these two systems are quite distinct. The former was judged to be especially appropriate for environments of change in which novel problems continually arise and was described as follows:

Organic systems are adapted to unstable conditions, when problems and requirements for action arise which cannot be broken down and distributed among specialist roles within a clearly defined hierarchy. Individuals have to perform their special tasks in the light of their knowledge of the tasks of the firm as a whole. Jobs lose much of their formal definition in terms of methods, duties, and powers, which have to be redefined continually by interaction with others participating in a task. Interaction runs laterally as much as vertically. Communication between people of different ranks tends to resemble lateral consultation rather than vertical command. Omniscience can no longer be imputed to the head of the firm.[20]

In contrast, mechanistic systems, containing many bureaucratic elements, seemed to be particularly appropriate for stable environments.

In mechanistic systems the problems and tasks facing the concern as a whole are broken down into specialisms. Each individual pursues his task as something distinct

---

[19]T. Burns and G. M. Stalker, *The Management of Innovation* (London: Tavistock, 1961).
[20]Ibid., pp. 5–6. Reprinted by permission of Tavistock Publications Ltd.

Table 6–3 *Comparison of Mechanistic and Organic Systems of Organization*

Mechanistic	Organic
1. Tasks are highly fractionated and specialized; little regard paid to clarifying relationship between tasks and organizational objectives.	1. Tasks are more interdependent; emphasis on relevance of tasks and organizational objectives.
2. Tasks tend to remain rigidly defined unless altered formally by top management.	2. Tasks are continually adjusted and redefined through interaction of organizational members.
3. Specific role definition (rights, obligations, and technical methods prescribed for each member).	3. Generalized role definition (members accept general responsibility for task accomplishment beyond individual role definition).
4. Hierarchic structure of control, authority, and communication. Sanctions derive from employment contract between employee and organization.	4. Network structure of control, authority, and communication. Sanctions derive more from community of interest than from contractual relationship.
5. Information relevant to situation and operations of the organization formally assumed to rest with chief executive.	5. Leader not assumed to be omniscient; knowledge centers identified where located throughout organization.
6. Communication is primarily vertical between superior and subordinate.	6. Communication is both vertical and horizontal, depending upon where needed information resides.
7. Communications primarily take form of instructions and decisions issued by superiors, of information and requests for decisions supplied by inferiors.	7. Communications primarily take form of information and advice.
8. Insistence on loyalty to organization and obedience to superiors.	8. Commitment to organization's tasks and goals more highly valued than loyalty or obedience.
9. Importance and prestige attached to identification with organization and its members.	9. Importance and prestige attached to affiliations and expertise in external environment.

Source: R. M. Steers, *Organizational Effectiveness: A Behavioral View* (Santa Monica, Calif.: Goodyear. 1977), p. 90. Adapted from T. Burns and G. M. Stalker, *The Management of Innovation* (London: Tavistock, 1961), pp. 119–122. Used by permission of Tavistock Publications Ltd.

from the real tasks of the concern as a whole, as if it were the subject of a sub-contract. "Somebody at the top" is responsible for seeing to its relevance. The technical methods, duties and power attached to each functional role are precisely defined. Interaction within management tends to be vertical, i.e., between superior and subordinate. Operations and working behavior are governed by instructions and decisions issued by supervisors. This command hierarchy is maintained by the implicit assumption that all knowledge about the situation of the firm and its tasks is, or should be, available only to the head of the firm. Management, often visualized as the complex hierarchy familiar in organization charts, operates a simple control system, with information flowing up through a succession of filters, and decisions and instructions flowing downwards through a succession of amplifiers.[21]

As conceptualized by Burns and Stalker, organic and mechanistic systems are seen as ideal types defining two ends of a continuum containing a variety of intermediate points. In actuality, Burns and Stalker suggest that few, if any, management systems are purely mechanistic or purely organic. In addition, they strongly emphasize that *no part of their research indicates that one system is superior to another.* Rather, they insist that there is no one optimum form of management system, and that the nature of an organization's environment largely determines whether its structure is appropriate.

We have endeavored to stress the appropriateness of each system to its own specific set of conditions. Equally, we desire to avoid the suggestion that either system is superior under all circumstances to the other. In particular, nothing in our experience justifies the assumption that mechanistic systems should be superseded by organic systems in conditions of stability. The beginning of administrative wisdom is the awareness that there is no one optimum type of management system.[22]

Lawrence and Lorsch Study

Building on the findings of Burns and Stalker and others, Lawrence and Lorsch undertook a much more systematic and quantitative investigation of the relationship between environmental differences and effective organization design.[23] These researchers studied ten firms with various levels of economic effectiveness in three divergent industrial environments: six in the plastics industry, two in the consumer foods industry, and two in the container industry. The plastics industry was chosen because it operates in a diverse environment characterized by both rapid rates of technological and scientific innovation and high degrees of uncertainty. The container industry, on the other hand, was selected because of its relatively greater stability. Further, unlike those in the plastics industry, the major competitive factors in this industry were customer service and consistent product quality. Finally, the consumer foods industry was chosen because it was in an environment of intermediate stability characterized by a moderate rate of growth and change; slower than that of the plastics industry, but faster than that of the container industry.

---

[21]Ibid., p. 5.

[22]Ibid., p. 125.

[23]P. R. Lawrence and J. W. Lorsch, *Organization and Environment: Managing Differentiation and Integration* (Boston: Division of Research, Graduate School of Business Administration, Harvard University, 1967); P. R. Lawrence and J. W. Lorsch, "Differentiation and Integration in Complex Organizations," *Administrative Science Quarterly* 12 (1967): 1–47.

Viewing organizations as open systems, Lawrence and Lorsch argued that organizations, rather than facing their environment as a single unit, tend to segment themselves into functional subunits, each concentrating on a particular sector of the relevant external environment. For example, in each of the ten organizations studied, Lawrence and Lorsch were able to identify a *market* subenvironment (the task of the sales unit), a *technoeconomic* subenvironment (the task of the production unit), and a *scientific* subenvironment (the task of the research and development unit). This is depicted in Figure 6–1.

Utilizing data collected via questionnaires and interviews with middle- and upper-level management, Lawrence and Lorsch hypothesized, and later substantiated by their research findings, that the greater the *differentiation* among functional subunits, the more difficult it would be to bring about the *integration* of their efforts. "*Differentiation* is defined as the state of segmentation of the organizational system into subsystems, each of which tends to develop particular [behavioral] attributes in relation to the requirements posed by its relevant external environment," while "*integration* is defined as the process of achieving unity of effort among various subsystems in the accomplishment of the organization's task."[24] Degree of differentiation was measured by computing difference scores for all relevant pairs of functional subunits in terms of four behavioral attributes: structure, members' interpersonal orientation, members' orientation toward time, and members' orientation toward goals. Degree of integration was measured by asking respondents for their appraisal of the general state of interdepartmental relations among all possible pairs of functional subunits; the evaluation was made on a seven-point scale ranging from "sound—full unity of effort is achieved" to "couldn't be worse—bad relations—serious problems exist that are not being solved."

In addition, Lawrence and Lorsch found that organizations operating in highly diverse and uncertain environments were more differentiated than those operating in less diverse and more stable or certain environments were. Environmental certainty-uncertainty was measured in each organization using the nine-item scale reproduced as Table 2–1 in Chapter 2 of this book. Top executives in each organization were asked to judge the degree to which the subenvironments corresponding to the various functional subunits varied along three dimensions: (1) the rate of change in the subenvironment over time; (2) the certainty of information about subenvironment conditions at any given time; and (3) the time span of feedback from the subenvironment on the results of subunit behavior. Thus, as indicated in Table 6–4, the organizations operating in the plastics industry were more highly differentiated than firms in the consumer foods industry were; and the latter, in turn, were more highly differentiated than firms in the container industry were. In other words, the greater the variation across the three subenvironments in terms of environmental uncertainty (that is, rate of change, certainty of information, and time span of feedback), the greater the variation across the three subenvironments in terms of the behavioral

---

[24]Lawrence and Lorsch, "Differentiation and Integration," pp. 3–4.

Figure 6–1 *A Conceptualization of the Lawrence and Lorsch Model*

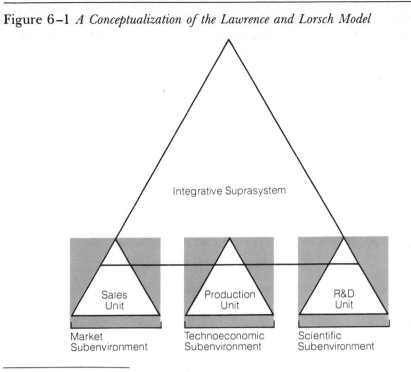

Source: Adapted from J. L. Gibson, J. M. Ivancevich, and J. H. Donnelly, *Organizations: Behavior, Structures, Processes* (Dallas, Tex.: Business Publications, 1979), p. 320. © 1979 by Business Publications, Inc. Used by permission.

attributes mentioned earlier (that is, formality of structure, interpersonal orientation, time orientation, and goal orientation).

Perhaps more important, Lawrence and Lorsch also found, as shown in Table 6–4, that the more effective organizations in each industry, with one exception, exhibited a higher degree of integration than less effective organizations did. Effectiveness was judged using such economic criteria as change in profits over the preceding five years, change in sales volume over the preceding five years, and number of new products introduced in the preceding five years as a percentage of total current sales. Thus, having established that a higher degree of differentiation was needed to deal with diverse and task environments, Lawrence and Lorsch found that a high degree of integration was needed to bring together an organization's various differentiated functional subunits in achieving effective performance.

Finally, by comparing the three most effective organizations in each environment, Lawrence and Lorsch discovered that they each differed in their primary mode of integration (see Table 6–5). In the dynamic and uncertain environment of the plastics industry, the more effective (and highly differentiated) organization largely relied on a formal integrating department to coordinate subunit activities. In the moderately stable consumer foods industry, the effective (and less differentiated) firm principally utilized individual integrators, while in the more stable and more certain container industry, the better-performing (and least differentiated) organization mainly employed direct managerial contact through the formal chain of command. Thus, a comparison of these mechanisms in these three effective organizations suggests that they should be more elaborate when the focal organization is highly differentiated and integration is, hence, more difficult. However, when the functional subunits in the organization are not highly differentiated, less elaborate mechanisms appear to work quite well.

In summary, Lawrence and Lorsch's findings imply that no single "type" of organization is appropriate under all conditions, but that appropriate patterns of orga-

Table 6–4   *Average Differentiation and Integration Across Three Environments*

Industry	Organization	Average Differentiation[a]	Average Integration[a]
Plastics	High performer	10.7	5.6
	Low performer	9.0	5.1
Foods	High performer	8.0	5.3
	Low performer	6.5	5.0
Containers	High performer	5.7	5.7
	Low performer	5.7	4.8

[a]Higher differentiation scores indicate greater differentiation between functional units. Higher integration scores indicate tighter integration between functional units.

Source: Reprinted by permission of Harvard University Press from *Organization and Environment,* p. 103, by Paul R. Lawrence and Jay W. Lorsch. Boston: Division of Research, Graduate School of Business Administration, Harvard University. Copyright © 1967 by the President and Fellows of Harvard College.

Table 6–5 *Comparison of Integrative Devices in Three High-Performing Organizations*

	Plastics	Foods	Containers
Degree of Differentiation[a]	10.7	8.0	5.7
Major Integrative Devices	1. Integrative department	1. Individual integrators	1. Direct managerial contact
	2. Permanent cross-functional teams at three levels of management	2. Temporary cross-functional teams	2. Managerial hierarchy
	3. Direct managerial contact	3. Direct managerial contact	3. Paper system
	4. Managerial hierarchy	4. Managerial hierarchy	
	5. Paper system	5. Paper system	

[a]High score means greater actual differentiation.

Source: Reprinted by permission of Harvard University Press from *Organization and Environment*, p. 138, by Paul R. Lawrence and Jay W. Lorsch. Boston: Division of Research, Graduate School of Business Administration, Harvard University. Copyright © 1967 by the President and Fellows of Harvard College.

nization vary and are contingent upon environmental uncertainty. Thus, Lawrence and Lorsch's findings are consistent with those of Burns and Stalker. That is to say, both suggest that the environment in which an enterprise functions is of foremost importance in selecting the structure appropriate for achieving organizational success.

Contradictory Evidence

While other studies have uncovered relationships consistent with the findings of Lawrence and Lorsch and of Burns and Stalker, the hypothesis that the effectiveness of an organization is related to the match between environmental demands and relevant structural and behavioral attributes has not received unequivocal, widespread support.[25] Hall, for instance, has been especially critical of Lawrence and Lorsch's failure to provide information on the supposed mechanisms by which environmental influences enter organizations.[26] He further points out that, in the design of their study, Lawrence and Lorsch failed to take into consideration other environmental pressures, original structural differences among the organizations studied,

[25]For a review see A. C. Filley, R. J. House, and S. Kerr, *Managerial Process and Organizational Behavior,* 2nd ed. (Glenview, Ill.: Scott Foresman, 1976), pp. 290–293.

[26]R. H. Hall, Review of *Organization and Environment: Managing Differentiation and Integration* by P. R. Lawrence and L. W. Lorsch, *Administrative Science Quarterly* 13 (1968): 180–186.

historical factors influencing the development of the organizations, and intra-industry differences in orientation and practice.

In addition, the failure of subsequent researchers to replicate Lawrence and Lorsch's findings has raised doubts concerning the reliability (degree of accuracy) and validity (degree to which a measurement actually reflects the phenomenon intended) of the measure of environmental uncertainty that they employed.[27] Whereas Lawrence and Lorsch administered a nine-item *perceptual scale* to top managers as a means of assessing environmental uncertainty, other researchers have constructed so-called *objective measures* based on such indicators as investment patterns and performance criteria.[28] Aldag and Storey, among others, suggest that the failure to replicate Lawrence and Lorsch's results may largely be a function of the use of "perceptual" as opposed to "objective" measures of environmental uncertainty.[29] The significance of this point is well made by Snow and Darran. Based on a review of the relevant literature, they conclude that using managers' perceptions to describe environmental conditions "is appropriate when an investigator is attempting to determine how an organization (its managers) views the *behavior* of the environment, because any response subsequently developed will be consistent with these perceptions. However, this approach is less appropriate when the investigation is trying to describe the *nature* of the environment; in these cases, it is preferable to have both perceptual and objective measures."[30]

Thus, the divergence of results reported in the literature serves not only to stress the questionable nature of uncertainty measures, but also makes the point that defining certainty-uncertainty criteria is not simple. Further, and perhaps most significantly, it suggests that an organization's structure may not solely reflect its response to objectively appraised environmental conditions; structure may also be influenced by an organization's subjective perceptions of its surrounding environment. In complex situations, an organization's reactions to environmental influences may well be a function of the self-selected and subjective perceptions of its managers, rather than of its interaction with a combination of "real" contingencies and constraints. It is this issue that provides the focus of the following discussion.

---

[27]See, for example, H. L. Tosi, R. J. Aldag, and R. G. Storey, "On the Measurement of the Environment: An Assessment of the Lawrence and Lorsch Environmental Subscale," *Administrative Science Quarterly* 18 (1973): 27–36; J. M. Pennings, "The Relevance of the Structural-Contingency Model for Organizational Effectiveness," *Administrative Science Quarterly* 20 (1975): 393–410.

[28]These include H. K. Downey and J. W. Slocum, "Uncertainty: Measures, Research, and Sources of Variation," *Academy of Management Journal* 18 (1975): 562–578; H. K. Downey, D. Hellriegel, and J. W. Slocum, "Individual Characteristics as Sources of Perceived Uncertainty Variability," *Human Relations* 30 (1977): 161–174; H. K. Downey, D. Hellriegel, and J. W. Slocum, "Environmental Uncertainty: The Construct and Its Application," *Administrative Science Quarterly* 20 (1975): 613–629.

[29]R. J. Aldag and R. G. Storey, "Environmental Uncertainty: Comments on Objective and Perceptual Indices," in *Proceedings of the Annual Meeting of the Academy of Management,* ed. A. G. Bedeian et al. (Auburn, Ala.: Academy of Management, 1975), pp. 203–205.

[30]C. C. Snow and D. C. Darran, "Organizational Adaptation to the Environment: A Review," *Proceedings of the American Institute for Decision Sciences,* ed. M. W. Hopfe and H. C. Schneider (Cincinnati, Ohio: American Institute for Decision Sciences, 1975), p. 279.

Chapter 6

Environmental Perception: The Enacted Environment

In support of the above line of reasoning, Starbuck and others (most notably Weick) have argued that an organization responds only to what it perceives, and that such perceptions may or may not reflect the "objective reality" of its environment (the world as God or some other omniscient observer sees it).[31] Consequently, those environmental factors not perceived are not considered in an organization's deliberations and actions. Under such circumstances, as Starbuck notes, "the same environment one organization perceives as unpredictable, complex, and evanescent, another organization might see as static and easily understood."[32] This in itself may be a major reason that researchers using nonperceptual measures of environmental uncertainty have been unsuccessful in replicating the findings of Lawrence and Lorsch.

In describing how organizations conceptualize their environments, Weick has argued that particular attention should be paid to how and why individual managers focus their attention on specific aspects of an environment to the exclusion of others, and how they acquire and process information necessary for learning about "what is really out there" and "what they have to do to deal with it."[33] In this regard, Weick has coined the phrase *enacted environment* to refer to that portion of the external environment that is perceived by an organization's managers. Weick states that "the human actor does not *re*act to an environment, he *en*acts it. It is this enacted environment and nothing else that is worked upon by the processes of organizing."[34]

With respect to how individual managers acquire, perceive, and interpret bits of information pertaining to various aspects of an organization's environment, little empirical information is available. Based on the findings of a laboratory simulation, Huber, O'Connell, and Cummings have suggested that the amount of environmental information available may affect an individual's judgment of perceived uncertainty.[35] Miles, Snow, and Pfeffer have further argued that organizations which are highly differentiated are more likely to produce highly differentiated managerial perceptions of their environment.[36] This is consistent with the work of Kefalas and Schoderbeck, who found that managers working for organizations in a dynamic environment (and thus more likely to be highly differentiated) not only spend a greater proportion of

[31]Starbuck, "Organizations and Their Environments"; K. E. Weick, *The Social Psychology of Organizing* (Reading, Mass.: Addison-Wesley, 1969); K. E. Weick, "Enactment Processes in Organizations," in *New Directions in Organizational Behavior,* ed. B. M. Staw and R. Salancik (Chicago: St. Clair Press, 1977), pp. 267–300.

[32]Starbuck, "Organizations and Their Environments," p. 1080.

[33]Weick, "Enactment Processes," p. 267.

[34]Weick, *Social Psychology,* p. 64.

[35]G. P. Huber, M. J. O'Connell, and L. L. Cummings, "Perceived Environmental Uncertainty: Effects of Information and Structure," *Academy of Management Journal* 18 (1975): 725–740.

[36]R. E. Miles, C. C. Snow, and J. Pfeffer, "Organization-Environment: Concepts and Issues," *Industrial Relations* 13 (1974): 244–264.

their time acquiring external information than do managers working for organizations in stable environments, but also that most of the information they acquire is relevant only to their own speciality or functional area.[37] Thus, as Miles, Snow, and Pfeffer speculate, "structure may not only be a consequence of the environment but may also influence the environment through its effect on managerial attention processes."[38]

Environmental Selection: Strategic Choice

Following Weick, Child has likewise argued that managerial perceptions play an important role in influencing the responses of an organization to its environment.[39] Child, however, further argues that, contrary to what is typically implied by contemporary theories, managers often have considerable latitude in making *strategic choices.* This "strategic choice" includes not only structural considerations, but also decisions with respect to the location of facilities, the market(s) to be served, and the types of employees to be recruited. Child's position thus emphasizes the importance of managerial decision makers who function as a critical link between an organization and its environment. Moreover, he argues (in line with Cyert and March, as discussed in Chapter 4) that managerial decisions regarding strategic choices are primarily the result of an "essentially political process, whereby power-holders within organizations decide upon courses of strategic action."[40]

A convincing body of evidence supporting Child's (and Weick's) position has begun to accumulate. Duncan's model (see Table 6–2) of environmental dimensions, discussed earlier, emphasizes that organizational decisions (strategic choices) are greatly affected by perceived uncertainty. Similarly, studies by Anderson and Paine and Montanari suggest that managerial perceptions are a key input in understanding strategy formulation in response to organization-environment interaction.[41] Finally, Miles and Snow, based on interviews with the top managers of sixteen college textbook publishing companies, have concluded that the strategies or "actions an organization takes in responding to its environment are much more likely to be consistent with top management perceptions of the environment than any 'objective' indicator of environmental conditions is likely to predict."[42]

---

[37]A. Kefalas and P. P. Schoderbeck, "Scanning the Business Environment—Some Empirical Findings," *Decision Sciences* 4 (1973): 63–74.

[38]Miles, Snow, and Pfeffer, "Organization-Environment," p. 250.

[39]J. Child, "Organizational Structure, Environment and Performance: The Role of Strategic Choice," *Sociology* 6 (1972): 1–21.

[40]Ibid., p. 2.

[41]C. R. Anderson and F. T. Paine, "Managerial Perceptions and Strategic Behavior," *Academy of Management Journal* 18 (1975): 811–823; J. R. Montanari, "Strategic Choice: A Theoretical Analysis," *Journal of Management Studies* 16 (1979): 202–221.

[42]Miles, Snow, and Pfeffer, "Organization-Environment," p. 257; see also R. E. Miles and C. C. Snow, *Organizational Strategy, Structure, and Process* (New York: McGraw-Hill, 1978), pp. 171–192.

Limits to Perceived Reality and Strategic Choice

Overall, much of the available evidence suggests that the way managerial decision makers conceptualize or perceive the environment influences their strategic choices (that is, decisions) of the most appropriate structure for achieving organizational success. It should be pointed out, however, that the concepts of perceived reality and strategic choice are subject to certain severe constraints. Indeed, as Aldrich and Pfeffer observe, a concern with perceptions of organizational reality is only meaningful to the degree that an organization is immune to, or at least partially insulated from, environmental effects. "If the organization is severely constrained by the environment, as in a very competitive market, then perception is not important. The personnel in the organization will operate and perceive effectively or else it will soon go out of existence."[43]

With respect to strategic choice, Child fails to recognize several inherent limitations. While managerial decision makers may be free to select certain aspects of their environment, they are also subject to certain constraints.[44] Two are particularly relevant for the present discussion. First, while Child assumes that the time frame is unlimited, once their resources are committed (plants built and personnel hired), most organizations are severely limited with respect to making major modifications in their strategic behavior. Hence, rather than being determined by them, size and technology may often serve to constrain an organization's (its manager's) strategic choices. Secondly, Child fails to consider that certain potential environments are effectively excluded by legal and economic barriers. Economies of scale and legal funding restrictions may be insurmountable for all but the largest organizations. Examples are the aluminum and steel industries. The cost of entry to achieve economies of scale in either industry is, for the most part, considered prohibitive.

Minimizing Environmental Uncertainty: Internal Strategies
Buffering, Smoothing, Forecasting, and Rationing

Putting aside the issue of perceived versus objective reality, it is important to realize that organizations employ a variety of internal strategies to minimize the uncertainties associated with their task environments. Under norms of rationality, they attempt to protect or seal off their *technical cores* (that is, central throughput processes) from environmental fluctuations.[45] While, ideally, an organization's inputs and outputs flow

---

[43]H.E. Aldrich and J. Pfeffer, "Environments of Organizations," *Annual Review of Sociology* 2 (1976): 92.

[44]Aldrich, *Organizations and Environments*, pp. 149–159; J. R. Montanari, "Managerial Discretion: An Expanded Model of Organizational Choice," *Academy of Management Review* 3 (1978): 231–241; J. Pfeffer and G. R. Salancik, *The External Control of Organizations: A Resource Dependence Perspective* (New York: Harper & Row, 1978), pp. 78–83; H. R. Bobbitt and J. D. Ford, "Decision-maker Choice as a Determinant of Organizational Structure," *Academy of Management Review*, in press.

[45]Thompson, *Organizations in Action*, p. 20.

at a continuous and steady rate from or to its environment, realistically they seldom do. Organizations, however, have been shown to regulate such exchanges with their environment through such internal responses as *buffering, smoothing, forecasting,* and *rationing.*[46]

Buffering

Buffering on the input side usually takes the form of accumulating and maintaining a stockpile of materials and supplies for future use. On the output side, buffering typically involves building and keeping up warehouse and distributor inventories. By buffering, then, environmental uncertainties are *absorbed* because an organization's technical core produces at a constant rate, steadily working from and putting into stock both inputs and outputs. At the same time, however, it should be realized that this advantage must be weighed against the cost of maintaining excess raw materials and finished products. This, of course, has long been the focal point of material requirements planning (MRP).

Smoothing

Whereas buffering is used to absorb environmental uncertainties, *smoothing* (also called leveling) involves efforts to *manage* environmental uncertainties. Examples of organizations that attempt to level the demand for their output (products or services) include utilities, airlines, and resorts. The telephone industry, for instance, attempts to smooth fluctuations in demand by charging lower rates during "trough periods" (11 P.M. to 8 A.M. and weekends) and relatively higher rates during "peak periods" (8 A.M. to 11 P.M. weekdays). Similarly, both airlines and resorts offer inducements such as reduced tariffs or special promotions on light days or during off seasons. Through smoothing, organizations attempt to manage their environment by protecting their technical core from cyclical interruptions.

Forecasting

When neither buffering nor smoothing proves effective in protecting an organization's technical core from environmental fluctuations, organizations can often reduce uncertainty and behave in a logical, rational manner by developing accurate *forecasting* capabilities. To the degree that environmental fluctuations can be predicted, they can be treated as constraints and adapted to accordingly. Organizations such as banks, package delivery services, supermarkets, and police departments are able to anticipate heavy demands for their services at predictable times and, consequently, schedule their operations. To the extent that such environmental fluctuations are foreseen and considered as contingencies, an organization's technical core can be sealed off and its performance maintained.

---

[46]Ibid., pp. 20–22.

Rationing

Finally, when neither buffering, smoothing, nor forecasting is sufficient to prevent environmental penetration, organizations can turn to *rationing*. The allocation or assignment of resources according to established priorities is seen in organizations such as hospitals, which may be forced to ration beds; social welfare departments, where case workers ration their time and effort according to client need; restaurants and theaters, which require the advance booking of reservations; and manufactories that, when products suddenly become popular, may have to ration deliveries to wholesalers or dealers, and, if inputs are scarce, may establish a system of priorities for their use. In general, rationing is a less than satisfactory solution, because it signifies that an organization is not fully serving its task environment.

Minimizing Environmental Uncertainty: External Strategies

Whereas the preceding section principally deals with *internal* strategies for responding to environmental uncertainties, as part of a larger social system, organizations also employ a variety of *external* strategies when interacting with other entities—persons, groups, and organizations—in their task environment. The strategies used range from *direct* attempts to deal with organizational interdependence to *indirect* methods designed to influence or regulate the broader context within which interactions take place. These direct and indirect strategies are the subject of the following two-part discussion. As a prologue to our upcoming comments, we turn to a brief consideration of interorganizational relations.

Interorganizational Relations: A Brief Comment

The survival of an organization operating in an uncertain environment largely depends on its ability to anticipate and counteract the behavior of the organizations with which it interacts.[47] Using the earlier idea of role-set,[48] both Blau and Scott and Evan have introduced the concept of *organization-set* to describe this interaction.[49] By extension, an organization-set refers to the network of organizations to which any one organization is related. "Thus all universities, all American universities, or all state

---

[47]F. E. Emery and E. L. Trist, "The Causal Texture of Organizational Environments," *Human Relations* 18 (1965): 21–32; S. Terreberry, "The Evolution of Organizational Environments," *Administrative Science Quarterly* 12 (1968): 590–613.

[48]R. K. Merton, "The Role-Set: Problems in Sociological Theory," *British Journal of Sociology* 8 (1957): 106–120.

[49]P. M. Blau and W. R. Scott, *Formal Organizations* (San Francisco: Chandler, 1962), p. 195; W. M. Evan, "The Organization-Set: Toward a Theory of Interorganizational Relations," in *Approaches to Organizational Design*, ed. J. D. Thompson (Pittsburgh: University of Pittsburgh Press, 1966), pp. 173–191.

universities constitute different sets and subsets."[50] Another example is that of professional major league baseball where teams in the American and National Leagues and their respective East and West Divisions also compose different organization-sets and -subsets.

As suggested, the utility of this concept derives from the fact that it defines the particular set of organizations with which interorganizational relationships will occur, and thus the context in which the resulting interactions will take place. As an illustration, the organization-set of a police operated social control system for problem youth is presented in Figure 6–2. The frequency of contact is also indicated. The actual relations, or interactions, between the organizations depicted occur within the role-sets of boundary personnel (i.e., persons serving as organizational representatives). These so-called *boundary spanners* are important because they mediate the flow of information, products or services, and personnel between organizations and their environment. As external representatives, boundary spanners, such as sales representatives, purchasing agents, labor negotiators, talent scouts, truant officers, lobbyists, promoters, personnel recruiters, press coordinators, public relations specialists, and credit managers serve to maintain an organization's boundaries against environmental pressures. Recent findings especially highlight the role of boundary spanners in gathering and processing required environmental information and in relaying that information to organization decision units.[51]

It is clear that the ability of an organization to anticipate and to appropriately deal with environmental conditions and with the actions of the organizations with which it must interact is largely determined by the behavior of boundary role personnel. This is highlighted in Figure 6–3. The spanners in this model are interacting with one another (at point 4) and serving as communication links with their respective organizations. In turn, they are relaying the information received to various organization decision units, which respond accordingly. As a point of interest, note that boundary spanning also occurs *within* an organization's internal environment between decision units (for example, Unit A_1 ↔ Unit A_2).

Organizational Interdependence: Direct Strategies

In developing a conceptual framework for the analysis of interorganizational relations, Thompson and McEwen have distinguished two direct strategies for dealing with organizational interdependence—*competitive* and *cooperative,* with the latter includ-

---

[50]F. W. Riggs, "Organizational Structures and Contexts," *Administration and Society* 7 (1975): 183.

[51]See, for example, H. E. Aldrich and D. Herker, "Boundary Spanning Roles and Organization Structure," *Academy of Management Review* 2 (1972): 217–230; R. Leifer and G. P. Huber, "Relations among Perceived Environmental Uncertainty, Organization Structure, and Boundary-Spanning Behavior," *Administrative Science Quarterly* 22 (1977): 235–247; J. S. Adams, "Interorganizational Processes and Organization Boundaries Activities," in *Research in Organizational Behavior,* vol. 2, ed. B. M. Staw and L. L. Cummings (Greenwich, Conn: JAI Press, in press).

Figure 6–2 *An Organization-Set Showing Frequency of Interaction*

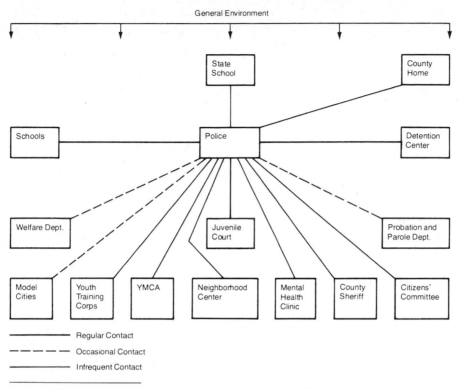

Source: R. H. Hall, *Organizations: Structure and Process,* 2nd ed. © 1977, p. 323. Reprinted by permission of Prentice-Hall, Inc., Englewood Cliffs, New Jersey.

The Organization and Its External Environment

Figure 6–3 *The Boundary Spanner*

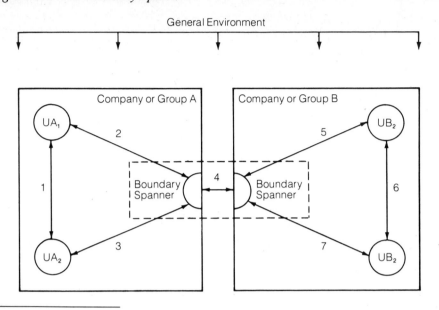

Source: Adapted from *Organizational Behavior and Performance* by J. M. Ivancevich, A. D. Szilagyi, Jr., and M. J. Wallace, Jr., p. 324. Copyright © 1977 by Goodyear Publishing Co. Reprinted by permission.

Chapter 6

ing three subtypes: *bargaining, coopting,* and *coalescing.*[52] Whereas competition is a means by which an organization can deal directly with environmental uncertainties through the use of its own resources, the three subtypes of cooperative strategy all require interaction between organizations.

Competition

As used here, competition implies rivalry among organizations which is mediated by an outside (third) party (for example, a customer, distributor, supplier, or client). The possibility of economic failure is a serious environmental threat to almost all organizations operating in a free market system. Competition prohibits the unilateral choice of organizational goals. It involves an element of rivalry in securing both resources *and* customers. As more fully developed by Porter, "The nature and degree of competition in an industry hinge on five forces: the threat of new entrants, the bargaining power of customers, the bargaining power of suppliers, the threat of substitute products or services (where applicable), and the jockeying among current contestants."[53] These forces are shown diagrammatically in Figure 6–4. Their combined strength establishes the "ultimate profit potential" of a field or industry and varies from mild, in industries such as soft drinks, toiletries, and oil field services where earnings have recently been quite high, to intense, in industries such as steel, metal cans, and tires where returns have traditionally been low. In either circumstance, organizations that are unable to successfully compete in obtaining raw materials and, in turn, to produce goods and services consumers are willing to accept, are soon confronted with the uncomfortable prospect of either changing their product line or being eliminated.

Cooperation

Bargaining.   In an effort to limit the uncertainty caused by competition, organizations often respond by entering into cooperative relationships. *Bargaining* refers to direct negotiation between organizations for the exchange of goods and services. Such contractual arrangements, to the extent that they are binding and enforceable, serve to reduce environmental uncertainty for the organizations involved. Thus, a long-term sales contract enables the selling organization to more accurately predict sales demand (and hence gross income) and assures the purchasing organization of a source of supply at a set price. Bargaining also includes other activities such as collective negotiations between labor and management and agreements between producers and distributors. In both cases, the groups involved represent a certain amount of uncertainty to one another. Management, for instance, needs a steady,

---

[52]J. D. Thompson and W. J. McEwen, "Organizational Goals and Environment: Goal-Setting as an Interaction Process," *American Sociological Review* 23 (1958): 23–31.

[53]M. E. Porter, "How Competitive Forces Shape Strategy," *Harvard Business Review* 57, no. 2 (1979): 137. See also D. Jacobs, "Dependency and Vulnerability: An Exchange Approach to the Control of Organizations," *Administrative Science Quarterly* 19 (1974): 45–59.

efficient work force in order to achieve its economic goals. Conversely, labor seeks acceptable benefits and wages, adequate working conditions, and job security (see the earlier discussion of this point in Chapter 4). Through collective negotiations, the uncertainty each group represents to the other is controlled for a mutually agreed upon period of time.

Although much is known about how target organizations respond to various bargaining tactics, very little is known about the means of influence that are actually used.[54] Recent work by Wilkinson and Kipnis, however, has provided an interesting insight into this area.[55] Classifying influence tactics into two major groupings, strong and weak (see Table 6–6), they predicted and found that strong influence tactics were invoked significantly more often when: (a) the target organization resisted attempts at being influenced; (b) the influencing organization was more powerful than the target organization; and (c) the influencing organization was trying to convince the target organization to undertake some new action, such as buying its products, rather than trying to change the target organization's behavior. As can be seen in Table 6–6, strong means of influence involve tactics in which control over a target organization rests primarily in an influencing organization (threaten to end relationship, withhold service or product), whereas weak means of influence represent tactics in which control is either shared (negotiations, compromise) or control resides in a target organization (be cooperative/act nice).

Coopting.   The second cooperative strategy for dealing with organizational inter-dependence—*coopting*—is defined as "the process of absorbing new elements into the leadership or policy-determining structure of an organization as a means of averting threats as to its stability or existence."[56] If the threatening elements from the surrounding task environment are actually absorbed or coopted into the organization, the effects of uncertainty can be more tightly controlled. Selznick's study of the Tennessee Valley Authority is a classic illustration of cooptation.[57] Initially encountering strong local opposition to its "socialistic" experiments, the authority adjusted to its hostile environment by coopting leading representatives of the opposition into its policy-making structure. Similarly, a series of studies by Pfeffer suggests that candidates for corporate directorships are often selected not only for their ability, but also for their potential influence in an organization's task environment.[58] Pfeffer found that organizations tend to select a higher proportion of outside directors from financial institutions when they are dependent on the external environment for financial resources. When they are in a highly regulated industry, they tend to select a higher

[54]H. Guetzkow, "Relations among Organizations," in *Studies on Behavior in Organizations: A Research Symposium,* ed. R. Bowers (Athens, Ga.: University of Georgia Press, 1966), pp. 13–44; S. Macaulay, "Non-Contractual Relations in Business: A Preliminary Study," *American Sociological Review* 28 (1963): 55–67.

[55]I. Wilkinson and O. Kipnis, "Interfirm Use of Power," *Journal of Applied Psychology* 63 (1978): 315–320.

[56]P. Selznick, "Foundations of the Theory of Organizations," *American Sociological Review* 13 (1948): 34.

[57]P. Selznick, *TVA and the Grass Roots: A Study in the Sociology of Formal Organization* (Berkeley, Calif.: University of California Press, 1949).

[58]J. Pfeffer, *Organizational Design* (Arlington Heights, Ill.: AHM Publishing, 1978), p. 154.

Figure 6–4 *Forces Governing Competition in an Industry*

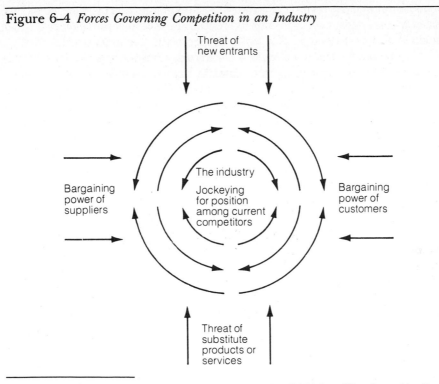

Table 6–6 *Tactics of Influence Used by Organizations in Their Attempts to Influence Other Organizations*

Strong Tactics	Weak Tactics
Threaten to end relation/punish	Face-to-face negotiation
Withhold payments	Use of higher status officers to negotiate
Withhold service, product, or business	Compromise
Legal action	Request compliance
Apply group pressure	Make target aware of problem
Demand compliance	Logical arguments
Dictate terms	Use of good name/reputation
Persistence	Be cooperative/act nice
Use of deceit	Offer benefits or deals
Surveillance of target	Make other party feel ashamed

proportion of attorneys.[59] Finally, publicly-regulated organizations, such as electric utilities that are dependent upon continued social approval to ensure their right to use valued resources, tend to coopt a higher proportion of media representatives.[60]

These practices illustrate a few of the many ways in which organizations attempt to absorb, and therefore to adapt to, threatening elements in their task environments. By selecting representatives from financial institutions for their boards, organizations are able to establish important links with sources of funding. By choosing attorneys as directors, organizations operating in government-regulated industries are better able to cope with and, in some instances, even influence specific regulation. Finally, the importance of mass-media "gatekeepers" in disseminating favorable information, whether related to public utility rate hikes or simply to the release of new books, phonograph records, or motion pictures, is well recognized.[61]

Coalescing.   The last form of cooperative strategy for dealing with organizational interdependence—*coalescing* or the combination of two or more organizations for a single purpose—requires a mutual commitment for joint action. Examples include mergers,[62] joint ventures,[63] interlocking directorships,[64] price fixing,[65] and other activities such as market-sharing conspiracies.[66] Although the complete extent of organizational involvement in such activities is difficult, if not impossible, to determine, certain information is available. For instance, it has been shown that there is a higher incidence of mergers in industries in which an intermediate, as opposed to a very large or very small, number of organizations operate.[67] That is, as Galbraith explains,

In highly concentrated industries, there is little merger activity because it is either unneccessary or illegal. It can be unnecessary because implicit cooperation and price leadership may be sufficient to generate stability. In highly competitive industries with many firms, there is also little merger activity. This time there is none because it is

---

[59]J. Pfeffer, "Size and Composition of Corporate Boards of Directors: The Organization and Its Environment," *Administrative Science Quarterly* 17 (1972): 218–228; J. Pfeffer, "Size, Composition and Function of Hospital Boards of Directors: A Study of Organization-Environment Linkage," *Administrative Science Quarterly* 18 (1973): 349–364.

[60]J. Pfeffer, "Cooption and the Composition of Electric Utility Boards of Directors," *Pacific Sociological Review* 17 (1974): 333–363.

[61]P. M. Hirsch, "Processing Fads and Fashions: An Organization-Set Analysis of Cultural Industry Systems," *American Journal of Sociology* 77 (1972): 639–659.

[62]J. Pfeffer, "Merger as a Response to Organizational Interdependence," *Administrative Science Quarterly* 17 (1972): 382–394.

[63]S. V. Berg and P. Friedman, "Part I: Joint Ventures in American Industry," *Mergers & Acquisitions* 13, no. 2 (1978): 28–41; "Part II: Case Studies of Managerial Policy," 13, no. 3 (1978): 9–17; "Part III: Public Policy Issues," 14, no. 1 (1979): 18–29.

[64]Pfeffer, "Size and Composition."

[65]G. A. Hay and D. Kelley, "An Empirical Study of Price Fixing Conspiracies," *Journal of Law & Economics* 17 (1974): 13–38.

[66]M. D. Ermann and R. J. Lundman, "Deviant Acts by Complex Organizations: Deviance and Social Control at the Organizational Level of Analysis," *Sociological Quarterly* 19 (1978): 55–67.

[67]Pfeffer, "Merger as a Response."

useless. The merger of several small firms still leaves a small firm among many others with no reduction in uncertainty. It is only in the intermediate range that large numbers of mergers take place.[68]

Evidence is also available on interlocking directorships among U.S. corporations. A recent Congressional committee investigation identified 530 direct (two organizations having a common director) and 12,193 indirect (two organizations, each having a director on the board of a third company) interlocks among the nation's 130 largest corporations. An analysis of this common pattern of directorate concentration disclosed the existence of both extensive coalescing and cooption among U.S. firms.[69]

1. On an average, 123 of the firms were each connected with half of the other companies in the study.

2. The 13 top firms were not only linked together, but accounted for 240 direct and 5,547 indirect interlocks, involving an average of 70 percent of the other 117 companies.

3. The nation's "Big Three" automotive manufacturers and top steel and electronic equipment producers met extensively on the boards of major financial institutions, suppliers, and contractors.

4. Directors of the 16 largest commercial banks clustered on major insurance company boards, and insurance directors met on bank boards.

5. The nation's largest airlines and electric utilities were substantially interlocked with major lending institutions.

As with bargaining and cooptation, it should be clear that the goal of coalescing is to help stabilize interorganizational relations, and, thus, make the environment less uncertain and more predictable. It should be further evident that, like other cooperative strategies for dealing with interorganizational relations, coalescing involves certain trade-offs.

Trade-offs. In stressing the importance of establishing the appropriate form of interaction with the surrounding task environment, Thompson and McEwen suggest that competition, bargaining, cooptation, and coalescing represent a continuum of "increasingly 'costly' methods of gaining support in terms of decision-making power."[70] Competition is seen as being the least costly method and coalescing as the most costly (see Figure 6–5). Whereas competition does prevent unilateral organizational choices from being made, it does not affect the autonomy of an organization's internal

---

[68]J. R. Galbraith, *Organization Design* (Reading, Mass.: Addison-Wesley, 1977), p. 219.

[69]U.S. Congress, Senate, Committee on Government Affairs, *Interlocking Directorates among the Major U.S. Corporations* (Washington, D.C.: U.S. Government Printing Office, 1978), p. 280. For an international review in this area, see M. Fennema and H. Schijf, "Analysing Interlocking Directorates: Theory and Methods," *Social Networks* 1 (1978–79): 297–332.

[70]Thompson and McEwen, "Organizational Goals and Environment," p. 29.

The Organization and Its External Environment

Figure 6–5 *Continuum of Decision-making Autonomy Associated with Four Direct Strategies for Dealing with Organizational Interdependence*

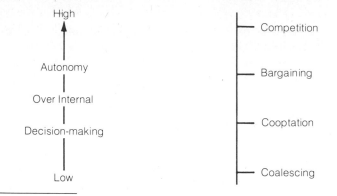

Source: Based on J. D. Thompson, *Organizations in Action* (New York: McGraw-Hill, 1967), pp. 32–36.

decision-making process. On the other hand, when organizations join together, or coalesce in mergers or through interlocking directorates, they "are not only related but actually interpenetrate one another through overlapping memberships."[71] As a consequence, the internal decision-making power of each of the organizations involved is fundamentally altered, and the decision-making autonomy of each reduced.

Bargaining and cooptation also have associated costs. Bargaining affects the decision process to the extent that the support of a second party is necessary for final action. Without *mutual* agreement, any final choice is effectively vetoed. By the same token, cooptation even further reduces an organization's decision-making discretion. The placement, for instance, of a coopted element on an organization's board or in some other policy-making capacity clearly places it in a position to exert influence on a much broader range of issues than is the case in either competition or bargaining. In this regard, "it would be naive to think that the financial institution representatives on a board of directors of an organization would limit their influence and interactions to financial procurement or allocation issues alone. By the nature of their position on the board, they have the right to impact on such decisions as management succession, new product development, dividend policies, and so on."[72]

In sum, while each of the processes described results in some decrease in environmental uncertainty, each also involves certain trade-offs. The loss of decision-making autonomy that is associated with each strategy must be carefully balanced against its probable benefits. The selection, by an organization, of strategies to follow in interacting with the many relevant parts of its task environment is, to be sure, a major organizational decision.

---

[71]Blau and Scott, *Formal Organizations,* p. 198.

[72]J. M. Ivancevich, A. D. Szilagyi, and M. J. Wallace, *Organizational Behavior and Performance* (Santa Monica, Calif.: Goodyear, 1977), p. 253.

Chapter 6

Organizational Interdependence: Indirect Strategies

Indirect strategies for dealing with organizational interdependence involve attempts by organizations to influence their surrounding task environment through the activities of third parties such as trade organizations, professional associations, organized lobbies, coordinating groups, and government regulatory agencies. When gearing into such larger systems, organizations reduce environmental uncertainty by taking advantage of control mechanisms more powerful than their own.[73] In this regard, organizations press for government regulations such as protective tariffs,[74] quotas,[75] and occupational licensing[76] to restrict competition. Indeed, Hirsch has shown that much of the success of the typical pharmaceutical firm has been a result of the pharmaceutical industry's ability to exert control over patent and copyright laws.[77] Furthermore, organizations act through trade associations (for example, National Association of Manufacturers), professional associations (American Medical Association), organized lobbies (Tobacco Institute), and coordinating groups (Consumer Federation of America) to protect themselves from unfavorable legislation and to gain various economic advantages, including direct cash subsidies, tax credits, rate hikes, and rate exemptions.[78] It is also important to note that, in addition to acting as representatives in issues of common concern, such collective structures allow a pooling and sharing of expenses and information, and serve to promote both a common identity and a common set of values and norms.[79]

Strategic Coping Behavior

Before closing our discussion of strategies for minimizing environmental uncertainty, at least some mention should be made of those instances in which organizations find that they cannot contend with some element of their task environment. In certain situations organizations may actually find it easier to *alter,* rather than attempt to cope with, their environment. Indeed, Starbuck and Dutton argue that "there are at least

---

[73]D. Katz and R. L. Kahn, *The Social Psychology of Organization,* 2nd ed. (New York: John Wiley & Sons, 1978), p. 131.

[74]R. A. Bauer, S. I. de Pool, and L. A. Dexter, *American Business and Public Policy: The Politics of Foreign Trade,* 2nd ed. (New York: Atherton, 1972).

[75]I. Mintz, *U.S. Import Quotas: Costs and Consequences* (Washington, D.C.: American Enterprise Institute for Public Policy Research, 1973).

[76]J. Pfeffer, "Some Evidence on Occupational Licensing and Occupational Incomes," *Social Forces* 53 (1974):102–111; J. Pfeffer, "Administration Regulation and Licensing: Social Problem or Solution?" *Social Problems* 21 (1974): 468–479.

[77]P. M. Hirsch, "Organizational Effectiveness and the Institutional Environment," *Administrative Science Quarterly* 20 (1975): 327–343.

[78]K. J. Meier and J. R. Van Lohuizen, "Interest Groups in the Appropriations Process: The Wasted Profession Revisited," *Social Science Quarterly* 5 (1978): 482–495.

[79]Pfeffer, *Organizational Design,* p. 147.

as many manipulable variables in the environment and in the organization-environment links as in the organization itself, and these extraorganizational variables are often easier to change than the intra-organizational ones."[80] For example, a manufacturing firm having a difficult time securing a steady supply of raw materials at an acceptable price may decide to diversify (expand its boundaries) and become its own supplier. The vertical integration of oil companies, aluminum manufacturers, and even grocery chains such as Kroger and A&P are illustrative of this process.[81] Similarly, an organization may change its clientele, location, products, services, or even financing. Finally, if all else fails and environmental pressures become too great, an organization always has the option of totally withdrawing from its present domain and entering a new line of activity.

An Appraisal

The major theme of the preceding discussion is perhaps best reflected in Caplow's simple dictum that "no organization exists in a vacuum."[82] All must respond to the demands of their environment. The managerial processes going on within every organization are significantly affected by the uncertainties stemming from environmental factors. While a considerable body of research suggests that an appropriate "fit" between an organization's structure and its task environment does affect its operational effectiveness, the influence of managerial perceptions and strategic choice must also be considered.

In reflecting on this appraisal, it is apparent that our understanding of an organization's ability to adapt to its task environment is still limited. In too many instances, the relationship between environment and structure has been unclear. In recognizing this dilemma, Montanari and Morgan have noted that "inconsistent measures of environmental characteristics, small sample size and unique conceptualizations of structure (e.g. Differentiation and Integration by Lawrence and Lorsch) confound the environment-structure research results."[83]

In addition, while previous research has shown that organizations utilize a variety of strategies to deal with environmental uncertainty, as shown in Table 6–7, little is known of how organizations initially perceive, subsequently select, and finally imple-

[80]W. H. Starbuck and J. M. Dutton, "Designing Adaptive Organizations," *Journal of Business Policy* 3, no. 4 (1973): 21–28.

[81]R. A. Pitts, "Strategies and Structures for Diversification," *Academy of Management Journal* 20 (1977): 197–208.

[82]T. Caplow, *How to Run Any Organization: A Manual of Practical Sociology* (Hinsdale, Ill.: Dryden Press, 1976), p. 176.

[83]J. R. Montanari and C. P. Morgan, "An Expanded Theory of Structural Determination: An Empirical Investigation," (Paper presented at the 39th Annual Academy of Management Meeting, San Francisco, August 1978), pp. 5–6.

Table 6-7 *A Summary of Strategies for Minimizing Environmental Uncertainty*

Internal Strategies

1. Buffering
2. Smoothing
3. Forecasting
4. Rationing

External Strategies

Direct	*Indirect*
1. Competition	1. Favorable government regulations

2. Cooperation
   a. Bargaining
   b. Coopting
   c. Coalescing
	2. Trade and professional associations
	3. Lobbies and coordinating groups
	4. Etc.

ment such responses as buffering, smoothing, forecasting, rationing, bargaining, coopting, and coalescing. Specifically, as Miles and Snow note: "It is not known why specific responses are employed by some organizations but not others. Furthermore, there is little research evidence pertaining to the impact of these responses on either the organization or the environment. Of particular interest would be data suggesting the relative contribution of different forms of adjustment to organizational effectiveness."[84]

Another major limitation is that, while it is realized that organizational environments are continually evolving, there is little knowledge of how organizations modify themselves in response to environmental demands and opportunities over time. Most research has focused on a single point in time. Moreover, environment has been generally viewed as the "cause" (independent variable) of organizational uncertainty. As a result, the possibility of treating particular environmental elements as dependent variables and, thus, susceptible to organizational manipulation, has been largely overlooked. As mentioned earlier, there are organizations that have the capacity to alter their environment or at least to create environmental circumstances which better suit their needs. Such *proactive* organizations, particularly those operating in monopolistic and oligopolistic markets, often possess the ability to stimulate or even to manufacture demand for their products or services.

A final limitation concerns the role of managerial perceptions in influencing organizational responses. A much more thorough understanding is needed of how and why individual managers focus their attention on specific aspects of an environment to the exclusion of others, and of how they process the information received.

---

[84]Miles and Snow, *Organization Strategy,* p. 256.

Summary

In this chapter, we discussed the importance of an organization having the ability to adapt to changes that take place in the external environment in which it functions. It has been repeatedly stressed that organizations do not exist in isolation. As open systems they affect and are affected by the properties of their surrounding environment.

Throughout our discussion we have thus highlighted the continual interaction between organizations and their external environment. After first establishing what is meant by environment, the effect of social structure on the rate at which organizations are founded was briefly discussed. The focus here was on how environmental conditions affect the formation rate of new organizations. Next, we reviewed the various approaches that have been taken describing the dimensions and characteristics of the external environment in which organizations occur. Following this, we examined the more important studies exploring the relationship between an organization and its environment. At this point, we introduced the concepts of "enacted environment" and "strategic choice." Finally, we considered interorganizational relationships and discussed specific strategies used by organizations to minimize the uncertainties associated with their external environment.

Review and Discussion Questions

1. What is the relationship between an organization's environment and its task environment?
2. Distinguish between organizational domain and domain consensus.
3. Describe the two-way relationship that apparently exists between societal development and the emergence of organizations.
4. What is the primary conceptual difference between viewing an organization's environment in terms of major dimensions versus viewing it in terms of specific physical components?
5. Why would an organic system be inefficient in a stable environment?
6. Explain the relationship between environmental stability and degree of organizational subunit differentiation.
7. Explain the difference between the concepts "environment" and "perceived environment."
8. Contrast buffering and smoothing.
9. What is the relationship between smoothing and forecasting?
10. Why is rationing considered a "last resort" move?

References

Adams, J. S., "Interorganizational Processes and Organization Boundaries Activities." In *Research in Organizational Behavior*, vol. 2, edited by B. M. Staw and L. L. Cummings. Greenwich, Conn.: JAI Press, in press.

Aldag, R. J., and Storey, R. G. "Environmental Uncertainty: Comments on Objective and Perceptual Indices." In *Proceedings of the Annual Meeting of the Academy of Management,* edited by A. G. Bedeian, A. A. Armenakis, W. H. Holley, Jr., and H. S. Feild. Auburn, Ala.: Academy of Management, 1975.

Aldrich, H. E. *Organizations and Environments.* Englewood Cliffs, N.J.: Prentice-Hall, 1979.

Aldrich, H. E., and Herker, D. "Boundary Spanning Roles and Organization Structure." *Academy of Management Review* 2 (1977): 217–230.

Aldrich, H. E., and Pfeffer, J. "Environments of Organizations." *Annual Review of Sociology* 2 (1976): 79–105.

Anderson, C. R., and Paine, F. T. "Managerial Perceptions and Strategic Behavior." *Academy of Management Journal* 18 (1975): 811–823.

Bauer, R. A., Pool, S. I. de, and Dexter, L. A. *American Business and Public Policy: The Politics of Foreign Trade.* 2nd ed. New York: Atherton, 1972.

Berg, S. V., and Friedman, P. "Joint Ventures in American Industry—Part I." *Mergers & Acquisitions* 13, no. 2 (1978): 28–41.

Berg, S. V., and Friedman, P. "Joint Ventures in American Industry—Part II: Case Studies of Managerial Policy." *Mergers & Acquisitions* 13, no. 3 (1978): 9–17.

Berg, S. V., and Friedman, P. "Joint Ventures in American Industry—Part III: Public Policy Issues." *Mergers & Acquisitions* 14, no. 1 (1979): 18–29.

Blau, P. M., and Scott, W. R. *Formal Organizations.* San Francisco: Chandler, 1962.

Bobbitt, H. R., and Ford, J. D. "Decision-maker Choice as a Determinant of Organizational Structure." *Academy of Management Review,* in press.

Burns, T., and Stalker, G. M. *The Management of Innovation.* London: Tavistock, 1961.

Caplow, T. *How to Run Any Organization: A Manual of Practical Sociology.* Hinsdale, Ill.: Dryden Press, 1976.

Child, J. "Organizational Structure, Environment and Performance: The Role of Strategic Choice." *Sociology* 6 (1972): 1–21.

Cyert, R. M., and March, J. G. *A Behavioral Theory of the Firm.* Englewood Cliffs, N.J.: Prentice-Hall, 1963.

Dill, W. R. "Environment as an Influence on Managerial Autonomy." *Administrative Science Quarterly* 3 (1958): 409–443.

Dill, W. R. "The Impact of Environment on Organizational Development." In *Concepts and Issues in Administrative Behavior,* edited by S. Mailick and E. H. Van Ness. Englewood Cliffs, N.J.: Prentice-Hall, 1962.

Downey, H. K., and Slocum, J. W. "Uncertainty: Measures, Research, and Sources of Variation." *Academy of Management Journal* 18 (1975): 562–578.

Downey, H. K., Hellriegel, D., and Slocum, J. W. "Environmental Uncertainty: The Construct and Its Application." *Administrative Science Quarterly* 20 (1975): 613–629.

Downey, H. K., Hellriegel, D., and Slocum, J. W. "Individual Characteristics as Sources of Perceived Uncertainty Variability." *Human Relations* 30 (1977): 161–174.

Duncan, R. B. "Characteristics of Organizational Environments and Perceived Environmental Uncertainty." *Administrative Science Quarterly* 17 (1972): 313–327.

Duncan, R. B. "Modifications in Decision Structure in Adapting to the Environment: Some Implications for Organizational Learning." *Decision Sciences* 5 (1974): 705–725.

Duncan, R. B. "Multiple Decision Making Structures in Adapting to Environmental Uncertainty: The Impact of Organizational Effectiveness." *Human Relations* 26 (1973): 273–291.

Duncan, R. B. "What Is the Right Organization Structure? Decision Tree Analysis Provides the Answer." *Organizational Dynamics* 7, no. 3 (1979): 59–80.

Eldridge, J. E. T., and Crombie, A. D. *A Sociology of Organisations.* London: George Allen & Unwin, 1975.

Emery, F. E., and Trist, E. L. "The Causal Texture of Organizational Environments." *Human Relations* 18 (1965): 21–32.

Ermann, M. D., and Lundman, R. J. "Deviant Acts by Complex Organizations: Deviance and Social Control at the Organizational Level of Analysis." *Sociological Quarterly* 19 (1978): 55–67.

Evan, W. M. "The Organization-Set: Toward a Theory of Interorganizational Relations." In *Approaches to Organizational Design,* edited by J. D. Thompson. Pittsburgh: University of Pittsburgh Press, 1966.

Fennema, M., and Schijf, H. "Analysing Interlocking Directorates: Theory and Methods." *Social Networks* 1 (1978–79): 297–332.

Filley, A. C., House, R. J., and Kerr, S. *Managerial Process and Organizational Behavior.* 2nd ed. Glenview, Ill.: Scott Foresman, 1976.

The Organization and Its External Environment

Galbraith, J. R. *Organization Design.* Reading, Mass.: Addison-Wesley, 1977.

Gibson, J. L., Ivancevich, J. M., and Donnelly, J. H. *Organizations: Behavior, Structure, Processes.* 3rd ed. Dallas, Tex.: Business Publications, 1979.

Guetzkow, H. "Relations among Organizations." In *Studies on Behavior in Organizations: A Research Symposium,* edited by R. Bowers. Athens, Ga.: University of Georgia Press, 1966.

Hall, R. H. *Organizations: Structure and Process.* 2nd ed. Englewood Cliffs, N.J.: Prentice-Hall, 1977.

Hall, R. H. Review of *Organization and Environment: Managing Differentiation and Integration* by P. R. Lawrence and J. W. Lorsch. *Administrative Science Quarterly* 13 (1968): 180–186.

Hay, G. A., and Kelley, D. "An Empirical Study of Price Fixing Conspiracies." *Journal of Law & Economics* 17 (1974): 13–38.

Hirsch, P. M. "Organizational Effectiveness and the Institutional Environment." *Administrative Science Quarterly* 20 (1975): 327–343.

Hirsch, P. M. "Processing Fads and Fashions: An Organization-Set Analysis of Cultural Industry Systems." *American Journal of Sociology* 77 (1972): 639–659.

Huber, G. P., O'Connell, M. J., and Cummings, L. L. "Perceived Environmental Uncertainty: Effects of Information and Structure." *Academy of Management Journal* 18 (1975): 725–740.

Ivancevich, J. M., Szilagyi, A. D., and Wallace, M. J. *Organizational Behavior and Performance.* Santa Monica, Calif.: Goodyear, 1977.

Jacobs, D. "Dependency and Vulnerability: An Exchange Approach to the Control of Organizations." *Administrative Science Quarterly* 19 (1974): 45–59.

Kast, F. E., and Rosenzweig, J. E. *Organization and Management: A Systems and Contingency Approach.* 3rd ed. New York: McGraw-Hill, 1979.

Katz, D., and Kahn, R. L. *The Social Psychology of Organizations.* 2nd ed. New York: John Wiley & Sons, 1978.

Kefalas, A., and Schoderbeck, P. P. "Scanning the Business Environment—Some Empirical Findings." *Decision Sciences* 4 (1973): 63–74.

Lawrence, P. R., and Lorsch, J. W. "Differentiation and Integration in Complex Organizations." *Administrative Science Quarterly* 12 (1967): 1–47.

Lawrence, P. R., and Lorsch, J. W. *Organization and Environment: Managing Differentiation and Integration.* Boston: Division of Research, Graduate School of Business Administration, Harvard University, 1967.

Leifer, R., and Huber, G. P. "Relations among Perceived Environmental Uncertainty, Organization Structure, and Boundary-Spanning Behavior." *Administrative Science Quarterly* 22 (1977): 235–247.

Levine, S., and White, P. E. "Exchange as a Conceptual Framework for the Study of Interorganizational Relationships." *Administrative Science Quarterly* 5 (1961): 395–420.

Litterer, J. A. *The Analysis of Organizations.* 2nd ed. New York: John Wiley & Sons, 1973.

Macaulay, S. "Non-Contractural Relations in Business: A Preliminary Study." *American Sociological Review* 28 (1963): 55–67.

Meier, K. J., and Van Lohuizen, J. R. "Interest Groups in the Appropriations Process: The Wasted Profession Revisited." *Social Science Quarterly* 59 (1978): 482–495.

Merton, R. K. "The Role-Set: Problems in Sociological Theory." *British Journal of Sociology* 8 (1957): 106–120.

Miles, R. E., and Snow, C. C. *Organizational Strategy, Structure, and Process.* New York: McGraw-Hill, 1978.

Miles, R. E., Snow, C. C., and Pfeffer, J. "Organization-Environment: Concepts and Issues." *Industrial Relations* 13 (1974): 244–264.

Mintz, I. *U.S. Import Quotas: Costs and Consequences.* Washington, D.C.: American Enterprise Institute for Public Policy Research, 1973.

Montanari, J. R. "Managerial Discretion: An Expanded Model of Organizational Choice." *Academy of Management Review* 3 (1978): 231–241.

Montanari, J. R. "Strategic Choice: A Theoretical Analysis." *Journal of Management Studies* 16 (1979): 202–221.

Montanari, J. R., and Morgan, C. P. "An Expanded Theory of Structural Determination: An Empirical Investigation." Paper presented at the 39th Annual National Academy of Management Meeting, August 1978, San Francisco, Calif.

Pennings, J. M. "The Relevance of the Structural-Contingency Model for Organizational Effectiveness." *Administrative Science Quarterly* 20 (1975): 393–410.

Pfeffer, J. "Administration Regulation and Licensing: Social Problem or Solution?" *Social Problems* 21 (1974): 468–479.

Chapter 6

Pfeffer, J. "Cooptation and the Composition of Electric Utility Boards of Directors." *Pacific Sociological Review* 17 (1974): 333–363.

Pfeffer, J. "Merger as a Response to Organizational Interdependence." *Administrative Science Quarterly* 17 (1972): 382–394.

Pfeffer, J. *Organizational Design.* Arlington Heights, Ill.: AHM Publishing, 1978.

Pfeffer, J. "Size and Composition of Corporate Boards of Directors: The Organization and Its Environment." *Administrative Science Quarterly* 17 (1972): 218–228.

Pfeffer, J. "Size, Composition and Function of Hospital Boards of Directors: A Study of Organization-Environment Linkage." *Administrative Science Quarterly* 18 (1973): 349–364.

Pfeffer, J. "Some Evidence on Occupational Licensing and Occupational Incomes." *Social Forces* 53 (1974): 102–111.

Pfeffer, J., and Salancik, G. R. *The External Control of Organizations: A Resource Dependence Perspective.* New York: Harper & Row, 1978.

Pitts, R. A. "Strategies and Structures for Diversification." *Academy of Management Journal* 20 (1977): 197–208.

Porter, M. E. "How Competitive Forces Shape Strategy." *Harvard Business Review* 57, no. 2 (1979): 137–145.

Riggs, F. W. "Organizational Structures and Contexts." *Administration & Society* 7 (1975): 150–190.

Selznick, P. "Foundations of the Theory of Organizations." *American Sociological Review* 13 (1948): 25–35.

Selznick, P. *TVA and the Grass Roots: A Study in the Sociology of Formal Organization.* Berkeley, Calif.: University of California Press, 1949.

Sethi, N. S. "A Research Model to Study the Environmental Factors in Management." *Management International Review* 10, no. 6 (1970): 75–81.

Silverman, D. *The Theory of Organisations.* New York: Basic Books, 1971.

Snow, C. C., and Darran, D. C. "Organizational Adaptation to the Environment: A Review." In *Proceedings of the Annual Meeting of the American Institute for Decision Sciences,* edited by M. W. Hopfe and H. C. Schneider. Cincinnati, Ohio: American Institute for Decision Sciences, 1975.

Starbuck, W. H. "Organizations and Their Environments." In *Handbook of Industrial and Organizational Psychology,* edited by M. D. Dunnette. Chicago: Rand McNally, 1976.

Starbuck, W. H., and Dutton, J. M. "Designing Adaptive Organizations." *Journal of Business Policy* 3, no. 4 (1973): 21–28.

Staw, B. M., and Szawjkowski, E. "The Scarcity-Munificence Component of Environments and the Commission of Illegal Acts." *Administrative Science Quarterly* 20 (1975): 345–353.

Steers, R. M. *Organizational Effectiveness: A Behavioral View.* Santa Monica, Calif.: Goodyear, 1977.

Stinchcombe, A. L. "Social Structure and Organizations." In *Handbook of Organization,* edited by J. G. March. Chicago: Rand McNally, 1965.

Terreberry, S. "The Evolution of Organizational Environments." *Administrative Science Quarterly* 12 (1968): 590–613.

Thompson, J. D. *Organizations in Action.* New York: McGraw-Hill, 1967.

Thompson, J. D., and McEwen, W. J. "Organizational Goals and Environment: Goal-Setting as an Interaction Process." *American Sociological Review* 23 (1958): 23–31.

Tosi, H. L., Aldag, R. J., and Storey, R. G. "On the Measurement of the Environment: An Assessment of the Lawrence and Lorsch Environmental Subscale." *Administrative Science Quarterly* 18 (1973): 27–36.

U.S. Congress, Senate, Committee on Government Affairs. *Interlocking Directorates among the Major U.S. Corporations.* Washington, D.C.: U.S. Government Printing Office, 1978.

Weick, K. E. "Enactment Processes in Organizations." In *New Directions in Organizational Behavior,* edited by B. M. Staw and G. R. Salancik. Chicago: St. Clair Press, 1977.

Weick, K. E. *The Social Psychology of Organizing.* Reading, Mass.: Addison-Wesley, 1969.

Wilkinson, I., and Kipnis, O. "Interfirm Use of Power." *Journal of Applied Psychology* 63 (1978): 315–320.

The Growth and Development of Organizations

The Growth and Development of Organizations

Chapter 7

As suggested in Chapter 6, organizations do not exist in a steady state. Assuming that they are able to successfully adapt to their surrounding environment, organizations not only endure, they also tend to grow and develop. [1] *It is this growth and development that forms the basis for the discussion in the first part of this chapter. Echoing the earlier observation of Blau and Scott, it is specifically noted that "large and complex formal organizations do not spring into existence full-blown but develop out of simpler ones."* [2] *With large organizations increasing in number as well as significance, it is important to better understand the patterns and forces of organizational growth. Through such an understanding, we will be better able to predict, and thus may be better able to control, what happens as an organization develops.*

Belief in the existence of a process of organizational evolution and development may be traced to the works of such early economists as Alfred Marshall (1842–1924). [3] *More recently, however, renewed interest in a "life cycle" of organizational development and in the forces that determine an organization's birth, growth, and decline can be credited to the research of Chandler.* [4] *Based on an analysis of the historical growth and configuration of some seventy large U.S. companies —particularly DuPont, General Motors, Standard Oil of New Jersey, and Sears, Roebuck— Chandler was able to identify several characteristic business strategies, each associated with a distinctive organization structure. He was also able to identify a characteristic developmental sequence. For example, he found that the strategy of vertical integration administered through a centralized structure tends to be followed by a strategy of diversification administered via a decentralized structure. Chandler's work thus suggested a developmental model of organization growth based on two areas of managerial choice: strategy and structure.* [5]

---

[1] H. G. Hicks and C. R. Gullett, *Organizations: Theory and Behavior* (New York: McGraw-Hill, 1975), p. 65.

[2] P. M. Blau and W. R. Scott, *Formal Organizations: A Comparative Approach* (San Francisco: Chandler, 1962), p. 224.

[3] E. T. Penrose, *The Theory of the Growth of the Firm* (New York: John Wiley & Sons, 1959), p. 89n.

[4] A. D. Chandler, *Strategy and Structure: Chapters in the History of the American Enterprise* (Cambridge, Mass.: M.I.T. Press, 1962).

[5] B. R. Scott, "The Industrial State: Old Myths and New Realities," *Harvard Business Review* 51, no. 2 (1973):133–149.

The two final parts of the present chapter will be devoted to a discussion of organizational size. An obvious and important aspect of growth, size, unlike other organizational attributes, can be easily observed and measured. In reviewing the literature dealing with the structural evolution of organizations, it is frequently evident, however, that much confusion has resulted from the almost interchangeable use of the terms "growth" and "size." As noted by Litterer: "Growth is a process internal to the organization which brings about certain directions of development. . . . Size, on the other hand, is something which results from growth. To suggest, as is sometimes done, that a change from one size to another is growth confuses effect with cause. Such a view may also obscure the fact that growth can be manifest in ways other than changes in size."[6] Thus, while size (number of employees) may be one aspect of growth, other important aspects include sales volume, net assets, market share, units of production or service, and so on.

Organizational Growth
Motives for Growth

Given that there is a lack of empirical evidence concerning the specific goals of either individual organizational members or dominant coalitions within organizations, it seems reasonable to argue that there are probably numerous motives for organizational growth. In what is undoubtedly still the most extensive review of the literature in this area, Starbuck enumerated ten possible alternative and complementary goals related to growth. Three are associated with the motives of individual organizational members: the desire for (1) adventure and risk; (2) prestige, power, and job security; and (3) increased compensation. Three are associated with the "problems and aesthetics" of administering an organization: the desire for (4) "organizational self-realization"; (5) a stable environment; and (6) organizational survival. And four are associated with "organizational purpose and effectiveness": (7) increased profit; (8) increased revenue; (9) decreased costs via economies of scale; and (10) monopolistic power.[7]

As should be obvious from the foregoing, the growth of an organization is more than a chance occurrence. As stated by Starbuck: "Growth is not spontaneous. It is a consequence of decisions."[8] That is, organizational expansion is dependent upon a host of specific managerial decisions (for example, decisions to increase output to meet demand, decisions to hire or fire, and so on) combined with the appropriate execution of the actions that follow from them. These decisions, in turn, are related to the goals pursued by an organization's members. This latter point serves to underscore the very important fact that organizational growth can continue only so long as the goals of an organization are met or the goals of at least some of its members are achieved.

---

[6]J. A. Litterer, *The Analysis of Organizations,* 2nd ed. (New York: John Wiley & Sons, 1973), pp. 651–652.
[7]W. H. Starbuck, "Organizational Growth and Development," in *Handbook of Organizations,* ed. J. G. March (Chicago: Rand McNally, 1965), pp. 451–533.
[8]Ibid., p. 453.

Models of Growth

As suggested earlier, as organizations grow in response to their environment, they follow certain patterns of evolution and development. Numerous models have been created to describe this process. Three of the most meaningful form the basis of the following discussion.

The Lippitt-Schmidt Model

Based on the corporate life cycle concept, the Lippitt-Schmidt model suggests that organizations normally experience three stages in their development: birth, youth, and maturity.[9] Lippitt and Schmidt contend that, as an organization enters each of these stages, it encounters a predictable series of "critical concerns" accompanied by recognizable "key issues" and "results" (see Table 7–1). Of fundamental importance to understanding this model is the thesis that a true measure of an organization's stage of development is best gained through an analysis of how it handles predictable organizational crises, rather than through simply making judgments based on its age or economic size. Consequently, a relatively small (or newly-founded) organization may (rapidly) achieve developmental maturity, and a relatively large (or comparatively older) organization may remain youthful. In addition, Lippitt and Schmidt emphasize that the managerial capabilities required at the various stages in an organization's life cycle vary according to the "critical concerns" encountered and the needs for action that are precipitated (see Table 7–2). As a result, they contend that the knowledge, skills, and attitudes that serve to make managers effective at one developmental stage may make them ineffective at another stage.

The Scott Model

Perhaps the most popular and widely quoted of the corporate life cycle theories, the Scott model of organizational growth and development, was derived directly from Chandler's research discussed earlier. The model, initially formulated in 1963, is summarized in Table 7–3.[10] It states that, as an organization grows, it will move from Stage I to Stage II to Stage III in sequence. As can be seen from the descriptions provided, the characteristics of a given company at each stage tend to be quite distinct from one another. As described by Scott, the three stages of growth are not small, medium, and large but *small, integrated,* and *diversified.* The major feature of the Stage I organization is that it is largely a "one person show." Typically a small, owner run concern, its strengths and weaknesses are primarily reflections of the personality, knowledge, and financial resources of its founder. As illustrated in Figure

---

[9] G. L. Lippitt and W. H. Schmidt, "Crises in a Developing Organization," *Harvard Business Review* 45, no. 6 (1967): 102–112; G. L. Lippitt, *Organizational Renewal* (New York: Appleton-Century-Crofts, 1969), pp. 26–41.
[10] B. R. Scott, *Stages of Corporate Development—Part I,* case no. 9–371–294 (Boston: Intercollegiate Case Clearing House, Harvard Business School, 1971).

Table 7-1 *Stages of Organizational Development and Results of Handling Critical Issues*

Developmental Stage	Critical Concerns	Key Issues	Result If the Issue Is Resolved	
			Correctly	Incorrectly
Birth	1. To create a new organization	What to risk	New corporate system comes into being and begins operating.	Idea remains abstract. Company is under-capitalized and cannot adequately develop and expose product or service.
	2. To survive as a viable system	What to sacrifice	Organization accepts realities, learns from experience, becomes viable.	Organization fails to adjust to realities of its environment and either dies or remains marginal – demanding continuing sacrifice.
Youth	3. To gain stability	How to organize	Organization develops efficiency and strength, but retains flexibility in face of change.	Organization overextends itself and returns to survival stage, or establishes stabilizing patterns that block future flexibility.
	4. To gain reputation and develop pride	How to review and evaluate	Organization's reputation reinforces efforts to improve quality of goods and service.	Organization places more emphasis on image creation than on quality product, or it builds an image that misrepresents its true capability.
Maturity	5. To achieve uniqueness and adaptability	Whether and how to change	Organization changes to take fuller advantage of its unique capability and provides growth opportunities for its personnel.	Organization develops too narrow a specialty to ensure security in future, fails to discover its uniqueness and spreads its effort into inappropriate areas, or develops a paternalistic stance that inhibits growth.
	6. To contribute to society	Whether and how to share	Organization gains public respect and appreciation as an institution contributing to society.	Organization may be accused of "public be damned" and similar attitudes.

Source: Adapted by permission of the *Harvard Business Review*. Exhibit from "Crises in a Developing Organization" by G. L. Lippitt and W. H. Schmidt, November–December 1967, pp. 103, 109. Copyright © 1967 by the President and Fellows of Harvard College; all rights reserved.

Chapter 7

Table 7–2 *The Knowledge, Skills, and Attitudes Required to Deal with Each Critical Concern*

Critical Concern	Knowledge	Skills	Attitudes
1. To create a system	Clearly perceived short-range objective in mind of top man	Ability to transmit knowledge into action by self and into orders to others	Belief in own ability, product, and market
2. To survive	The short-range objectives that need to be communicated	Communications know-how; ability to adjust to changing conditions	Faith in future
3. To stabilize	How top man can predict relevant factors and make long-range plans	Ability to transmit planning knowledge into communicable objectives	Trust in other members of organization
4. To earn good reputation	Planning know-how and understanding of goals on part of whole executive team	Ability to allow others a voice in decision making, involve others in decision making and obtain commitments from them, and communicate objectives to customers	Interest in customers
5. To achieve uniqueness	Understanding on part of policy team of how others should set own objectives, and of how to manage sub-units of the organization	Ability to teach others to plan; proficiency in integrating plans of subunits into objectives and resources of organization	Self-confidence
6. To earn respect and appreciation	General understanding of the larger objectives of organization and of society	Ability to use own organization and resources in dealing with the problems of the larger community	Sense of responsibility to society and to mankind

7–1, the organization chart of a Stage I company is generally a simple one-unit concern with a single product or limited line of products and with most employees operating under the direct supervision of the company's owner-manager. Well-known business figures who began their careers as Stage I company managers include Henry Ford, Andrew Carnegie, John D. Rockefeller, and the Krupps.

The distinguishing feature of the Stage II organization is that it is an integrated, multi-functional company operating with a single product line (see Figure 7–1). Staffed by professional managers, Stage II organizations grow through both product and geographical diversification. As noted by Thain:

The size, scope, and resources of Stage II companies vary widely—some of the largest companies in the world in industries such as steel, oil, and agricultural implements are basically Stage II. Ownership is usually public, but may be private or personal. The great strength of a Stage II company lies in its concentration and specialization in one field. Its great vulnerability is that all its eggs are in one basket. Stage II companies tend to be strong in solving functional and product problems and

The Growth and Development of Organizations

Table 7–3 *The Three Stages of Organizational Development*

Company Characteristics	Stage I	Stage II	Stage III
Product line	Single product or single line	Single product line	Multiple product lines
Distribution	One channel or set of channels	One set of channels	Multiple channels
Organization structure	Little or no formal structure; "one-man show"	Specialization based on function	Specialization based on product market relationships
Product-service transactions	Not applicable	Integrated pattern of transactions [A → B → C → Markets]	Nonintegrated pattern of transactions [A B C → Markets]
R&D organization	Not institutionalized; guided by owner-manager	Increasingly institutionalized search for product or process improvements	Institutionalized search for *new* products as well as for improvements
Performance measurement	By personal contact and subjective criteria	Increasingly impersonal, using technical and/or cost criteria	Increasingly impersonal, using *market* criteria (return on investment and market share)
Rewards	Unsystematic and often paternalistic	Increasingly systematic, with emphasis on stability and service	Increasingly systematic, with variability related to performance
Control system	Personal control of both strategic and operating decisions	Personal control of strategic decisions, with increasing delegation of operating decisions through policy	Delegation of product-market decisions within existing businesses, with indirect control based on analysis of "results"
Strategic choices	Needs of owner versus needs of company	Degree of integration; market-share objective; breadth of product line	Entry and exit from industries; allocation of resources by industry; rate of growth

weak in coping with basic market changes and the general management problems related to strategic changes.[11]

John Deere, Kennecott Copper, and General Foods are well-known examples of Stage II organizations.

The major characteristic of the Stage III organization is the shift to a large multi-unit structure having a general office and decentralized product divisions (see Figure 7–1). Each division represents a largely autonomous functional organization producing a single product or single line. In addition, each division is a relatively

[11]D. H. Thain, "Stages of Corporate Development," *Business Quarterly* 34 (1969): 35–36.

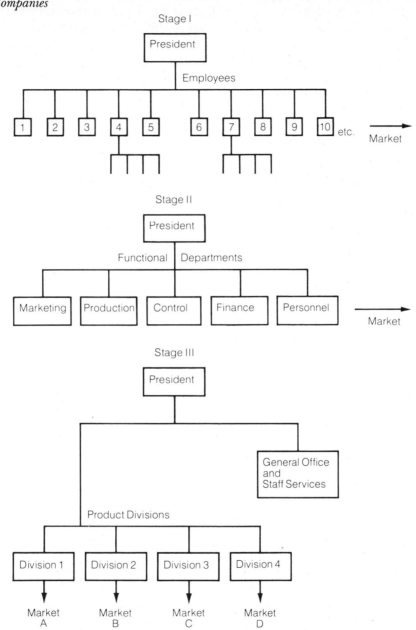

Source: D. H. Thain, "Stages of Corporate Development," *Business Quarterly* 34 (1969): 36. Reprinted by permission of the *Business Quarterly,* published by the School of Business, the University of Western Ontario.

The Growth and Development of Organizations

independent profit center. Examples of well-known Stage III organizations include General Motors, DuPont, Westinghouse, IBM, and Xerox.

Upon reflection, it is clear that the essence of the Scott model involves the same two critical areas of managerial choice emphasized by Chandler—strategy and structure.[12] Thus, Scott refers to each of the three stages of his model as consisting of a "distinctive set of managerial characteristics," as a "distinctive way of life."[13] Each stage is considered to represent not just a phase of potential historical transition but, in Scott's words, a "way of managing."[14] In this regard, it is important to realize that the Scott model suggests that an organization's strategy shapes its structure, rather than vice versa. Stated differently, the Scott model suggests that management adjusts structures to suit strategies, rather than modifying strategies to match established structures. In the main, the interpretation that structure follows strategy is clearly consistent with the central findings in the work of Chandler mentioned earlier.

The Greiner Model

Based on an analysis of numerous case studies of corporate development, the Greiner model is essentially a theory of organizational adjustment.[15] It argues that growing organizations pass through at least five successive phases of development. Each phase is comprised of a relatively calm and prolonged period of growth, referred to as an *evolutionary stage,* which ends with a management crisis characterized by substantial internal turmoil. This period of crisis is referred to as *revolution.* Greiner argues that only a limited range of alternatives are available to solve the crises associated with each period of growth and that decisions made in any one period strongly influence the alternatives available in succeeding periods. Moreover, it is Greiner's contention that the future growth of an organization, in all likelihood, will be determined more by these past decisions than by present events or outside forces, such as market conditions. Thus, somewhat paradoxically, Greiner avers that the management of an organization, by learning more about its past, will be in a better position to determine its future.

There are five key dimensions in the Greiner model:

1. Organizational age
2. Organizational size
3. Stages of evolution
4. Stages of revolution
5. Industry growth rate

---

[12]Chandler, *Strategy and Structure,* p. 49.
[13]Scott, "The Industrial State," p. 137.
[14]Scott, *Stages of Corporate Development,* p. 4.
[15]L. E. Greiner, "Evolution and Revolution as Organizations Grow," *Harvard Business Review* 50, no. 4 (1972): 37–46.

Age is considered to be the most essential dimension in the model, since current management problems are believed to be a function of past decisions. *Size* is also adjudged to be important, since an organization's problems (and their potential solutions) are thought to vary markedly as work force and sales volume increase. For instance, as such changes in size occur, problems of communication and coordination intensify, new roles develop, and jobs invariably become more interrelated. Greiner contends that, as organizations age and increase in size, they tend to enter a period of uninterrupted growth, or what he refers to as an *evolutionary stage.* Smooth evolution, however, is not inevitable. As an organization increases in both age and size, it finds that the management practices appropriate to an earlier phase of development become inappropriate for sustained growth. The ensuing economic setback and internal disruption mark what Greiner refers to as a *stage of revolution.* The critical task for management in such periods is identifying and implementing new procedures for a new stage of evolutionary growth. Ironically, these new procedures will eventually become inappropriate in turn, leading to another period of revolution. Thus, in a very real sense, each stage of evolution is seen as "breeding" its own revolution. The speed with which periods of evolution are punctuated by revolution is believed to be closely related to the *growth rate* of an organization's task environment. That is, periods of evolution tend to be shorter in rapidly expanding industries than they are in mature or slowly growing industries. The combined effects of the five dimensions critical to the Greiner model are illustrated in Figure 7–2.

The five phases of organizational growth identified by the model are shown in Figure 7–3. As explained by Greiner, "Each evolutionary period is characterized by the dominant *management style* used to achieve growth, while each revolutionary period is characterized by the dominant *management problem* that must be solved before growth can continue."[16] As Figure 7–3 suggests, the *first* problem or crisis typically confronted by a new organization following its birth is leadership. In such situations, an organization's founders are usually technically oriented, devoting a majority of their time to the manufacture and selling of the concern's new product. Since the organization is loosely organized, communication is frequent and informal. The organization is comprised of a small group of dedicated workers. *Esprit de corps* is high. As the company grows, however, each of the individualistic activities essential for a new undertaking quickly becomes ineffective. Steady increase in the number of employees makes it more and more difficult to manage by relying only on informal means of communication. Moreover, the organization's founders find themselves saddled with unwanted management responsibilities requiring skills that they most likely do not possess. The first critical developmental choice occurs at this point—a qualified professional manager must be located and enticed to join the organization.

The *second* crisis encountered is one of autonomy. While directive management techniques enable the organization to embark on a second period of growth, they

---

[16]Ibid., p. 40.

The Growth and Development of Organizations

Figure 7–2 *Model of Organizational Development*

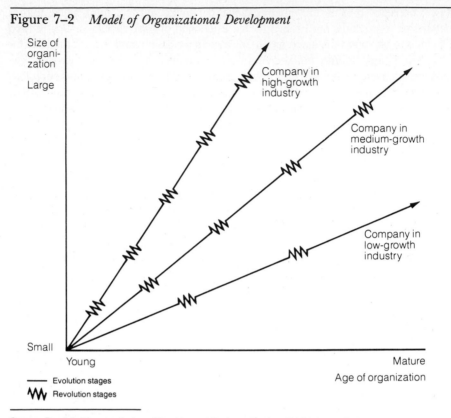

Source: Reprinted by permission of the *Harvard Business Review*. Exhibit from "Evolution and Revolution as Organizations Grow" by L. E. Greiner, July–August 1972, p. 39. Copyright © 1972 by the President and Fellows of Harvard College; all rights reserved.

Chapter 7

Figure 7–3 *The Five Phases of Growth*

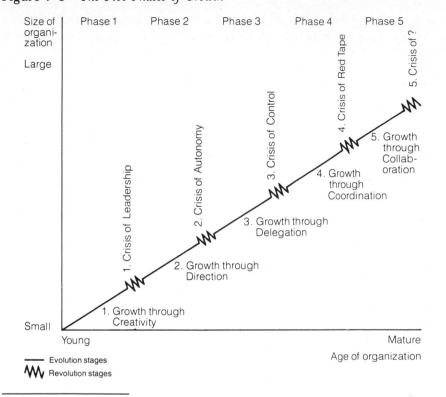

Evolution stages
Revolution stages

The Growth and Development of Organizations

eventually become inappropriate as the organization becomes larger and more diverse. Lower level managers, often possessing more knowledge than executives at the top do, find themselves burdened with an overly centralized and impersonal hierarchy. A solution to this crisis is most often achieved through a greater delegation of authority.

The *next* crisis that evolves is the crisis of control. As an organization continues to grow through various forms of diversification, upper level management fears that it may be losing control over a highly decentralized field operation. Being highly independent, field managers prefer running their own shows and resent having to coordinate their activities with the rest of the organization. Special coordinating techniques, such as product groups, formal planning procedures, and company-wide control programs, are generally the solution to this management problem.

The *fourth* crisis is one of red tape. While the introduction of formal systems for increasing coordination leads to a more efficient allocation of resources, a lack of trust gradually develops between headquarters and the field, and as a consequence, line-staff conflicts gradually emerge. Line managers increasingly resent the paperwork and programs originated by staff personnel unfamiliar with local conditions. Staff, in turn, complain about what they consider to be uncooperative and uninformed line managers. Soon, both groups condemn the bureaucratic maze that has developed. Unless the existing situation is quickly brought under control, means become ends unto themselves and procedures take precedence over problem solving.

The solution to the red-tape crisis involves moving into the *final* observable phase of the model. Whereas Phase 4 was characterized by formal systems and procedures, the dominant style used to achieve growth in Phase 5 involves strong interpersonal collaboration. Formal control is replaced by social control and self-discipline. As Figure 7–3 implies, the nature of the revolution in response to this stage of evolution is still unclear. While both U.S. and European companies are experimenting with new practices to encourage greater spontaneity within organizations, there is as yet little clear evidence concerning the outcome of their efforts.[17]

Like both the Lippitt-Schmidt model and the Scott model, the Greiner model is clearly an oversimplification intended to underscore the problems that organizations encounter in the process of evolution. The central message of the foregoing discussion, however, seems clear: Basic changes in structure are required as growing organizations develop new strategies for coping with the fluctuating demands of their task environment. It may thus be reasonably argued that, to the extent that researchers continue to explore the specific problems associated with the processes of development, our ability to understand, predict, and more effectively control the evolution of organizations will be enhanced.

---

[17]W. F. Dowling, "Job Redesign on the Assembly Line: Farewell to Blue-Collar Blues," *Organizational Dynamics* 2, no. 2 (1973): 51–67.

Organizational Decline and Death

Before ending our discussion of organizational growth and development, some comment on organizational decline and death seems appropriate. This is particularly so since the bankruptcies of the Penn Central, once our nation's largest railroad, and W. T. Grant, once one of the world's largest retailers, in 1970 and 1975 respectively, have led to an increased interest in business failures.

As reported by Dun & Bradstreet, 7,919 businesses failed in the United States during 1977, down 17.7 per cent from 9,628 in 1976 and off 30.7 per cent from an eight-year peak of 11,432 reached in 1975. This slackening of casualties, however, was offset by a 2.8 per cent increase in aggregate dollar liabilities of $3.1 billion. At the same time, these failures resulted in a higher average liability per failure, $390,872 in 1977 versus the 1976 average of $312,762. These totals, along with similar data for the years 1920 through 1976, are presented in Table 7–4. As indicated, business failures reached a peak in 1932 (an annual rate of 1.5 per cent) and stood at a twenty-five-year low in 1977.

It should be noted, however, that the statistics contained in Table 7–4 are somewhat misleading, masking what Stinchcombe has termed the *liability of newness*.[18] That is, Dun & Bradstreet records reveal that over half (53.1 per cent) of the businesses that failed in 1977 were five years of age or less.[19] This compares with a mortality rate of 19.4 per cent for businesses that have weathered at least ten years of operation. Without doubt, the first five years of a business's existence are its hardest. As Gross has observed, new businesses are "particularly subject to economic fluctuations, strong competition, and unforeseen technological changes."[20] In addition, many new businesses attempt to compete in markets dominated by established firms with established economies of scale, credit sources, channels of distribution, and product lines. Organizations capable of displacing such competition are rarely built quickly. This point is underscored by Hannan and Freeman's finding that, of the 500 industrial corporations identified by *Fortune* magazine in 1955 as being our nation's largest, almost 90 per cent—excluding the effects of mergers—were still among this group in 1975.[21] Almost identical results have been reported for the United Kingdom.[22]

While those factors are primarily external, internal factors also contribute to the downfall of many businesses. As shown in Table 7–5, over 90 per cent of the 7,919 business failures occurring in 1977 resulted from managerial inexperience and

---

[18]A. L. Stinchcombe, "Social Structures and Organizations," in *Handbook of Organizations*, ed. J. G. March (Chicago: Rand McNally, 1965), p. 148.

[19]*The Business Failure Record* (New York: Dun & Bradstreet, 1978), p. 10.

[20]B. M. Gross, *Organizations and Their Managing* (New York: Free Press, 1968), p. 459.

[21]M. T. Hannan and J. H. Freeman, "The Population Ecology of Organizations," *American Journal of Sociology* 82 (1977): 929–964.

[22]G. Whittington, "Changes in the Top 100 Quoted Manufacturing Companies in the United Kingdom 1948 to 1968," *Journal of Industrial Economics* 21 (1972): 17–34.

Table 7-4 *Trends in Business Failure, 1920–1977*

Year	Number of Failures	Total Failure Liabilities	Failure Rate per 10,000 Listed Concerns	Average Liability per Failure
1920	8,881	$ 295,121,000	48	$ 33,230
1921	19,652	627,401,000	102	31,926
1922	23,676	623,895,000	120	26,351
1923	18,718	539,387,000	93	28,817
1924	20,615	543,226,000	100	26,351
1925	21,214	443,744,000	100	20,918
1926	21,773	409,233,000	101	18,795
1927	23,146	520,105,000	106	22,471
1928	23,842	489,559,000	109	20,534
1929	22,909	483,252,000	104	21,094
1930	26,355	668,282,000	122	25,357
1931	28,285	736,310,000	133	26,032
1932	31,822	928,313,000	154	29,172
1933	19,859	457,520,000	100	23,038
1934	12,091	333,959,000	61	27,621
1935	12,244	310,580,000	62	25,366
1936	9,607	203,173,000	48	21,148
1937	9,490	183,253,000	46	19,310
1938	12,836	246,505,000	61	19,204
1939	14,768	182,520,000	70	12,359
1940	13,619	166,684,000	63	12,239
1941	11,848	136,104,000	55	11,488
1942	9,405	100,763,000	45	10,713
1943	3,221	45,339,000	16	14,076
1944	1,222	31,660,000	7	25,908
1945	809	30,225,000	4	37,361
1946	1,129	67,349,000	5	59,654
1947	3,474	204,612,000	14	58,898
1948	5,250	234,620,000	20	44,690
1949	9,246	308,109,000	34	33,323
1950	9,162	248,283,000	34	27,099
1951	8,058	259,547,000	31	32,210
1952	7,611	283,314,000	29	37,224
1953	8,862	394,153,000	33	44,477
1954	11,086	462,628,000	42	41,731
1955	10,969	449,380,000	42	40,968
1956	12,686	562,697,000	48	44,356
1957	13,739	615,293,000	52	44,784
1958	14,964	728,258,000	56	48,667
1959	14,053	692,808,000	52	49,300
1960	15,445	938,630,000	57	60,772
1961	17,075	1,090,123,000	64	63,843
1962	15,782	1,213,601,000	61	76,898
1963	14,374	1,352,593,000	56	94,100
1964	13,501	1,329,223,000	53	98,454

1965	13,514	1,321,666,000	53	97,800
1966	13,061	1,385,659,000	52	106,091
1967	12,364	1,265,227,000	49	102,332
1968	9,636	940,996,000	39	97,654
1969	9,154	1,142,113,000	37	124,767
1970	10,748	1,887,754,000	44	175,638
1971	10,326	1,916,929,000	42	185,641
1972	9,566	2,000,244,000	38	209,099
1973	9,345	2,298,606,000	36	245,972
1974	9,915	3,053,137,000	38	307,931
1975	11,432	4,380,170,000	43	383,150
1976	9,628	3,011,271,000	35	312,762
1977	7,919	3,095,317,000	28	390,872

Source: *The Business Failure Record* (New York: Dun & Bradstreet, 1978), p. 2. Used by permission of Dun & Bradstreet.

ineptitude, as evidenced by such factors as inadequate sales, heavy operating expenses, and receivables difficulties. Interestingly, a longitudinal analysis of Dun & Bradstreet data indicates that these same causes have persisted for at least the last twenty years, maintaining a similar level of importance across all industry groups.[23]

Two conclusions can be drawn from these data. First, on a practical level, many new ventures are in trouble from the beginning, seemingly unable to survive the traumas associated with birth. Second, on a more theoretical level, while the figures presented do attest to a certain dynamism within the business world, they at the same time suggest that the ability of the business environment to support its population is undeniably limited.

Organizational Size and Structural Configuration

As the preceding discussion clearly suggests, organizational growth by its very nature involves increasing complexity. "As an organization grows, its structure naturally becomes more complicated. Jobs that could once be handled by a single person are split and split again; new layers of supervision are inserted between the top man and

---

[23]J. R. Cesta and V. P. Apilado, "Business Bankruptcies: Variations and Associative Factors," paper presented at the Midwest Finance Association annual meeting, St. Louis, Mo., April 1977, pp. 17–18.

Table 7—5
Causes of 7,919 Business Failures in 1977[a]

Underlying Causes	Percent		Apparent Causes	Percent
Neglect	0.9	Due to—	Bad habits	0.2
			Poor health	0.3
			Marital difficulties	0.2
			Other	0.2
Fraud	0.4	On the part of the principals, reflected by—	Misleading name	—
			False financial statement	0.1
			Premeditated overbuy	0.0
			Irregular disposal of assets	0.1
			Other	0.2
Lack of experience in the line	11.3	Evidenced by inability to avoid conditions which resulted in—	Inadequate sales	53.9
Lack of managerial experience	14.6		Heavy operating expenses	17.0
			Receivables difficulties	7.7
Unbalanced experience[b]	22.6		Inventory difficulties	6.3
Incompetence	44.6		Excessive fixed assets	2.8
			Poor location	1.9
			Competitive weakness	24.0
			Other	1.4
Disaster	0.5	Some of these occurrences could have been provided against through insurance—	Fire	0.3
			Flood	0.0
			Burglary	—
			Employees' fraud	0.0
			Strike	0.0
			Other	0.2
Reason unknown	5.1			
Total	100.0		Percent of total failures	100.0[c]
Number of failures	7,919			
Average liabilities per failure	$390,872			

Source: Adapted from *The Business Failure Record* (New York: Dun & Bradstreet, 1978), pp. 12–13. Used by permission of Dun & Bradstreet.

[a]Classification failures based on opinion of informed creditors and information in Dun & Bradstreet reports.

[b]Experience not well rounded in sales, finance, purchasing, and production on the part of the individual in case of a proprietorship, or of two or more officers constituting a management unit.

[c]Because some failures are attributed to a combination of apparent causes, the totals of these columns exceed the totals of the corresponding columns on the left.

the rank and file."[24] The remaining sections of this chapter are devoted to a discussion of the relative influence of size as it affects organization structure. As previously noted, size (as used here, number of employees) is an obvious and important aspect of growth. Extensive research has been devoted to the study of the relationships between size and (a) various dimensions of structure and (b) what has been termed *administrative intensity.* Each of these relationships will be discussed in turn.

[24]E. Dale, ed., *Readings in Management: Landmarks and New Frontiers,* 3rd ed. (New York: McGraw-Hill, 1975), p. 214.

Simple to Complex

Systematic change in structural configuration as a function of organizational size has been the focus of considerable study. In general, research supports the view that the transition from a simple organization to a complex one is a function of size. As an organization increases in size, there comes a point at which a simple structure is no longer effective, and it is forced to realign duties and responsibilities and, more often than not, add new integrating (coordinating) units. The transition from a simple to a complex system has been well documented by Herbst. In an investigation of the efficiency of retail stores in Great Britain, he provides data which indicate that

as the size of the simple system increases, and depending on the extent of both its internal and external linkages, more and more work has to be carried out on the coordination of component functioning, so that a critical boundary value with respect to size is reached, beyond which intrinsic regulation breaks down. An increase in size beyond this point will become possible by differentiating out a separate integrating unit, which takes over the function of both control and coordination of component units, thus leading to a transition from a simple to a complex system.[25]

The nature of the actual transition Herbst speaks of is illustrated in Figures 7–4 through 7–6. Beginning with Figure 7–4, it is clear that for a simple system such as a small retail store, the relationship between sales and number of employees (size) is perfectly linear. As demand increases sales, additional employees are hired. As demand decreases, employment is reduced, thus maintaining an equilibrium between sales and number of employees. In this context, the efforts of each employee contribute directly to increased sales.

As an organization increases in size, however, a critical point is soon reached beyond which it cannot maintain itself without establishing a separate integrating unit concerned exclusively with the control and coordination of ongoing processes. It is this event, implying the withdrawal of selected components from direct output-producing functions, that Herbst sees as marking the transition from a simple to a complex system. The effect of this shift is shown in Figure 7–5. It should be noted that, although initially the withdrawal of component units from output-producing functions may briefly result in a relative decrease in output, this loss is quickly offset by the increase in output efficiency of the components that are retained in productive functions (see Figure 7–6). If this were not the case, the creation of integrating units would lead to reduced, rather than to increased, efficiency, and large complex systems would not come into being. These findings thus clearly suggest that size increases complexity *and* influences structure.

---

[25]P. G. Herbst, "Measurement of Behavior Structures by Means of Input-Output Data," *Human Relations* 10 (1957): 337.

Figure 7–4 *Input-Size-Output Functions of Simple Systems:*
Relation between Sales Turnover and Size of Shop[a]

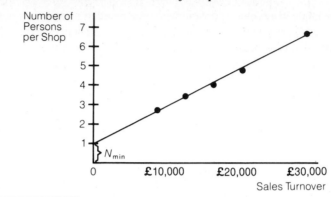

Source: P. G. Herbst, "Measurement of Behavior Structures by Means of Input-Output Data," *Human Relations*
10 (1957): 340. Used by permission of Plenum Publishing Corporation.
[a]Data are based on records for shops of a retail chain ($n = 404$).

Figure 7–5 *Size-Output Function of Complex Systems:*
Relation between Sales Turnover and Size of Establishment

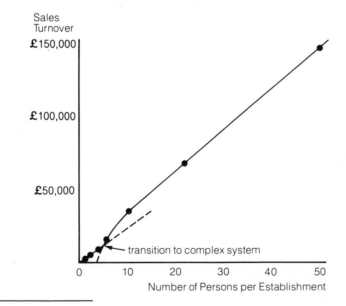

Source: Adapted from P. G. Herbst, "Measurement of Behavior Structures by Means of Input-Output Data,"
Human Relations 10 (1957): 343. Used by permission of Plenum Publishing Corporation.

Figure 7–6 *Size-Output Function of Complex Systems: Comparative Efficiency of Simple and Complex Organizations*

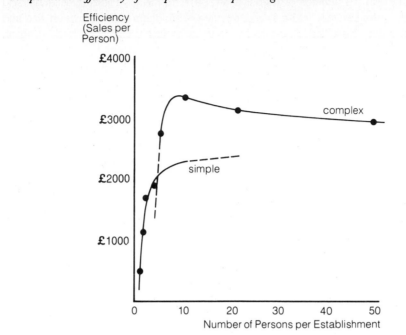

Source: Adapted from P. G. Herbst, "Measurement of Behavior Structures by Means of Input-Output Data," *Human Relations* 10 (1957): 343. Used by permission of Plenum Publishing Corporation.

The Growth and Development of Organizations

Structuring of Activities

Consistent with the findings of Herbst, the research of Pugh, Hickson, Hinings, and Turner supports the view that a strong, positive relationship exists between size and organization structure. Based on a sample of forty-six organizations in the English Midlands, they found that size was highly correlated with a composite measure of *structuring of activities* that included such elements as greater specialization of roles and functions, greater specialization of operations through rules and procedures, and greater formalization (paperwork). From these findings, Pugh et al. hypothesize that "an increased scale of operation increases the frequency of recurrent events and the repetition of decisions, which are then standardized and formalized. . . . Once the number of positions and people grows beyond control by personal interaction, the organization must be more explicitly structured."[26] This conclusion has been given additional support in a more recent report of essentially the same findings[27] and is also consistent with the previously mentioned work of both Greiner and Herbst.

Structural Differentiation

In an effort to develop a formal theory of organizations, Blau has provided additional information underlining the relationship of size to organization structure.[28] Blau studied the formal structure of the fifty-three state and territorial employment security agencies in the United States. Information pertaining to the operation and structure of the agencies was collected primarily through interviews with key informants and supplemented, as necessary, by analysis of organizational records. The results of his investigation revealed that increasing size is related to increasing *structural differentiation* along various dimensions, but at decreasing rates. The dimensions of differentiation measured were the number of hierarchical levels (*vertical differentiation*), departments (*functional differentiation*), and occupational positions *(horizontal differentiation)* within the organizations studied.

Additional evidence supporting Blau's findings has been provided by Child, by Mileti, Gillespie, and Haas and by Meyer.[29] In a study of British labor unions, business organizations, and engineering firms, Child consistently found that with increases in size, horizontal and vertical differentiation increase at a decreasing rate. Mileti et al. report identical results for a heterogeneous sample of federal and state agencies in California. Meyer likewise found that increases in size lead to structural differentiation.

---

[26]D. S. Pugh et al., "The Context of Organization Structures," *Administrative Science Quarterly* 14 (1969): 112.

[27]C. R. Hinings and G. L. Lee, "Dimensions of Organization Structure and Their Context: A Replication," *Sociology* 5 (1971): 83–93.

[28]P. M. Blau, "A Formal Theory of Differentiation in Organizations," *American Sociological Review* 35 (1970): 201–218; P. M. Blau and R. Schoenherr, *The Structure of Organizations* (New York: Basic Books, 1971), pp. 55–81.

[29]J. Child, "Predicting and Understanding Organizational Structure," *Administrative Science Quarterly* 18 (1973): 165–168; D. S. Mileti, D. F. Gillespie, and J. E. Haas, "Size and Structure in Complex Organizations," *Social Forces* 56 (1977): 208–217; M. W. Meyer, "Size and the Structure of Organizations: A Causal Model," *American Sociological Review* 37 (1972): 434–441.

Using path analysis (a statistical technique to help test the consequences of proposed causal relations among a set of variables), on information collected from 194 government finance departments in 1966 and 1971, he found size more likely to be a cause of differentiation than vice versa. Furthermore, when the effect of size was controlled, apparent causal relationships between other parameters (number of subunits, levels of hierarchy, and number of supervisors) of organization structure vanished.

Contradictory Evidence

Although the preceding results suggest the existence of a strong relationship between size and organization structure, the evidence is not unequivocal. Using data from a group of seventy-five highly diverse organizations, Hall, Haas, and Johnson examined the relationships between size and several measures of organizational *complexity* and *formalization* (as defined below).[30] The set of organizations studied included a newspaper, a public school system, a post office, a private country club, a state hospital, and a government regulatory agency; they ranged in size from 6 to over 9,000 members. The researchers justified using such a heterogeneous sample by arguing that, if size bore an important relationship to organization structure, "this importance should be demonstrable in a large sample of varying types of organizations."[31] Data were collected via personal interviews and through the review of official documents. Based on the information thus collected, indicators of organizational complexity and formalization were constructed. *Complexity* was defined as "the degree of internal segmentation—the number of separate 'parts' of the organization as reflected by the division of labor, number of hierarchical levels, and the spatial dispersion of the organization."[32] On examination of these factors, it is apparent that this variable is essentially the same as Blau's structural differentiation. *Formalization* was defined to be consistent with the meaning of the same concept as used by Pugh et al., that is, the degree to which procedures are codified in writing. Based upon a critical evaluation of their findings, Hall, Haas, and Johnson conclude, contrary to Pugh et al. and Blau, that "size may be rather irrelevant as a factor in determining organizational structure" and that "neither complexity nor formalization can be implied from knowledge of organizational size."[33]

Mayhew, McPherson, Levinger, and James also question the notion that size is a major influence on structure.[34] Using calculations from a computer algorithm, they were able to determine that Blau's statement of the relation of structural differentia-

---

[30]R. H. Hall, J. E. Haas, and N. J. Johnson, "Organizational Size, Complexity and Formalization," *American Sociological Review* 32 (1967): 903–912.

[31]Ibid., p. 905.

[32]Ibid., p. 906.

[33]Ibid., pp. 912, 911.

[34]B. H. Mayhew et al., "System Size and Structural Differentiation in Formal Organizations: A Baseline Generator for Two Major Theoretical Propositions," *American Sociological Review* 37 (1972): 629–633.

tion to size (increasing at a decreasing rate) was a mathematical certainty when equal probabilities were assigned to all possible structural combinations regardless of size.

Similarly, Aldrich has questioned the contention that size has a major impact on structure.[35] In a reanalysis of the Pugh et al. data,[36] he concluded that size is much less important than technology in influencing structure. Using path analysis, Aldrich found that the positive relationships between size and various dimensions of organization structure are due to nothing more than the fact that "more highly structured firms, with their greater degree of specialization, formalization, and monitoring of role performance, simply need to employ a larger work force than less structured firms."[37]

While the significance of technology in influencing structure will be explored at length in the following chapter, it should be noted that the results of several recent studies strongly suggest that the "technology-structure" versus "size-structure" issue is even more complex than previous studies had revealed. For instance, Dewar and Hage, in an analysis of three waves (for the years 1964, 1967, 1970) of data for each of sixteen social service organizations, report finding that task scope (a dimension of technology) is a more important determinant of the number of departments or divisions (what Blau termed "functional differentiation") in an organization than size is.[38] Moreover, they report finding virtually no relationship between organizational size and complexity (that is, number of occupational specialties, or what Blau termed "horizontal differentiation"). To complicate the pattern of these relationships even further, Paulson, using a sample of seventy-seven retail firms, reports results suggesting that the Dewar and Hage findings may partially be a function of the type of organizations selected for study—public versus private sector.[39] This would seem to imply that the relative effect of technology (as opposed to size) on structure may vary by industry type. Finally, based on a reexamination and replication of Blau's original findings, Beyer and Trice, in the belief that organizations have considerable latitude in the strategies they adopt, have concluded that a more reasonable and fruitful approach to understanding the relationship between size and structure (and at the same time technology and structure) would be to simply focus on those activities of decision makers that result in the hiring of additional employees, the creation of new hierarchical levels, the development of new job titles, the establishment of new departments, and so on.[40]

---

[35]H. E. Aldrich, "Technology and Organization Structure: A Reexamination of the Findings of the Aston Group," *Administrative Science Quarterly* 17 (1972): 26–43.

[36]Pugh et al., "The Context"; D. S. Pugh et al., "Dimensions of Organization Structure," *Administrative Science Quarterly* 13 (1968): 65–105; D. S. Pugh et al., "A Scheme for Organization Analysis," *Administrative Science Quarterly* 8 (1963): 289–315.

[37]Aldrich, "Technology and Organization Structure," p. 38.

[38]R. Dewar and J. Hage, "Size, Technology, Complexity, and Structural Differentiation: Toward a Theoretical Synthesis," *Administrative Science Quarterly* 23 (1978): 328–346.

[39]S. K. Paulson, "Organizational Size, Technology and Structure: Replication of a Study of Social Service Agencies among Small Retail Firms," *Academy of Management Journal,* in press.

[40]J. M. Beyer and H. M. Trice, "A Reexamination of the Relations between Size and Various Components of Organizational Complexity," *Administrative Science Quarterly* 24 (1979): 48–64.

As is evident from the preceding discussion, the relationship between organization size and structure is questionable. While the available evidence (including studies not cited here) does suggest that size has some relation to certain dimensions of structure, the exact nature of this relationship is far from clear-cut. In short, an exact understanding of the issues involved seems yet a long way from being achieved.

Organizational Size and Administrative Intensity

As noted by Child, more studies have probably been conducted on the relationship between organizational size and the proportion of employees in administrative or supportive roles (*administrative intensity* or, as it is called in the military, the "teeth to tail ratio") than on any other aspect of organization structure.[41] Early research and conjecture, bolstered by popular satirical statements such as *Parkinson's Law,* gave support to the general view that, as organizations increase in size, the number of administrative and staff employees increases more than proportionately.[42] The basic assumption underlying this reasoning is that, since administrators and staff are responsible for providing coordination, and since coordination becomes more and more difficult as the number of employees increases, it follows that administrative and support components increase out of proportion to increases in size.

Following this reasoning, Terrien and Mills were among the first researchers to explore the relationship between size and administrative intensity on an empirical basis.[43] Using data on 428 California public school districts, they found that the percentage of employees holding administrative jobs, such as superintendents, their assistants and staff, principals, business managers, and so on, increased with size regardless of school type (elementary, high, and unified). More recently, Raphael, in a study of sixty-five local unions, and Hinings and Bryman, in a study of the Anglican and Methodist churches in England, have reported similar findings.[44]

---

[41]J. Child, "Parkinson's Progress: Accounting for the Number of Specialists in Organizations," *Administrative Science Quarterly* 18 (1973): 328–346. It should be noted that the use of ratio variables in the measurement of administrative intensity has become an area of increased debate. For both sides of this issue see: —pro, J. D. Kasarda, "Ratio Measurement and Theoretical Inference in Social Research," *Social Forces* 58 (1979): 212–227; A. MacMillan and R. L. Daft, "Administrative Intensity and Ratio Variables: The Case against Definitional Dependency," *Social Forces* 58 (1979): 228–248; —con, J. H. Freeman and J. E. Kronenfeld, "Problems of Definitional Dependency: The Case of Administrative Intensity," *Social Forces* 52 (1973): 108–121.

[42]F. W. Terrien and D. L. Mills, "The Effect of Changing Size upon the Internal Structure of Organizations," *American Sociological Review* 20 (1955): 11–13; T. Caplow, "The Effects of Increasing Size on Organisational Structure in Industry," *Transactions of the Third World Congress of Sociology,* vol. 2 (London: International Sociological Organization, 1956), pp. 157–164; T. Caplow, "Organizational Size," *Administrative Science Quarterly* 1 (1957): 484–505.

[43]Terrien and Mills, "The Effect of Changing Size."

[44]E. Raphael, "The Anderson-Warkov Hypothesis in Local Unions: A Comparative Study," *American Sociological Review* 32 (1967): 768–776; C. R. Hinings and A. Bryman, "Size and the Administrative Component in Churches," *Human Relations* 27 (1974): 457–475.

Other investigators, however, argue differently, presenting data which suggest that large organizations contain a smaller proportion of personnel engaged in administrative functions. According to this opposing view, economies of scale are achieved, as are many other improvements, at the administrative level as supervisors increase their span of control. Hence, an increase in output may require using additional operating employees but not necessarily more managerial personnel. Empirical support for this proposition comes from a variety of sources.[45]

Indik, in a study of two businesses and three voluntary organizations, and Blau, in the previously mentioned study of state employment security agencies, found that as unit size increased, the ratio of supervisors to total personnel decreased, regardless of function.[46] This finding is consistent with Bendix's analysis of German industrial statistics which shows that the ratio of salaried administrative personnel to production workers in industries employing six or more persons consistently decreased during the first half of the twentieth century. It is also consistent with Melman's even earlier analysis showing an identical inverse relationship between size and administrative overhead for U.S. and British manufacturing concerns over roughly the same period.[47] This same negative relationship has been reported in studies of hospitals, urban school systems, school districts, institutions of higher education, occupational associations, and various other commercial and noncommercial concerns (see Appendix 7–A). Nevertheless, while almost all studies indicate that larger organizations contain a smaller proportion of employees engaged in administration, the relationship between size and administrative intensity is not as clear as it might seem at first sight.

Anderson-Warkov Hypotheses

In a study of forty-nine Veterans Administration hospitals, Anderson and Warkov found that, while administrative intensity was negatively related to organizational size, it was positively related to *functional complexity*—the number of tasks performed, degree of structural differentiation, and extent of combined effort.[48] Given these findings, and assuming functional complexity to intervene between organizational size and the proportion of persons occupying administrative roles, Anderson and Warkov offered three new hypotheses: (1) administrative intensity would *decrease* as the number of persons performing similar tasks in the same place increased; (2) it would

---

[45]S. Melman, "Production and Administration Cost in Relation to Size of Firm," *Applied Statistics* 3 (1954): 1–10; M. R. Smith, "Profits and Administrative Intensity: A Longitudinal Analysis," *Sociology* 9 (1978): 509–521.

[46]B. P. Indik, "The Relationship between Organizational Size and Supervision Ratio," *Administrative Science Quarterly* 9 (1964): 301–312; Blau, "A Formal Theory."

[47]R. Bendix, *Work and Authority in Industry* (New York: John Wiley & Sons, 1956), Table 7, p. 222; S. Melman, "The Rise of Administrative Overhead in the Manufacturing Industries of the United States, 1899–1947," *Oxford Economic Papers,* new series 3 (1951): 61–112; S. Melman, *Dynamic Factors in Industrial Productivity* (Oxford: Basil Blackwell, 1956), pp. 69–94.

[48]T. R. Anderson and S. Warkov, "Organizational Size and Functional Complexity: A Study of Administration in Hospitals," *American Sociological Review* 26 (1961): 23–28.

Chapter 7

increase as the number of operating sites increased; and (3) it would *increase* as the number of persons performing different tasks increased. Anderson and Warkov thus suggested that the relationship between size and administrative intensity may be a function of a third variable—complexity (see Figure 7–7). Interestingly, this proposition is consistent with the previously discussed findings of Herbst.

Administrative Subgroup Differences

In an elaboration of the Anderson-Warkov hypotheses, Rushing investigated the possibility that the relative number of employees in *different* administrative subgroups may be differentially related to organizational size.[49] Using data from forty-one industries, Rushing identified three primary administrative subgroups: managerial, clerical, and professional personnel. *Managerial personnel* coordinate throughout the managerial hierarchy. The primary coordinative mechanism for *professional employees* is professional authority based on technical knowledge and expertise. *Clerical personnel* are concerned with coordination of paperwork and formal communication. An

Figure 7–7   *A Graphic Representation of the Anderson-Warkov Hypotheses*

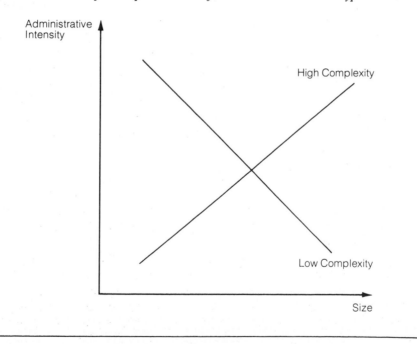

[49]W. A. Rushing, "Organizational Size and Administration: The Problems of Causal Homogeneity and a Heterogeneous Category," *Pacific Sociological Review* 9 (1966): 100–108; W. A. Rushing, "The Effects of Industry Size and Division of Labor on Administration," *Administrative Science Quarterly* 12 (1967): 273–275; W. A. Rushing, "Two Patterns of Industrial Administration," *Human Organization* 26 (1967): 32–39.

analysis of the resulting categories revealed administrative intensity to be inversely related to size but directly related to complexity. More specifically, as complexity increased, the proportion of clerical and professional personnel relative to production personnel increased at a faster rate than did the proportion of managerial personnel (see Figure 7–8).

This suggests that with increases in the division of labor, managerial activities may be increasingly supplemented with the activities of clerical and professional personnel. Thus, relative to managerial authority and supervision, formal communication and professional authority may become increasingly important in coordination as industries become increasingly complex. Decisions may be made and coordination may be effected less and less on the basis of direct observation of the work process by the managerial hierarchy and more and more indirectly on the basis of information processed by professional and clerical personnel. [50]

Such an interpretation implies that as an organization grows in size and complexity, the knowledge and technical skills of *professional personnel* and the procedures of *clerical personnel* may be "functional substitutes" for increases in *managerial personnel.* This reasoning is consistent with the findings of Kasarda on the effect of increases in size and complexity on the administrative structure of school systems in Colorado; Child on the effect of size and various measures of complexity on specific areas of specialist employment in fifty-four British manufacturing firms; Champion and Betterton on the influence of size and complexity on the administrative ratios of fifty hospitals of varying sizes; Reimann on the differential effect of such situational variables as technology and technological change on the size of various staff components in twenty manufacturing concerns; and, finally, Klatzky on the joint influence of size and complexity on the administrative intensity of the same sample of state employment security agencies examined by Blau.[51] In summary, while Anderson and Warkov assumed that complexity intervened between the effects of organizational size and administrative intensity (see Figure 7–7), the findings cited above clearly suggest that organizational size and complexity interact (see Figure 7–8) in their effect on the relative proportion of personnel occupying specific administrative or supportive roles.[52]

[50]Rushing, "The Effects of Industry Size and Division of Labor," p. 292.

[51]J. D. Kasarda, "The Effects of Personnel Turnover, Employee Qualifications, and Professional Staff Ratios on Administrative Intensity and Overhead," *Sociological Quarterly* 14 (1973): 350–358; J. D. Kasarda, "The Structural Implications of Social System Size: A Three-Level Analysis," *American Sociological Review* 39 (1974): 19–28; Child, "Parkinson's Progress"; D. Champion and H. Betterton, "On Organization Size and Administrative Ratios," *Pacific Sociological Review* 17 (1974): 98–106; B. C. Reimann, "Parkinson Revisited: A Component Analysis of the Use of Staff Specialists in Manufacturing Organizations," *Human Relations* 32 (1979): 625–641; S. R. Klatzky, "Relationships of Organizational Size to Complexity and Coordination," *Administrative Science Quarterly* 15 (1970): 428–438.

[52]W. V. Heydebrand, *Comparative Organizations: The Results of Empirical Research* (Englewood Cliffs, N.J.: Prentice-Hall, 1973), pp. 379–380.

Chapter 7

Figure 7–8 *The Influence of Administrative Subgroup Differences on Administrative Intensity*

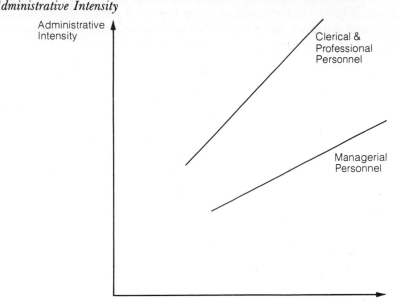

Source: The original version of this material appeared under the title "Organizational Size and Administration: The Problems of Causal Homogeneity and a Heterogenous Category," by William A. Rushing, published in the *Pacific Sociological Review,* vol. 9, no. 2 (Fall 1966), pp. 100–109, and is reprinted herewith by permission of the publisher, Sage Publications, Inc.

Administrative Intensity and Other Factors

Building on the above studies, Freeman has revealed that a variety of technological and environmental factors also influence administrative intensity.[53] Using a sample of forty-one manufacturing companies located in southern California, he presents evidence to suggest that administrative intensity increases as a function both of environmental complexity and of technological sophistication. Based on this finding, Freeman reasons that other factors, such as the nature of the product or service being provided, may also be an important influence on an organization's administrative structure. As he observes: "A brewery and a chemical firm may use very similar production systems, but one would expect the chemical firm to have a wider variety of products, a more diverse set of raw materials, and a more elaborate research and development operation. Administrative intensity may be higher, then, because administrative functions are linked to these product-related variables."[54] (It should be noted

[53]J. Freeman, "Environment, Technology, and the Administrative Intensity of Manufacturing Organizations," *American Sociological Review* 38 (1973): 750–763.
[54]Ibid., p. 761.

that, in fact, available information does suggest that the relative proportion of administrative personnel differs widely among industries. Pondy, for instance, reports that "for a sample of 45 manufacturing industries, the number of administrative personnel per 100 production workers varies from 8.7 for the logging industry to 131.1 for the drug industry, with a mean of 37.7 and a standard deviation of 28.8.")[55]

Longitudinal Changes

A majority of the studies discussed so far have been static in nature, using data drawn from a cross section of firms in one or more industries at a single point in time. Being time bound, they not only neglect changing relationships that may develop between periods but assume that, among the organizations sampled, the conditions of all other factors which could influence administrative intensity are either the same or are randomly distributed. As a result, they may produce, as Haire has pointed out, "a spurious growth curve. It is not a curve of growth representing the dynamics within an organization, but a set of static measurements arranged by size."[56] In contrast, the ideal basis for examining changes in administrative intensity as a function of size would be to study longitudinal changes in a representative sampling of organizations over time.[57] Such analyses would give a dynamic perspective of the true relationship between organizational size and administrative intensity. The few longitudinal investigations that have been undertaken lend credence to this contention, reflecting the existence of a much more complex relationship than simpler cross sectional studies might suggest.

Tsouderos' study of growth and change in voluntary associations is an excellent case in point.[58] In an attempt to link a series of selected variables to changes in membership size, he found that, while membership first increased (during an initial phase of growth) and then decreased (during a phase of decline), the number of administrative personnel continued to grow. In other words, during an initial period of growth, changes in administrative employment were positively associated with changes in size, while in a period of decline they were negatively associated. This suggests that the relationship between size and administrative intensity may in fact be curvilinear, taking the form of a U-shaped curve that is first positive and then negative. Other longitudinal studies, however, offer differing interpretations. Akers and Campbell, using data on seventy-five occupational associations at two points in

---

[55]L. R. Pondy, "Effects of Size, Complexity and Ownership on Administrative Intensity," *Administrative Science Quarterly* 14 (1969): 47–60.

[56]M. Haire, "Biological Models and Empirical Histories of the Growth of Organizations," in *Modern Organization Theory*, ed. M. Haire (New York: John Wiley & Sons, 1959), p. 292.

[57]J. R. Kimberly, "Issues in the Design of Longitudinal Organizational Research," *Sociological Methods and Research* 4 (1976): 321–347.

[58]J. E. Tsouderos, "Organizational Change in Terms of a Series of Selected Variables," *American Sociological Review* 20 (1955): 206–210.

time fifteen years apart, report finding a "negative association" between relative staff size and membership expansion, regardless of rate of growth.[59] A third study, by Holdaway and Blowers, presents an even different interpretation.[60] In a study of forty-one Canadian urban school systems, they report finding that, despite general system size increases over a five-year period, there was no consistent tendency for administrative intensity to increase or decrease.

Finally, a fourth and a fifth study offer additional interpretations. Hendershot and James present longitudinal data on the effects of organizational growth and size (student enrollment) on the ratio of administrative staff to teachers in 299 school districts.[61] While their results reveal a negative relationship between size and administrative intensity, they also disclose that size and rate of growth contributed independently to this outcome. School districts that experienced slow growth tended to increase administrative intensity, while those that experienced rapid growth tended to show decreases. Freeman and Hannan examined the effects of enrollment growth and decline on the number of teachers (direct component) versus the number of professional, administrative, and nonprofessional staff (supportive component) employed in 769 California school districts over a five-year period.[62] On the basis of their results, they argue that the effects of growth and decline on the structure of an organization are quite different. With regard to the relationship between size and administrative intensity, Freeman and Hannan equate changes in enrollment with demand for school services and contend that "when demand is increasing, the size of the direct component increases as does the supportive component. But when demand declines, the loss in direct component is not matched by loss in the supportive component. That is, the supportive component tends to increase on the upswings but decreases less on the downswings."[63]

Taken together, the preceding results clearly suggest that the relationship between organizational size and administrative intensity is not *static* in nature; rather it is highly complex and dynamic. That size and the proportion of personnel occupying administrative roles have been shown to vary according to an organization's rate of growth (decline) casts doubt on the more simplistic, but more common, explanations of administrative intensity discussed earlier. Unquestionably, further efforts in this area are needed for a richer and more complete understanding of size as a dimension of organization structure. Of particular note is the follow-up research of Freeman, using essentially the same sample of California school districts, and the recent work

[59]R. Akers and F. L. Campbell, "Size and the Administrative Component in Occupational Associations," *Pacific Sociological Review* 13 (1970): 241–251; F. L. Campbell and R. Akers, "Organizational Size, Complexity, and the Administrative Component in Occupational Associations," *Sociological Quarterly* 11 (1970): 435–451.

[60]E. Holdaway and T. A. Blowers, "Administrative Ratios and Organizational Size: A Longitudinal Examination," *American Sociological Review* 36 (1971): 278–286.

[61]G. E. Hendershot and T. F. James, "Size and Growth as Determinants of Administrative-Production Ratios in Organizations," *American Sociological Review* 37 (1972): 149–153.

[62]J. H. Freeman and M. T. Hannan, "Growth and Decline Processes in Organizations," *American Sociological Review* 40 (1975): 215–288.

[63]Ibid., p. 227.

The Growth and Development of Organizations

of Jones concerning other dimensions which may influence administrative intensity.[64] Freeman's findings suggest that not only are the effects of growth and decline on the structure of an organization quite different but such environmental constraints as changes in funding (local, state, or federal revenues) are also possible influences on the size of an organization's supportive component. Jones similarly reports results which indicate that level of administrative intensity may be influenced not only by the relationship between an organization and its environment but also by an organization's core technology. If this is so, it would seem reasonable to argue not only that growing organizations may perhaps also be distinguished from declining organizations by other underlying factors but that differences in environment and technology may also account for variations in administrative intensity.[65]

Toward Conceptual Clarity: A Summary and Appraisal

As the previous review suggests, there are numerous unresolved issues beclouding the relationship between administrative intensity and organizational size. A summary of the studies discussed is presented in Appendix 7–A. For each entry, the investigators, the sample(s) employed, the definitions of size and administrative component employed, and the more important relationships found between administrative intensity and size are listed.

An evaluation of the empirical evidence presented in Appendix 7–A highlights a number of issues that are a large part of the problem confronting research on organizations in general. First, definitional ambiguities abound. Many of the studies listed have failed to agree on a definition of any of the central concepts involved. While the most common definition of *size* is "total number of employees," other measures have been used, including annual average daily patient load, total student enrollment, total assets, and total number of dues-paying members. An even greater lack of consensus exists as to exactly what comprises an organization's administrative component. While each study identified in the appendix focused on the proportion (ratio) of employees performing administrative or supportive roles, these have been classified in a wide variety of ways. A brief quote from Child offers a representative sample of the divergent classification schemes that have been employed.

Some investigators have worked with a classification of indirect personnel for which the proportion of nondirect employees taken together has been the operational measure (for example, Melman, 1951; Rushing, 1967[a]; Pondy, 1969). Other researchers have employed the concept of a "supportive" or "staff" component from which managers of direct areas of work are excluded (Haas, Hall, and Johnson, 1963;

---

[64]J. H. Freeman, "Going to the Well: School District Administrative Intensity and Environmental Constraint," *Administrative Science Quarterly* 24 (1979): 119–133; R. E. Jones, "Determinants of Administrative Intensity," *Journal of Management* 3, no. 2 (1977): 15–23.

[65]For a discussion of this point see J. D. Ford, "The Occurrence of Structural Hysteria in Declining Organizations," *Academy of Management Review,* in press.

Pugh et al., 1968; Klatzky, 1970; Blau and Schoenherr, 1971). Still other studies have focused upon the "administrative" component, a concept which is usually operationalized to exclude not only line managers but also staff who are providing professional services rather than administration per se (Anderson and Warkov, 1961; Hawley, Boland, and Boland, 1965; Tosi and Patt, 1967; Holdaway and Blowers, 1971). A few studies have, finally, employed measures of the ratio between managers and employees (Indik, 1964; Blau, 1972).[66]

It hardly seems inappropriate to argue that such extensive definitional confusion may in fact be responsible for the ambiguous empirical findings concerning the relationship of size to administrative intensity. As stated by Kimberly: "It is not unreasonable to speculate that were concepts and measures more closely aligned, a significant portion of the empirical ambiguity might be resolved. What currently appear to be contradictory or inconsistent findings, might, with closer fit between concepts and measures, turn out to be more consistent and interpretable."[67]

In addition to the issue of consistency and problems of interpretation, such extensive variation raises two related questions.[68] *First,* to what extent may it be assumed that administrative or supportive staff is a homogeneous category? Is what is true of the whole administrative component true of its subcomponent parts? As suggested by the previously cited research of Rushing, Child, Kasarda, Champion and Betterton, and Klatzky, administrative subgroup differences do exist. It is thus highly probable that the use of broad classifications may result in misleading conclusions. The *second,* related, point concerns the extent to which the relation of size to administrative intensity may be expected to vary as a function of organizational type.[69] Public agencies and service and manufacturing organizations often differ in rather significant ways. To draw certain distinctions in this regard, one need only contrast the highly competitive environment faced by an aerospace manufacturer with that typically confronted by a government bureau or other civil service organization. In addition, tax-supported organizations typically operate within distinct geographical boundaries and often with stipulated staff sizes. Furthermore, they traditionally have very little budgetary autonomy. Each of these differences clearly carry important implications for a discussion of size-structure relationships.[70]

In closing we are left with several conclusions:

1. Large organizations *generally* contain a smaller proportion of personnel engaged in administrative or supportive positions. That is, larger organizations *generally* have smaller administrative intensities than do smaller organizations.

---

[66]Child, "Parkinson's Progress," p. 329.

[67]J. R. Kimberly, "Organizational Size and the Structuralist Perspective: A Review, Critique, and Proposal," *Adminstrative Science Quarterly* 21 (1976): 571–596.

[68]Hinings and Bryman, "Size and the Administrative Component."

[69]Kimberly, "Organizational Size and the Structuralist Perspective."

[70]C. Argyris, *The Applicability of Organizational Sociology* (Cambridge: Cambridge University Press, 1972), pp. 11–12; H. G. Rainey, R. W. Backoff, and C. H. Levine, "Comparing Public and Private Organizations," *Public Administration Review* 36 (1976): 233–244.

The Growth and Development of Organizations

2. Size, however, is not the only factor that influences administrative intensity. Other factors include organizational type, organizational complexity, degree of environmental uncertainty, extent of technological constraints, and the nature of the service being provided or the product being produced.
3. Administrative intensity varies according to an organization's rate and stage of growth. As organizations grow and develop, so do the structural dimensions that comprise them.
4. The relative proportion of personnel occupying specific administrative or supportive roles is a joint function of an organization's size and complexity.

Summary

The purpose of this chapter has been threefold. It has sought (1) to familiarize the reader with several of the more meaningful models of organizational growth, (2) to review the literature dealing with the relative influence of size on structural configuration, and (3) to examine the relationship between organizational size and administrative intensity.

Opening with a brief discussion of the motives for growth, the first part of the chapter presented three models of the organizational growth process: the Lippitt-Schmidt Model, the Scott Model, and the Greiner Model. Each was an attempt to deal with the basic changes in structure that are necessary as organizations grow and must develop new strategies for coping with the changing demands of their task environment. This section concluded with a discussion of the specific causes of the decline and death of organizations.

The second and third parts of the chapter were devoted to a discussion of organizational size. In particular, the relationship between size (number of employees) and various dimensions of structure and what has been termed administrative intensity was examined.

Review and Discussion Questions

1. "Growth is not spontaneous. It is a consequence of decisions." What is meant by this statement? Comment on several motives that are typically associated with decisions to grow.
2. The Lippitt-Schmidt model follows a life cycle concept in discussing stages of organizational growth. What causes an organization to pass from one stage to another?
3. Characterize organizations at each stage of the Scott model of organizational growth and development. What, according to Scott, determines the structure of an organization?
4. The Greiner model of organizational growth is composed of five periods, each of which is composed of two phases. What are these two phases?
5. In 1977 over half of the business failures in the United States were firms less than five years old. Why are young firms so vulnerable? What are some factors that could result in the death of an organization?

6. What is meant by an "integrating unit," and how does it relate to size?
7. Discuss the impact of size on organization structure. Is there a relationship between size and structural differentiation?
8. What are the Anderson-Warkov hypotheses?
9. Do longitudinal studies show any clear-cut relationship between administrative intensity and organizational size? Between administrative intensity and growth rate? Elaborate.
10. What conclusions can be drawn concerning the effect of organization size on administrative intensity?

References

Akers, R., and Campbell, F. L. "Size and the Administrative Component in Occupational Associations." *Pacific Sociological Review* 13 (1970): 241–251.

Aldrich, H. E. "Technology and Organizational Structure: A Reexamination of the Findings of the Aston Group." *Administrative Science Quarterly* 17 (1972): 26–43.

Anderson, T. R., and Warkov, S. "Organizational Size and Functional Complexity: A Study of Administration in Hospitals." *American Sociological Review* 26 (1961): 23–28.

Argyris, C. *The Applicability of Organizational Sociology.* Cambridge: Cambridge University Press, 1972.

Bendix, R. *Work and Authority in Industry.* New York: John Wiley & Sons, 1956.

Beyer, J. M., and Trice, H. M. "A Reexamination of the Relations between Size and Various Components of Organizational Complexity." *Administrative Science Quarterly* 24 (1979): 48–64.

Blau, P. M. "A Formal Theory of Differentiation in Organizations." *American Sociological Review* 35 (1970): 201–218.

Blau, P. M. "Interdependence and Hierarchy in Organizations." *Social Science Research* 1 (1972): 23–45.

Blau, P. M., and Schoenherr, R. *The Structure of Organizations.* New York: Basic Books, 1971.

Blau, P. M., and Scott, W. R. *Formal Organizations: A Comparative Approach.* San Francisco: Chandler, 1962.

The Business Failure Record. New York: Dun & Bradstreet, 1978.

Campbell, F. L., and Akers, R. L. "Organizational Size, Complexity, and the Administrative Component in Occupational Associations." *Sociological Quarterly* 11 (1970): 435–451.

Caplow, T. "The Effect of Increasing Size on Organisational Structure in Industry." *Transactions of the Third World Congress of Sociology,* vol. 2. London: International Sociological Association, 1956.

Caplow, T. "Organizational Size." *Administrative Science Quarterly* 1 (1957): 484–505.

Cesta, J. R., and Apilado, V. P. "Business Bankruptcies: Variations and Associative Factors." Paper presented at the Midwest Finance Association annual meeting, St. Louis, Mo., April 1977.

Champion, D., and Betterton, H. "On Organization Size and Administrative Ratios." *Pacific Sociological Review* 17 (1974): 98–106.

Chandler, A. D. *Strategy and Structure: Chapters in the History of the American Enterprise.* Cambridge, Mass.: M.I.T. Press, 1962.

Child, J. (a) "Parkinson's Progress: Accounting for the Number of Specialists in Organizations." *Administrative Science Quarterly* 18 (1973): 328–346.

Child, J. (b) "Predicting and Understanding Organizational Structure." *Administrative Science Quarterly* 18 (1973): 168–185.

Dale, E., ed. *Readings in Management: Landmarks and New Frontiers.* 3rd ed. New York: McGraw-Hill, 1975.

Dewar, R., and Hage, J. "Size, Technology, Complexity, and Structural Differentiation: Toward a Theoretical Synthesis." *Administrative Science Quarterly* 23 (1978): 111–136.

Dowling, W. F. "Job Redesign on the Assembly Line: Farewell to Blue-Collar Blues." *Organizational Dynamics* 2, no. 2 (1973): 51–67.

Evers, F. T., Bohlen, J. M., and Warren, R. D. "The Relationships of Selected Size and Structure Indicators in Economic Organizations." *Administrative Science Quarterly* 21 (1976): 326–342.

Ford, J. D. "The Occurrence of Structural Hysteria in Declining Organizations." *Academy of Management Review,* in press.

Freeman, J. H. "Environment, Technology, and the Administrative Intensity of Manufacturing Organizations." *American Sociological Review* 38 (1973): 750–763.

Freeman, J. H. "Going to the Well: School District Administrative Intensity and Environmental Constraint." *Administrative Science Quarterly* 24 (1979): 119–133.

Freeman, J. H., and Hannan, M. T. "Growth and Decline Processes in Organizations." *American Sociological Review* 40 (1975): 215–228.

Freeman, J. H., and Kronenfeld, J. E. "Problems of Definitional Dependency: The Case of Administrative Intensity." *Social Forces* 52 (1973): 108–121.

Goldman, P. "Size and Differentiation in Organizations: A Test of a Theory." *Pacific Sociological Review* 16 (1973): 89–105.

Greiner, L. E. "Evolution and Revolution as Organizations Grow." *Harvard Business Review* 50, no. 4 (1972): 37–46.

Gross, B. M. *Organizations and Their Managing.* New York: Free Press, 1968.

Haas, J. E., Hall, R. H., and Johnson, N. J. "The Size of the Supportive Component in Organizations: A Multi-organizational Analysis." *Social Forces* 42 (1963): 9–17.

Haire, M. "Biological Models and Empirical Histories of the Growth of Organizations." In *Modern Organization Theory,* edited by M. Haire. New York: John Wiley & Sons, 1959.

Hall, R. H., Haas, J. E., and Johnson, N. J. "Organizational Size, Complexity and Formalization." *American Sociological Review* 32 (1967): 903–912.

Hannan, M. T., and Freeman, J. H. "The Population Ecology of Organizations." *American Journal of Sociology* 82 (1977): 929–964.

Hawley, A. H., Boland, W., and Boland, M. "Population Size and Administration in Institutions of Higher Education." *American Sociological Review* 30 (1965): 252–255.

Herbst, P. G. "Measurement of Behavior Structures by Means of Input-Output Data." *Human Relations* 10 (1957): 335–346.

Hendershot, G. E., and James, T. F. "Size and Growth as Determinants of Administrative-Production Ratios in Organizations." *American Sociological Review* 37 (1972): 149–153.

Heydebrand, W. V., ed. *Comparative Organizations: The Results of Empirical Research.* Englewood Cliffs, N.J.: Prentice-Hall, 1973.

Hicks, H. G., and Gullett, C. R. *Organizations: Theory and Behavior.* New York: McGraw-Hill, 1975.

Hinings, C. R., and Bryman, A. "Size and the Administrative Component in Churches." *Human Relations* 27 (1974): 457–475.

Hinings, C. R., and Lee, G. L. "Dimensions of Organization Structure and Their Context: A Replication." *Sociology* 5 (1971): 83–93.

Holdaway, E. A., and Blowers, T. A. "Administrative Ratios and Organizational Size: A Longitudinal Examination." *American Sociological Review* 36 (1971): 278–286.

Indik, B. P. "The Relationship between Organizational Size and Supervision Ratio." *Administrative Science Quarterly* 9 (1964): 301–312.

James, T. F. "The Administrative Component in Complex Organizations." *Sociological Quarterly* 13 (1972): 533–539.

Jones, R. E. "Determinants of Administrative Intensity." *Journal of Management* 3, no. 2 (1977): 15–23.

Kasarda, J. D. "Effects of Personnel Turnover, Employee Qualifications, and Professional Staff Ratios on Administrative Intensity and Overhead." *Sociological Quarterly* 14 (1973): 350–358.

Kasarda, J. D. "Ratio Measurement and Theoretical Inference in Social Research." *Social Forces* 58 (1979): 212–227.

Kasarda, J. D. "The Structural Implications of Social System Size: A Three-level Analysis." *American Sociological Review* 39 (1974): 19–28.

Kimberly, J. R. "Issues in the Design of Longitudinal Organizational Research." *Sociological Methods and Research* 4 (1976): 321–347.

Kimberly, J. R. "Organizational Size and the Structuralist Perspective: A Review, Critique, and Proposal. *Administrative Science Quarterly* 21 (1976): 571–596.

Klatzky, S. R. "Relationship of Organizational Size to Complexity and Coordination." *Administrative Science Quarterly* 15 (1970): 428–438.

Lindenfield, F. "Does Administrative Staff Grow as Fast as Organization?" *School Life* 43, no. 8 (1961): 20–23.

Lippitt, G. L. *Organizational Renewal.* New York: Appleton-Century-Crofts, 1969.

Chapter 7

Lippitt, G. L., and Schmidt, W. H. "Crises in a Developing Organization." *Harvard Business Review* 45 (1967): 102–112.

Litterer, J. A. *The Analysis of Organizations*. 2nd ed. New York: John Wiley & Sons, 1973.

MacMillan, A., and Daft, R. L. "Administrative Intensity and Ratio Variables: The Case against Definitional Dependency." *Social Forces* 58 (1979): 228–248.

Mayhew, B. H., McPherson, J. M., Levinger, R. L., and James, T. F. "System Size and Structural Differentiation in Formal Organizations: A Baseline Generator for Two Major Theoretical Propositions." *American Sociological Review* 37 (1972): 629–633.

Melman, S. "Production and Administration Cost in Relation to Size of Firm." *Applied Statistics* 3 (1954): 1–10.

Melman, S. *The Rise of Administrative Overhead in the Manufacturing Industries of the United States, 1899–1947*. Oxford Economic Papers. New series 3 (1951): 61–112.

Melman, S. *Dynamic Factors in Industrial Productivity*. Oxford: Basil Blackwell, 1956.

Meyer, M. W. "Size and the Structure of Organizations: A Causal Model." *American Sociological Review* 37 (1972): 434–441.

Parkinson, C. N. *Parkinson's Law and Other Studies in Administration*. Boston: Houghton Mifflin, 1957.

Paulson, S. K. "Organizational Size, Technology and Structure: Replication of a Study of Social Service Agencies among Small Retail Firms." *Academy of Management Journal,* in press.

Penrose, E. T. *The Theory of the Growth of the Firm*. New York: John Wiley & Sons, 1959.

Pondy, L. R. "Effects of Size, Complexity and Ownership on Administrative Intensity." *Administrative Science Quarterly* 14 (1969): 47–60.

Pugh, D. S., Hickson, D. J., Hinings, C. R., and Turner, C. "The Context of Organization Structures." *Administrative Science Quarterly* 14 (1969): 91–114

Pugh, D. S., Hickson, D. J., Hinings, C. R., and Turner, C. "Dimensions of Organization Structure." *Administrative Science Quarterly* 13 (1968): 65–105.

Pugh, D. S., Hickson, D. J., Hinings, C. R., Macdonald, K. M., Turner, C., and Lupton, T. "A Scheme for Organizational Analysis." *Administrative Science Quarterly* 8 (1963): 289–315.

Rainey, H. G., Backoff, R. W., and Levine, C. H. "Comparing Public and Private Organizations." *Public Administration Review* 36 (1976): 233–244.

Raphael, E. "The Anderson-Warkov Hypotheses in Local Unions: A Comparative Study." *American Sociological Review* 32 (1967): 768–776.

Reimann, B. C. "Parkinson Revisited: A Component Analysis of the Use of Staff Specialists in Manufacturing Organizations." *Human Relations* 32 (1979): 625–641.

Rushing, W. A. (a) "The Effects of Industry Size and Division of Labor on Administration." *Administrative Science Quarterly* 12 (1967): 273–295.

Rushing, W. A. (b) "Two Patterns of Industrial Administration." *Human Organization* 26 (1967): 32–39.

Rushing, W. A. "Organizational Size and Administration: The Problems of Causal Homogeneity and a Heterogeneous Category." *Pacific Sociological Review* 9 (1966): 100–108.

Scott, B. R. "The Industrial State: Old Myths and New Realities." *Harvard Business Review* 51, no. 2 (1973): 133–149.

Scott, B. R. *Stages of Corporate Development—Part I*. Boston: Intercollegiate Case Clearing House, Harvard Business School, 1971, 9–371–294.

Smith, M. R. "Profits and Administrative Intensity: A Longitudinal Analysis." *Sociology* 9 (1978): 509–521.

Starbuck, W. H. "Organizational Growth and Development." In *Handbook of Organizations,* edited by J. G. March. Chicago: Rand McNally, 1965.

Stinchcombe, A. L. "Social Structure and Organizations." In *Handbook of Organizations,* edited by J. G. March. Chicago: Rand McNally, 1965

Terrien, F. W., and Mills, D. L. "The Effect of Changing Size upon the Internal Structure of Organizations." *American Sociological Review* 20 (1955): 11–13.

Thain, D. H. "Stages of Corporate Development." *Business Quarterly* 34 (1969): 33–45.

Tosi, H. L., and Patt, H. "Administrative Ratios and Organizational Size." *Academy of Management Journal* 10 (1967): 161–168.

Tsouderos, J. E. "Organizational Change in Terms of a Series of Selected Variables." *American Sociological Review* 20 (1955): 206–210.

Whittington, G. "Changes in the Top 100 Quoted Manufacturing Companies in the United Kingdom 1948 to 1968." *Journal of Industrial Economics* 21 (1972): 17–34.

The Growth and Development of Organizations

Appendix 7-A *Summary of Selected Studies Examining the Relationship between Administrative Intensity and Organizational Size and Other Selected Variables*

Author and Date Published[a]	Sample	Definition of Size	Definition of Administrative Component	Relationship(s)
1. Akers & Campbell (1970), and Campbell & Akers (1970)	Occupational associations N = 75	Total number of full-fledged members	Number of full-time staff employed at the national office of each association	Negative, regardless of rate of growth
2. Anderson & Warkov 1961	19 tuberculosis and 30 general Veterans Administration hospitals	Annual average daily patient load—highly correlated ($r > .96$) with total hospital labor force	General hospital administration (e.g., employees in the registrar's office, fiscal department, and supply units)	Size: Negative Complexity: Positive
3. Bendix 1956	Manufacturing industries in the U.S., France, Great Britain, Germany, and Sweden, 1895–1950	Total number of production workers	Number of administrative (or salaried) employees, excluding owners and top executives	Negative
4. Blau (1970), Blau & Schoenherr (1971), and Klatzky (1970)	53 state and territorial employment security agencies and 1,201 local branches of the above offices	Total number of employees	Staff component, i.e., total number of administrative and managerial (supervisory) personnel	Negative
5. Blau 1972	53 state and territorial employment security agencies (same as Blau, 1970); 1,201 local branches of the above agencies (same as Blau, 1970); 124 retail department stores (same as Goldman, 1973); 115 universities and colleges; 1,279 teaching hospitals	Total number of employees	Proportion of personnel responsible for administering the organization in all cases except universities and colleges (administration-faculty ratio) and teaching hospitals (percent of administrative nurses)	Negative
6. Champion & Betterton 1974	9 general hospitals; 41 tuberculosis hospitals	Annual average daily patient load	Number of full-time personnel	Size: Negative Complexity: Positive

Author and Date Published[a]	Sample	Definition of Size	Definition of Administrative Component	Relationship(s)
7. Child 1973b	Manufacturing companies N = 53 (Great Britain)	Total employees, counting part-time people as half	Total number of employees minus the combination of all direct employees and all managers of direct employment—or production—areas of work	*Size:* Overall (positive) *Subcomponents:* Positive *Contextual:* Mixed
8. Evers, Bohlen, & Warren 1976	Farm cooperatives N = 153	Total number of employees	Number of personnel in managerial (e.g., manager, foreman, department head), and clerical (e.g., bookkeeper, secretary, business machine operator) positions	Negative
9. Freeman 1973	Manufacturing organizations N = 41	Total number of employees	Total number of employees minus production workers (i.e., employees who physically change the form or location of materials or products) and maintenance personnel	*Size:* Positive *Environment:* Positive *Technology:* Positive *Environment × Technology:* Positive
10. Freeman & Hannan 1975	School districts N = 805	Total number of employees	Total full-time equivalent count of professional staff (e.g., guidance counselors, librarians), administrators (e.g., principals, superintendents), and nonprofessional staff (e.g., janitors, cafeteria workers)	*Growth:* Positive *Decline:* Negative
11. Freeman 1979	School districts N = 518	Total number of employees	Total full-time equivalent count of professional staff	*Growth:* Positive *Decline:* Negative *Revenues:* Positive

Author and Date Published[a]	Sample	Definition of Size	Definition of Administrative Component	Relationship(s)
12. Goldman 1973	Retail department stores N = 124	Total number of employees	Executive and supervisory personnel	*Size:* Middle levels (positive); lower levels (negative) *Complexity:* Positive
13. Haas, Hall, & Johnson 1963	30 organizations of various types, ranging from a large hotel to a railroad	Total number of full-time workers or the equivalent	Supportive component, i.e., total number of persons who contributed indirectly to goal attainment (e.g., employees engaged in payroll, auditing, filing, and office management)	Negative
14. Hawley, Boland, & Boland 1965	Tax-supported institutions of higher education N = 97	Number of full- and part-time faculty—highly correlated ($r > .94$) with student body size	Total number of professional administrators, excluding department chairperson and heads of research institutes and bureaus.	*Size:* Negative *Complexity:* Negative
15. Hendershot & James 1972	School districts N = 299	Total number of students enrolled—assumed to be correlated with number of employees	Total number of supervisory faculty (i.e., principals and supervisors)	*Size:* Negative *Rate of Growth:* slow (positive); rapid (negative)
16. Hinings & Bryman 1974	42 Anglican dioceses; 26 Methodist districts (Great Britain)	Number of paid and unpaid personnel employed	Administrative, professional, and technical staff outside the parish or circuit system	*Size:* Positive *Complexity:* Negative

Author and Date Published[a]	Sample	Definition of Size	Definition of Administrative Component	Relationship(s)
17. Holdaway & Blowers 1971	Urban school systems $N = 41$ (Canada)	Variety of intercorrelated measures: number of schools, pupils, professional and administrative staff, and classroom teachers (excluding principals)	Defined in three ways: (1) Central office administrative personnel (2) Central office professional employees (i.e., university-trained, nonadministrative staff), and (3) Central office administrative personnel plus school principals. Personnel who could not be classified as teachers, professional employees or administrators were excluded (e.g., nonprofessional clerical and custodial employees)	No consistent tendency to rise or fall
18. Indik 1964	32 package delivery firms, 36 automobile sales dealerships, 12 volunteer fire companies, 8 industrial labor union locals, 28 nonpartisan political organization chapters	Number of members of the organization unit	Number of supervisors whose role involved mainly direct interpersonal supervision or key organizational administrative decision making	Negative
19. James 1972	General hospitals $N = 91$	Number of personnel employed, plus part-time equivalents	Number of personnel in managerial (e.g., administrator, department manager, director of nursing) and clerical (e.g., accountant, clerk, typist) positions	Negative
20. Jones 1977	Manufacturing companies $N=32$	Total number of employees	Nonworkflow personnel	Perceived environmental uncertainty and mass-output orientation of production technology were found to be significant determinants of administrative intensity

206

Author and Date Published[a]	Sample	Definition of Size	Definition of Administrative Component	Relationship(s)
21. Kasarda 1973	School systems N = 130	Total number of classroom teachers, administrators, professionals,[b] and clerical staff employed by each system	Proportion of personnel who perform administrative duties	*Turnover:* Positive *Number of professional staff:* Positive
22. Kasarda 1974	School systems N = 178	Total number of workers	Total number of marginal, communication, and professional[b] and technical workers	*Size:* Overall (negative) *Subcomponents:* Professional & technical employees (positive); communication workers (positive); managerial workers (negative)
23. Lindenfeld 1961	School systems N = 323	Total of institutional and administrative staff	Total administrators, principals, and supervisors	Negative
24. Melman 1951 & 1956	Manufacturing industries, 1899–1947 N = 69	Total assets	Administrative personnel, including all salaried and clerical office employees	Negative
25. Pondy 1969	Manufacturing industries, 1960 N = 45	Number of production personnel per organization	Census categories: managerial, professional and clerical personnel	*Size:* Negative *Complexity:* Positive
26. Raphael 1967	Local unions N = 65	Total number of dues-paying members	Active (as opposed to formally designated) administrative component	Positive
27. Reimann 1979	Manufacturing concerns N = 20	Total number of employees	Full-time employees engaged in 17 specialist functions representing 4 components (i.e., general staff, planning & control, development, and maintenance)	*Size:* Overall (positive) *Subcomponents:* Mixed *Structural Variables:* Mixed *Situational Variables:* Mixed

Author and Date Published[a]	Sample	Definition of Size	Definition of Administrative Component	Relationship(s)
28. Rushing 1966, 1967, & 1972	Manufacturing industries $N = 41$	Total number of production personnel per organization	Census categories: managerial, professional, and clerical personnel	*Size:* Negative *Complexity:* Positive
29. Terrien & Mills 1955	School districts $N = 2,061$	Total number of employees	Administrative personnel (e.g., superintendent, principal, business manager)	Positive
30. Tosi & Patt 1967	Army hospitals $N = 36$	Full-time personnel or equivalents, excluding dental, veterinary, sanitary, research, and full-time training services	Full-time personnel or equivalents used for administrative functions (e.g., office work, supply, and planning personnel)	Negative
31. Tsouderos 1955	Voluntary associations $N = 10$	Annual membership	Not defined	*Growth:* Positive *Decline:* Negative

[a]Complete citations are listed in the reference section at the end of Chapter 7.
[b]For example, guidance counselors, social workers, speech therapists, etc.

Technology and Structure

Technology and Structure

Chapter 8

The impact of technology on society can scarcely be questioned. We are living in a world where technological development and change are more conspicuous by their absence than by their presence. Technologically based developments are responsible for the "movement of people from farms to cities and from industrial to service occupations. They have stimulated the evolution of the modern economic organization, altered class structures, and affected political institutions."[1] The corresponding effects of technology on organizations and job structures have been almost equally profound. It is the study of these effects and organizational responses to them that provides the focus of the present chapter.

Technology Defined

As has been frequently noted, there is a great lack of clarity and virtually no agreement as to the *exact* meaning of organizational technology.[2] This confusion reflects both the diversity of orientations in the study of organizations and the divergent approaches that have been developed to measure it. One set of definitional parameters, however, that has gained at least some measure of *general* acceptance conceives of technology as the means by which an organization transforms inputs into outputs. Building on this base, the concept of technology employed here refers to the techniques or processes used in the transformation of material or informational inputs into various outputs (either goods or services).

The relevance of the concept of technology to organizations in general is often unappreciated. Regardless of type or kind, *all* organizations are vehicles of technology. This point is well stated by Porter, Lawler, and Hackman.

---

[1] P. M. Blau et al. "Technology and Organization in Manufacturing," *Administrative Science Quarterly* 21 (1976): 20.

[2] D. F. Gillespie and D. S. Mileti, "Technology and the Study of Organizations: An Overview and Appraisal," *Academy of Management Review* 2 (1977): 7–16.

It must be emphasized that technology is a term that is applicable to all types and kinds of organizations, not just industrial or manufacturing. All organizations, whether production-oriented or service-oriented, are presumed to involve individuals in some sort of activities that result in the transformation of "things" (requests, raw materials, people, communication, symbols, etc.) coming in into things going out. The fact that some of these techniques and activities deal with less tangible objects in no sense obviates the necessity to consider the technology of operations used to deal with them. [3]

Why Technology Is Important

There are several major reasons why technology is of particular importance to the study of organizations. One immediate and obvious reason is that, within the industrial sector, technology has been and continues to be the main source of increases in productivity. Despite changes in the means used to motivate people and the variety of incentives that have been offered to stimulate production, the resulting increase has been negligible when compared to that created by technology. Over the thirty-year period 1948 to 1977, the index of manufacturing output per work-hour in the private sector increased almost 70 percentage points, from 58.0 to 126.9. While not all of this increase can be attributed to improved technology, unquestionably the lion's share can. Furthermore, the exponential growth of technology has made the exploitation of increasingly more marginal resources economically feasible, thereby ensuring continued material benefits at acceptable costs. [4] Perhaps more importantly, technological change has created what Roy has characterized as an "irresistible force toward continued innovations." [5] A conjectural model of this progression of technology is presented in Figure 8-1.

In addition to the influence of technology on productivity, there is a second reason why technology is of importance to the study of organizations. Technology is often a dominant determinant of job structure. As Litterer succinctly notes, "If technology and machines are changed, then jobs are changed." [6] One need only review the evolution of technology from the first use of rudimentary hand tools to the present application of computer-based manufacturing systems to appreciate the truth of this statement.

A third reason that technology is important in the study of organizations is its influence on employee attitudes and behavior. While the assembly line immediately comes to mind in this respect, the effect of technology on the nature of work extends

[3]L. W. Porter, E. E. Lawler, and J. R. Hackman, *Behavior in Organizations* (New York: McGraw-Hill, 1975), pp. 232-233.
[4]C. Starr and R. Rudman, "Parameters of Technological Growth," *Science* 182 (October 26, 1973): 358-364.
[5]R. H. Roy, *The Cultures of Management* (Baltimore, Md.: Johns Hopkins University Press, 1977), p. 155.
[6]J. A. Litterer, *The Analysis of Organizations,* 2nd ed. (New York: John Wiley & Sons, 1973), p. 280.

Figure 8–1 *Conjectural Representation of Technological Evolution*

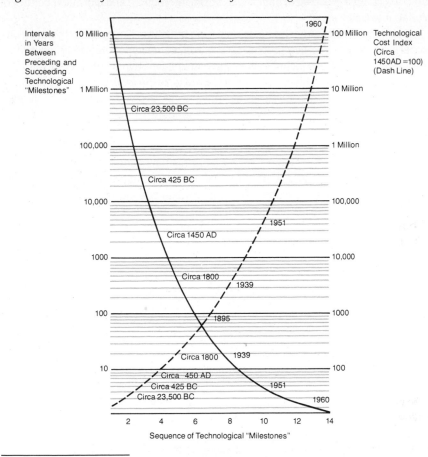

Source: R. H. Roy, *The Cultures of Management* (Baltimore, Md.: Johns Hopkins University Press, 1977), p. 161. Copyright © 1970, 1977 by the Johns Hopkins University Press. All rights reserved. Used by permission.

Note: The *solid line* and its related ordinate scale at the left show "intervals between preceding and succeeding technologies, that is, the number of years that the *preceding* technology has survived before the advent of its successor. Thus, the scale reading for the point designated as circa 1450 is 2000; this means that the technologies that preceded (e.g., manuscript writing, the distaff and spindle, and catapult) those introduced about 1450 (e.g., printing, the spinning wheel and flyer, the hand gun) had characterized society for about 2000 years. Analogously, the reading for circa 1895 is about 90 years, the period of dominance of predecessor technologies introduced at the time of the Revolution." The *dashed line* and its related ordinate scale at the right show index numbers for the increasing capital cost of each successive technology. "The assumption of an index number of 100 for circa 1450 says, in effect, that the technology that cost 100 units then has been supplanted by the technology of 1960 (e.g., satellite communication and space travel) at a cost two million times as great." (Roy, *Cultures of Management,* pp. 161, 162)

Technology and Structure

beyond the obvious subjugation of man to machine. Technology exerts influence on group composition, group size, patterns of social interaction, and individual control of personal activities.[7]

A final reason is its effect on basic operating structure. Research in this area can be separated roughly into *two* groups. *One* group, sometimes referred to as *technological determinists*, views technology as the primary determinant of an organization's structure and processes. This is frequently referred to as the *technological imperative*.[8] Representatives of this group hold that "technology evolves according to its own internally derived logic and needs, quite independent of social environment and culture."[9] The position of the *second* group is much less extreme. Viewing organizations as open systems, it recognizes the existence of a mutual interdependence between technology and structure. This group thus maintains that "technology can both influence the organization and be influenced by the organization."[10] The remaining sections of this chapter will further explore these two views.

Two Important Points

Before proceeding further in our discussion two important points deserve mention: (a) the manner in which information on the technological sophistication and structure of an organization is collected; and (b) the level of analysis employed in studies dealing with the relationships between technology and organization structure.

With respect to point a, organization theorists have developed two very different approaches for judging the technological characteristics and structural properties of a firm.[11] Commonly labeled *objective* and *perceptual*, each has its weaknesses. The *objective approach* primarily relies on company documents such as organization charts, job descriptions, and personnel folders in measuring various dimensions. The *perceptual approach* is largely based on the aggregation of interview and questionnaire data from a representative sampling of organizational members. Care should be taken here not to interpret the word "objective" to mean more reliable or valid. While the interview-questionnaire approach has been criticized for possibly reflecting personal biases and role idiosyncrasies, company records are often obsolete. Given the potential for error in each instance, one approach should not be arbitrarily preferred over the other. Furthermore, it should be realized that the results that they yield may not be comparable.[12]

---

[7]J. M. Shepard, "Technology, Alienation and Job Satisfaction," *Annual Review of Sociology* 3 (1977): 1–21.

[8]D. J. Hickson, D. S. Pugh, and D. C. Pheysey, "Operations Technology and Organization Structure: An Empirical Reappraisal," *Administrative Science Quarterly* 14 (1969): 378.

[9]L. F. Davis and J. C. Taylor, "Technology, Organization and Job Structure," in *Handbook of Work Organization and Society,* ed. R. Dubin (Chicago: Rand McNally), p. 380.

[10]R. Albanese, *Managing toward Accountability for Performance,* 2nd ed. (Homewood, Ill.: Richard D. Irwin, 1978), p. 497.

[11]J. M. Pennings, "Measures of Organizational Structure: A Methodological Note," *American Journal of Sociology* 79 (1973): 686–704; J. D. Ford, "Institutional versus Questionnaire Measures of Organizational Structure: A Reexamination," *Academy of Management Journal* 22 (1979): 601–610.

[12]V. Sathe, "Institutional versus Questionnaire Measures of Organization Structure," *Academy of Management Journal* 21 (1978): 227–238.

With respect to point b, level of analysis, *three* quite different approaches have been taken in assessing the basic nature of the relationship of technology to structure. Technology has been conceptualized as a variable at three different levels: (1) organization-wide or systems level, (2) work group or subunit level, and (3) individual level. This is primarily a distinction between the *overall* or *core technology* of an organization, the basic character of subunit work flow, and the nature of individual jobs. Thus, the *first* approach is an organization level analysis. For example, Woodward classified the technology of industrial plants on the basis of the technological complexity of their dominant mode of production.[13] Similarly, Hickson, Pugh, and Pheysey studied the relationship between technology and structure using such organization level dimensions as ownership and total number of employees.[14] Subunit or work flow level analysis, the *second* approach, recognizes that different work groups within the same organization may have different technologies. Thus, Grimes and Klein as well as Van de Ven and Delbecq measured technology at the work flow level using such variables as subunit task variability and subunit task difficulty.[15] The *third* and final approach, individual level analysis, is typically concerned with the characteristics of the tasks performed by individual employees. As examples of this approach, technology has been conceptualized at the individual level using such variables as task interdependence, task predictability, and task manageability.[16]

In comparing and evaluating the results of the various studies to be discussed in this chapter, it should be noted that, although all three approaches are similar in that they treat technology as an independent variable affecting specific aspects of organization structure (dependent variables), the results that they provide and the relationships that they suggest may very well be different.[17]

Technological Typologies

Finally, before beginning a discussion of studies dealing with the relationship between technology and organization structure, it would seem beneficial to briefly review the various ways in which technologies can be classified. Not only will this provide an

---

[13]J. Woodward, *Management and Technology* (London: Her Majesty's Stationery Office, 1958), p. 12.

[14]Hickson, Pugh, and Pheysey, "Operations Technology and Organization Structure."

[15]A. J. Grimes and S. M. Klein, "The Technological Imperative: The Relative Impact of Task Unit, Modal Technology, and Hierarchy on Structure," *Academy of Management Journal* 16 (1973): 583–597; A. Van de Ven and A. L. Delbecq, "A Task Contingent Model of Work Unit Structure," *Administrative Science Quarterly* 19 (1974): 183–197.

[16]L. G. Hrebiniak, "Job Technology, Supervision and Work Group Structure," *Administrative Science Quarterly* 19 (1974): 395–410; L. Mohr, "Organizational Technology and Organization Structure," *Administrative Science Quarterly* 16 (1971): 444–459.

[17]See, for example, D. E. Comstock and W. R. Scott, "Technology and the Structure of Subunits," *Administrative Science Quarterly* 22 (1977): 177–202; B. C. Reimann, "Organization Structure and Technology in Manufacturing: Systems versus Workflow Level Perspectives," *Academy of Management Journal*, in press; D. M. Rousseau, "Measures of Technology as Predictors of Employee Attitude," *Journal of Applied Psychology* 63 (1978): 213–218; D. M. Rousseau, "Assessment of Technology in Organizations: Closed versus Open Systems Approaches," *Academy of Management Review* 4 (1979): 531–542.

overview of variations in technology, but it will also serve to introduce several common terms used in describing technical systems.

It should be noted that classification schemes are not inherently right or wrong, but rather useful or useless. As is true with so many other areas of organization theory, there is no single agreed upon technological classification system. In general, however, the following classifications are the ones that are most commonly used at the present time, and have been shown to be the most beneficial in understanding the technology-organization relationship.

Thompson—Technological Interdependence

Of the several technological typologies that have been employed, Thompson's is generally considered to be the richest conceptually.[18] Although essentially a systems level model focusing on the overall or core technology of an organization, it is also adaptable to the categorization of subsystem units such as departments. In addition, it has the important advantage of being applicable to a wide variety of industries and service organizations, not being bound exclusively to a single organizational setting.

Thompson classified technologies according to a threefold scheme based on the way in which work systems are structured for task accomplishment.

Long-Linked Technology. Typified by the mass production assembly line, long-linked technology is characterized by the *sequential interdependence* of a variety of tasks, operations, or motions. The procedures necessary to complete a unit of output are highly standardized and must be performed in a specified serial order. Figure 8–2 (a) depicts such a system. The most obvious example of this form of technology is the automobile assembly line. Other examples include cafeterias, relay teams, petroleum refineries, and automated car washes.

Mediating Technology. Characterized by a *pooled interdependence,* mediating technology, as illustrated in Figure 8–2(b), entails the joining together of otherwise independent units such as clients and customers. Examples of organizations using this type of technology include banks, commodity brokers, insurance claim units, post offices, computer dating services, employment agencies, and even auction companies. Each performs a mediating or interchange function linking units that are otherwise independent. Banks, for instance, serve as a nexus between depositors and borrowers. It should be noted that, to be effective, mediating technologies require both a measure of categorization and a degree of standardization. For instance, continuing with the example of a bank, customers are first categorized as either depositors or borrowers, but are subsequently treated according to a standardized process.

---

[18]J. Thompson, *Organizations in Action* (New York: McGraw-Hill, 1967), pp. 15–18.

Figure 8–2 *Thompson's Technological Typology and Three Types of Technological Interdependence*

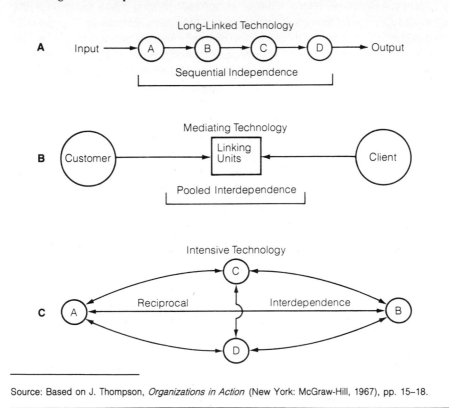

Source: Based on J. Thompson, *Organizations in Action* (New York: McGraw-Hill, 1967), pp. 15–18.

Technology and Structure

Intensive Technology.   Exemplified by the use of a variety of different techniques and skills to effect a change in a specific object, intensive technology is characterized by *reciprocal interdependence*. That is, in contrast to long-linked technology that achieves coordination through planning, and to mediating technology that relies on standardization, intensive technology secures coordination through mutual adjustment. The selection, mix, and the sequence of techniques and skills used to achieve change in an object are largely affected by feedback from the object itself. Thus, the outputs of individuals or units are based on inputs (feedback) from the individuals or units themselves and vice versa. "The intensive technology is most dramatically illustrated by the general hospital. At any moment an emergency admission may require some combination of dietary, x-ray, laboratory, and housekeeping or hotel services, together with the various medical specialties, pharmaceutical services, occupational therapies, social work services, and spiritual or religious services. Which of these, and when, can be determined only from evidence about the state of the patient."[19]

Other examples of intensive technologies are military combat teams, mental health centers, basketball teams, and certain research and development units. Their general structure is shown in Figure 8–2(c).

As has been noted by Rousseau and others, the underlying distinction between Thompson's three types of technology "is essentially based on the amount of discretionary or problem-solving behavior required of the human operator in the production process."[20] In addition, as observed by Jelinek, each type is increasingly contingent, increasingly difficult to coordinate (responding increasingly to uncertainty), and thus increasingly costly.[21]

Organizations characterized by *long-linked technology,* therefore, typically seek to offset significant uncertainties through vertical integration—broadening their operations so as to include a larger number of processing stages—in order to encompass important sources of uncertainty within their boundaries. Examples of this are the move backward of some automobile manufacturers into the production of parts and accessories to assure reasonably priced stocks of supplies; the move forward of aluminum companies into the marketing of finished products to cultivate a demand for their product; and the emergence through acquisition and merger of large integrated producers in the oil and forest products industries. Similarly, organizations with *mediating technologies* characteristically cope with uncertainty by increasing the number of units served. Thus, the stability of an insurance company is a function of its ability "to find enough poolers of risk to avoid the possibility of any one loss destroying the coverage of the others."[22] Finally, organizations founded on *intensive technology* generally increase their tolerance for uncertainty by ensuring the availabil-

[19]Thompson, *Organizations in Action*, p. 17.
[20]Rousseau, "Measures of Technology," p. 214.
[21]M. Jelinek, "Technology, Organizations, and Contingency," *Academy of Management Review* 2 (1977): 17–26.
[22]Thompson, *Organizations in Action*, p. 42.

ity of a variety of specialized services and skills in order to be prepared for any contigency. A much publicized recent example is the tendency for an increasing number of general hospitals to acquire such sophisticated and specialized equipment as computer-assisted transaxial tomography units—"C.A.T. scanners."

Woodward—Technical Complexity

One of the earliest and most popular technological typologies was offered by Woodward.[23] Drawing on an empirical study of the organization structures of 100 British manufacturing firms, Woodward developed a scale of technology based on three related variables: "(1) stages in the historical development of production processes, (2) the interrelation between the items of equipment used for these processes, and (3) the extent to which the operations performed in the processes were repetitive or comparable from one production cycle or sequence to the next."[24] The application of this scale to the firms' typical mode of production resulted in a threefold classification of technology with numerous subgroups, as illustrated in Figure 8–3. These various subgroups were viewed by Woodward as systems of production increasing in both order of chronological development and technical complexity, that is, "the extent to which [a] production process is controllable and its results predictable."[25] Thus, technical complexity is conceptualized as ranging from, at one extreme, the production of single units according to customer specifications (the oldest and simplest method of production) through an intermediate category involving large batch and mass production to the opposite extreme, that of continuous flow process production (the most recent and most technically advanced).

Organizations falling in the unit production category are typically called *job-order* shops. Products are designed and manufactured on a "custom-made" basis. As a result, they are relatively heterogeneous, and the tasks performed on each unit are typically noncomparable. Examples of job-order shop output include custom-made accessories, custom-tailored clothing, prototype electronic components, and special order machine tools. At the opposite end of the technological continuum, *process* or continuous flow manufacturing systems produce highly standardized outputs following a uniform and repetitive sequence. Production is characteristically maintained at a set level, and lot sizes are generally large. Illustrations of process production include the manufacture of petroleum products, chemicals, and pharmaceuticals. *Mass production* systems fall between these two extremes. Equivalent to Thompson's "long-linked" technology, the operations performed in this type of manufacturing are generally routine, repetitive, and predictable. In addition to the assembly line manu-

---

[23]Woodward, *Management and Technology;* J. Woodward, *Industrial Organization: Theory and Practice* (London: Oxford University Press, 1965), pp. 35–40.

[24]J. Woodward, "Automation and Technical Change—The Implications for the Management Process," in *Organization Structure and Design,* ed. G. W. Dalton, P. R. Lawrence, and J. W. Lorsch (Homewood, Ill.: Richard D. Irwin, 1970), p. 299.

[25]Woodward, *Management and Technology,* p.12.

Figure 8-3 *Woodward's Classification of 100 British Firms According to Their System of Production*

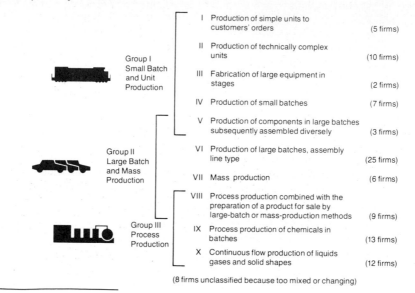

Group I
Small Batch
and Unit
Production

   I   Production of simple units to customers' orders   (5 firms)

   II   Production of technically complex units   (10 firms)

   III   Fabrication of large equipment in stages   (2 firms)

   IV   Production of small batches   (7 firms)

Group II
Large Batch
and Mass
Production

   V   Production of components in large batches subsequently assembled diversely   (3 firms)

   VI   Production of large batches, assembly line type   (25 firms)

   VII   Mass production   (6 firms)

Group III
Process
Production

   VIII   Process production combined with the preparation of a product for sale by large-batch or mass-production methods   (9 firms)

   IX   Process production of chemicals in batches   (13 firms)

   X   Continuous flow production of liquids gases and solid shapes   (12 firms)

(8 firms unclassified because too mixed or changing)

Source: J. Woodward, *Management and Technology* (London: Her Majesty's Stationery Office, 1958), p. 11. Diagram is reproduced with the permission of the Controller of Her Britannic Majesty's Stationery Office.

facturing of automobiles, other examples of mass production include large bakeries and mass produced clothing.

In reflecting on Woodward's classification of production systems, it should be realized that its application is much narrower than Thompson's, being appropriate primarily for industrial organizations. Furthermore, while Woodward's data suggest that the distinction between the batch plants she studied was clear enough to differentiate small from large batch production, she provides no cutoff point to guide in making this judgment. In reality, we would expect to find a few plants where production runs would make it difficult, if not impossible, to unequivocally make this distinction. Finally, the argument that technical complexity increases from unit, through mass, to continuous process production has been challenged by Harvey, who has argued that this sequence can also be viewed "as a move toward technical simplicity rather than complexity," in that "it is, after all, the frequent emergence of problems calling for innovation that characterize unit rather than process production."[26] A somewhat similar view is also expressed by Starbuck who says that "it is not really accurate to call the technological variable 'complexity,' since this complexity seems to correspond to *smoothness* of production, but this was Woodward's term."[27]

[26]E. Harvey, "Technology and the Structure of Organizations," *American Sociological Review* 33 (1968): 249.
[27]W. H. Starbuck, "Organizational Growth and Development," in *Handbook of Organizations,* ed. J. G. March (Chicago: Rand McNally, 1965), p. 503.

Other Technology Typologies

Numerous other technological typologies have been proposed. In general, like Woodward's, they primarily focus on industrial operations. For instance, Hickson, Pugh, and Pheysey have advanced a three-part typology based on technology of *work flow*: (1) *operations technology,* "the equipping and sequencing of activities in the workflow," (2) *materials technology,* "characteristics of the materials used in the workflow," and (3) *knowledge technology,* "characteristics of the knowledge used in the workflow."[28] A somewhat broader typology has been suggested by Perrow.[29] It classifies the kind of work performed in an organization or unit on the basis of two dimensions: (1) the number of exceptional cases encountered and (2) the extent to which the search for solutions to these exceptions is analyzable in task performance. A third, widely-referenced typology has been developed by Harvey.[30] It employs a complexity dimension ranging from "technical diffuseness to specificity." A firm is considered to be technically diffuse when it utilizes a number of techniques or processes to produce a wide range of outputs that vary over time. In contrast, technical specificity implies a firm in which only one or a small number of outputs are produced consistently. Thus, Harvey's typology considers not only the *form* of technology (as did Woodward's), but also the amount of "changefulness" *within* a form.[31]

Although other schemes for the classification of technology could be mentioned, the approaches discussed above are the most widely used. In reviewing the typologies presented, the reader should recognize that, in general, each deals with two primary dimensions: (a) degree of simplicity/complexity and (b) degree of uniformity/nonuniformity. A generic representation of these dimensions with an accompanying interpretation is contained in Table 8–1.

Technology and Organization Structure

Having clarified the meaning of technology and established its importance, and having reviewed the various ways in which technology can be classified, we are now ready to examine the literature dealing with the relationship between technology and organization structure. While there is little disagreement that the historical evolution from craft to more advanced technologies has resulted in an increased complexity of organizations, as Eldridge and Crombie observe, "the extent to which technology determines structure has been disputed by organisation theorists for some years."[32] To begin our analysis of this dispute, we first turn to the studies done by Woodward.

---

[28]Hickson, Pugh, and Pheysey, "Operations Technology and Organization Structure," p. 380.

[29]C. Perrow, *Organizational Analysis: A Sociological View* (Monterey, Calif.: Brooks/Cole, 1970), pp. 75–80; C. Perrow, "A Framework for the Comparative Analysis of Organizations," *American Sociological Review* 32 (1967): 194–208.

[30]Harvey, "Technology and Structure."

[31]R. Hunt, "Technology and Organization," *Academy of Management Journal* 13 (1970): 236–252.

[32]J. E. T. Eldridge and A. D. Crombie, *A Sociology of Organisations* (London: George Allen & Unwin, 1975), p. 107.

Table 8–1 *Technology Continuum*

	Craft	Machine Tending	Mass Production Assembly Line	Continuous Process	Advanced Technology	
Simple technology	●○○○○	●●○○○	●●●○○	●●●●○	●●●●●	Complex technology
Stable, uniform technology	●○○○○	●●○○○	●●●○○	●●●●●	●●●●●	Dynamic, nonuniform technology

Source: Adapted from F. E. Kast and J. F. Rosenzweig, *Organization and Management: A Systems Approach,* 2nd ed. (New York: McGraw-Hill, 1974), p. 187. Used by permission.

Note: The simple-complex continuum relates to the degree of complexity of a technological system—both its mechanical and intellectual aspects. Thus craft technology is the simplest form, and the technology in such undertakings as atomic energy and space exploration is the most complex. The stable-dynamic dimension refers to the frequency of change in technology. Here again, craft technology is the most stable. The most dynamic is found in industries such as aerospace and electronics.

The Woodward Studies

Begun in 1953 by the Human Relations Research unit at the South East Essex College of Technology in Great Britain, the Woodward studies represent the first major attempt to view organization structure from a technological perspective.[33] Their results have had a major influence on the subsequent course of organization theory and research.

The findings of the Woodward studies are based on an analysis of the organization structure and operating procedures of 100 South Essex manufacturing firms ranging in size from less than 250 employees (40 per cent of the sample) to over 1,000 employees (20 per cent of the sample). Information pertaining to the operation of the firms was collected using a variety of research methods, including surveys, longitudinal analyses, and case studies. Data were collected on each firm with regard to the following:

1. *History, background, and objectives.*
2. *Description of the manufacturing process and methods.*
3. *Forms and routines through which the firm was organized and operated.*
4. *Facts and figures that could be used to make an assessment of the firm's commercial success.*[34]

The central focus of the initial Woodward study was to determine the validity of the basic concepts (for example, unity of command, number of hierarchical levels, optimum span of control, etc.) typically associated with traditional views of organization.

---

[33]Woodward, *Management and Technology;* Woodward, *Industrial Organization.*
[34]Woodward, *Industrial Organization,* p. 11.

The firms were classified into three groups—"average," "above average," and "below average"—in terms of success, depending on such factors as the state of the industry in which each firm operated, changes in market share, annual reports and financial accounts, and fluctuation of shares on the stock exchange. An attempt was then made to correlate success with structural form and organizational size. No systematic relationships were found in either instance. The variability in the form and size of the firms examined was so great that it was impossible to establish any interrelationship between business success and what traditionally had been regarded as sound organizational structure.

It was only after Woodward and her associates tried to classify the firms according to technological complexity (using the typology described earlier) that clear, strong relationships began to appear between organizational structure and success *within* each technological grouping—unit, mass, and continuous process production.

For example, *the number of levels of management authority increased with technical complexity.* As illustrated in Figure 8–4, the twenty-four unit production firms had a median of three levels, which resulted in short and broadly based structures. The thirty-one mass production firms had an average of four levels; firms engaged in process production were tall and narrowly based, typically averaging six levels. Perhaps most significantly, however, the firms classified as above average in each category had at least one characteristic in common. That is, the number of levels of management authority in each tended to cluster around the median for their production group.

Similarly, *the span of control of first-line supervisors varied in relation to technology.* As shown in Figure 8–5, the span of control of first-line supervisors displayed a curvilinear relationship, increasing from unit to mass production and then decreasing from mass to process production. The primary explanation of this difference is the fact that, as technology reaches the process production level, an increasing number of activities are machine or system controlled. Most importantly, however, there was a marked tendency for above average firms in each production group to approximate the median for their category. In contrast, the supervisory spans of firms judged below average tended to vary widely from the median.

Likewise, *the ratio of managers and supervisors to other personnel varied with type of technology.* A positive linear relationship (similar to that for levels of management) was found between technical complexity and the ratio of managers and supervisors to nonsupervisory staff. In unit production firms, the ratio ranged from 1:24 to as low as 1:49, whereas in mass production firms the ratio ranged from 1:14 to 1:18. In process production firms, the ratio ranged from 1:7 to 1:8. In explanation, an analysis of the Woodward data revealed that, as technological level increased, so did the proportion of clerical and administrative employees and the percentage of professional and technical personnel. A summary of Woodward's findings is provided in Table 8–2.

Subsequent to this analysis, Woodward and her associates selected 20 firms, employing more than 250 employees, for a more detailed analysis. The firms chosen for study, although not randomly selected, were representative of each category of

Technology and Structure

Figure 8–4 *Number of Levels of Management Authority in Relation to System of Production in Woodward Study*

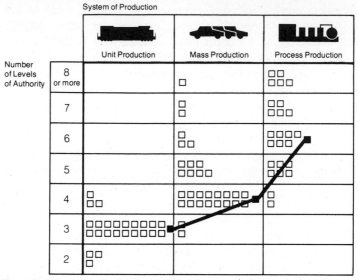

The median is the number of levels in the middle firm in the range—for instance, the sixteenth of the 31 mass-production firms

☐ 1 Firm
■ Median

Source: J. Woodward, *Management and Technology* (London: Her Majesty's Stationery Office, 1958), p. 14. Diagram is reproduced with the permission of the Controller of Her Britannic Majesty's Stationery Office.

Figure 8–5 *Span of Control in First-Line Supervision in Relation to System of Production in Woodward Study*

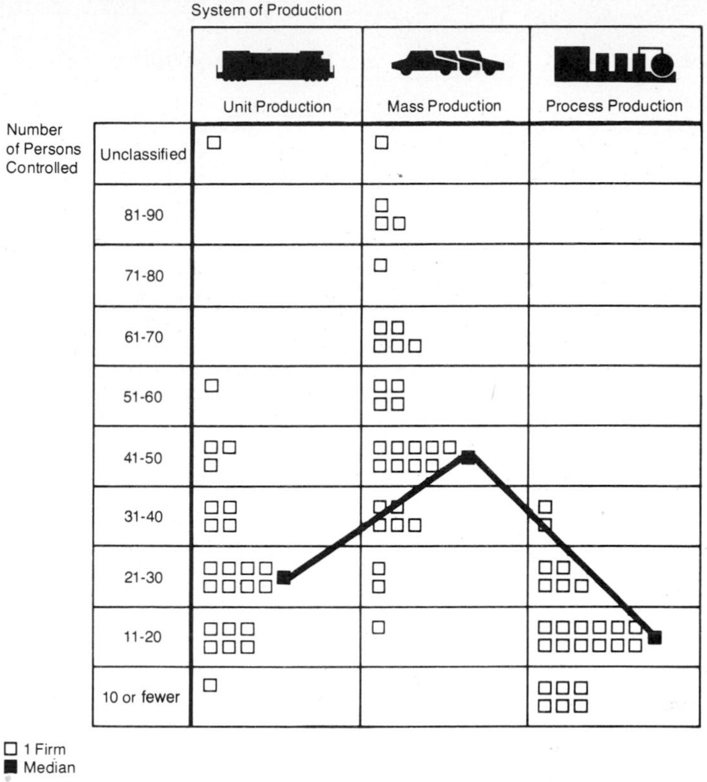

System of Production

Number of Persons Controlled		Unit Production	Mass Production	Process Production
	Unclassified	□	□	
	81-90		□ □ □	
	71-80		□	
	61-70		□ □ □ □ □	
	51-60	□	□ □ □ □	
	41-50	□ □ □	□ □ □ □ □ □ □ □ □	
	31-40	□ □ □ □	□ □ □ □ □	□ □
	21-30	□ □ □ □ □ □ □ □	□ □	□ □ □ □ □
	11-20	□ □ □ □ □ □	□	□ □ □ □ □ □ □ □ □ □ □ □
	10 or fewer	□		□ □ □ □ □ □

□ 1 Firm
■ Median

Source: J. Woodward, *Management and Technology* (London: Her Majesty's Stationery Office, 1958), p. 15. Diagram is reproduced with the permission of the Controller of Her Britannic Majesty's Stationery Office.

Technology and Structure

Table 8–2 *Organizational Characteristics as Related to System of Production in Woodward Study*

Organizational Characteristic	System of Production		
	Unit and Small Batch	Large Batch	Process
Number of firms in study	24	31	25
Levels of management authority			
Median	3	4	6
Range	2-4	3-8	2-17
Median span of control	23	48	15
Range of ratio of managers and supervisory personnel to other personnel	1:24 to 1:49	1:14 to 1:18	1:7 to 1:8

Source: After M. P. Charns, "The Theories of Joan Woodward and James Thompson," in *Organization Planning: Cases and Concepts,* ed. J. W. Lorsch and P. R. Lawrence (Homewood, Ill.: Richard D. Irwin, 1972), p. 31, with permission of the copyright holder, the President and Fellows of Harvard College.

technological complexity and each category of success. One or more research teams spent roughly a month in each firm collecting additional information through observation and interviews. In addition to further examining each firm's technology of production, the teams made a more detailed analysis of both the history and the structural evolution of each firm and the manner in which it reached decisions. Finally, an intensive study was conducted in three firms, all employing 2,001–4,000 workers, in which manufacturing methods were either changing or mixed. These were selected because it was felt that, if organization and technology were linked in the way suggested by the earlier findings, the most difficult organizational problems would arise in such firms.

The results of the second and third phases of the research not only confirmed the findings of the initial study, but also revealed that *for certain characteristics the most successful firms at each end (the extremes) of the technical continuum were quite similar.* Specifically, for successful firms Woodward found:

1. There was a tendency for organic management systems [in Burns and Stalker's sense; see Chapter 6] to predominate in jobbing and continuous flow production, while mechanistic systems predominated in the middle ranges.

2. Clear cut definition of duties and responsibilities was characteristic of firms in the middle ranges, while flexible organisations with a high degree of delegation, both of authority and of the responsibility for decision making and with permissive and participating management, was characteristic of firms at the extremes.

3. There was less organisation at the extremes, and it was extremely difficult to distinguish between executive and advisory responsibility.

4. In both process and unit production, stress was laid on the importance of line managers' being technically competent. The technical competence required was, however, of a different kind in the two types of production. In process

production, the technical competence was intellectual, based upon qualifications and knowledge, whereas in unit production it was intuitive, based on long experience and know-how.

5. The two groups of firms at the extremes tended to be homogeneous in organisational and behavioural patterns. The physical work flow and the nature of the manufacturing operations appeared to place considerable restrictions on organisational choice. Between the two extremes, however, in the batch production area, the physical work flow did not impose such rigid restrictions, with the result that technology did not as much determine organisation as define the limits within which it could be determined.[35]

Woodward summarized these findings by concluding:

As far as the organisation of production [is] concerned, situational demands impose themselves more rigidly and obviously at the extremes than in the middle of the scale. Those responsible for organisation planning have less room for maneuver. There are few alternative ways of organising production in a special order production firm, and an unsatisfactory structure seems to show itself immediately in a decline in business success. [36]

After having made the above observations, Woodward and her associates turned their attention toward an examination of the relationship among what were considered to be the three main task functions of the manufacturing cycle: development, production, and marketing. This investigation (involving fifteen of the twenty-five firms) revealed that, in the technically advanced systems, the three task functions could be separated rather easily; however, in the unit production firms this separation was much more difficult to achieve. In addition, it was discovered that different relationships existed *among* the various task functions of the manufacturing cycle. In short, the relative importance and sequence of the three functions were found to be related to the system of production, and, within each production group, one function was central and critical to both success and survival. The three sequences felt to characterize the three main production categories are shown in Table 8–3.

In unit and small batch firms, marketing was the first phase of the cycle, since products are designed and manufactured on a custom-made basis. Sales personnel must first secure orders. Products must be developed according to specifications and then manufactured. Research and development are the central and critical activities since success depends upon the ability to transform customer specifications into acceptable finished products. This close integration of functions necessitates both frequent interdepartmental communication and close contact between the firm and its customers.

At the other extreme of the technical scale, in process-production firms, the

---

[35]Each numbered item is quoted from Woodward, "Automation and Technical Change," pp. 300–301.
[36]Woodward, *Industrial Organization,* p. 155.

Table 8–3 *Characteristics of Manufacturing Cycle as Related to System of Production in Woodward Study*

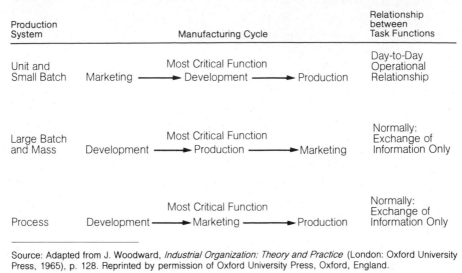

Production System	Manufacturing Cycle	Relationship between Task Functions
Unit and Small Batch	Marketing ⟶ Development (Most Critical Function) ⟶ Production	Day-to-Day Operational Relationship
Large Batch and Mass	Development ⟶ Production (Most Critical Function) ⟶ Marketing	Normally: Exchange of Information Only
Process	Development ⟶ Marketing (Most Critical Function) ⟶ Production	Normally: Exchange of Information Only

Source: Adapted from J. Woodward, *Industrial Organization: Theory and Practice* (London: Oxford University Press, 1965), p. 128. Reprinted by permission of Oxford University Press, Oxford, England.

manufacturing cycle begins with research and development. The firms' major activities were associated more with the extension of knowledge than with the development of any particular new products. As a result, however, the most critical function of the cycle was marketing, because the continued existence of the firms depended on establishing markets that would steadily absorb their production output. The relationships between the functions of the cycle were based on the routine exchange of information.

Between these extremes are the large batch and mass production firms. For this group, the first phase of the manufacturing cycle was product development; the second, production; the third, marketing. The importance of the manufacture of standardized outputs through programmed and controlled procedures puts the production function into a dominant position. Although new products required initial development and some marketing, neither of these functions was as important as production itself. The main responsibility of the development function in mass production firms was largely the modification of existing products. The primary task of the marketing function was to persuade consumers that they needed the goods produced. The independence of functions resulted in self-contained units requiring only a normal exchange of information.

These findings clearly emphasize that the nature of interactions within a firm will be greatly influenced by the function that is central and critical for its success and survival, and this in turn will be greatly affected by the firm's level of technology.

In summary, the Woodward studies suggest that technology was a dominant factor affecting the organizational structures of the firms studied. Of greatest import is the finding not only that the structures of the firms studied were affected but that the success of each firm was also directly related to a proper match between technology and certain organizational characteristics. Within each technological classification—unit, mass, process—there was a marked tendency for the most effective firms to have the appropriately structured technical systems.

Before closing our discussion of the Woodward studies, mention should be made of several of its weaknesses. Some of these were acknowledged by Woodward in her own analysis of the data.[37] Others have been raised by subsequent researchers.[38] In general, these weaknesses fall into six categories:

1. The methods employed to measure commercial success were imprecise. The study lacked rigorous measures of performance.

2. Information pertaining to the reliability and validity of the measures of technology and structure employed was not reported. In particular, the measure of technology used has been criticized as unreliable.

3. Although the results were quantified, few statistical tests were used to assess the data. The study primarily relied on subjective observational methods and interviews.

4. The methodology employed identified association and not causation. The analyses were static in nature and failed to evaluate the dynamics of change. Thus, the studies do not reveal *evolutionary* shifts in structure as technological complexity has advanced.

5. The extent to which a firm's organization structure was deemed appropriate to its technology was determined solely on the basis of economic success (for example, profits and rate of growth). Social success in terms of social benefits and abuses was not considered.

6. The firms studied (almost exclusively in manufacturing) cannot be regarded as representative of industry as a whole, either in Great Britain or the United States. This, of course, does not mean that the conclusions presented are irrelevant to similar organizations in other locations, but that their generalizability (external validity) *may be* limited.

Finally, one may argue that the differences in structure by technological type may have occurred, not as a result of the inherent characteristics of the production systems themselves, but through the mistakes of incapable organization planners. How-

---

[37]Ibid., p. 10; Woodward, "Automation and Technical Change," p. 301.

[38]See, for example, Davis and Taylor, "Technology Organization and Job Structure"; L. Donaldson, "Woodward Technology, Organizational Structure and Performance—A Critique of the Universal Generalization," *Journal of Management Studies* 13 (1976): 255–273; S. Eilon, "Structural Determinism," *Omega* 5 (1977): 499–504.

ever, as Whyte has correctly noted, "If we accept this argument, we would have to explain why it is that organization planners in a certain type of production system consistently deviate . . . in a single direction."[39]

Despite these criticisms, the Woodward studies are still significant as the first major attempt to view organization from a technological perspective. Since the publication of Woodward's work, the study of the relationship between organization structure and technology has expanded both theoretically and empirically.[40] Our discussion continues with an analysis of the Aston studies.

The Aston Studies

One of the most ambitious and intensive studies of the relationship between organization structure and technology has been conducted for over a decade and a half by another group of English researchers under the direction of Pugh and Hickson.[41] Known as the Aston Group because its early work was carried out at the Industrial Administration Research Unit of the University of Aston in Birmingham, England, the efforts and findings of this research team have become a mainstay of organization theory literature.

The Aston researchers are perhaps best known for their study of the structural and technological characteristics of forty-six diverse and randomly selected firms located in the British Midlands. This sample included a variety of retail stores, transportation companies, public utilities, commercial offices, and factories, ranging in number of employees from roughly 240 to over 25,000.

Based on data collected via personal interviews with the chief executives of the firms and department heads, the researchers attempted to distinguish between two major facets of *operations technology:* work flow integration and production continuity. (The Hickson et al. companion concepts of *materials technology* and *knowledge technology* were not measured.) *Work flow integration* was conceptualized as a general factor comprising level of automation of work flow equipment, the rigidity of the work flow, the degree of interdependence of work flow segments, and the precision or specificity of criteria used in evaluating operations. *Production continuity* was measured using Woodward's ten organizational level categories of production technology illustrated in Figure 8–3.

In an effort to determine the extent to which *operations technology* and structure were related, the Aston researchers compared the technology variable *work flow integration* to various measures of organization structure for the thirty-one manufacturing firms included in their sample. Surprisingly, only three of sixty-four structural variables had even a weak relationship with this facet of technology. These were the

[39]W. F. Whyte, *Organizational Behavior: Theory and Application* (Homewood, Ill.: Richard D. Irwin, 1969), p. 63.

[40]K. Azumi and J. Hage, *Organizational Systems* (Lexington, Mass.: Heath, 1972), p. 103.

[41]The original statement of the goals of this research program appeared in D. S. Pugh et al., "A Conceptual Scheme for Organizational Analysis," *Administrative Science Quarterly* 8 (1963): 289–315.

proportion of personnel in employment work, storekeeping, and buying and stock control. This finding is, of course, directly counter to that of Woodward.

In an attempt to reconcile this result with Woodward's conclusions, the researchers were prompted to further examine their data. In doing so, they realized that, although the three types of production systems—unit, batch, and mass—exhibit linear differences in complexity, their influence on organization structure appeared to be curvilinear (⌒-shaped). Indeed, these curvilinear effects had been observed by Woodward. For example, both the Hickson et al. and Woodward results revealed a curvilinear relationship between the span of control of first-line supervisors and production technology, with the largest spans in mass production and smaller ones in unit and continuous process. In addition, consistent with Woodward's findings, the Aston research team uncovered similar curvilinear relationships between technological type and such "job counts" as the number of workers per first-line supervisor, the proportion of personnel having inspection duties, and the proportion of personnel in maintenance capacities. In still further reanalysis, the researchers also noted that there were proportionately fewer large firms in the South East Essex sample as compared to the number in the Birmingham sample. Combined, these findings led the research team to suggest that Woodward's findings were valid only for smaller organizations where "everyone is closer to the 'shop-floor,' and structural responses to the problems of size (for example) have not begun to show."[42] This, the researchers believed, was in contrast to the situation in larger organizations where "managers and administrators are buffered from the technology itself by the specialist departments, standard procedures, and formalized paperwork that size brings with it."[43] Thus, based on the belief that small organizations are more affected by technology than large organizations, Hickson et al. concluded:

Structural variables will be associated with operations technology only where they are centered on the workflow. The smaller the organization the more its structure will be pervaded by such technological effects: the larger the organization, the more effects will be confined to variables such as job-counts of employees on activities linked with the workflow itself, and will not be detectable in variables of the more remote administrative and hierarchical structure.[44]

The Aston Group interpreted their findings to suggest that technology is much less important than size in affecting organization structure. More specifically, the smaller the organization, the greater the structural effects of technology; the larger the organization, the more such effects will be confined to production-related activities or departments. This interpretation thus represents a synthesis of the Woodward and the earlier Aston findings and is consistent with research reported in the previous chapter.

---

[42]Hickson, Pugh, and Pheysey, "Operations Technology and Organization Structure," p. 395.
[43]Ibid.
[44]Ibid., pp. 394–395.

As encouraging as these results may at first seem, the Aston studies, like those of Woodward, have also received their share of criticism. In a complete reexamination of the Aston data, Aldrich has argued that the relationship between size, structure, and technology may be largely a result of the analysis (for example, unreliable measures of technology and structure) and research design employed.[45] Aldrich examined numerous plausible rival models and found that indeed technology, as opposed to size, emerged as a key determinant of structure, thus supporting Woodward's initial thesis.

Based on this reexamination, Aldrich proposed the revised model of organizational development shown in Figure 8–6. In this model, technology (work flow integration and production continuity) was assumed to be a primary precursor of (a) the structuring of activities, (b) concentration of authority, and (c) line control of authority. Dependence, in terms of relationships with other organizations such as suppliers, creditors, and labor unions, was presented as having a positive causal impact on both production continuity and concentration of authority. Size was hypothesized as dependent on work flow integration, the structuring of activities, and production continuity. In turn, both size and production continuity were seen as having a causal impact on line control of authority. In reply to the general issues raised by Aldrich, Pugh and Hickson, while conceding that his underlying theory "seems likely in some instances," nevertheless continued to defend the position that "the suggestion that size causes structure . . . is also likely in some instances."[46]

Figure 8–6   *A Revised Model of Organizational Development Based on the Findings of the Aston Group*

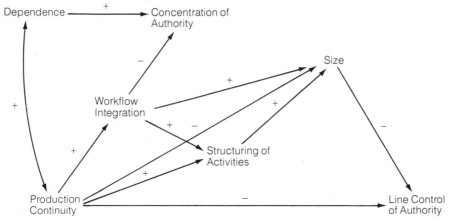

Source: Adapted from "Technology and Organizational Structure: A Reexamination of the Findings of the Aston Group" by H. E. Aldrich, published in *Administrative Science Quarterly* 17 (1972) by permission of *Administrative Science Quarterly.* Copyright © 1972 by *Administrative Science Quarterly.*

[45]H. E. Aldrich, "Technology and Organizational Structure: A Reexamination of the Findings of the Aston Group," *Administrative Science Quarterly* 17 (1972): 26–43.

[46]D. S. Pugh and D. J. Hickson, "Causal Inference and the Aston Studies," *Administrative Science Quarterly* 17 (1972): 275.

In closing our discussion, it should also be noted that many of the weaknesses that plague the Woodward findings are also common to the Aston studies. In particular, questions have been raised concerning (a) the operational structure of the variables work flow integration and production continuity;[47] (b) the reliability and validity of the numerous structural measures used in the study;[48] (c) the applicability (generalizability) of the study's findings to other types (and sizes) of organizations;[49] and (d) the overall research design of the study.[50]

Other Studies of Technology and Structure: A Summary and Evaluation

The relationship of structure to technology has been examined in numerous other studies. Ideally, a detailed analysis and explanation of each would be presented. More realistically, however, the extent of the literature in this area makes such an undertaking virtually impossible within the present context.[51] Instead, a summary of relevant studies (including all those reviewed above) is presented in Appendix 8–A. For each study this appendix lists the investigator(s), the sample(s) employed and level of analysis, the theoretical dimension(s) of technology analyzed, the manner in which technology was made operational, the type of measure of technology utilized, the theoretical dimension(s) of structure analyzed, the manner in which the dimensions of structure were made operational, the measure of structure utilized, and the more important relationships found between the structure variables and the measures of technology.

An appraisal of the empirical evidence presented in Appendix 8–A reveals most strikingly the wide variety of theoretical and operational dimensions that have been employed to measure technology and structure. An analysis of this has led Stanfield, among others, to point out that many of the apparently contradictory conclusions concerning the relationship between technology and structure may be largely a result of the tendency on the part of researchers to generalize their findings to technological dimensions they have not measured and to fail to provide clear definitions that delimit the variables measured.[52] Stanfield believes that "both of these practices result from *unrationalized categorization of variables,* which is the practice of providing no substantial, explicit explanation for one's conceptual groupings and separations, as if the

---

[47]Aldrich, "Technology and Organizational Structure"; C. W. Osmond, "Organization—Is Technology the Key?" *Personnel Management* 2, no. 5 (1970): 43–44.

[48]Aldrich, "Technology and Organizational Structure."

[49]Holdaway et al., "Dimensions of Organizations in Complex Societies: The Educational Sector," *Administrative Science Quarterly* 20 (1975): 47–58.

[50]J. L. Kmetz, "A Critique of the Aston Studies and Results with a New Measure of Technology," *Organization and Administrative Sciences* 8, no. 4 (1977/78): 123–144.

[51]For one such effort see B. C. Reimann and G. Inzerilli, "A Comparative Analysis of Empirical Research on Technology and Structure," *Journal of Management* 5 (1979): 167–192.

[52]G. G. Stanfield, "Technology and Structure as Theoretical Categories," *Administrative Science Quarterly* 21 (1976): 489–493.

system of categories had consensual validity."[53] Unrationalized categorization is further aggravated by the implicit assumption of many researchers that each of the categories employed is homogeneous. This presupposition is reflected in the mistaken belief that "the operation of one or a few variables in a category adequately represents the operations of the category as a whole."[54] This results in the misrepresentation of both technology and structure as unidimensional rather than as being complex aggregates of variables and produces apparently contradictory results that are not what they appear to be. Thus, as can be seen in Appendix 8–A, researchers have not only used different theoretical constructs of technology and structure, but have even in some instances employed dimensions that tend to overlap. As an example, Billings, Klimoski, and Breaugh treat task interdependence as a structural variable, whereas Mohr; Overton, Schneck, and Hazlett; and Van de Ven, Delbecq, and Koenig classify the same construct as a subdimension of technology.[55] Unrationalized categorization has thus led to the use of noncomparable sets of variables under common or similar names, making comparisons difficult and replication impossible.

In addition to the above theoretical differences, further examination of Appendix 8–A reveals divergences with respect to the level of analysis (organization, subunit, individual) employed and the manner in which information pertaining to the technological sophistication and structure of an organization has been obtained (objectively versus perceptually). As has been previously noted, the results yielded under such circumstances may very well be different and largely noncomparable. Indeed, the research dealing with the influence of technology on structure not only is conflicting, but is in extensive disarray.

A final methodological problem reflected in Appendix 8–A is the great diversity of contexts in which the various studies reported have been conducted. While a majority of researchers have studied manufacturing firms, others have studied service, or people-processing, organizations such as hospitals and employment security agencies. A problem in comparing the results of such studies arises, as Reimann and Inzerilli observe, in that "there is a fundamental qualitative difference between product and service industry technologies."[56] Whereas manufacturing firms typically transform various material inputs into outputs (that is, products) that go to customers, service organizations typically perform some type of transformation on individual customers who are both input into and output from the process. Consequently, as Reimann and Inzerilli further note, "It may be difficult and even misleading to try and

---

[53]Ibid., p. 489. Italics added.

[54]Ibid.

[55]R. S. Billings, R. S. Klimoski, and J. A. Breaugh, "The Impact of a Change in Technology on Job Characteristics: A Quasi-experiment," *Administrative Science Quarterly* 21 (1976): 20–40; Mohr, "Organizational Technology"; P. Overton, R. Schneck, and C. B. Hazlett, "An Empirical Study of the Technology of Nursing Subunits," *Administrative Science Quarterly* 22 (1977): 203–219; A. Van de Ven, A. L. Delbecq, and R. Koenig, "Determinants of Coordination Modes within Organizations," *American Sociological Review* 41 (1976): 322–338.

[56]B. C. Reimann and G. Inzerilli, "Technology and Organization: A Review and Synthesis of Major Research Findings" (Department of Management and Labor, Cleveland State University, Cleveland, Ohio, 1978), p. 11.

compare technology-structure relationships observed in manufacturing firms with those from service organizations."[57]

Returning to the subject that began this chapter, the impact of technology on society can scarcely be questioned. The main focus of our present discussion, however, has been on the hypothesized effects of technology on organization structure. While both technology and structure are increasingly viewed as complex aggregates with multiple dimensions, further refinements are needed not only in terms of the way these constructs are made operational, but also to more clearly define the mode of data collection utilized and the level of analysis employed. In addition, it should be noted that the relationship between technology and structure and the interactive effects of other variables, such as environment and strategic choice (discussed in Chapter 6), have seldom been considered. Furthermore, until recently, structure has almost invariably been conceived of as being dependent on technology. The adequacy of this conceptualization, however, has been increasingly questioned. At least one study has shown that structural dimensions within an organization may be manipulated in such a manner as to lessen the effects of technology.[58]

In summarizing our evaluation, we are thus led to conclude, as have Porter, Lawler, and Hackman, that available empirical evidence suggests that technology "does have some relationship to certain features of structure. But it is particularly difficult to estimate how many of the structural features have been caused by technology, how much technology has been the effect of structure, and, especially, how much other factors have affected or caused both the nature of the technology and the design of organizations."[59]

Summary

In this chapter we have examined the effects of technology on organizations and job structures. After first defining "technology," several major reasons were offered for the particular importance of technology to the study of organizations. Specifically, it was noted that: (1) technology has been and continues to be the main source of productivity increases; (2) technology is often a dominant determinant of job structure; (3) technology exerts influence on employee attitudes and behavior; and (4) an organization's technology affects its basic operating structure.

Following a brief comment on (a) the manner in which information pertaining to the technological sophistication and structure of organizations is collected (objectively versus perceptually), and (b) the level of analysis (organization, subunit, individual) employed in studies dealing with the relationships between technology and structure, a review of the various ways in which technologies can be classified was

---

[57]Ibid.

[58]C. A. Glisson, "Dependence of Technological Routinization on Structural Variables in Human Service Organizations," *Administrative Science Quarterly* 23 (1978): 383–395.

[59]Porter, Lawler, and Hackman, *Behavior in Organizations,* p. 242.

presented. Although the Thompson (see Figure 8–2) and Woodward (see Figure 8–3) technological typologies were the primary focus of our discussion, other similar schemes were also mentioned.

Having clarified the meaning of technology and established its importance, and having considered the various ways in which technology can be classified, our attention then turned to an analysis of the major literature concerning the relationship between technology and organization structure. In particular, the work of Woodward and of the Aston Group was extensively reviewed. Finally, a summary and an evaluation of other studies of technology and structure were presented.

Review and Discussion Questions

1. Why is technology important to the study of organizations?
2. The text discusses two important points dealing with the methodology commonly employed in the study of the technology-structure relationship. What are these two points, and how can they affect the results of a study?
3. Explain the Thompson Technological Interdependence typology. Provide examples of organizations in each technological classification, and comment on how they typically cope with uncertainty.
4. Compare Thompson's technological typology with that of Woodward. Which typology would more likely be applicable to all types of organizations?
5. What approach did Woodward use for collecting the information utilized for judging the technological characteristics and structural properties of the firms she studied? Do you think this is a valid approach? Why?
6. Contrast the central focus of the initial Woodward study with the final results obtained.
7. Woodward identified a curvilinear relationship between span of control and technological complexity. Explain how this relationship might have been predicted.
8. The third phase of the Woodward studies dealt with the relationship among the three main task functions of the manufacturing cycle. Discuss this relationship for each of Woodward's production systems (job-order, large batch, and process production).
9. How were the Aston Group's findings similar to Woodward's findings?
10. Why does the text conclude that it is difficult to sort out whether structure is shaped by or shapes technology? How much do other factors affect technology and structure?

References

Albanese, R. *Managing toward Accountability for Performance.* 2nd ed. Homewood, Ill.: Richard D. Irwin, 1978.

Aldrich, H. E. "Technology and Organizational Structure: A Reexamination of the Findings of the Aston Group." *Administrative Science Quarterly* 17 (1952): 26–43.

Amber, G. H., and Amber, T. S. *Anatomy of Automation.* Englewood Cliffs, N.J.: Prentice-Hall, 1962.

Azumi, K., and Hage, J. *Organizational Systems.* Lexington, Mass.: Heath, 1972.

Bell, G. D. "Determinants of Span of Control." *American Journal of Sociology* 73 (1967): 100–109.

Billings, R. S., Klimoski, R. J., and Breaugh, J. A. "The Impact of a Change in Technology on Job Characteristics: A Quasi-experiment." *Administrative Science Quarterly* 22 (1977): 318–339.

Blau, P. M., Falbe, C. M., McKinley, W., and Tracy, P. K. "Technology and Organization in Manufacturing." *Administrative Science Quarterly* 21 (1976): 20–40.

Blau, P. M., and Schoenherr, R. *The Structure of Organizations.* New York: Basic Books, 1971.

Charns, M. P. "The Theories of Joan Woodward and James Thompson." In *Organization Planning: Cases and Concepts,* edited by J. W. Lorsch and P. R. Lawrence. Homewood, Ill.: Richard D. Irwin, 1972.

Child, J. "Organizational Structure and Strategies of Control: A Replication of the Aston Study." *Administrative Science Quarterly* 17 (1972): 163–177.

Child, J. "Strategies of Control and Organizational Behavior." *Administrative Science Quarterly* 18 (1973): 1–17.

Child, J., and Mansfield, R. "Technology, Size and Organization." *Sociology* 6 (1972): 369–393.

Comstock, D. E., and Scott, W. R. "Technology and the Structure of Subunits." *Administrative Science Quarterly* 22 (1977): 177–202.

Davis, L. E., and Taylor, J. C. "Technology, Organization, and Job Structure." In *Handbook of Work, Organization, and Society,* edited by R. Dubin. Chicago: Rand McNally, 1976.

Donaldson, L. "Woodward Technology, Organizational Structure and Performance—A Critique of the Universal Generalization." *Journal of Management Studies* 13 (1976): 255–273.

Eilon, S. "Structural Determinism." *Omega* 5 (1977): 499–504.

Eldridge, J. E. T., and Crombie, A. D. *A Sociology of Organisations.* London: George Allen & Unwin, 1975.

Ford, J. D. "Institutional versus Questionnaire Measures of Organizational Structure," *Academy of Management Journal* 22 (1979): 601–610.

Freeman, J. H. "Environment, Technology, and the Administrative Intensity of Manufacturing Organizations." *American Sociological Review* 38 (1973): 750–763.

Fry, L. W. "Technology-Structure Research: An Example of Unrationalized Categorization." College Station, Tex.: Department of Management, Texas A&M University, 1979.

Fullan, M. "Industrial Technology and Worker Integration in the Organization." *American Sociological Review* 35 (1970): 1028–1039.

Gillespie, D. F., and Mileti, D. S. "Technology and the Study of Organizations: An Overview and Appraisal." *Academy of Management Review* 2 (1977): 7–16.

Glisson, C. A. "Dependence of Technological Routinization on Structural Variables in Human Service Organizations." *Administrative Science Quarterly* 23 (1978): 383–395.

Grimes, A. J., and Klein, S. M. "The Technological Imperative: The Relative Impact of Task Unit, Modal Technology, and Hierarchy on Structure." *Academy of Management Journal* 16 (1973): 583–597.

Hage, J., and Aiken, M. "Routine Technology, Social Structure and Organizational Goals." *Administrative Science Quarterly* 14 (1969): 368–379.

Harvey, E. "Technology and the Structure of Organizations." *American Sociological Review* 33 (1968): 241–259.

Hickson, D. J., Hinings, C. R., McMillan, C. J., and Schwittzer, J. P. "The Culture-free Context of Organization Structure: A Tri-national Comparison." *Sociology* 8 (1974): 59–80.

Hickson, D. J., Pugh, D. S., and Pheysey, D. C. "Operations Technology and Organization Structure: An Empirical Reappraisal." *Administrative Science Quarterly* 14 (1969): 378–397.

Holdaway, E. A., Newberry, J. F., Hickson, D. J., and Heron, R. P. "Dimensions of Organizations in Complex Societies: The Educational Sector." *Administrative Science Quarterly* 20 (1975): 37–58.

Hrebiniak, L. G. "Job Technology, Supervision and Work Group Structure." *Administrative Science Quarterly* 19 (1974): 395–410.

Hunt, R. "Technology and Organization." *Academy of Management Journal* 13 (1970): 236–252.

Inkson, J. H. K., Pugh, D. S., and Hickson, D. J. "Organizational Context and Structure: An Abbreviated Replication." *Administrative Science Quarterly* 15 (1970): 318–329.

Jelinek, M. "Technology, Organizations, and Contingency." *Academy of Management Review* 2 (1977): 17–26.

Kast, F. E., and Rosenzweig, J. E. *Organization and Management: A Systems Approach.* 2nd ed. New York: McGraw-Hill, 1974.

Technology and Structure

Keller, R. T., Slocum, J. W., and Susman, G. I. "Uncertainty and Type of Management System in Continuous Process Organizations." *Academy of Management Journal* 17 (1974): 56–68.

Khandwalla, P. N. "Mass Output Orientation of Operations Technology and Organization Structure." *Administrative Science Quarterly* 19 (1974): 74–97.

Kmetz, J. L. "A Critique of the Aston Studies and Results with a New Measure of Technology." *Organization and Administrative Sciences* 8, no. 4 (1977/78): 123–144.

Litterer, J. A. *The Analysis of Organizations.* 2nd ed. New York: John Wiley & Sons, 1973.

Lynch, B. P. "An Empirical Assessment of Perrow's Technology Construct." *Administrative Science Quarterly* 19 (1974): 338–356.

Mahoney, T. A., and Frost, P. J. "The Role of Technology in Models of Organizational Effectiveness." *Organizational Behavior and Human Performance* 11 (1974): 122–138.

Mohr, L. "Organizational Technology and Organization Structure." *Administrative Science Quarterly* 16 (1971): 444–459.

Negandhi, A. R., and Reimann, B. C. "Correlates of Decentralization: Closed and Open Systems Perspectives." *Academy of Management Journal* 16 (1973): 570–582.

Osmond, C. W. "Organization—Is Technology the Key?" *Personnel Management* 2, no. 5 (1970): 43–44.

Overton, P., Schneck, R., and Hazlett, C. B. "An Empirical Study of the Technology of Nursing Subunits." *Administrative Science Quarterly* 22 (1977): 203–219.

Pennings, J. M. "Measures of Organizational Structure: A Methodological Note." *American Journal of Sociology* 79 (1973): 686–704.

Perrow, C. *Organizational Anaylsis: A Sociological View.* Monterey, Calif.: Brooks/Cole, 1970.

Perrow, C. "A Framework for the Comparative Analysis of Organizations," *American Sociological Review* 32 (1967): 194–208.

Porter, L. W., Lawler, E. E., and Hackman, J. R. *Behavior in Organizations.* New York: McGraw-Hill, 1975.

Pugh, D. S., Hickson, D. J., Hinings, C. J., McDonald, K., Turner, C., and Lupton, T. "A Conceptual Scheme for Organizational Analysis." *Administrative Science Quarterly* 8 (1963): 289–315.

Pugh, D. S., Hickson, D. J., and Turner, C. "The Context of Organization Structure." *Administrative Science Quarterly* 14 (1969): 91–114.

Reimann, B. C. "Dimensions of Organizational Technology and Structure: An Explanatory Study." *Human Relations* 30 (1977): 545–566.

Reimann, B. C. "Organization Structure and Technology in Manufacturing: Systems versus Workflow Level Perspectives." *Academy of Management Journal,* in press.

Reimann, B. C. and Inzerilli, G. "Technology and Organization: A Review and Synthesis of Major Research Findings." Cleveland, Ohio: Department of Management and Labor, Cleveland State University, July 1978.

Reimann, B. C. and Inzerilli, G. "A Comparative Analysis of Empirical Research on Technology and Structure." *Journal of Management* 5 (1979): 167–192.

Rousseau, D. M. "Assessment of Technology in Organizations: Closed versus Open Systems Approaches." *Academy of Management Review* 4 (1979): 531–542.

Rousseau, D. M. "Measures of Technology as Predictors of Employee Attitude." *Journal of Applied Psychology* 63 (1978): 213–218.

Rousseau, D. M. "Technological Differences in Job Characteristics, Employee Satisfaction and Motivation: A Synthesis of Job Design Research and Sociotechnical Systems Theory." *Organizational Behavior and Human Performance* 19 (1977): 18–42.

Roy, R. H. *The Cultures of Management.* Baltimore, Md.: Johns Hopkins University Press, 1977.

Rushing, W. A. "Hardness of Material as Related to Division of Labor in Manufacturing Industries." *Administrative Science Quarterly* 13 (1968): 229–245.

Sathe, V. "Institutional versus Questionnaire Measures of Organizational Structure." *Academy of Management Journal* 21 (1978): 227–238.

Shepard, J. M. "Technology, Alienation, and Job Satisfaction." *Annual Review of Sociology* 3 (1977): 1–21.

Stanfield, G. G. "Technology and Structure as Theoretical Categories." *Administrative Science Quarterly* 21 (1976): 489–493.

Starbuck, W. H. "Organizational Growth and Development." In *Handbook of Organizations,* edited by J. G. March. Chicago: Rand McNally, 1965.

Starr, C., and Rudman, R. "Parameters of Technological Growth." *Science* 182 (October 26, 1973): 358–364.

Thompson, J. *Organizations in Action.* New York: McGraw-Hill, 1967.

Van de Ven, A., and Delbecq, A. L. "A Task Contingent Model of Work Unit Structure." *Administrative Science Quarterly* 19 (1974): 183–197.

Van de Ven, A., Delbecq, A. L., and Koenig, R. "Determinants of Coordination Modes within Organizations." *American Sociological Review* 41 (1976): 322–338.

Whyte, W. F. *Organizational Behavior: Theory and Application.* Homewood, Ill.: Richard D. Irwin, 1969.

Woodward, J. "Automation and Technical Change—The Implications for the Management Process." In *Organization Structure and Design,* edited by G. W. Dalton, P. R. Lawrence, and J. W. Lorsch. Homewood, Ill.: Richard D. Irwin, 1970.

Woodward, J. *Industrial Organization: Theory and Practice.* London: Oxford University Press, 1965.

Woodward, J. *Management and Technology.* London: Her Majesty's Stationery Office, 1958.

Zwerman, W. *New Perspectives on Organization Theory.* Westport, Conn.: Greenwood, 1970.

Appendix 8–A   *Summary of Studies Examining Technology-Structure Relationships*

Author and Date Published[a]	Level of Analysis and Sample	Theoretical Technology Dimensions[b]	Operational Technology Dimensions[b]	Type of Measure	Theoretical Structure Dimensions[b]	Operational Structure Dimensions[b]	Type of Measure	Results
1. Woodward 1965	Organizational; N = 100 manufacturing firms	Technical complexity	Unit, mass production, continuous process	Interviews with managers	Organic-mechanistic	Span of control; ratio of supervisory personnel; levels of management	Interviews with managers	Technical complexity curvilinearly related to levels of management, span of control of chief executive, and ratio of supervisory to nonsupervisory personnel.
2. Bell 1967	Subunit; N = 30 departments in a general hospital	Job complexity	1. Predictability of work demands; 2. Number of different tasks performed; 3. Amount of discretion; 4. Extent of responsibility	Observations, interviews, and questionnaires	1. Span of control; 2. Closeness of supervision	Same as theoretical dimensions	1. Number of subordinates under each supervisor; 2. Category rankings based on questionnaire responses	The more complex the task the smaller the span of control; closeness of supervision is unrelated to span of control; the more complex the administrators' task the fewer subordinates they regulate.
3. Harvey 1968	Organizational; N = 43 industrial organizations	Technical specificity-diffuseness	Same as theoretical	Number of product changes in last 10 years	1. Horizontal differentiation; 2. Vertical differentiation; 3. Ratio of managers to total number of personnel; 4. Formalization	Same as theoretical	1. Number of specialized subunits; 2. Number of levels of authority; 3. Numerical ratio; 4. Amount of program specification (expert ratings)	Found as technical specificity increased there was a corresponding increase in structure measures; no relationship between size and structure or size and technology was found.

Author and Date Published[a]	Level of Analysis and Sample	Theoretical Technology Dimensions[b]	Operational Technology Dimensions[b]	Type of Measure	Theoretical Structure Dimensions[b]	Operational Structure Dimensions[b]	Type of Measure	Results
4. Rushing 1968	Industry; N = 44 manufacturing industries	Hardness of material	Ease with which substance could be pierced or broken	Expert rankings	Division of labor: 1. Structural differentiation 2. Individual differentiation	Same as theoretical	1. Number of occupations 2. Formula for dispersion-concentration	Found a positive relationship between technology measure and both measures of division of labor.
5. Hage and Aiken 1969	Organizational; N = 16 health and welfare agencies	Routinization (based on Perrow, 1967)	Same as theoretical dimension	Questionnaire	1. Social structure 2. Organizational goals	1. Centralization; formalization; stratification; complexity 2. System goals; product-characteristic goals	Structured interviews with department heads, supervisors and other department professionals	Found routineness of technology influences structure. The more routine the organization the more centralized and formalized are organizational policies and the more specified are jobs within the social structure. The more routine the organization the more emphasis on efficiency and quantity, and the less emphasis on quality service and staff morale.
6. Hickson et al. 1969	Organizational; N = 46 manufacturing and service organizations	1. Operations 2. Materials 3. Knowledge	1. Work flow integration; level of automation; work flow rigidity; interdependence of work flow segments; specificity of criteria of quality; production continuity (same criteria as Woodward, 1965) 2.-3. Not operationalized	Interviews with chief executives and department heads	1. Structuring of activities 2. Concentration of authority 3. Line control of work flow	1. Standardization; role specialization; formalization 2. Centralization; autonomy 3. Subordinate-supervisor ratio; percentage of work flow superordinates	Interviews with chief executives and department heads	Technological imperative not supported. Operations technology affects only those structural variables centered on work flow. The effect becomes less pronounced as size increases. Impact of size on structure variables is more pronounced than that of technology.

Author and Date Published[a]	Level of Analysis and Sample	Theoretical Technology Dimensions[b]	Operational Technology Dimensions[b]	Type of Measure	Theoretical Structure Dimensions[b]	Operational Structure Dimensions[b]	Type of Measure	Results
7. Pugh et al. 1969	Same as Hickson et al. 1969	1. Operations 2. Charter, i.e., goals, ideology, and value systems	1. Work flow integration 2. Operating variability; consumer-producer outputs; customer orientation of outputs; type of output	Interviews with chief executives and department heads	← Same as Hickson et al. (1969) →			Found aspects of organization context to be related to structure. Operating variability was negatively related to line control of work flow. Work flow integration was positively related to structuring of activities and negatively related to concentration of authority and line control of work flow.
8. Fullan 1970	Individual; N = 1,491 workers from 12 plants in 3 industries	Production process; manual and machine operations performed on an object in the process of turning out a final product	Unit, mass production, continuous-process	A priori classification by authors	Worker integration	Relationship with workers; relationship with first-line supervisors; labor-management relations; status structure; evaluation of company	Self-administered questionnaire	Technology is an important factor that affects worker integration. Continuous process workers experienced the most integration, with mass production firms experiencing the least and craft firms in between but closer to the continuous process firms.
9. Inkson et al. 1970	Organizational; N = 40 manufacturing and service organizations	Operations	Work flow integration; level of automation; evaluation of operations	Interviews with chief executives and department heads	1. Structuring of activities 2. Concentration of authority	1. Functional specialization; formalization 2. Lack of organization autonomy	Interviews with chief executives and department heads	Findings supportive of Hickson et al. (1969). Use of abbreviated scales successful.
10. Zwerman 1970	Organizational; N = 55 manufacturing firms	← Same as Woodward (1965) →						Findings consistent with Woodward (1965).

Author and Date Published[a]	Level of Analysis and Sample	Theoretical Technology Dimensions[b]	Operational Technology Dimensions[b]	Type of Measure	Theoretical Structure Dimensions[b]	Operational Structure Dimensions[b]	Type of Measure	Results
11. Blau and Schoenherr 1971	Organizational; N = 53 state and territorial employment security agencies; N = 1,201 local branches of the above agencies	Operations technology	Automation of operations	Scope of computer installations; based on number of computers and input/output units	1. Division of labor 2. Vertical differentiation 3. Horizontal differentiation 4. Managerial span of control	Same as theoretical	1. Number of occupational positions 2. Number of hierarchical levels 3. Number of major subdivisions; number of sections per division 4. Number of officials reporting to director or director's deputy; supervisory ratio; clerical ratio	Found size to be the most important condition affecting structure.
12. Mohr 1971	Individual; N = 144 subunits in 13 local health departments	1. Manageability of tasks and materials 2. Interdependence 3. Noise level	1. Uniformity; complexity; analyzability 2. Same as theoretical 3. Same as theoretical	1. Assignment to 8 separate groups by author; expert ratings 2. Questionnaire 3. Questionnaire	Participativeness of supervisory style	Participativeness of supervisory style	Questionnaire	Found a weak relationship between manageability and participation. The technological imperative hypotheses were not supported. Found a positive relationship between participation and effectiveness. Technology does not appear to be a unidimensional concept.

Author and Date Published[a]	Level of Analysis and Sample	Theoretical Technology Dimensions[b]	Operational Technology Dimensions[b]	Type of Measure	Theoretical Structure Dimensions[b]	Operational Structure Dimensions[b]	Type of Measure	Results
13. Aldrich 1972		———————— Same as Hickson et al. (1969) ————————						Used path analysis to reanalyze Hickson et al. (1969) data. Showed several alternative models could fit the data. Found technology to reemerge as an important organizational variable.
14. Child 1972	Organizational; N = 82	———————— Same as Hickson et al. (1969) ————————						Supportive of Hickson et al. (1969). Size exerted a dominant influence on complexity (specialization and formalization). Distinguished complexity from other aspects of structure (i.e., formalization and decentralization). Complexity levels were influenced by integration and automation of technology.
15. Child and Mansfield 1972	Organizational; N = 82	———————— Same as Hickson et al. (1969) ————————						Supportive of Hickson et al. (1969). Technology was found to be moderately related to role and functional specialization. There was a stronger relationship between technology and structure in smaller organizations.

Author and Date Published[a]	Level of Analysis and Sample	Theoretical Technology Dimensions[b]	Operational Technology Dimensions[b]	Type of Measure	Theoretical Structure Dimensions[b]	Operational Structure Dimensions[b]	Type of Measure	Results
16. Child 1973	Organizational; N = 787 managers in 78 firms	——— Same as Hickson et al. (1969) ———			1. Structuring of activities 2. Centralization of decision making	1. Specialization; standardization of procedures; formalization 2. Centralization	Interviews with chief executives and department heads	Overall study examined relationships between organizational work role and behavioral variables. Study supportive of Hickson et al. (1969). Found a stronger relationship between size and structure variables than between technology and structure. Found a positive relationship between work flow integration and centralization.
17. Freeman 1973	Organizational; N = 41 manufacturing firms	Mechanization	1. Substance produced; 2. Level of automation; 3. Extent of automation	Structured interviews with executives: 1. Integral or dimensional 2. Existence of automated lines 3. Proportion of automated lines	Administrative intensity	Number of managers, professionals and clerical workers divided by number of laborers	Structured interviews with executives	Found a positive relationship between mechanized production technology and administrative intensity. Also, as degree of mechanized production increased so did the effect of environmental diversity and change variables on administrative intensity.
18. Grimes and Klein 1973	Subunit and organizational; unit N = 828, model organization N = 25	Task variability; variation in personnel discretion	Routine Engineered Craft	Classification by authors	Autonomy	Autonomy	Questionnaire	Found autonomy increased as technological routinization decreased. The relationship was stronger at the task unit level but still observed at the organization level. The technological imperative was generally not supported.

Author and Date Published[a]	Level of Analysis and Sample	Theoretical Technology Dimensions[b]	Operational Technology Dimensions[b]	Type of Measure	Theoretical Structure Dimensions[b]	Operational Structure Dimensions[b]	Type of Measure	Results
19. Negandhi and Reimann 1973	Organizational; N = 30 manufacturing firms in India	Technical complexity	Unit, mass production, continuous-process	Interviews with managers	Decentralization	Nine factors related to the decision-making hierarchy	Interviews with managers	Decentralization was primarily influenced by a firm's concern for task environmental agents and the degree of dependence on other organizations. Technical complexity exerted a relatively minor influence on decentralization.
20. Hickson et al. 1974	Organizational and cross-cultural; N = 70 American, Canadian and British manufactures	Automation	Level of automation (same criteria as Amber and Amber, 1962)	Interviews with chief executives and senior managers	1. Structuring of activities 2. Concentration/dispersion of authority (autonomy)	1. Functional specialization; formalization 2. Autonomy	Interviews with chief executives and senior managers	Results show similar patterns of correlations between context and structure variables for all 3 countries. The data support Hickson et al. (1969). Size had a greater impact on formalization and specialization than technology did.
21. Hrebiniak 1974	Individuals (N = 174) and subunits (N = 36) of a general hospital	1. Technological level 2. Task predictability 3. Task interdependence 4. Task manageability	1. Uniformity; analyzability; choice of methods; discretion in task assignment 2. Questionnaire 3. Questionnaire 4. Questionnaire	1. Expert ratings 2. Questionnaire 3. Questionnaire 4. Questionnaire	1. Autonomy; participation; closeness of supervision; extent of rule usage; unity of control	Same as theoretical	Questionnaire	Failed to support the technological imperative at the individual level. Found perceived independence and decisional participation of supervisors related to measures of structure, independent of subordinate technology at the subunit level. Technological level, task manageability and interdependency variables were also related to various structural dimensions at this level.

Author and Date Published[a]	Level of Analysis and Sample	Theoretical Technology Dimensions[b]	Operational Technology Dimensions[b]	Type of Measure	Theoretical Structure Dimensions[b]	Operational Structure Dimensions[b]	Type of Measure	Results
22. Keller et al. 1974	Organizational; $N = 44$ continuous process plants	Continuous-process	Continuous-process	Data derived from *Pennsylvania Industrial Directory*	Organic versus mechanistic	Impersonal hierarchy; group decision making; rules for decision making	Questionnaire to chief executive and two immediate subordinates	Results supported Woodward (1965). Organic systems were associated with success for the 44 continuous process firms. Size and environmental uncertainty (measured by Harvey's, 1968, number of product changes) had no effect on the type of managerial system. The association between organic systems and success was stronger for nonautonomous plants with responsibility for production only.
23. Khandwalla 1974	Organizational; $N = 79$ manufacturing firms	Mass output orientation of operations	Custom; small batch; large batch; mass-production; continuous-process	Questionnaire ratings by chief executives	1. Vertical integration; 2. Decentralization 3. Use of sophisticated controls	1. Questionnaire 2. Delegation of authority 3. 9 types of control	Questionnaire to chief executives	Found significant positive correlations between the technology and structure measures for high performing companies. Found some support for the technological imperative.
24. Lynch 1974	Subunit; $N = 15$ library subunits from 3 libraries	1. Task predictability 2. Operations routinization 3. Knowledge 4. Overall routinization 5. Task interdependence	Same as theoretical	Questionnaire	Discretion	1. Rules 2. Autonomy	Questionnaire	Developed a technology measure of Perrow's (1967) construct that exhibited some degree of reliability and validity. The dimensions of technology were interrelated. Did not report data concerning technology-structure relationships. Did find existence of multiple organizational technologies.

Author and Date Published[a]	Level of Analysis and Sample	Theoretical Technology Dimensions[b]	Operational Technology Dimensions[b]	Type of Measure	Theoretical Structure Dimensions[b]	Operational Structure Dimensions[b]	Type of Measure	Results
25. Mahoney and Frost 1974	Subunit; $N = 297$ subunits from 17 business and industrial firms	1. Long-linked 2. Mediating 3. Intensive	Same as theoretical	A priori classification by authors	——————— Did not measure structure ———————			This study examined the relationship between technology and dimensions of organizational effectiveness. It was found that criteria of subunit effectiveness vary with the nature of the technology of a unit. No direct relationships were observed between technology and effectiveness.
26. Van de Ven and Delbecq 1974	Subunit; $N = 120$ subunits within a large government employment security agency	1. Number of exceptions 2. Search analyzability	1. Task variability 2. Task difficulty	Questionnaire	Systemized mode, service mode, group mode	Six group structures were used: 1. routine system 2. technical system 3. routine service 4. technical service 5. intensive service 6. design groups	A priori classification by authors	Support was found for a taxonomy of work unit structures that can be classified on the basis of the technology dimensions.

Author and Date Published[a]	Level of Analysis and Sample	Theoretical Technology Dimensions[b]	Operational Technology Dimensions[b]	Type of Measure	Theoretical Structure Dimensions[b]	Operational Structure Dimensions[b]	Type of Measure	Results
27. Blau et al. 1976	Organizational; $N = 110$ manufacturing firms	1. Technical complexity 2. Automation of functions through computers	Same as theoretical	Structured questionnaire to top managers: 1. Degree of mechanization of manufacturing equipment; unit, mass, continuous-process (same as Woodward, 1965) 2. Number of different computer functions on and off site; total number of computer functions	1. Structural differentiation 2. Personnel components 3. Span of control 4. Decentralization of operations and personnel matters	Same as theoretical	Structured interviews: 1. 6 indices 2. 10 indices 3. 5 indices 4. 2 indices	The technological imperative hypothesis was rejected, although curvilinear relationships were observed between production technology and numerous structure measures. Automation technology was positively related to specialization, vertical differentiation, decentralization from corporate headquarters to top management and ratios of supervisor and staff personnel.
28. Van de Ven et al. 1976	Subunits; $N = 197$ subunits of an employment security agency	1. Task uncertainty 2. Task interdependence	1. Task variability; task difficulty 2. Pooled, sequential, reciprocal, team	1. Interviews with supervisors; 2. Classification by authors	Coordination processes: 1. programming through impersonal modes 2. feedback through personal and group modes	1. Rules and procedures; plans and schedules 2. Vertical channels; horizontal channels; scheduled and unscheduled meetings	Interviews with supervisors	Found a difference in degree and kind of influence of the technology measures on modes of coordination. Increases in task uncertainty resulted in the use of horizontal communication channels and group meetings in lieu of coordination by the hierarchy and impersonal modes. As interdependence increased there was an additive increase in the use of all coordination modes combined. Technology measures had a much greater effect on use of coordination mechanisms than on size.

Author and Date Published[a]	Level of Analysis and Sample	Theoretical Technology Dimensions[b]	Operational Technology Dimensions[b]	Type of Measure	Theoretical Structure Dimensions[b]	Operational Structure Dimensions[b]	Type of Measure	Results
29. Billings et al. 1977	Individual; $N = 85$	Technological complexity	Change from large batch to mass production	A priori classification by authors	1. Work structure 2. Social structure	1. Job importance; task variety; task interdependence; mobility; task effort; time pressure; feedback 2. Closeness of supervision; supervisor relations; co-worker relations	Employee interviews over 4 time periods	The authors used a quasi-experimental design. While 6 of the 7 work structure variables were in the predicted direction, only time pressure showed the hypothesized specific shape of change. Elements of social structure were unaffected by the technology change
30. Comstock and Scott 1977	Mixed; $N = 142$ patient care subunits in 16 acute-care general hospitals	Technological predictability	1. Task predictability 2. Work flow predictability	1. Questionnaires; interviews; census of type of patients, independent nurse ratings 2. Ratings by authors		1. Qualifications 2. Differentiation index 3. Organizational influence 4. Explicitness of 8 nursing procedures	1. Interviews, questionnaires 2. Formula 3. Interviews, questionnaires 4. Interviews, questionnaires	Results provide support for argument that different measures of technology correspond to the work of individuals and groups. Task predictability was negatively related to staff qualifications and routine decisions and positively related to differentiation. Predictable work flow was positively related to standardization and centralization. Independent effects of size on qualifications, differentiation, and centralization of routine decisions were also found.

Author and Date Published[a]	Level of Analysis and Sample	Theoretical Technology Dimensions[b]	Operational Technology Dimensions[b]	Type of Measure	Theoretical Structure Dimensions[b]	Operational Structure Dimensions[b]	Type of Measure	Results
31. Overton et al. 1977	Subunit; 7 types of nursing subunits; $N = 71$	1. Raw materials 2. Techniques 3. Task interdependence	1. Uncertainty 2. Instability 3. Variability	1. Number of patients requiring frequent observations; frequency of emergencies 2. Type of nursing skills involved (technical judgmental, and communicative); programmability of activities 3. Degree nurses rely on each other for assistance; dependence on patient feedback, physician communication, and services from other departments	———————— Structure not studied ————————			The hypothesized factors were not found in the data; the empirically derived factors pointed to the general organizational constructs of uncertainty, instability, and variability. These factors were found to be useful in distinguishing and classifying the sample subunits.

Author and Date Published[a]	Level of Analysis and Sample	Theoretical Technology Dimensions[b]	Operational Technology Dimensions[b]	Type of Measure	Theoretical Structure Dimensions[b]	Operational Structure Dimensions[b]	Type of Measure	Results
32. Reimann 1977	Organizational; N = 19 manufacturing firms	1. Degree of mass production 2. Degree of technical change	1. Adapted from Khandwalla (1974) 2. Rate of productivity change	1. Personal interviews with high ranking executives; direct observation 2. Bureau of National Affairs (1973) Standard Industrial Classification (SIC) codes	1. Centralization 2. Specialization 3. Formalization	1. Delegation of authority; centralization index 2. Number of hierarchical levels; number of functional specialties; professionalization 3. Formalization of role definition; lack of autonomy	Executive interviews; company documents	Results indicate neither dimension of technology is strongly related to structure. Hickson et al. (1969) was generally supported. However, there was an interactive effect between the two technology dimensions and centralization.
33. Rousseau 1977	Mixed; 19 subunits from 13 organizations; N = 201	1. Long-linked 2. Mediating 3. Intensive	Same as theoretical	A priori classification by author	———— Did not measure structure ————→			This study examined the relationship between technology and job characteristics. Results showed that characteristics of jobs vary across technology, as do levels of employee satisfaction and motivation.

[a]Complete citations are listed in the reference section at the end of Chapter 8.

[b]For studies with multiple theoretical and operational definitions of technology and/or structure, numbers are used to match the operational with the theoretical definition. In addition, numbers given under the type of measure columns correspond to numbers assigned to their respective theoretical and operational definitions.

Source: Adapted by permission from L. W. Fry, "Technology-Structure Research: An Example of Unrationalized Categorization," paper presented at 1978 National Academy of Management Meeting, San Francisco, California.

Organizational
Communication

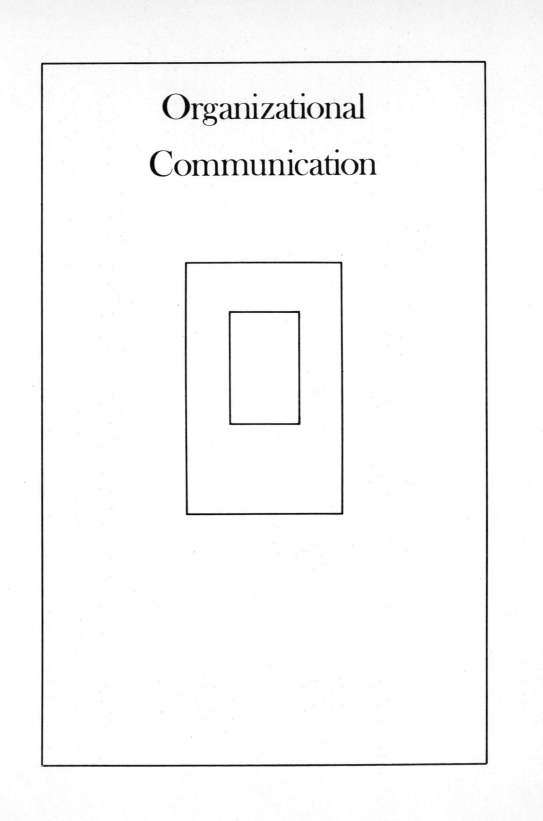

Organizational
Communication
Chapter 9

Communication in most organizations is clearly a dynamic process. The accurate transfer of information and understanding from one unit (sender) to another (receiver) is not only vital in formulating and implementing organizational goals but is also the principal means through which other organizational activities are carried out. As authority and responsibility are delineated and specific groupings and subgroupings of activities are differentiated, the coordination of output becomes an increasingly complex task that can be achieved only through communication. The subgrouping of activities also leads enterprises to develop specific structural characteristics that, as will be discussed, serve to further influence organizational communications.

Communication also serves as the primary means by which an organization—successfully or unsuccessfully—relates to its task environment. Further, as an organization's task environment changes, necessitating new operational responses, its communication system must also adapt to provide the flow of necessary information. A well-developed communication system is the prime mechanism available to an organization for sensing external conditions and, as necessary, effecting changes in its operations. In this chapter, therefore, we turn our attention to the role of communication with and between organizations. Table 9–1 shows the contexts and types of communication to be discussed, along with primary influences on information transfer. Table 9–2 expands on Table 9–1 by indicating the communication, individual, organizational, and environmental variables associated with the various levels of analysis—interpersonal, interunit, and interorganizational—to be considered. Rather than treating each type separately, an effort will be made to focus on the major areas they have in common. Thus, the chapter begins with a review and discussion of the directions of communication flow within an organization. Particular emphasis is placed on the characteristics and implications of vertical, horizontal, and diagonal flow as they relate to effective communication. Discussion then centers on the many barriers to accurate communication. Next, there is a review of techniques for improving communication, followed by a section on the importance of feedback as an essential means for confirming the accuracy of interpersonal transfer of information. Then follows a survey and analysis of research findings concerning the exchange of information between organizations.

Table 9–1 *Communication Context, Types of Communication, and Primary Influences on Transmission of Information*

Context for Communication	Type of Communication (Level of Analysis)	Primary Influences on Information Transmission
Independent of the organization	a. Interpersonal	a. Cognitive phenomena, and social roles and norms
Within the organization	a. Interpersonal	a. Organizational roles and norms plus applicable social norms
	b. Interunit	b. Interdepartmental relations, aggregate effects of information exchanged
External to the individual organization	a. Interorganizational	a. Relations among organizations
	b. Organizational–environmental	b. Environmental components

Source: K. H. Roberts et al., "Organizational Theory and Organizational Communication: A Communication Failure?" *Human Relations* 27 (1974): 515. Reprinted by permission of Plenum Publishing Corporation.

Directions of Formal Communication Flow

The basic hierarchical structure of most organizations largely prescribes the nature of their internal communication flow. Formal communication channels are generally designed to provide vertical, horizontal, and diagonal exchanges of information. The characteristics and implications of each of these directional flows, as they relate to effective communication, will be discussed next. The hypothetical organization depicted in Figure 9–1 will be used to illustrate the examples that follow.

Vertical Flow

Vertical communication flow includes all transactions involving both the downward and upward flow of information occurring between superiors and subordinates in an organization. The *downward* transmission of information is usually conceived of as paralleling an organization's authority flow, extending from its highest to its lowest echelons. For example, in Figure 9–1, there would be a downward vertical flow of communication from the president to the vice-president for production, then to the plant manager, the production manager, the superintendents, the first-line supervisors, and, ultimately, to the operative personnel. Although the downward transmission of information may serve any of several functions, it is used principally to command and instruct. Katz and Kahn suggest that downward communication flow serves five basic purposes:

Table 9–2 *Communication, Individual, Organizational, and Environmental Variables Relatable within Each Level of Analysis*

Context (1)	Level of Analysis (2)	Variables			
		Communication (3)	Individual (4)	Organizational (5)	Environmental (6)
Independent of the organization	Interpersonal	Message characteristics Feedback Information overload Source credibility Information processing Nonverbal	Personality variables Perceptions Needs Social roles and norms Social goals Attitudes		Culture Spatial arrangements
Within the organization	Interpersonal	Message characteristics Feedback Overload Information processing Source credibility Modality choice Gatekeeping Distortion Speed Directionality Coding Network alignment Activity level Accuracy	Organizational rules, norms, goals Status-authority Influence Expectations Mobility Satisfaction	Hierarchy –number of levels –line/staff Size –total organization –subunit Structure –tall-flat –centralized/ decentralized Performance criteria Reward structure Technology/work flow Formalization	
	Interunit	Aggregate effects of information by organizational members on the above variables	Liaison roles	Interdepartmental relations Departmental status Work group relations	
External to the organization	Interorganizational	Aggregated information Processing Sensing mechanism Uncertainty absorption –rules –cycles		Interorganizational relations –dependency –status and influence Climate –satisfaction –leadership style	
		Organizational-environmental		Structure Hierarchy Technology Performance criteria Organizational maturity	Rate of change –technology –market Perceived equivocality of the environment

Source: K. H. Roberts et al., ''Organizational Theory and Organizational Communication: A Communication Failure?'' *Human Relations* 27 (1974): 516–517. Reprinted by permission of Plenum Publishing Corporation.

Figure 9–1 *Flows of Communication in a Hypothetical Organization Consisting of Five Medium-Sized Production Plants*

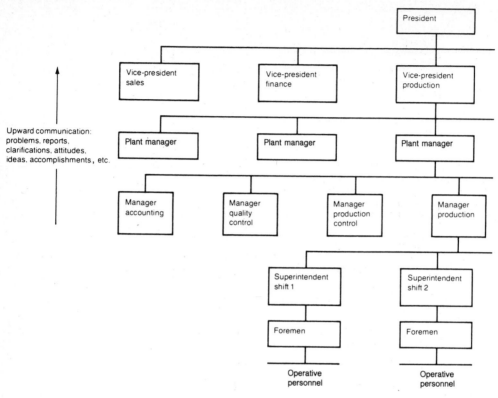

Source: Adapted from *Management: The Act of Working with and through People* by D. C. Mosley and P. H. Petri, Jr. Copyright © 1975 by Wadsworth, Inc. Reprinted by permission of Brooks/Cole Publishing Company, Monterey, California.

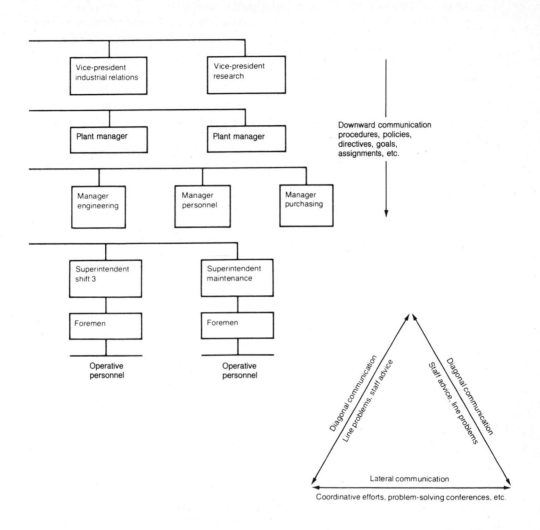

1. to provide specific task directives or job instructions;
2. to provide information about the rationale of a job;
3. to provide information about organizational procedures and practices;
4. to provide subordinates with performance feedback;
5. to present information of an ideological nature to assist in the inculcation of goals.[1]

Downward flowing communication may be either written or oral. Examples of written communication are memoranda, manuals, magazines, newspapers, bulletin boards, and information displays. Some examples of downward flowing oral communication include media verbal directives, conferences, speeches, and telephone contacts.

The movement of information *upward* through levels in the organizational hierarchy most frequently takes the form of performance feedback and is principally associated with the control function. For instance, the upward transmission of production output data is essential for production control. Similarly, the upward flow of information concerning matters such as a firm's cash balance and accounts receivable is necessary for investment control. While primarily utilized for control purposes, the upward flow of communication also performs an integrative role by providing a means for the expression of employee concerns. Management by objectives, attitude surveys, suggestion systems, and grievance hearings are all examples of upward communication that serve an integrative role and further encourage upward communication.

The quality of vertical communication (upward and downward) has been the subject of numerous investigations. Research has focused on both its *efficiency* and its *effectiveness.* One study of the *efficiency* of vertical communication in one hundred business and industrial firms calculated the average loss of information sent from the top of these companies through five layers of management to operative personnel to be an astonishing 80 per cent.[2] On the average, only 67 per cent of a message sent by their board of directors was understood at the vice-presidential level. At the general supervisory level, 56 per cent was understood; at the plant manager level, 40 per cent was understood; at the general first-line supervisory level, 30 per cent was understood; and at the operative level, only 20 per cent was understood. Findings concerning the *effectiveness* or *accuracy* of vertical transmission are equally discouraging. Studies have demonstrated that the accuracy of superior-subordinate communication is affected by both the nature of information communicated and the characteristics of the communicators. For example, research indicates that transmissions about observable and objective subject matter (for example, job duties) are more likely to be accurate than messages involving subjective views and opinions (for example, work-related attitudes).[3] With respect to communicator characteristics,

---

[1]D. Katz and R. L. Kahn, *The Social Psychology of Organizations,* 2nd ed. (New York: John Wiley & Sons, 1978), p. 440.

[2]R. G. Nichols, "Listening Is Good Business," *Management of Personnel Quarterly* 1, no. 2 (1962): 2–10.

[3]N. R. F. Maier et al., *Superior-Subordinate Communications in Management,* Research Study No. 52 (New York: American Management Association, 1961).

available research suggests that the accuracy of upward transmissions is related to both the level of trust existing between a superior and a subordinate and the subordinate's aspirations toward upward mobility.[4] This evidence suggests a tendency for ambitious subordinates to distort or refrain from communicating potentially threatening information in order to preserve a favorable image, especially when they are uncertain of the extent to which a disclosure would affect their opportunities for promotion.

An earlier study of the activities of 330 professional scientists provides support for this reasoning.[5] Its results show that accurate information is less likely to be communicated between two individuals under conditions of distrust than under conditions of trust. The results also show that subordinates with aspirations toward upward mobility perceive a special threat to their security or progress when required to communicate unfavorable matters to a superior they do not trust, since they think the information might be used against them at a later date.

Horizontal (Lateral) Flow

Horizontal communication includes all transmissions that flow laterally within an organization. These transmissions may be classified as occurring: (a) among peers within the same work group and (b) between groups of equivalent status across departmental boundaries. For example, in a structure like that represented in Figure 9–1, there would be a horizontal flow of communication within and across units such as sales, finance, and production; among the managers of quality control, production, and engineering; or among shift superintendents. Such communication is typically coordinative, because it is most often associated with the flow of work. Since horizontal communication takes place primarily between persons of equal or nearly equal status, it tends to be less threatening, more accurate, and faster than vertical communication.

The most prevalent form of lateral communication within organized work settings is the interchange between members of the same work group. Research in this area has focused primarily on the relationship between communication and work group size. Porter has stated the belief that small size facilitates communication within peer groups.[6] His basis for this belief is drawn largely from research conducted in the field of small group behavior. Several studies, for example, have shown that work group cohesion is inversely related to group size. After an extensive review of the literature on small groups, Hare has concluded that "as size increases, there is a tendency toward a more mechanical method of introducing information . . . , a less sensitive

[4]W. H. Read, "Upward Communication in Industrial Hierarchies," *Human Relations* 15 (1962): 3–16.
[5]G. Mellinger, "Interpersonal Trust as a Factor in Communication," *Journal of Abnormal and Social Psychology* 52 (1956): 304–309.
[6]L. W. Porter, "Communication: Structure and Process," in *Integrating the Organization,* ed. H. L. Fromkin and J. J. Sherwood (New York: Free Press, 1974), pp. 216–246.

exploration of the point of view of the other, and a more direct attempt to control others and reach [a] solution whether or not all group members indicate agreement."[7] Likewise, Porter and Lawler noted in their review of group size in industrial enterprises that "the literature on subunit size shows that when blue-collar workers are considered, small size subunits are characterized by higher job satisfaction, lower absence rates, lower turnover rates, and fewer labor disputes."[8] Taken together, these findings strongly imply the value of limiting the size of work groups to facilitate effective communication among members.

The second type of horizontal communication occurs between units of equivalent status across departmental boundaries. While it has long been suspected that this form of lateral communication is much more common than organization charts imply, recent evidence suggests that interdepartmental communication increases as organizations become more structurally diversified and personal specialization becomes more common.[9] This increase is largely attributed to the necessity for coordinating diverse functional and occupational specialties.

The focus of much of the additional research in this area has been concerned largely with interdepartmental rivalry and conflict. On the basis of an analysis of the interdepartmental relations in three engineering plants, Landsberger has argued that much of the competitiveness and conflict that arise is an inevitable consequence of functional specialization, which leads to the development of loyalty to individual departments rather than to the larger enterprise.[10] One of the clearest, most complete descriptions of this occurrence and its effects on interdepartmental communication has been provided by Strauss.[11] Using purchasing agents as an example (in this instance acting as internal boundary spanners), he has illustrated the forms that rivalry between functional groups can take and has outlined various tactics that agents have developed for dealing with other departments—for example, distorting information provided to other units, making restrictive rules for other units, and using personal contacts and persuasion to subvert the activities of other units. The implications of such activities for communication, and thus for organizational effectiveness, are obvious. In the case studied by Strauss, individual agents who were their firm's sole contact with suppliers not only blocked lines of communication but deliberately filtered information to benefit their own departmental interests!

[7]A. P. Hare, *Handbook of Small Group Research,* 2nd ed. (New York: Free Press, 1976), p. 226.

[8]L. W. Porter and E. E. Lawler, "Properties of Organization Structure in Relation to Job Attitudes and Job Behavior," *Psychological Bulletin* 64 (1965): 39.

[9]J. Hage, M. Aiken, and C. Marrett, "Organizational Structure and Communications," *American Sociological Review* 36 (1971): 860–871; B. Stymne, "Interdepartmental Communication and Intraorganizational Strain," *Acta Sociologica* 11 (1968): 82–100.

[10]H. Landsberger, "The Horizontal Dimension in Bureaucracy," *Administrative Science Quarterly* 6 (1961): 299–332.

[11]G. A. Strauss, "Tactics of Lateral Relationships: The Purchasing Agent," *Administrative Science Quarterly* 7 (1962): 161–186.

Chapter 9

Diagonal Flow

The diagonal flow of communication includes all transmissions that cut across an organization's chain of command. Diagonal communication most often takes the form of interactions between line managers and members of staff or service units. For example, in Figure 9–1, diagonal channels may be said to exist between the industrial relations department and each lower level line unit. Since it is typically advisory in nature, the potential for conflict in diagonal line-staff communication has long been realized. Dalton, in a study of four firms, observed that staff managers are often required to monitor and report on the performance of line units.[12] For fear of being shown up, line units often resist innovations introduced by staff. The power struggles that result frequently lead to the distortion of information for essentially the same reasons that information is distorted in interactions across departments. The most frequently noted finding from studies of line-staff communication is that staff employees have greater communication activity and greater knowledge of organization events than do their counterparts in the line.[13] Typical is Davis's analysis of the communication patterns of the managerial group of an unidentified leather goods manufacturer employing approximately six hundred people.[14] He found that staff executives usually knew more than line about any company event. This was true not only at each level of management, but also for the management group as a whole. He offered several explanations for this finding:

1. Communication is the primary function of many staff specialists. They routinely gather data and perform activities such as preparing reports and issuing directives.
2. Staff specialists usually have shorter communication channels to upper management, largely because staff personnel generally occupy higher positions in the management hierarchy.
3. Many staff specialists have to move regularly through the various departments of an enterprise to perform their tasks. This mobility allows them greater opportunity to receive and spread information and thus to develop a wider range of communication contacts.
4. Because of their particular expertise, staff specialists are usually more involved in carrying out decisions than are their line counterparts.

A clear implication of these findings is that, while the nature of the staff relationship may be advisory, staff's greater communication activity and knowledge of events in

---

[12]M. Dalton, *Men Who Manage: Fusions of Feeling and Theory in Administration* (New York: John Wiley & Sons, 1959), pp. 71–109.

[13]Porter, "Communication," p. 239.

[14]K. Davis, "Management Communication and the Grapevine," *Harvard Business Review* 31, no. 5 (1953): 43–49.

an organization provides staff specialists with an unofficial source of power in dealing with line managers.

Communication Barriers

Ineffective communication may be attributed to many different types of human and technical barriers. A complete identification of all forms of obstacles to human communication is beyond the scope of this chapter. For this reason, only those forms of communication difficulties that frequently occur in complex structures will be discussed. They may be classified into four categories: intrapersonal, interpersonal, organizational, and technological.[15]

Intrapersonal Factors
Selective Perception

The relationship between perception and communication is complex. The way in which we perceive a subject or an event affects not only the way we conceive of it but also the way in which our thoughts about it are converted into a form of meaningful communication. For example, it is a well-known fact that people have a tendency to see and hear only what they are emotionally prepared (or want) to see and hear. Furthermore, research suggests that people seek out favorable messages and ignore unpleasant ones.[16] In other words, they reject or inaccurately perceive information that is inconsistent with their previously established beliefs and expectations.

An interesting example of selective perception is presented by one study that asked twenty-three managers from a single firm to analyze a standard business case from the company-wide perspective of a new president and then to identify the most important problem presented by the case.[17] Despite this open attempt to influence the scope of their analyses, the executives still tended to perceive the most important problem facing the company in terms of the goals of their own particular departments. With evidence such as this, it is easy to understand how selective perception can cause many interdepartmental conflicts.

---

[15]L. Thayer, "Communication and Organization Theory," in *Human Communication Theory: Original Essays,* ed. F. E. X. Dance (New York: Holt, Rinehart and Winston, 1967), pp. 70–115.

[16]H. J. Leavitt, *Managerial Psychology,* 4th ed. (Chicago: University of Chicago Press, 1978), pp. 25–54.

[17]D. C. Dearborn and H. A. Simon, "Selective Perception: A Note on the Departmental Identifications of Executives," *Sociometry* 21 (1958): 140–144; for similar examples see A. K. Korman, "Selection Perceptions among First-Line Supervisors," *Personnel Administration* 26 (1963): 31–36; R. A. Webber, "Perceptions of Interaction between Supervisors and Subordinates," *Human Relations* 23 (1970): 235–248.

Chapter 9

Individual Differences in Communication Skills

In addition to differing in their perceptual ability, people also differ in their ability to develop and apply basic communication skills. Some people are incapable of expressing themselves verbally but are able to write very clear and concise messages. Others are effective speakers but poor listeners. In addition, many people read slowly and find it difficult to understand what they have read. When such difficulties exist, they are potential barriers to effective communication. Research suggests that such difficulties and their effects in industry have not been adequately taken into account.[18] In addition, numerous analyses of company bulletins, magazines, employee handbooks, and training manuals have shown that much of this literature is aimed at a level of comprehension above that of its intended audience. Without understanding, there can be no communication. Unless employees comprehend the information directed at them, they certainly cannot be expected to act effectively upon it.

Interpersonal Factors
Climate

Within an organizational context, the relationship between a superior and a subordinate largely derives from the treatment each receives from the other and from the way in which this reciprocal behavior is interpreted. As superior and subordinate interact, the feelings that arise either limit or encourage both the content and the frequency of their communications, as well as the methods in which they attempt to communicate with each other.[19] This combination of attitudes comprises the climate of an interpersonal relationship. The lack of a positive climate can easily lead to a restricted flow of communication, subordinate gamesmanship in the manipulation of information, and widespread distrust and antagonism. The resulting decay of group and enterprise effectiveness has been well documented.[20]

Trust

The communication process is a transactional relationship between a sender and a receiver. The transfer of information is meant to have a reciprocal effect on both interacting parties. A major characteristic of all such relationships is trust. Distrust and suspicion between a superior and subordinate can serve only to increase defensive-

---

[18]K. Davis, "Readability Changes in Employee Handbooks of Identical Companies during a Fifteen Year Period," *Personnel Psychology* 21 (1968): 413–420.

[19]F. M. Jablin, "Superior-Subordinate Communication: The State of the Art," *Psychological Bulletin* 86 (1979): 1201–1222.

[20]See, for example, C. Argyris, "Interpersonal Barriers to Decision Making," *Harvard Business Review* 44, no. 2 (1966): 84–97; R. D. Willits, "Company Performance and Interpersonal Relations," *Industrial Management Review* 8, no. 2 (1967): 91–108.

Organizational Communication

ness and decrease the frequency of open expression, subsequently decreasing the likelihood of effective communication. It may be recalled from the preceding discussion of upward communication flow that the distortion of information resulting from such distrust is often a result of subordinates attempting to cope with the uncertainty of having to communicate information that might serve to damage their careers. Recent research in the area of superior-subordinate communication has further advanced understanding of message distortion.[21] The evidence suggests that experience with the distortion of organizational messages (both sending and receiving) has led many managers to almost automatically apply counter-biases to adjust for biases they assume to exist in the information they receive. For instance, many superiors perceive messages that are favorable to their subordinates as probably less accurate than messages that are unfavorable. Subordinates, they have observed, are more likely to maximize information that reflects their strengths and minimize information that reflects their weaknesses. From the perspective of the entire enterprise, it is readily apparent that the elimination of this type of distortion is essential for effective performance. From the more basic interpersonal perspective, reestablishment of trust must be emphasized as crucial to individual and work group development.

Credibility

Closely related to trust, "credibility" refers to the perceived characteristics of a source of information. Empirical research has identified four distinct elements of source credibility: honesty or general trustworthiness, expertise or competence, dynamism or enthusiasm, and objectivity or open-mindedness.[22] These characteristics are not necessarily possessed by a given source but are attributed to that source by individual receivers. Thus, the credibility of a source is actually receiver determined. For example, when presented with identical communications from different sources, employees will most often believe the one coming from the source that *they perceive* to be the most qualified, honest, fair, and forceful.

Of particular importance to the study of organizational communication are findings that relate credibility to individual and group behavior. At the individual level, subordinate perceptions of supervisor credibility have been shown to be directly related to subordinate satisfaction with immediate supervision.[23] At the group level, highly credible work units or departments have been shown to experience greater communication openness, information accuracy, and higher within-group interaction rates than do other units.[24] As a result, they are generally found to be more accurate

[21]L. Sussman, "Perceived Message Distortion or You Can Fool Some of the Supervisors Some of the Time . . . ," *Personnel Journal* 53, no. 9 (1974): 679–682, 688.

[22]J. L. Whitehead, "Factors of Source Credibility," *Quarterly Journal of Speech* 54 (1968): 59–63.

[23]R. L. Falcione, "The Relationship of Supervisor Credibility to Subordinate Satisfaction," *Personnel Journal* 52, no. 9 (1973): 800–803.

[24]C. A. O'Reilly, "The Intentional Distortion of Information in Organizational Communication: A Laboratory and Field Investigation," *Human Relations* 31 (1978): 173–193.

in the transmission of information and more efficient in problem solving and to experience a greater degree of group accomplishment.

Sender-Receiver Similarity

Research generally indicates that the accuracy of communication between two communicators is directly related to the extent to which they perceive themselves to be similar.[25] The degree of similarity between communicators in terms of such characteristics as age, sex, intelligence, race, and socioeconomic status and such factors as common attitudes, interests, values, and abilities influences the ease and openness with which they communicate. Communicators who perceive themselves as being similar are generally more willing to accept the viewpoints of one another and to express common agreement.

Likewise, studies conducted within organizational settings indicate that the greater the degree of similarity between a superior and subordinate, the more effective communication will be. Of particular interest is the finding that differences in values and thinking between persons at varying organizational levels result in different criteria for making judgments. For instance, one study found that upper- and mid-level managers tend to judge jobs on the basis of power, whereas lower-level employees judge jobs on the basis of work requirements.[26] Similarly, the study revealed that upper-level managers tend to judge people on the basis of class and background, while lower-level employees tend to judge others on the basis of reliability, authority, and pay. Care should be taken to avoid over-generalizing the specific results of any research; however, simply knowing that significant differences in attitude do exist between superiors and their subordinates can be a great aid to understanding why they are sometimes unable to communicate with one another.

Organizational Factors

Status

A person's status in an organization depends largely upon the prestige associated with the position he or she occupies. The influence of status on the direction and frequency of organizational communication has been the subject of numerous studies. Evidence indicates that (a) people generally prefer to direct their communication to individuals of higher status; (b) persons of high status generally communicate more with one another than they do with persons of lower status; (c) the wider the status differential, the greater the likelihood that information will flow from the higher to the lower status persons rather than vice versa; (d) high status persons generally dominate conversations with lower status persons; and (e) low status persons often

---

[25]For a review of findings in this area see A. Mehrabian and H. Reed, "Some Determinants of Communication Accuracy," *Psychological Bulletin* 70 (1968): 109–114.

[26]H. C. Triandis, "Similarity in Thought Processes and Boss-Employee Communication," in *Communication in Organizations: Some New Research Findings* (Ann Arbor, Mich.: Foundation for Research on Human Behavior, 1959), pp. 25–32.

attempt to gain the favor of those with higher status by displaying respect, offering praise, and agreeing with their views.[27]

These findings clearly suggest that status is a major influence on the process of communication. From an organizational viewpoint, there are at least two reasons that employees prefer to communicate with individuals of higher status. First, such interactions can be an effective way to gain peer group recognition and prestige. Second, communicating with higher status superiors who possess the capacity to gratify or deprive is often perceived as a means of increasing one's chances of satisfaction. Since status differences are inherent in hierarchical structures, managers should be keenly aware of the effect status has upon their interactions with both subordinates and superiors.

Hierarchical Transmission

Hierarchical differentiation is a central structural aspect of the development of an organization. As organizations grow, hierarchies develop not only to facilitate the accomplishment of broadened activities but also because they are necessary to communication. Information must be systematically channeled to all parts of an organization. Although hierarchical transmission is thus desirable, it does give rise to numerous communication difficulties. For instance, the more levels a message must pass through, the longer it takes to reach its destination and the less likely it is to be accurate.

In addition to the factors associated with both the efficiency and the effectiveness of vertical information flow discussed earlier, certain individual processes also serve to distort the hierarchical transmission of information. Such distortions have been shown to take a number of systematic forms: condensation, closure, expectation, and association.[28] These distortions contribute to both the selective retention *(sharpening)* of certain details in a message and the selective omission *(leveling)* of other details.

Condensation.   Research indicates that the recipient of a message who in turn is responsible for passing it on to another person typically distorts its content (especially in word-of-mouth transmissions) in a predictable manner. That is, what he or she repeats will be shorter and less detailed than what he or she received. Often only the salient points of the message are forwarded, and most often in a condensed form; certain portions of the message are therefore intensified, and others are ignored. March and Simon have labeled this editing process *uncertainty absorption.*[29] Such

---

[27]For a review of findings in this area see H. Guetzkow, "Communication in Organizations," in *Handbook of Organizations,* ed. J. G. March (Chicago: Rand McNally, 1965), pp. 534–573; P. R. Monge, J. A. Edwards, and K. K. Kirste, "The Determinants of Communicational Structure in Large Organizations: A Review of Research," in *Communication Yearbook 2,* ed. B. D. Ruben (New Brunswick, N.J.: Transaction Books, 1973), pp. 311–331.

[28]B. M. Bass and E. C. Ryterband, *Organizational Psychology,* 2nd ed. (Boston: Allyn & Bacon, 1979), pp. 175–177; D. T. Campbell, "Systematic Error on the Part of Human Links in Communication Systems," *Information and Control* 1 (1958): 334–369.

[29]J. G. March and H. A. Simon, *Organizations* (New York: John Wiley & Sons, 1958), pp. 164–166.

absorption frequently occurs in situations where inferences are drawn from a sum of evidence and the inferences, rather than the evidence itself, are communicated. Interestingly, it seems that, as a message is relayed, its midsection is more likely to be condensed (that is, edited) than either its beginning or its end. In addition, the longer the period between the time a message is received and the time it is relayed to the next level and the larger the number of people involved in its transmission, the more likely it is to be distorted.

Closure. Relayers of ambiguous messages, which rumors quite often are, tend to fill in—that is, to close gaps in the information that they are transmitting. As an illustration, if a message that an unknown official from the home office may arrive sometime next week on an unannounced inspection tour leaks, the news may be transmitted that a staff manager, *probably* John Henry, is coming next week to conduct a surprise inspection. After several transmissions, the message may be that John Henry is *definitely* coming to conduct a surprise inspection.

Expectation. Evidence further suggests that relayers of information are often prone to bias communications in the direction of their own attitudes and expectations. As a message flows up or down through the layers of an enterprise, it passes through various way stations, each with its own unique frame of reference. Frames of reference differ because of variations in needs, values, and opinions, as well as because of variations in job requirements.

A laboratory study involving thirty-two graduate business students provides an interesting example of this point.[30] The students were asked to make either cost or sales estimates using identical figures, at one time taking the role of a chief market analyst, at another time taking the role of a chief cost analyst. The results of the study clearly highlight the influence of job requirements on expectations. When acting as cost analysts, the students tended to overestimate costs. When acting as sales analysts, they tended to underestimate sales. In other words, the students interpreted the same information according to the biases inherent in two different roles and arrived at two very different conclusions. In an enterprise, this sort of prejudice inevitably exists in both the transmission and reception of information.

Association. Research further indicates that when events or outcomes have occurred together in the past, they are often associated with one another at a later date. For instance, if past errors have been attributable to a particular person, that person is likely to be linked to any recurrence of the original errors, often without justification. In such instances, associated cues serve to suggest guilt by prior association. Communication, unfortunately, more easily serves to reinforce unjustified associations than to repudiate them.

---

[30]R. M. Cyert, J. G. March, and W. H. Starbuck, "Two Experiments on Bias and Conflict in Organization Estimation," *Management Science* 7 (1961): 254–264.

Group Size

The effect of work group size on the accuracy of communications is often underestimated. As the earlier discussion of horizontal information flow indicated, interpersonal communication becomes increasingly difficult as the size of a work group increases. This occurs in part because the number of possible communication channels between individual members increases more rapidly than group size does. For a group of five people, there are $n(n-1)/2$, or 10, channels of communication possible. When group size increases to ten, 45 potential channels exist. When a group is composed of twenty members, 190 channels are opened. Furthermore, as the size of a work unit increases, communication patterns become increasingly complicated by the formation of subgroups. Their development not only creates new communication channels —for instance, between subgroups or between an individual and a subgroup—but also increases the likelihood of inner group conflict. Allowing for the formation of inner circles, the number of possible communication channels within a gathering of five people is $(3^n - 2^{n+1})/2$, or 90. This represents a rapid increase over the number of potential relationships calculated when consideration was being given only to interactions between individuals. In most groups, however, not all possible communication channels are utilized; indeed, available evidence suggests the existence of a negative relationship between group size and the percentage of total possible communication channels employed.[31]

In addition, studies indicate that as group size increases, the amount of time available for open communication per member decreases. As groups become larger, each member has less opportunity to participate in discussions; and in larger groups, there is a tendency for communication to be dominated by a few members. Furthermore, studies suggest that, as size increases, group members often experience feelings of threat accompanied by a reluctance to participate.[32] Interestingly, one study has shown that communication activity may also be related to overall organization size.[33] The larger an organization, the less likelihood there is that adequate communication will be achieved; reduced levels of interpersonal attraction are the result of less adequate communication, and this in turn further contributes to decreased communication among organization members.

Spatial Constraints

The physical characteristics of a job often necessitate that it be performed in a specific area. Spatial constraints are felt most noticeably in situations in which it is necessary to remain in a single location for the manipulation of controls or for moving between machines or work pieces. Such requirements establish physical distances between workers and thus serve to restrict the amount and quality of communication

---

[31]For a review of findings in this area see Hare, *Handbook of Small Group Research*, pp. 214–219; M. E. Shaw, *Group Dynamics: The Psychology of Small Group Behavior*, 2nd ed. (New York: McGraw-Hill, 1976), pp. 154–162.

[32]Hare, *Handbook of Small Group Research*, p. 219; Shaw, *Group Dynamics*, p. 156.

[33]B. P. Indik, "Organization Size and Member Participation: Some Empirical Tests of Alternatives," *Human Relations* 18 (1965): 339–350.

Chapter 9

that can take place between work group members. Research on the relationship between spatial constraints and communication flow has been conducted in a wide range of settings. A review of past studies provides strong support for the more recent hypothesis that "the rate of information flow among components is less the farther they are from one another and the longer the channels between them."[34] For example, in an analysis of the social interaction of thirty-seven office workers, one study firmly concluded that "distance was the most important factor in determining the rate of interaction between any two employees."[35] Evidence that a similar phenomenon may affect intergroup interaction is also available. A study of Project Fifty, an applied research group composed of two units located several miles apart, revealed that many of its problems of coordination were the result of faulty communications.[36] In an effort to overcome such difficulties, the units were moved to a single site, with the result that all problems of coordination were resolved.

These findings clearly suggest that it may be possible for an organization to influence the interaction, and therefore the communication, between individuals or groups within its structure by manipulating or imposing spatial restrictions. Indeed, as Reitz has observed:

Arranging for people to share common facilities (copying machines, elevators, eating areas, desks) is a common method of encouraging communication. Separate facilities, physical distance, closed doors, walls, indirect lines of communication, and different working hours are devices which will usually discourage communication. Many of these factors are controllable by managers and administrators, and they are more effective than telling people that they should or should not communicate.[37]

Technological Factors
Language and Meaning

A major determinant of communication accuracy is the extent to which communicators assign similar meanings to the same words. Because language, like mathematics, is a symbol system, words in and of themselves have no meaning. They are simply labels we use to describe or symbolize our own personal view of reality. The meaning a person attaches to a message is uniquely determined by prior experiences, individual needs, social background, and so on. For this reason, the words used in a message rarely have exactly the same meaning to a sender as they do to a receiver; neither do they have the same meaning for different receivers.

---

[34]J. G. Miller, "Living Systems: The Organization," *Behavioral Science* 17 (1972): 3.
[35]J. T. Gullahorn, "Distance and Friendship as Factors in the Gross Interaction Matrix," *Sociometry* 15 (1952): 134.
[36]H. A. Shepard, "The Value System of a University Research Group," *American Sociological Review* 19 (1954): 456–462.
[37]H. J. Reitz, *Behavior in Organizations* (Homewood, Ill.: Richard D. Irwin, 1977), p. 344.

The imprecision of language is further complicated by the fact that, besides simply serving as labels, words are capable of evoking a vast array of emotions that may bias the interpretation of a message. For instance, one study examined the reactions of 488 hourly paid employees to 61 commonly used management terms.[38] The word *capitalism,* used by management to mean "private ownership of business . . . equal opportunity for all," aroused within 74 per cent of the workers feelings such as "the wealthiest people take over," "big business has so much money they freeze out the little fellow," and even "a dictatorship by the rich." The phrase *free enterprise* was much more acceptable to the workers. The word *corporation* carried a strong connotation of money, power, and selfishness; the term *company* was preferred. The phrase *work stoppage* was considered to be unfair; however, *strike* was seen as a practical means to an end.

Other studies have not only reconfirmed the existence of such differences in meaning between labor and management but also have suggested that similar discrepancies exist *between* levels of management with regard to words such as *incentives, quota, cooperation,* and *budget.*[39] Whereas top-level managers may speak of the need for incentives and quotas, such words may elicit feelings of resentment and unnecessary manipulation within lower level managers. Thus, the same word used in conversations and correspondence evokes an entirely different set of emotions and therefore carries a different meaning for each group.

There are other common barriers to comprehension. While it is correct to say that no two people assign exactly the same meaning to the same word or symbol, unless there is some uniformity in meaning—some public dimension—we will be unable to communicate. Indeed, the use of a common language implies a certain degree of regularity or agreement in word meanings. The extent of this regularity, however, varies widely. Few words have only one common meaning. One study reports that for the five hundred most frequently used words in the English language, the *Oxford English Dictionary* records an average of over twenty-eight separate and different meanings.[40] To further contribute to this confusion, many words either are spelled identically and pronounced differently—such as "read" (present tense) and "read" (past tense), "lead" (verb) and "lead" (noun), "wind" (verb) and "wind" (noun), and "live" (verb) and "live" (adjective)—or are spelled differently and pronounced identically—such as "to," "two," and "too"; "hear" and "here"; and "their" and "there." Given such obstacles, it is easy to understand why language and meaning can be major barriers to the successful transfer of intended meaning.

Nonverbal Cues

When people speak, their words are usually accompanied by a variety of meaningful nonverbal cues, such as physical posture, gestures, facial expressions, body move-

---

[38]M. Wright, "Do You Need Lessons in Shop Talk?" *Personnel* 42, no. 4 (1965): 58–62.

[39]A. K. Korman, "A Cause of Communication Failure," *Personnel Administration* 23, no. 3 (1960): 17–21; C. H. Weaver, "The Quantification of the Frame of Reference in Labor Management Communication," *Journal of Applied Psychology* 42 (1958): 1–19.

[40]C. C. Fries, *Linguistics and Reading* (New York: Holt, Rinehart and Winston, 1963), p. 57.

Chapter 9

ments, touch, and visual behavior. These nonverbal stimuli are "silent" messages that assist in the accurate transfer of meaning. For example, the degree of eye-to-eye contact between communicators may indicate interest, liking, involvement, or aggression. Similarly, body movements (shifts in position, hand gestures, head nods, etc.) may convey eagerness, anger, or feelings of relaxation.[41]

The importance of nonverbal communication is underscored by evidence which suggests that, in face-to-face communication, only 7 per cent of the content of a typical message is transmitted by verbal stimuli.[42] The remaining 93 percent is transmitted by tone of voice (38 percent) and facial expression (55 percent). Verbal and nonverbal cues thus interrelate to create a total message. Research indicates that, in a majority of instances, verbal and nonverbal cues will carry the same meaning. That is, they will repeat, complement, or accent one another. For example, a verbal expression of anger may be accompanied by a look of disgust, a rigid body stance, and a clenched fist accenting particular phrases. On the other hand, nonverbal stimuli may, in certain circumstances, contradict and even negate the intended meaning of a verbal message. For instance, a statement such as "That's great, just great!" said in a sarcastic tone of voice in reaction to an unfavorable outcome is almost always perceived as negative. In general, evidence suggests that when nonverbal cues are incongruent with an accompanying verbal message, reliance is placed primarily upon the nonverbal portion of the total communication. That is, observers are more inclined to believe nonverbal cues, because such cues are less subject to conscious control. Furthermore, research suggests that when a discrepancy between a sender's verbal and nonverbal behavior persists, the resulting ambiguity will almost invariably lead to feelings of tension and anxiety on the part of affected observers.[43]

Channel Effectiveness

Researchers have long been concerned with the comparative effectiveness of different channels of communication. Amid often conflicting results, evidence suggests that written and oral channels are each to be preferred for specific tasks.[44] Written channels (memoranda, charts and diagrams, bulletins, company newspapers, etc.) have been found to be most effective for transmitting lengthy and detailed material. A written communication provides readers with the opportunity to achieve understanding at their own rate (even rereading as needed) and by their own method. Written communications also allow ideas to be conveyed over distance and time. Wider distribution is possible (for example, directives to regional offices), as are storage and retrieval for use in making future decisions. By being open to the scrutiny of more than one person, written messages can be made more exact.

---

[41]For a further review of findings in this area see R. G. Harper, A. N. Wiens, and J. D. Matarazzo, *Nonverbal Communication: The State of the Art* (New York: John Wiley & Sons, 1978).

[42]A. Mehrabian, *Silent Messages* (Belmont, Calif.: Wadsworth, 1971), p. 44.

[43]A. Mehrabian and M. Winer, "Decoding of Inconsistent Communications," *Journal of Personality and Social Psychology* 6 (1967): 109–114.

[44]G. T. Vardaman and P. B. Vardaman, *Communication in Modern Organizations* (New York: John Wiley & Sons, 1973), pp. 328–340.

Oral channels (face-to-face discussion, telephone conversations, lectures, conferences, etc.) are especially appropriate for communications that require translation and elaboration in order to be understood by lower-level recipients with varying orientations and language skills. Oral channels are most effective when rapid transmission of information and immediate feedback are desired and are generally more appropriate for handling sensitive or confidential matters because their transitory nature makes the discussion of ticklish issues more acceptable. In addition, a degree of personalism is possible in oral communication that is difficult to achieve through written means. Feelings and ideas are often more accurately communicated orally than they are in writing, since discussion provides a maximum opportunity for interaction on the basis of both verbal and nonverbal cues.

Multi-media transmissions (written-oral, written-visual, oral-visual, written-oral-visual) have proven to be the most appropriate in situations such as settling work disputes, communicating major policy changes, and reprimanding for work deficiencies.[45] Some multi-media transmissions employ different channels consecutively to accomplish objectives; for example, a face-to-face discussion of work problems followed by a written memorandum identifying the means of overcoming the problems that were discussed serves first to verify understanding and second to ensure that compliance is agreed upon. Other multi-media transmissions employ different channels simultaneously to great advantage. The oral presentation of an annual operating report accompanied by a written handout and further complemented by charts and graphs depicting important trends, for instance, is a particularly effective means of reinforcing receiver comprehension. Research suggests that repetition of a transmission through various media increases the likelihood that a message not only will be received and comprehended but also will be recalled more accurately.[46]

Perhaps the prime conclusion to be drawn from available evidence is that the effectiveness of a particular communication channel depends to a great extent upon the type and purpose of the information to be transmitted as well as upon the circumstances and individuals involved. As Melcher and Beller have observed:

Administrative effectiveness probably is critically affected by how quickly a manager familiarizes himself with the orientation of his superiors, subordinates, and members in other departments, the extent to which he integrates himself into the social system, and his awareness of the functional aspects of the alternative channels. He is then in a position to use the channels and media that would best fit the nature of the communication.[47]

---

[45]D. A. Level, "Communication Effectiveness: Method and Situation," *Journal of Business Communication* 10, no. 1 (1972): 19–25; T. L. Dahle, "An Objective and Comparative Study of Five Methods of Transmitting Information to Business and Industrial Employees," *Speech Monographs* 21 (1954): 21–28.

[46]H. J. Hsia, "Redundancy: Is It the Lost Key to Better Communication?" *AV Communication Review* 25 (1977): 63–85.

[47]A. J. Melcher and R. Beller, "Toward a Theory of Communication: Consideration in Channel Selection," *Academy of Management Journal* 10 (1967): 52.

Information Overload

There is clearly a limit to the amount of information an individual can process and absorb at any given time. It has been observed that a typical executive can receive and absorb only 1/100 to 1/1000 of the available information relevant to his or her decisions.[48] Information overload is partly a product of the technological and scientific knowledge explosion of our times. Worldwide, there are over 66,000 periodicals publishing about 1,500,000 articles per year. In addition, over 500,000 books and about 10,000 general interest newspapers are published annually. Examples of the impact of information overload upon organizational effectiveness are readily available. For instance, based upon evidence that has recently been released, Steers has concluded that

an analysis of the events leading up to the Cuban missile crisis of 1962 reveals that the Central Intelligence Agency had sufficient information to assess accurately the deployment of missiles on Cuba and take quiet diplomatic steps to remedy the problem long before events reached crisis proportion. The problem was that the CIA possessed so much information that it was months behind in its processing of such intelligence. By the time the information was analyzed, opportunities for diplomatic conflict resolution had long passed.[49]

Information overload also has consequences for work group effectiveness. Roby and Lanzetta, drawing upon a series of experimental investigations, note that the "overloaded individual is as likely to neglect obligations to other group members, thereby increasing their errors, as he is to neglect his own control responsibilities."[50] As a result, what often occurs is what Shelly and Gilchrist refer to as a "self-perpetuating condition of communication confusion." They reason that

under the pressure of great amounts of required communication to be handled at once, the individuals in the group probably neglect to forward some problem relevant information and/or duplicate previously forwarded information; this in turn gives rise to information-seeking questions. These questions, because answers are required, further increase the communication load (a) leading to greater probability of neglecting to forward information and/or (b) forgetting to whom certain items have previously been sent, etc.[51]

---

[48]R. C. Raymond, "Betting on New Technologies," in *Technological Planning on the Corporate Level,* ed. J. R. Bright (Boston: Graduate School of Business Administration, Harvard University, 1962), p. 21.

[49]R. M. Steers, *Organizational Effectiveness: A Behavioral View* (Santa Monica, Calif.: Goodyear, 1977), pp. 150–151.

[50]T. B. Roby and J. T. Lanzetta, "Conflicting Principles in Man-Machine System Design," *Journal of Applied Psychology* 41 (1957): 176.

[51]M. W. Shelly and T. C. Gilchrist, "Some Effects of Communication Requirements in Group Structures," *Journal of Social Psychology* 48 (1958): 37–43.

As should be obvious, information overload may also have consequences for individual group members. Stress from the resulting confusion and overwork is often signaled by indicators such as increases in the frequency of errors and interdepartmental friction.[52] These difficulties manifest themselves in anger, aggression, or other more serious forms of personal distress.[53] The logical consequences of such pressures are increased absenteeism and employee turnover.

Numerous methods have been suggested for dealing with information overload.[54] A *first* response is *filtering,* whereby a scheme of priorities dictates the processing of certain types of information to the exclusion of others. Staff assistants may be employed as *gatekeepers* to screen or condense information so that only relevant matters are channeled to higher-level executives. In this way, peripheral details, redundancy, and opinions are eliminated. A drawback of filtering, however, is that unless the priorities on which filtering is based are established through a careful assessment of organization needs, critical information may be inadvertently eliminated.

A *second* approach to dealing with information overload is *queuing,* whereby, during periods of peak load, the processing of low priority messages is delayed or rescheduled. Under such conditions, some meetings may be postponed, some appointments rescheduled, and responses to selected written correspondence delayed. The effectiveness of a priority system for communications depends largely upon the accuracy of a manager's judgments in determining the relative importance of incoming messages and upon the occurrence of periodic lulls in which to catch up on previously deferred communications and other backlogged activities.

A *third* method of dealing with the problem of information overload is the establishment of multiple channels of input or output, such as the addition of special staff channels or the creation of parallel information channels when authority is decentralized. In addition to serving as gatekeepers, staff advisors can be called upon to furnish specialized and technical advice. Such assistance serves to relieve overloaded line channels by providing an alternative mechanism for processing information. An important point about communication in relation to decentralization of authority is that, while decentralization does not alter the total amount of information existing within an organization, it does affect the amount of information available for a particular decision. By restructuring the decision-making system of an organization, decentralization shortens communication channels and places decision-making power at those points in an enterprise where the most complete knowledge exists.[55] As is the case with filtering and queuing, the establishment of multiple channels of input and output also has certain limitations. For instance, the activities of specialized staff that are

[52]R. L. Meier, "Communications Stress," *Annual Review of Ecology and Systematics* 3 (1972): 289–314.
[53]D. A. Rothstein, "Psychiatric Implications of Information Theory," *Archives of General Psychiatry* 13 (1965): 87–94.
[54]J. G. Miller, "Input Overload and Psychopathology," *American Journal of Psychiatry* 116 (1960): 695–704.
[55]W. G. Scott, "Communication and Centralization of Communication," *Journal of Communication* 13 (1963): 3–11.

designed to increase channel capacity may in actuality promote information distortion. As Blau and Scott have observed:

The staff expert can submit accurate operational reports to management, but if he presents adverse information concerning the action of lower managers he will earn their antipathy and distrust, and these attitudes will prevent him from obtaining accurate information from them in the future. Alternatively, he can attempt to modify his report in order to maintain the goodwill of his informants, but in so doing he suppresses information that reflects adversely on lower managers, making his report hardly more accurate than their own communications. [56]

In the creation of parallel information channels through authority decentralization, both functional and dysfunctional changes in organization structure are likely to occur. One study of a university library's attempt to respond to the demands of an information input overload by attempting to decentralize authority has described some of the "unintended structural consequences" as follows:

The structural effects of being tested up to or even beyond the long run capacity for completing transactions can be expressed in various forms. Spatially, *the institution becomes decentralized, functionally differentiated in its various branches and outliers, develops a complex boundary for the receipt of messages, and evolves a strong headquarters unit.* Economically, *it accumulates deferred maintenance and generally transforms capital assets into a network of interdependencies with individuals and other institutions whose resources can be drawn upon in an emergency.* Status *within the institution depends much more upon functional effectiveness than upon official rank. As a* decision system *it is more complex and adaptive, having developed many alternative sets of rules during the test which can be reapplied as soon as the need arises. The* value *structure is permanently changed because operating at capacity has revealed the importance of conserving resources which were not otherwise scarce. Considered as a* network *of positions and relations, the institution develops a greater variety of relations, adds more positions, and greatly increases the centrality of some positions. Overload causes the destruction of relations more rapidly than they can be rebuilt through experience and instruction (internal communications).* [57]

Thus, it would seem that the advantages of either adding special staff channels or decentralizing authority in response to information overload would have to be carefully weighed against the probability of numerous unintended consequences.

---

[56] P. M. Blau and W. R. Scott, *Formal Organization: A Comparative Approach* (San Francisco: Chandler, 1962), p. 173.

[57] R. L. Meier, *Social Change in Communication Oriented Institutions,* Mental Health Research Institute Report no. 10 (Ann Arbor: University of Michigan, 1961), pp. 55–56.

Organizational Communication

Improving Communication Effectiveness

In general, research has supported the proposition that improved communication effectiveness facilitates the exchange of job relevant information, thereby facilitating organization performance.[58] For example, one study compared two plants of a large manufacturing firm that had been matched as closely as possible "except for one factor—communication."[59] Plant B had participated in an ongoing communications development program over a period of several years. Plant A had no such program. The results revealed striking differences, always in favor of Plant B, in the communication patterns of the two groups. For instance, 55 per cent of the workers in Plant B felt that the company did a good job of telling them of its current activities and future plans. Only 18 per cent of the Plant A workers agreed. In Plant B, 62 per cent of the workers felt that they really belonged and were part of the company. Less than 30 per cent of the Plant A workers expressed a similar feeling. When asked to compare their company with other places to work, 45 per cent of the Plant B workers thought that their company was "one of the very best" as compared to only 20 per cent in Plant A.

In another study, Indik, Georgopoulos, and Seashore investigated the relationship between superior and subordinate interaction and performance in twenty-seven operating units of a package delivery firm.[60] Each unit averaged thirty-six members and was responsible for performing the same general tasks. There was, however, a wide variation in their productivity. Based upon a comparison of superior-subordinate communication and performance, the researchers confirmed their hypothesis that the extent to which superiors and subordinates communicate tends to be positively related to performance.

Communication Audit

While the above results seem encouraging in their implications for developing a strong organization by improving its communication processes, the fact remains that all organizations, much like individuals, are different. Each is a product of its own history, technology, personnel, and industry. And as a result of their uniqueness, organizations have unique communication problems. One method of dealing directly with these unique problems before they become acute is the communication audit. It is designed to systematically and comprehensively assess the communication

---

[58]For a complete review of the literature see R. V. Farace, J. P. Stewart, and J. A. Taylor, "Criteria for Evaluation of Organizational Communication Effectiveness: Review and Synthesis," in Ruben, *Communication Yearbook 2,* pp. 271–292.

[59]S. Habbe, "Does Communication Make a Difference?" *Management Record* 14 (1952): 414–416, 442–444.

[60]B. P. Indik, B. S. Georgopoulos, and S. E. Seashore, "Superior-Subordinate Relationships and Performance," *Personnel Psychology* 14 (1961): 357–374.

processes within an organization.[61] A major advantage of the communication audit is that it allows an organization to determine whether specific communication problems are interrelated. Rather than being an attempt to deal with problems individually, the communication audit seeks solutions on a company-wide basis. Individually tailored for each client, audits utilize such procedures as survey questionnaires, communication diaries, in-depth interviews, critical incident techniques, and network analyses within the overall framework of each enterprise. Communication audits typically explore such issues as the adequacy of channels of communication, the accuracy and completeness of transmitted information, and the nature of communication relationships (for example, trust, openness, candor).

Techniques for Improving Communication Effectiveness

Typical recommendations arising from a communication audit are directed toward improvement in such areas as overall communication climate, upward and downward communication, and internal and external communication channels. A variety of techniques have been developed to implement recommendations in these and other areas.[62]

The Establishment of Private Lines that allow employees to question or comment anonymously on any issue ranging from job assignments to promotions, either by calling a special telephone number or by mailing their remarks on company-prepared forms. There may even be certain time periods when executives are available to answer telephone calls personally. Responses are either sent to employees directly or published in a company newsletter or other publication. A survey of employee attitudes toward the private line program in one company revealed that 79 per cent of the employees who had participated in the program were satisfied with the responses that they had received, and 93 per cent indicated that they would use the program again. Interestingly enough, of the private line queries that had been received, 25 per cent had originated within management ranks.[63]

The Establishment of Special Councils composed of managers and operative employees, special councils to provide an opportunity for managers and lower-level employees to get together regularly and discuss issues of mutual concern. Generally organized to meet two to six times per year, these councils normally have a formal

---

[61]G. M. Goldhaber et al., "Organizational Communications: 1978," *Human Communication Research* 5 (1978): 76–96; K. Brooks, J. Callicoat, and G. Siegerdt, "The ICA Communication Audit and Perceived Communication Effectiveness Changes in 16 Audited Organizations," *Human Communication Research* 5 (1979): 130–137.

[62]D. H. Fenn and D. Yankelovich, "Responding to the Employee Voice," *Harvard Business Review* 50, no. 3 (1972): 83–91.

[63]B. Harriman, "Up and Down the Communications Ladder," *Harvard Business Review* 52, no. 5 (1974): 143–151.

agenda jointly prepared by management and labor. The agenda is published prior to the meeting of the council, and the subsequent outcome for each item is publicly announced. In many companies the main council is undergirded by subcouncils of lower-level personnel. Issues that cannot be settled at lower levels flow up to the main council for resolution.

The Establishment of Employee Annual Meetings conducted at about the same time of year and in the same manner as regular stockholders' meetings. In addition to being available for questions, the president and other top officers brief organization members on the state of the company and outline their future plans for the company. In geographically dispersed organizations, several such meetings may be held. While these meetings do take time and involve a certain expense, they serve to reflect management's interest in improved communication.

The Establishment of Nonmanagement Task Teams to deal with specific high priority problems of the work force. Typically, the formation of the task teams and the problems they are to study are widely publicized. Most often, the teams are composed of volunteers who are allowed a certain amount of company time to conduct their investigation and report to management. In turn, management has a specified period of time in which to respond publicly. One company reports that over a five-year period more than 90 per cent of its task team's recommendations have been accepted and implemented.[64] Teams have dealt with problems such as labor-management relations, scheduling of maintenance work, and interdepartmental conflicts.

The Establishment of Interdepartmental Management Teams Designed to facilitate horizontal communication, these teams meet regularly to coordinate interdepartmental operations. These groups, which are also called coordinating action teams, generally have proven to be particularly successful as a vehicle for stimulating meaningful and effective first-line management participation. Furthermore, because of their person-to-person nature, coordinating action teams have been especially effective in resolving sensitive personal issues.

The Importance of Feedback

A common feature of each of the foregoing techniques is their recognition of feedback as an essential mechanism for establishing accuracy in organizational communications. Feedback is necessary for verifying the degree to which a communication has been both accurately transmitted and understood. Research comparing one-way communication (zero feedback) with two-way communication (free feedback) indicates that two-way communication is not only more accurate but also more satisfying

---

[64]Ibid.

for the participants.[65] Studies conducted as early as the 1920s further indicate that feedback is associated with improved performance.[66] Recent studies have confirmed this finding and also suggest that the frequency of performance feedback affects job attitudes and levels of aspiration.[67]

Feedback originates with numerous sources and is expressed in many ways. The comments and nonverbal communications of coworkers, immediate supervisors, clients, or perhaps subordinates may each be a source of feedback. Other possible feedback sources include performance appraisals, awards and promotions, and even personal evaluations of one's own feelings and ideas.[68] It is important to realize that feedback itself is communication and is subject to all the barriers that hinder other forms of communication.[69] Thus, in the role of message senders, managers must also serve as receivers in order to ensure that their communications have been received and accurately interpreted. For example, after explaining a job assignment, a manager might ask, "Are there any questions?" or "Is everything clear?" It should be realized, however, that such an approach will be useful only in instances in which a subordinate realizes that he or she has not interpreted a message properly. A more direct approach would be for a manager to ask a subordinate to repeat the assignment. However, rather than revealing a true understanding, this procedure might only reveal whether the message was received intact. Perhaps the best approach in such situations is for a manager to request that a subordinate restate the assignment in his or her own words, specifying the actions that need to be taken. Experience suggests that this procedure frequently results in a number of clarifications that neither the manager nor the subordinate realized were necessary.[70]

Interorganizational Communication

Whereas the preceding sections have dealt almost exclusively with various dimensions of interpersonal communication (that is, communication between individuals) and interunit communication (that is, communication within and across organizational subunits), this final section focuses upon the third communication context identified

---

[65]W. V. Haney, "A Comparative Study of Unilateral and Bilateral Communication," *Academy of Management Journal* 7 (1964): 128–136; H. J. Leavitt and R. H. Mueller, "Some Effects of Feedback on Communication," *Human Relations* 4 (1951): 401–410.

[66]See, for example, G. F. Arps, "Work with Knowledge of Results versus Work without Knowledge of Results," *Psychological Monographs* 28, no. 3 (whole no. 125; 1920).

[67]For a review of findings in this area see D. R. Ilgen, C. D. Fisher, and M. S. Taylor, "Consequences of Individual Feedback on Behavior in Organizations," *Journal of Applied Psychology* 64 (1979): 349–371; D. A. Clement and K. S. Frandsen, "On Conceptual and Empirical Treatments of Feedback in Human Communication," *Communication Monographs* 43 (1976): 11–28.

[68]M. M. Greller and E. M. Herold, "Sources of Feedback: A Preliminary Investigation," *Organizational Behavior and Human Performance* 13 (1975): 244–256.

[69]M. Bjorkman, "Feedforward and Feedback as Determiners of Knowledge and Policy: Notes on a Neglected Issue," *Scandinavian Journal of Psychology* 13 (1972): 152–158.

[70]K. M. Wexley and G. A. Yukl, *Organizational Behavior and Personnel Psychology* (Homewood, Ill.: Richard D. Irwin, 1977), pp. 64–65.

in Tables 9–1 and 9–2—communication between organizations. In stark contrast to other types of communication, our knowledge of information exchange between organizations is quite limited and for the most part is an incidental by-product of other investigations.[71] This is somewhat surprising, given the frequency with which most organizations must interact with other entities within their organization-set.[72] In addition to interacting with consumers or clients, most organizations typically communicate regularly with suppliers, competitors, and other external groups such as advisory boards and regulating agencies. A graphic model of such interorganizational communication is presented in Figure 9–2. As suggested in Chapter 6, this type of communication (the acquisition, importation, and processing of environmental information) is essential if an organization is not only to adapt to the needs and demands of its task environment, but also to exercise more than a minimum measure of control in molding events in the direction of preferred outcomes. With respect to this last point, access to and control of information have repeatedly been shown to be a power resource allowing an organization to protect its prerogatives and influence decisions.[73]

Organizations communicate with one another in several ways. Individuals occupying boundary roles—sales representatives, purchasing agents, labor negotiators, top corporate officers, credit managers—exchange information in their normal duties as external organizational representatives. In addition, many larger organizations communicate with their many publics through institutionalized communication officials.[74] Examples include public relations staffs, lobbyists, and consumer hot lines or ombudsmen. Finally, organizations may be said to communicate via their membership in information systems that cross company boundaries[75] and through their participation in computerized data banks.[76] The former encompasses the paperless recording of claims, processing of orders, payment of invoices, and other financial transactions that occur between buyers and sellers as well as between organizations performing similar functions—for instance, the reservation information system maintained by the nation's airlines. Illustrations of the latter include data banks dealing with consumer and business credit, marketing and econometric statistics, and stock, bond, and commodity prices.

---

[71]P. C. Morrow, "Interorganizational Communication and Interorganizational Research: A Propositional Inventory," in *Proceedings of the Annual Meeting of the Academy of Management,* ed. J. C. Susbauer (Cleveland, Ohio, 1978), pp. 334–338.

[72]J. L. Metcalfe, "Organizational Strategies and Interorganizational Networks," *Human Relations* 29 (1976): 327–343.

[73]A. M. Pettigrew, "Information Control as a Power Resource," *Sociology* 6 (1972): 187–204; R. E. Speckman, "Influence and Information: An Exploratory Investigation of the Boundary Role Person's Basis of Power," *Academy of Management Journal* 22 (1979): 104–117.

[74]J. E. Grunig, "A Multi-systems Theory of Organizational Communication," *Communication Research* 2 (1975): 99–136.

[75]F. Kaufman, "Data Systems That Cross Company Boundaries," *Harvard Business Review* 44, no. 1 (1966): 141–155.

[76]J. W. Darrow and J. R. Belilove, "The Growth of Databank Sharing," *Harvard Business Review* 31, no. 5 (1953): 180–194.

Figure 9–2 *A Graphic Representation of Interorganizational Communication*

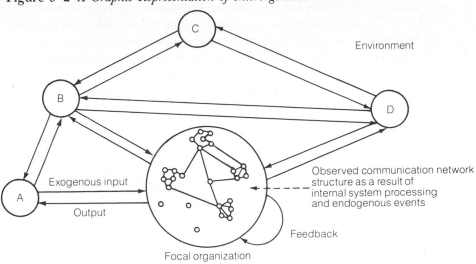

Source: R. Wigand, "A Model of Interorganizational Communication among Complex Organizations," in *Communication and Control in Society,* ed. K. Krippendorff (New York: Gordon and Breach, 1979), p. 342. Reprinted by permission.

Research Findings

While numerous organizational analysts argue as we do concerning the necessity of interorganizational communications,[77] carrying what Scott has referred to as their "freight of information, influence, and inducements,"[78] very few studies have been conducted in this area. Czepiel, in a study of thirty-two steel manufacturers, confirmed the operation of an industry-wide communication network and presented evidence to suggest that, in order to completely understand the dynamics of intraorganizational systems, one must take into account the flow of interorganizational information.[79] Studies by Mulford et al. and Morrow provide further support for this finding.[80] In an

---

[77]See, for example, R. T. Wigand, "A Cybernetic Model of Communication and Interorganizational Relationships among Complex Organizations," in *Proceedings of the 8th International Congress on Cybernetics of the International Association for Cybernetics* (Namur, Belgium, 1978), pp. 463–480; R. T. Wigand, "A Path-Analytic Evaluation of Communication among Social Service Organizations" (paper presented at the Annual Meeting of the International Communications Association, Berlin, Federal Republic of West Germany, May 29–June 4, 1977).

[78]W. R. Scott, "Theory of Organizations," in *Handbook of Modern Sociology,* ed. R. E. L. Faris (Chicago: Rand McNally, 1964), pp. 501–502.

[79]J. A. Czepiel, "Patterns of Interorganizational Communications and the Diffusion of a Major Technological Innovation in a Competitive Industrial Community," *Academy of Management Journal* 18 (1975): 6–24.

[80]C. L. Mulford et al. "A Multidimensional Evaluation of Effectiveness in a Noneconomic Organization," *Organization and Administrative Sciences* 7, no. 4 (1976): 125–145; P. C. Morrow, "Communication as an Organizational Construct: A Conceptual and Empirical Examination of Organizational Feedback" (paper presented at the 39th Annual National Academy of Management meeting, Atlanta, Georgia, August 1979).

effort to determine the effectiveness of a random sample of ninety local civil defense units, Mulford et al. found a significant relationship between unit preparedness and the number of linkages maintained with other services and local voluntary organizations. This finding was interpreted to suggest that "the extent to which the local disaster organization is able to establish strong relationships with other agencies and governmental services in the community may be a good indication of its attainment of other types of effectiveness."[81] Similarly, Morrow, in an investigation of ninety federated nonprofit organizations, found operational effectiveness (defined as goal attainment) to be significantly related not only to the amount of information received from customers and other "organizational peers" (termed "horizontal feedback") but also to the amount of information received from superordinate organizations such as regulatory agencies and higher level units (termed "vertical feedback").[82] Together, these findings clearly suggest that external feedback is as important to the effective exchange of information and outputs between organizations as our earlier discussion indicated it to be in establishing effective interpersonal and interunit communication.

Evidence is also available which indicates that frequency and type (personal or impersonal) of interaction are related not only to the quality of interorganizational communications but also to the actual number of joint programs in which an organization participates.[83] Paradoxically, however, these same data indicate that, while frequency of interaction is related to increased interorganizational coordination and good communications, it is also related to increased conflict. It thus appears that the exchange of information between organizations can be of high quality, be frequent, and yet, at the same time, center around conflict situations. This seems to suggest that interorganizational communications play a dual role—leading on one hand to more cooperative efforts and on the other to increased conflict.[84]

In an attempt to further ascertain the nature of this occurrence, as well as the types of organizations likely to be chosen as partners in such interdependent relations, some recently published studies have also provided support for the hypothesis that organizations are most likely to communicate with one another when *both* perceive benefits from interacting. Thus, Grunig, in a study of 26 low-income housing interest groups, governmental agencies, housing developers, and private employers, Schmidt and Kochan in an investigation of the interactions among 146 community organizations (for example, local unions, community action programs, social welfare services, and so on) and 23 district offices of the U.S. Training and Employment Service, and Molnar, in an analysis of the network membership of 39 public agencies involved in the field of natural resource management, all found general support for the prediction that organizations are most likely to interact with one another when confronted with a mutual problem or with a common constraint that might be elimi-

---

[81]Mulford et al., "A Multidimensional Evaluation," p. 113.

[82]Morrow, "Communication as an Organizational Construct."

[83]R. H. Hall and J. P. Clark, "Problems in the Study of Interorganizational Relationships," *Organization and Administrative Sciences* 5, no. 1 (1974): 45–68; R. H. Hall et al., "Patterns of Interorganizational Relationships," *Administrative Science Quarterly* 22 (1977): 457–474; Mulford et al., "A Multidimensional Evaluation."

[84]Hall and Clark, "Problems in the Study of Interorganizational Relationships," p. 53.

Chapter 9

nated through a cooperative exchange of information.[85] Such situations are thus two-sided, serving on one hand to reduce the probability of conflict and on the other to give rise to a mutual motivation for cooperative interaction.

Summary

The entire focus of this chapter has been directed at explaining the nature of communication within organizational settings. After establishing the importance of communication for the effective functioning of an organization, emphasis was placed upon the accurate transfer of information and understanding at three levels of analysis— interpersonal (communication between individuals), interunit (communication within and across organizational subunits), and interorganizational (communication between organizations). Within each of these levels a wide variety of individual, organizational, and environmental variables relating to the accurate transmission of information were discussed. Included were comments on the characteristics of the various directional flows (vertical, horizontal, and diagonal) within an organization, the host of communication barriers present in most organized settings, and techniques for overcoming such difficulties. In addition, a specific attempt was made to stress the importance of feedback in all types of communication settings.

In contrast to certain of the topics discussed in preceding chapters, the absence of adequate theoretical models to explain the nature of the findings presented is especially noteworthy. In commenting on basically this same point, Porter and Roberts, in a recent state of the art assessment, were forced to conclude that neither communication theorists nor organization theorists have provided the direction or impetus necessary for the development of acceptable conceptual systems for dealing with communication in organizational settings. The present state of this dilemma is reflected in both the unintegrated nature of the research that has been reported and the extensive extrapolation of findings from other areas that is necessary to make generalizations about organizations.[86] In this regard, the role of communication in organizations is an area of study desperately in need of theory development and further meaningful research.

Review and Discussion Questions

1. Distinguish between the efficiency and effectiveness of vertical communications.
2. List some possible reasons why staff personnel seem to know more about

---

[85]Grunig, "A Multi-systems Theory"; S. M. Schmidt and T. A. Kochan, "Interorganizational Relationships: Patterns and Motivations," *Administrative Science Quarterly* 22 (1977): 220–234; J. J. Molnar, "Comparative Organizational Properties and Interorganizational Interdependence," *Sociology and Social Research* 63 (1978): 24–48.

[86]L. W. Porter and K. H. Roberts, "Communication in Organizations," in *Handbook of Industrial and Organizational Psychology,* ed. M. D. Dunnette (Chicago: Rand McNally, 1976), p. 1553.

company events than their line counterparts. What are the implications of this increased knowledge?

3. Explain what is meant by selective perception.
4. What communication difficulties does hierarchical transmission cause?
5. Describe what happens when nonverbal cues are incongruent with an accompanying verbal message.
6. Comment on the advantages of written communications.
7. Explain how information overload serves as a barrier to effective communication. What causes information overload?
8. Comment on the advantages of oral communications.
9. Explain how the activities of specialized staff which are designed to increase channel capacity may in actuality promote information distortion.
10. Why is feedback important?

References

Argyris, C. "Interpersonal Barriers to Decision Making." *Harvard Business Review* 44, no. 2 (1966): 84–97.

Arps, G. F. "Work with Knowledge of Results versus Work without Knowledge of Results." *Psychological Monographs* 28, no. 3 (whole no. 125; 1920).

Bass, B. M., and Ryterband, E. C. *Organizational Psychology.* 2nd ed. Boston: Allyn & Bacon, 1979.

Bjorkman, M. "Feedforward and Feedback as Determiners of Knowledge and Policy: Notes on a Neglected Issue." *Scandinavian Journal of Psychology* 13 (1972): 152–158.

Blau, P. M., and Scott, W. R. *Formal Organization: A Comparative Approach.* San Francisco: Chandler, 1962.

Brooks, K., Callicoat, J., and Siegerdt, G. "The ICA Communication Audit and Perceived Communication Effectiveness Changes in 16 Audited Organizations." *Human Communication Research* 5 (1979): 130–137.

Campbell, D. T. "Systematic Error on the Part of Human Links in Communication Systems." *Information and Control* 1 (1958): 334–369.

Clement, D. A., and Frandsen, K. D. "On Conceptual and Empirical Treatments of Feedback in Human Communication." *Communication Monographs* 43 (1976): 11–28.

Cyert, R. M., March, J. G., and Starbuck, W. H. "Two Experiments on Bias and Conflict in Organization Estimation." *Management Science* 7 (1961): 254–264.

Czepiel, J. A. "Patterns of Interorganizational Communications and the Diffusion of a Major Technological Innovation in a Competitive Industrial Community." *Academy of Management Journal* 18 (1975): 6–24.

Dahle, T. L. "An Objective and Comparative Study of Five Methods of Transmitting Information to Business and Industrial Employees." *Speech Monographs* 21 (1954): 21–28.

Dalton, M. *Men Who Manage: Fusions of Feeling and Theory in Administration.* New York: John Wiley & Sons, 1959.

Darrow, J. W., and Belilove, J. R. "The Growth of Databank Sharing." *Harvard Business Review* 56, no. 6 (1978): 180–194.

Davis, K. "Management Communication and the Grapevine." *Harvard Business Review* 31, no. 5 (1953): 43–49.

Davis, K. "Readability Changes in Employee Handbooks of Identical Companies during a Fifteen Year Period." *Personnel Psychology* 21 (1968): 413–420.

Dearborn, D. C., and Simon, H. A. "Selective Perception. A Note on the Departmental Identifications of Executives." *Sociometry* 21 (1958): 140–144.

Falcione, R. L. "The Relationship of Supervisor Credibility to Subordinate Satisfaction." *Personnel Journal* 52, no. 9 (1973): 800–803.

Farace, R. V., Stewart, J. P., and Taylor, J. A. "Criteria for Evaluation of Organizational Communication Effectiveness: Review and Synthesis." In *Communication Yearbook 2,* edited by B. D. Ruben. New Brunswick, N.J.: Transaction Books, 1978.

Fenn, D. H., and Yankelovich, D. "Responding to the Employee Voice." *Harvard Business Review* 50, no. 3 (1972): 83–91.

Fries, C. C. *Linguistics and Reading*. New York: Holt, Rinehart and Winston, 1963.

Goldhaber, G. M., Yates, M. P., Porter, D. T., and Lesniak, R. "Organizational Communication: 1978." *Human Communications Research* 5 (1978): 76–96.

Greller, M. M., and Herold, D. M." Sources of Feedback: A Preliminary Investigation." *Organizational Behavior and Human Performance* 13 (1975): 244–256.

Grunig, J. E. "A Multi-systems Theory of Organizational Communication." *Communication Research* 2 (1975): 99–136.

Guetzkow, H. "Communications in Organizations." In *Handbook of Organizations,* edited by J. G. March. Chicago: Rand McNally, 1965.

Gullahorn, J. T. "Distance and Friendship as Factors in the Gross Interaction Matrix." *Sociometry* 15 (1952): 123–134.

Habbe, S. "Does Communication Make a Difference?" *Management Record* 14 (1952): 414–416, 442–444.

Hage, J., Aiken, M., and Marrett, C. "Organization Structure and Communications." *American Sociological Review* 36 (1971): 860–871.

Hall, R. H., and Clark, J. P. "Problems in the Study of Interorganizational Relationships." *Organization and Administrative Sciences* 5, no. 1 (1974): 45–66.

Hall, R. H., Clark, J. P., Giordans, P. C., Johnston, P. V., and Van Roekel, M. "Patterns of Interorganizational Relationships." *Administrative Science Quarterly* 22 (1977): 457–474.

Haney, W. V. "A Comparative Study of Unilateral and Bilateral Communication." *Academy of Management Journal* 7 (1964): 128–136.

Hare, A. P. *Handbook of Small Group Research.* 2nd ed. New York: Free Press, 1976.

Harper, R. G., Wiens, A. N., and Matarazzo, J. D. *Nonverbal Communication: The State of the Art.* New York: John Wiley & Sons, 1978.

Harriman, B. "Up and Down the Communications Ladder." *Harvard Business Review* 52, no. 5 (1974): 143–151.

Hsia, H. J. "Redundancy: Is It the Lost Key to Better Communication?" *AV Communication Review* 25 (1977): 63–85.

Ilgen, D. R., Fisher, C. D., and Taylor, M. S. "Consequences of Individual Feedback on Behavior in Organizations." *Journal of Applied Psychology* 64 (1979): 349–371.

Indik, B. P. "Organization Size and Member Participation: Some Empirical Tests of Alternatives." *Human Relations* 18 (1965): 339–350.

Indik, B. P., Georgopoulos, B. S., and Seashore, S. E. "Superior-Subordinate Relationships and Performance." *Personnel Psychology* 14 (1961): 357–374.

Jablin, F. M. "Superior-Subordinate Communication: The State of the Art." *Psychological Bulletin* 86 (1979): 1201–1222.

Katz, D., and Kahn, R. L. *The Social Psychology of Organizations.* 2nd ed. New York: John Wiley & Sons, 1978.

Kaufman, F. "Data Systems That Cross Company Boundaries." *Harvard Business Review* 44, no. 1 (1966): 141–155.

Korman, A. K. "A Cause of Communication Failure." *Personnel Administration* 23, no. 3 (1960): 17–21.

Korman, A. K. "Selective Perceptions among First-Line Supervisors." *Personnel Administration* 26 (1963): 31–36.

Landsberger, H. A. "The Horizontal Dimension in Bureaucracy." *Administrative Science Quarterly* 6 (1961): 299–332.

Leavitt, H. J. *Managerial Psychology.* 4th ed. Chicago: University of Chicago Press, 1978.

Leavitt, H. J., and Mueller, R. H. "Some Effects of Feedback on Communication." *Human Relations* 4 (1951): 401–410.

Level, D. A. "Communication Effectiveness: Method and Situation." *Journal of Business Communication* 10, no. 1 (1972): 19–25.

Maier, N. R. F., Hoffman, L. R., Hooven, J. J., and Read, W. H. *Superior-Subordinate Communications in Management.* Research Study No. 52. New York: American Management Association, 1961.

March, J. G., and Simon, H. A. *Organizations.* New York: John Wiley & Sons, 1958.

Mehrabian, A. *Silent Messages.* Belmont, Calif.: Wadsworth, 1971.

Mehrabian, A., and Reed, H. "Some Determinants of Communication Accuracy." *Psychological Bulletin* 70 (1968): 365–381.

Mehrabian, A., and Winer, M. "Decoding of Inconsistent Communications." *Journal of Personality and Social Psychology* 6 (1967): 109–114.

Meier, R. L. "Communications Stress." *Annual Review of Ecology and Systematics* 3 (1972): 289–314.

Meier, R. L. *Social Change in Communication Oriented Institutions.* Report No. 10. Ann Arbor: Mental Health Research Institute, University of Michigan, 1961.

Melcher, A. J., and Beller, R. "Toward a Theory of Communication: Consideration in Channel Selection." *Academy of Management Journal* 10 (1967): 39–52.

Metcalfe, J. L. "Organizational Strategies and Interorganizational Networks." *Human Relations* 29 (1976): 327–343.

Miller, J. G. "Input Overload and Psychopathology." *American Journal of Psychiatry* 116 (1960): 695–704.

Miller, J. G. "Living Systems: The Organization." *Behavioral Science* 17 (1972): 1–182.

Molnar, J. J. "Comparative Organizational Properties and Interorganizational Interdependence." *Sociology and Social Research* 63 (1978): 24–48.

Monge, P. R., Edwards, J. A., and Kirste, K. K. "The Determinants of Communication and Communication Structure in Large Organizations: A Review of Research." In *Communication Yearbook 2,* edited by B. D. Ruben. New Brunswick, N.J.: Transaction Books, 1978.

Morrow, P. C. "Communication as an Organizational Construct: A Conceptual and Empirical Examination of Organizational Feedback." Paper presented at the 39th Annual National Academy of Management Meeting, Atlanta, Georgia, August 1979.

Morrow, P. C. "Interorganizational Communication and Interorganizational Research: A Propositional Inventory." In *Proceedings of the Annual Meeting of the Academy of Management,* edited by J. C. Susbauer, Cleveland, Ohio, 1978.

Mosley, D. C., and Pietri, P. H. *Management: The Act of Working with and through People.* Encino, Calif.: Dickenson, 1975.

Mulford, C. L., Klonglan, G. E., Warren, R. D., and Padgitt, J. B. "A Multidimensional Evaluation of Effectiveness in a Non-economic Organization." *Organization and Administrative Sciences* 7, no. 4 (1976): 125–143.

Nichols, R. G. "Listening Is Good Business." *Management of Personnel Quarterly* 1, no. 2 (1962): 2–10.

O'Reilly, C. A. "The Intentional Distortion of Information in Organizational Communication: A Laboratory and Field Investigation." *Human Relations* 31 (1978): 173–193.

Pettigrew, A. M. "Information Control as a Power Resource." *Sociology* 6 (1972): 187–204.

Porter, L. W. "Communication: Structure and Process." In *Integrating the Organization,* edited by H. L. Fromkin and J. J. Sherwood. New York: Free Press, 1974.

Porter, L. W., and Lawler, E. E. "Properties of Organization Structure in Relation to Job Attitudes and Job Behavior." *Psychological Bulletin* 64 (1965): 23–51.

Porter, L. W., and Roberts, K. H. "Communication in Organizations." In *Handbook of Industrial and Organizational Psychology,* edited by M. D. Dunnette. Chicago: Rand McNally, 1976.

Raymond, R. C. "Betting on New Technologies." In *Technological Planning on the Corporate Level,* edited by J. R. Bright. Boston: Division of Research, Graduate School of Business Administration, Harvard University, 1962.

Read, W. H. "Upward Communication in Industrial Hierarchies." *Human Relations* 15 (1962): 3–16.

Reitz, H. J. *Behavior in Organizations.* Homewood, Ill.: Richard D. Irwin, 1977.

Roberts, K. H., O'Reilly, C. A., Bretton, G. E., and Porter, L. W. "Organizational Theory and Organizational Communication: A Communication Failure?" *Human Relations* 27 (1974): 501–524.

Roby, T. B., and Lanzetta, J. T. "Conflicting Principles in Man-Machine System Design." *Journal of Applied Psychology* 41 (1957): 170–178.

Rothstein, D. A. "Psychiatric Implications of Information Theory." *Archives of General Psychiatry* 13 (1965): 87–94.

Schmidt, S. M., and Kochan, T. A. "Interorganizational Relationships: Patterns and Motivations." *Administrative Science Quarterly* 22 (1977): 220–234.

Scott, W. G., "Communication and Centralization of Communication." *Journal of Communication* 13 (1963): 3–11.

Scott, W. R. "Theory of Organizations." In *Handbook of Modern Sociology,* edited by R. E. L. Faris. Chicago: Rand McNally, 1964.

Chapter 9

Shaw, M. E. *Group Dynamics: The Psychology of Small Group Behavior.* 2nd ed. New York: McGraw-Hill, 1976.

Shelly, M. W., and Gilchrist, T. C. "Some Effects of Communication Requirements in Group Structures." *Journal of Social Psychology* 48 (1958): 37–43.

Shepard, H. A. "The Value System of a University Research Group." *American Sociological Review* 19 (1954): 456–462.

Spekman, R. E. "Influence and Information: An Exploratory Investigation of the Boundary Role Person's Basis of Power." *Academy of Management Journal* 22 (1979): 104–117.

Steers, R. M. *Organizational Effectiveness: A Behavioral View.* Santa Monica, Calif.: Goodyear, 1977.

Strauss, G. A. "Tactics of Lateral Relationships: The Purchasing Agent." *Administrative Science Quarterly* 7 (1962): 161–186.

Stymne, B. "Interdepartmental Communication and Intraorganizational Strain." *Acta Sociologica* 11 (1968): 82–100.

Sussman, L. "Perceived Message Distortion or You Can Fool Some of the Supervisors Some of the Time. . . ." *Personnel Journal* 53, no. 9 (1974): 679–682, 688.

Thayer, L. "Communication and Organization Theory." In *Human Communication Theory: Original Essays,* edited by F. E. X. Dance. New York: Holt, Rinehart and Winston, 1967.

Triandis, H. C. "Similarity in Thought Processes and Boss-Employee Communication." In *Communication in Organizations: Some New Research Findings.* Ann Arbor, Mich.: Foundation for Research on Human Behavior, 1959.

Vardaman, G. T., and Vardaman, P. B. *Communication in Modern Organizations.* New York: John Wiley & Sons, 1973.

Weaver, C. H. "The Quantification of the Frame of Reference in Labor-Management Communication." *Journal of Applied Psychology* 42 (1958): 1–19.

Webber, R. A. "Perceptions of Interactions between Supervisors and Subordinates." *Human Relations* 23 (1970): 235–248.

Wexley, K. M., and Yukl, G. A. *Organizational Behavior and Personnel Psychology.* Homewood, Ill.: Richard D. Irwin, 1977.

Whitehead, J. L. "Factors of Source Credibility." *Quarterly Journal of Speech* 54 (1968): 59–63.

Wigand, R. T. "A Cybernetic Model of Communication and Interorganizational Relationships among Complex Organizations." In *Proceedings of the 8th International Congress on Cybernetics of the International Association for Cybernetics (1976).* Namur, Belgium, 1978.

Wigand, R. T. "A Model of Interorganizational Communication among Complex Organizations." In *Communication and Control in Society,* edited by K. Krippendorff. New York: Gordon and Breach, 1979.

Wigand, R. T. "A Path-Analytic Evaluation of Communication among Social Service Organizations." Paper presented at the Annual Meeting of the International Communication Association. Berlin, Federal Republic of Germany, May 29–June 4, 1977.

Willits, R. D. "Company Performance and Interpersonal Relations." *Industrial Management Review* 8, no. 2 (1967): 91–108.

Wright, M. "Do You Need Lessons in Shop Talk?" *Personnel* 42, no. 4 (1965): 58–62.

Organizational Change

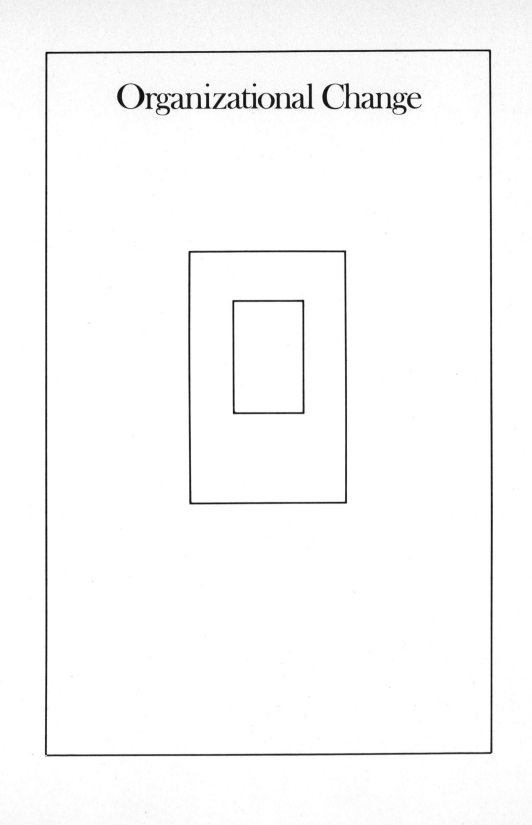

Organizational Change

Chapter 10

As the previous chapters have suggested and as Mann has so aptly observed, "Social organizations are functioning entities with interdependent structures and processes. They are not fixed, static structures, but rather continuously moving patterns of relationships in a much larger field of social activity."[1] Change, therefore, is a universal and continual aspect of all organizations. Regardless of its structural characteristics, no organization is exempt from change. Simply put, as open systems, organizations must either adapt to the inevitable changes that occur in their basic environmental, technological, and human parameters or perish. Indeed, as Cadwallader has recognized, "Any industrial corporation, such as International Business Machines or General Electric, that has survived the last fifty years of social change in the United States has done so through a process of self-transformation and not through the continuation of original organizational and operational patterns."[2]

The management of change is thus clearly an integral part of organizational functioning. Surprisingly, however, despite research dating back some thirty years, the process of organizational change has remained one of the least developed areas of organizational study.[3] No integrated theory of organizational change exists; nor are the attendant problems associated with the dynamics of the change process understood in more than a rough and ill-defined manner.

Nevertheless, change is part and parcel of the organizational process, and no discussion of organizations would be complete without some treatment of this complex topic. The challenge is clear—to create organizational systems that are capable of remaining current and viable, both internally and externally. For, as Porter, Lawler, and Hackman warn, "The pace of change will vary from organization to organization, but the fact of change will not."[4]

---

[1] F. C. Mann, "Studying and Creating Change: A Means to Understanding Social Organization," in *Research in Industrial Human Relations,* ed. C. M. Arensberg et al. (New York: Harper & Bros., 1957), p. 146.

[2] M. L. Cadwallader, "The Cybernetic Analysis of Change in Complex Social Systems," *American Journal of Sociology* 65 (1959): 155.

[3] See, for example, A. Bavelas, "Some Problems of Organizational Change," *Journal of Social Issues* 4, no. 3 (1948): 48–52; L. Coch and J. R. P. French, "Overcoming Resistance to Change," *Human Relations* 1 (1948): 512–532; R. N. McMurry, "The Problem of Resistance to Change in Industry," *Journal of Applied Psychology* 31 (1947): 589–593.

[4] L. W. Porter, E. E. Lawler, and J. R. Hackman, *Behavior in Organizations* (New York: McGraw-Hill, 1975), p. 437.

The purpose of this chapter is to explore the manifold nature of organizational change. After first discussing some frequent objectives of change, we will consider some of the reasons that people tend to resist change and will suggest a number of ways of dealing with this resistance. We will then consider two of the many approaches to introducing change and will examine a proposed model of the organizational change process. Finally, after identifying some additional aspects of change, we will briefly comment on the importance of its proper assessment and evaluation.

In so outlining the topics to be discussed, we in no way mean to imply that the analysis will be exhaustive. First, there are many other methods for introducing change besides the two basic approaches that will be discussed here. Furthermore, in focusing principally on organizational change, as opposed to individual or small group change, the chapter purposely neglects the vast literature associated with these latter two areas.

Objectives of Organizational Change

In attempting to identify the "objectives of organizational change," Greiner and Barnes note that while, on the surface, the purpose of organizational change is to facilitate the continued achievement of organizational goals, underlying the more obvious statements concerning greater profit and performance are two overarching objectives: (1) changes in the way an organization adapts to its external environment, and (2) changes in the behavioral patterns of its employees.[5] With respect to the former, and as emphasized throughout the preceding chapters, organizations are continually faced with the necessity of adapting to the changing contingencies and constraints of their surrounding environment. Because an organization cannot completely control its external environment, it must continually introduce internal organizational changes so that it can deal more effectively with new challenges arising from increased competition, technological innovations, mounting government regulations, and pressing social demands. Organizational responses to such pressures may be characterized as ranging from *reactive* (changes introduced in *reaction* to unanticipated events) to *proactive* (changes introduced in *anticipation* of future happenings). While the latter are certainly more difficult to achieve, they are unquestionably characteristic of an organization that seeks to influence environmental outcomes rather than simply react to events that have already occurred. This, of course, is the major difference between organizations that lead and those that follow their industries.

The second objective of organizational change is to achieve modifications in the behavioral patterns of individuals within an organization. Regardless of other factors, an organization's ability to cope with its environment will not be improved unless its members alter their relationships with one another and with their jobs. Organizations, to state the obvious, are run by human beings, not machines. Thus, as Greiner and

---

[5]L. E. Greiner and L. B. Barnes, "Organization Change and Development," in *Organizational Change and Development,* ed. G. W. Dalton, P. R. Lawrence, and L. E. Greiner (Homewood, Ill.: Richard D. Irwin, 1970), p. 2.

Barnes comment, "any organization change, whether it be introduced through a new structural design or a training program, is basically trying to get employees to adopt new patterns of behavior and ground rules for relating to each other and their jobs."[6] Consequently, in order for organization-wide effects to be felt, new behavioral patterns consistent with the requirements of an organization's environment must be developed. If this does not occur, an organization's level of adaptation will not be improved, since its operational stance will, in effect, be no different after than before change was attempted.

Resistance to Change

Although, as we have suggested, change is a universal and inevitable phenomenon, it rarely occurs in a smooth and balanced fashion. Resistance to change is a frequent and natural occurrence. The various causes of this resistance, however, are quite often difficult to determine. Nevertheless, resistance, soundly based or not, is always an important signal calling for further inquiry.[7] Managers are all too often unfamiliar with even the most basic reasons that resistance might be expected to occur. The following is an abbreviated discussion of four of the most common reasons.[8] To fully describe any one of them would require treatment at far greater length and depth than we can reasonably attempt here.

Parochial Self-Interest

It may be expected that virtually all organizational members will behave in ways that will maximize those goals that they personally consider most important. Consequently, to the extent that all proposals for change represent a threat to the status quo, individuals (and groups) are likely to resist if they believe they stand to lose something of value as a result. In such circumstances, the parties involved will for the most part focus on their own self-interest and only incidentally on the overall good of their organization. A sample listing of personal goals that, when threatened, will almost inevitably provoke resistance, would doubtlessly include:

1. *Power*—authority and control over organizational behavior
2. *Money*—increases in income or income substitutes
3. *Prestige*—respect and approval from those who are responsible for funding the agency, determining promotions, hiring and firing, and so on

---

[6]Ibid., p. 2.

[7]P. R. Lawrence, "How to Deal with Resistance to Change," *Harvard Business Review* 47, no. 1 (1969): 4–12, 166–176.

[8]J. P. Kotter and L. A. Schlesinger, "Choosing Strategies for Change," *Harvard Business Review* 57, no. 2 (1979): 106–114.

4. *Convenience*—avoidance of conditions that will require additional personal efforts
5. *Security*—protection against losses of personal power, prestige, or income
6. *Professional competence*—respect from peers for knowledge, technical proficiency, or professionally ethical behavior[9]

Another aspect of self-interest which often constitutes a source of resistance to change involves what March and Simon have labeled the *sunk costs doctrine*.[10] "Sunk costs refer to the investments that have been made by an organization (or its members) to develop and sustain any institutional arrangement or pattern of behavior that is currently in force."[11] Broadly defined, investments in this context include inputs of time, money, energy, or personal commitment. A simple example is the time and energy that organization members have devoted to developing and sustaining existing programs, procedures, and regulations. Such an investment may be viewed as a personal stake that may well be threatened by a proposed change in existing arrangements. Sunk costs thus foster an organizational bias toward continuity.

Misunderstandings and Lack of Trust

People also tend to resist when they do not understand the intended purpose, mechanics, or consequences of a planned change. Such a predicament is most likely to occur when there is a lack of trust between the parties involved in initiating and adopting a proposed modification. As suggested in the previous chapter, the distortion of information resulting from distrust and suspicion can serve only to increase defensiveness and decrease the frequency of open expression, thereby decreasing the likelihood of effective communication *and* of change. The important point here is that people do not resist change per se. They do, however, resist the uncertainties that change can bring.[12]

Different Assessments

Resistance to change also frequently occurs when organizational participants differ in their evaluation of the associated costs and benefits resulting from a proposed change. Responses to an attempted change, whatever the reality, are inevitably

---

[9]R. J. Patti, "Organizational Resistance and Change: The View from Below," *Social Service Review* 48 (1974): 371–372.

[10]J. G. March and H. A. Simon, *Organizations* (New York: John Wiley & Sons, 1958), p. 173.

[11]Patti, "Organizational Resistance," p. 378.

[12]A. C. Bartlett and T. A. Kayser, eds., *Changing Organizational Behavior* (Englewood Cliffs, N.J.: Prentice-Hall, 1973), p. 379.

related to the different parties' views of what the action will mean not only for themselves but for their organization as well.[13] Differing assessments of the effectiveness of proposed changes often occur when information concerning a change is inadequate. Unfortunately, this inadequacy is commonly compounded by the fact that, as Kotter and Schlesinger explain, change initiators "often assume both that they have all the relevant information required to conduct an adequate organization analysis and that those who will be affected by the change have the same facts, when neither assumption is correct." They go on to note that "in either case, the difference in information that groups work with often leads to differences in analyses, which in turn can lead to resistance."[14] It should be quickly pointed out, however, that situations such as that described raise the distinct possibility that opposition to change is not necessarily always bad. Constructive opposition that is grounded in an analysis more accurate than that made by the sponsoring initiators would obviously be good for an organization.

Low Tolerance for Change

Finally, a low tolerance for change on the part of an organization's members may also be a basis for opposition. This stems from the fact that different people have varying abilities to absorb change. As diagnosed by Student, "Facing the unknown consequences of change is a fundamental and disquieting psychological threat" to many individuals, challenging their sense of adequacy as well as threatening their self-esteem.[15] While it has been indicated that personal anxieties and apprehensions are to be expected in the face of change, there are certain types of individuals who, because of a low tolerance for ambiguity, will oppose a new plan or idea even though they recognize its soundness. These are often individuals who are afraid they will be unable to develop the new skills and behaviors that will be demanded of them if placed in a new position or if forced to work under altered circumstances such as might be associated with a reorganization.

For example, a person who receives a significantly more important job as a result of an organizational change will probably be very happy. But it is just as possible for such a person to also feel uneasy and to resist giving up certain aspects of the current situation. A new and very different job will require new and different behavior, new and different relationships, as well as the loss of some satisfactory current activities and relationships. If the changes are significant and the individual's tolerance for change is low, he might begin to actively resist change for reasons even he does not consciously understand.[16]

---

[13]G. A. Brager and H. Specht, *Community Organizing* (New York: Columbia University Press, 1973), p. 263.
[14]Kotter and Schlesinger, "Choosing Strategies," p. 108.
[15]K. R. Student, "Managing Change: A Psychologist's Perspective," *Business Horizons* 21, no. 6 (1978): 28–33.
[16]Kotter and Schlesinger, "Choosing Strategies," p. 109.

Again, it should be mentioned that these are just a few of the reasons that resistance to change might occur. There are doubtlessly innumerable others. They will vary in importance from situation to situation depending on the particular circumstances.

Dealing with Resistance to Change

Having discussed various causes for resistance to change, it is only appropriate that we also discuss the variety of approaches for overcoming such opposition. While in practice it may not always be possible to isolate the specific strategies being employed, for purposes of presentation we will separately treat six methods for influencing participant reactions to change.[17] These methods and their associated advantages and disadvantages are summarized in Table 10–1. The choice of a specific approach will, of course, depend on the combination of factors that obtains in each individual situation.

Table 10–1   *Methods for Dealing with Resistance to Change*

Approach	Commonly Used in Situations	Advantages	Drawbacks
Education + communication	Where there is a lack of information or inaccurate information and analysis.	Once persuaded, people will often help with the implementation of the change.	Can be very time-consuming if lots of people are involved.
Participation + involvement	Where the initiators do not have all the information they need to design the change, and where others have considerable power to resist.	People who participate will be committed to implementing change, and any relevant information they have will be integrated into the change plan.	Can be very time-consuming if participators design an inappropriate change.
Facilitation + support	Where people are resisting because of adjustment problems.	No other approach works as well with adjustment problems.	Can be time-consuming, expensive, and still fail.
Negotiation + agreement	Where someone or some group will clearly lose out in a change, and where that group has considerable power to resist.	Sometimes it is a relatively easy way to avoid major resistance.	Can be too expensive in many cases if it alerts others to negotiate for compliance.
Manipulation + cooptation	Where other tactics will not work, or are too expensive.	It can be a relatively quick and inexpensive solution to resistance problems.	Can lead to future problems if people feel manipulated.
Explicit + implicit coercion	Where speed is essential, and the change initiators possess considerable power.	It is speedy, and can overcome any kind of resistance.	Can be risky if it leaves people mad at the initiators.

Source: Reprinted by permission of the *Harvard Business Review*. Exhibit from "Choosing Strategies for Change" by J. P. Kotter and L. A. Schlesinger, March–April 1979, p. 111. Copyright © 1979 by the President and Fellows of Harvard College; all rights reserved.

---

[17]Ibid.

Education and Communication

Certainly the most basic approach to dealing with resistance, education is the sharing of knowledge or perceptions that a change initiator has acquired through means not typically available to other members of his or her general organization.[18] With this approach it is assumed that shared objectives are prevalent and implied that resistance can be overcome by training people to recognize the existence of problem areas and hence the necessity for change. This process furthermore assumes that resistance is based largely on misinformation or poor communication. Thus, as Warren advises, "appropriate action calls for 'getting the facts,' clearing up misunderstandings based on faulty or incomplete information, and reconciling different points of view on the basis of discussion."[19]

Depending on the nature of the change, this approach may involve mass media educational campaigns, one-on-one discussions, memos, group presentations, and reports. It should be noted, however, that to be successful such education and communication programs must be unquestionably and firmly grounded in mutual trust and credibility. Other advantages and disadvantages are identified in Table 10–1.

Participation and Involvement

The involvement of potential resistors in the planning and implementation of a proposed change is based on the notion that the most effective way to reduce anticipated opposition and to engender commitment to a proposed change is to work collaboratively with the members of a so-called target system. Intended to allay the fears of those to be affected and to capitalize on their specialized skills, the participation process is ideally designed to provide an opportunity for involvement in the discussion and planning of a proposed change in advance of its introduction. Theoretically, such activities are characterized by open communication and the exchange of perspectives on the part of all parties involved. Such interaction rests on the assumptions that the members of a target system are rational, possess the required expertise to contribute meaningfully, and are willing to act in good faith.[20] Additional drawbacks and benefits are given in Table 10–1.

---

[18]G. A. Brager and S. Holloway, *Changing Human Service Organizations: Politics and Practice* (New York: Free Press, 1978), p. 132.

[19]R. L. Warren, "Types of Purposive Social Change at the Community Level," in *Readings in Community Organization Practice*, ed. R. M. Kramer and H. Specht (Englewood Cliffs, N.J.: Prentice-Hall, 1969), p. 211.

[20]R. J. Patti and H. Resnick, "Changing the Agency from Within," *Social Work* 17, no. 4 (1972): 48–57.

Facilitation and Support

Another approach that has been shown to be helpful in decreasing resistance that arises in a changed situation involves the use of facilitative and supportive skills. Particularly appropriate when resistance develops as a result of fear and anxiety, the origins of the use of supportive methods such as employee counseling and therapy programs may be traced to the earliest stirrings of the human relations movement. Perhaps the clearest expression of the philosophy that underlies this approach is the following statement by Zander: *"Resistance will be prevented to the degree that the changer helps the changees to develop their own understanding of the need for change, and an explicit awareness of how they feel about it, and what can be done about those feelings."*[21]

Although written some thirty years ago, this one-sentence declaration is just as applicable now as it was then. It provides a nutshell description of the basic framework of the facilitative approach, underscoring its behavioral origin. Note, however, as indicated in Table 10–1, a major drawback of this approach: It can be time-consuming and expensive, and it can still fail.

Negotiation and Agreement

Negotiation as an approach to dealing with resistance to change involves "the sequential exchange of resources, sanctions, accommodations, and rewards, with the intent of reaching some mutually acceptable position" regarding a proposed change.[22] Since exchange implies reciprocity, this tactic necessarily suggests that an initiator is willing to tailor a change to meet the needs and interests of active or potential resisters. As stated in Table 10–1, negotiated agreements are particularly appropriate in situations "where someone or some group will clearly lose out in a change, and where that group has considerable power to resist." While negotiation is a relatively easy approach to initially avoiding resistance, in ongoing relationships, as Brager warns, "settlement by negotiation often entails a continuing process, for agreement is [more often] apparently, rather than actually, reached."[23] Once an initiator of change makes it known that he or she is willing to modify a stance to avoid resistance, the way is open for continued bargaining and even blackmail.

Manipulation and Cooptation

In the present context, manipulation involves the use of covert attempts to sidestep potential resistance to change. Manipulation is thus not simply a matter of persuasion

---

[21]A. Zander, "Resistance to Change—Its Analysis and Prevention," *Advanced Management* 15, no. 1 (1950): 9–11.

[22]Brager and Holloway, *Changing Human Service Organizations,* p. 132.

[23]G. A. Brager, "Institutional Change: Perimeters of the Possible," *Social Work* 12, no. 1 (1967): 68.

but more a devious tactic for persuading differently-minded groups that a proposed change should be adopted. As described by Brager and Holloway, manipulation often "involves advocating a position through a presentation designed to appeal to the particular interest and sensitivities" of a target system.[24] The selective distortion of information by both omission and commission may be involved, as may the conscious selection of facts and emotional appeals most likely to be convincing to the principal parties involved.

Cooptation, as described in Chapter 6, may be classified as a form of manipulation. The absorption of various key resisters into an organization's decision-making structure (recall the earlier example of TVA cited by Selznick) has long been a popular method to avert opposition.[25] Unlike participation, however, only the coopted element's endorsement, not its advice, is sought. It should be recalled, however, that along with its professed advantages (see Table 10–1) cooptation may reduce rather than enhance an organization's decision-making discretion.

Explicit and Implicit Coercion

Last on the list of approaches is the use of explicit and implicit coercion, which assumes that there is basic disagreement and that the principal parties involved are operating from relatively fixed positions. Typified by the abandonment, at least temporarily, of efforts at consensus, coercion involves the use of force or threats or both to impel the acceptance of an enacted change.[26] Tactics employed may involve virulent disagreements as well as threatened firings, transfers, and the loss of promotion possibilities. For reasons that are largely apparent (see Table 10–1), coercion is generally used sparingly in practice.[27]

In summary, the reader is again reminded that the six approaches discussed do not necessarily exist independently. Organizations often utilize a combination of approaches over time. The choice of a particular approach or approaches must be made with obvious concern for both the anticipated reaction of the parties involved and the principal goals being sought.

Approaches to Introducing Change

As one might suspect from the preceding discussion, there are any number of approaches to introducing change. It is perhaps no less surprising that methods for classifying these approaches are almost as numerous. One basis of such classification, which has gained at least some measure of acceptance, is to distinguish be-

---

[24]Brager and Holloway, *Changing Human Service Organizations*, p. 132.
[25]P. Selznick, *TVA and the Grass Roots: A Study in the Sociology of Formal Organization* (Berkeley, Calif.: University of California Press, 1949).
[26]Warren, "Types of Purposive Social Change."
[27]Brager and Holloway, *Changing Human Service Organizations*, p. 215.

tween the content of *what* is being changed (the variables) and the process of *how* change is initiated and implemented.[28]

Leavitt's Analysis

The most frequently cited example of the *what* approach is Leavitt's view of organizations as complex systems composed of four interacting variables: task, people, technology, and structure (see Figure 10–1).[29] *Task* refers to an organization's reason for existence, its production of goods and services; *people* to the human element operating within an organization; *technology* to technical tools and problem-solving inventions such as drill presses, work measurement techniques, and computers. Finally, *structure* refers to an organization's systems of communications, authority, and work flow.

It is Leavitt's contention that specific approaches to change can be developed and directed toward the alteration of any or all of these variables. Thus, change can be introduced *structurally* through the establishment of new systems of communication, authority, and responsibility and *technologically* by modifying an organization's tools and problem-solving instruments (for example, computers) and by influencing the *people,* or human element, within an organization. In that an organization's *task* (that is, manufacturing, education, transportation, and so on) is typically regarded as fixed, efforts at change are less frequently directed toward this area.

Given the highly interdependent nature of these four variables, Leavitt is quick to point out that a "change in any one usually results in compensatory (or retaliatory) change in others" and that "sometimes, the aim may be to change one as an end in itself, sometimes as a mechanism for effecting changes in one or more of the others."[30] As an illustration, he suggests that "the introduction of new technological tools—computers, for example—may effect changes in structure (e.g., in the communication system or decision map of the organization), changes in people (their numbers, skills, attitudes, and activities), and changes in task performance or even task definition, since some tasks may now become feasible of accomplishment for the first time."[31] It is important to note that any of these changes could be intended or could be an unanticipated outcome of changes in other variables whose relationships were previously unknown.

In brief, given their nearly total interdependence, it is Leavitt's position that each of the variables identified in Figure 10–1—task, people, technology, and structure—can be viewed as a possible entry point for an effort to effect change. The specific variable selected depends in part on the approach—new or modified people or machines, new tools, or new structures—that one may choose as a point of departure

---

[28]L. B. Barnes, "Organizational Change and Field Experiment Methods," in *Methods of Organizational Research,* ed. V. H. Vroom (Pittsburgh: University of Pittsburgh Press, 1967), p. 61.

[29]H. J. Leavitt, "Applied Organizational Change in Industry: Structural, Technological and Humanistic Approaches," in *Handbook of Organizations,* ed. J. G. March (Chicago: Rand McNally, 1965), pp. 1144–1170.

[30]Ibid., p. 1145.

[31]H. J. Leavitt, "Applied Organizational Change in Industry: Structural, Technical, and Human Approaches," in *New Perspectives in Organization Research,* ed. W. W. Cooper, H. J. Leavitt, and M. W. Shelly (New York: John Wiley & Sons, 1964), p. 56.

Figure 10–1 *Leavitt's Four Variable Conception of Organizational Change*

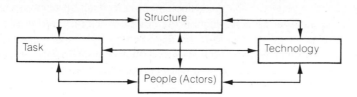

and on the underlying values that one may hold. Regardless of the point of intervention, however, one or more of the other variables will soon be affected.

Greiner's Analysis

In focusing on the process of *how* change is accomplished, as opposed to emphasizing *what* is being changed, Greiner's analysis goes one step beyond the consideration of the four variables identified by Leavitt.[32] In doing so, Greiner "suggests that change can be initiated by using various power distributions which may be as important or more important than the variable itself in determining the outcomes."[33]

Drawing on a survey of the organizational change literature, Greiner identified the seven major approaches most frequently used by managers to introduce change. He then further classified these approaches in terms of their position along a *power distribution continuum* such as that shown in Figure 10–2.

Figure 10–2 *Greiner's "Power Distribution Continuum" for Introducing Organizational Change with Corresponding Approaches*

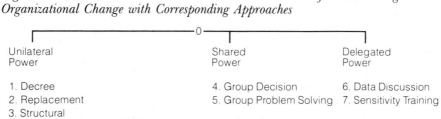

---

[32]L. E. Greiner, "Patterns of Organization Change," *Harvard Business Review* 45, no. 3 (1967): 119–130.
[33]Barnes, "Organizational Change," p. 61.

Unilateral Power

At the one extreme of the power distribution continuum are the approaches that rely on *unilateral power,* whereby: "Change is implemented through an emphasis on the authority of a man's hierarchical position in the company. Here, the definition and solution to the problem at hand tend to be specified by the upper echelons and directed downward through formal and impersonal control mechanisms."[34] The use of unilateral power to initiate change may take any of three forms:

1. The Decree Approach. *A "one-way" announcement originating with a person with high formal authority and passed on to those in lower positions.*
2. The Replacement Approach. *Individuals in one or more key organizational positions are replaced by other individuals. The basic assumption is that organizational changes are a function of a key man's ability.*
3. The Structural Approach. *Instead of decreeing or injecting new blood into work relationships, management changes the required relationships of subordinates working in the situation. By changing the structure of organizational relationships, organizational behavior is also presumably affected.*[35]

Shared Power

Located near the middle of the power distribution continuum are those approaches which rely on *shared power,* where "authority is still present and used, yet there is also interaction and sharing of power."[36] The shared exercise of power as a means of implementing change may take either of two forms:

4. The Group Decision Approach. *Here we have participation by group members in selecting from several alternative solutions specified in advance by superiors. This approach involves neither problem identification nor problem solving, but emphasizes the obtaining of group agreement to a particular course of action.*
5. The Group Problem Solving Approach. *Problem identification and problem solving through group discussion. Here the group has wide latitude, not only over choosing the problems to be discussed, but then in developing solutions to these problems.*[37]

Delegated Power

Finally, at the other extreme are the approaches that rely on *delegated power,* "where almost complete responsibility for defining and acting on problems is turned over to the subordinates."[38] The use of delegated power may take one of two forms:

---

[34]Greiner, "Patterns of Organization Change," p. 120.
[35]Greiner and Barnes, "Organization Change," p. 3.
[36]Greiner, "Patterns of Organization Change," p. 121.
[37]Greiner and Barnes, "Organization Change," p. 4.
[38]Greiner, "Patterns of Organization Change," p. 121.

6. The Data Discussion Approach. *Presentation and feedback of relevant data to the client system either by a change catalyst or by change agents within the company. Organizational members are encouraged to develop their own analyses of the data, presented in the form of case materials, survey findings, or data reports.*

7. The Sensitivity Training Approach. *Managers are trained in small discussion groups to be more sensitive to the underlying processes of individual and group behavior. Changes in work patterns and relationships are assumed to follow from changes in interpersonal relationships. Sensitivity approaches focus upon interpersonal relationships first, then hope for, or work toward, improvements in work performance.* [39]

Originally proposed in the context of business organizations, Greiner's scheme seems equally applicable to introducing change into all forms of complex systems. Perhaps most importantly, as an analytical aid, this system of classifying approaches to change not only indicates the extent to which power is retained by a change initiator or shared with those individuals who will be affected by a change effort, but also serves to suggest the type of tactics that might be most appropriate to achieve a proposed alteration. Moreover, it highlights the type of resources and facilities necessary to undertake a modification, as well as underscores the degree of personal commitment that will be necessary—for both changer and changees—to ensure a successful program of change.

In considering the Leavitt and Greiner schemes together, it should be emphasized that implementing successful organizational change is a much more complex process than merely selecting a particular method. In this regard, certain managerial steps have been identified that set necessary conditions for the effective introduction of change. When combined, these steps may be viewed as forming a conceptual framework or model of the change process. It is this subject which forms the basis of the next section.

The Change Process: A Model

There have been many attempts to develop a model of the organizational change process. Perhaps the model that is the most general in its application is a by-product of the Greiner study. Building upon the evidence collected in his initial survey of the organizational change literature, Greiner sought to identify the conditions that distinguished successful from less successful change efforts. This analysis led to the finding that the successful process of change almost invariably hinges on two key factors:

---

[39]Greiner and Barnes, "Organization Change," p. 4.

1. A redistribution of power within an organization such that traditional decision-making practices move toward the greater use of *shared power.*
2. Such power redistribution within the structure of an organization occurs through a *developmental process of change.* (This implies that successful organizational changes do not take place in one fell swoop. Rather, as will be discussed, they involve a pattern consisting of a number of specific and interrelated phases.)[40]

Treating this evidence further, Greiner was able to identify six phases common to successful change efforts, each involving a *stimulus* to the power structure and a *reaction* from the power structure of an organization. A general overview of this process is presented in Figure 10–3.

As indicated, the process begins *(first phase)* as a result of pressures on top management. These pressures may arise either externally from environmental factors such as lower sales or internally from events such as interdepartmental disagreements. In successful changes, the result is the same: arousal to take action.

Arousal in itself, of course, does not automatically ensure a proper response. It is quite likely that "top management, when under severe pressure, may be inclined to rationalize its problems by blaming them on a group other than itself, such as 'that lousy union' or 'that meddling government.' "[41] As a consequence, a *second phase* in successful change patterns emerges: intervention by an outsider. It is important that this individual be known for his or her ability to introduce improvements and that he or she enter an organization at the top or as a consultant who reports directly to the highest level of management. This type of entry places the newcomer in an ideal position to encourage top managers to reevaluate their past practices as possible causes of current internal problems.

Their reorientation consequently leads to a *third phase* common to successful changes—namely, the diagnosis and recognition of specific organizational problems. This phase is characterized by a *shared approach to power,* as the newcomer, with top management support and active personal involvement, engages members at several lower levels in collaborative, fact-finding, problem-solving discussions in order to recognize and diagnose current and potential organizational problems and, as suggested earlier, to reduce any anticipated opposition. By way of contrast, Greiner reports finding that less successful change experiences are generally typified by top managements that exercise *unilateral* or *delegated power.*

Once current and potential problem areas are diagnosed and identified, a *fourth phase* emerges: the invention of new solutions capable of generating and sustaining a high commitment to new courses of action. As in the previous phase, the newcomer again plays an active role, involving all management levels in developing new ideas and methods for solving problems and taking action. Solutions are thus based on *shared power,* emphasizing participation in the invention of group solutions to the

---

[40]Greiner, "Patterns of Organization Change," p. 126.
[41]Ibid., p. 127.

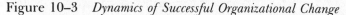

Figure 10–3 *Dynamics of Successful Organizational Change*

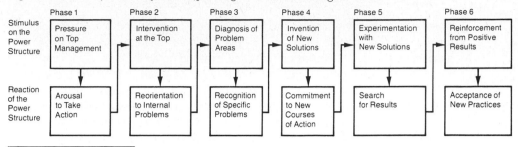

	Phase 1	Phase 2	Phase 3	Phase 4	Phase 5	Phase 6
Stimulus on the Power Structure	Pressure on Top Management	Intervention at the Top	Diagnosis of Problem Areas	Invention of New Solutions	Experimentation with New Solutions	Reinforcement from Positive Results
Reaction of the Power Structure	Arousal to Take Action	Reorientation to Internal Problems	Recognition of Specific Problems	Commitment to New Courses of Action	Search for Results	Acceptance of New Practices

problems recognized in phase 3. Such collaboration has been shown to be particularly effective in developing both quality solutions and, as previously suggested, high commitment to action. The latter factor is generally attributed to the notion that people are much more likely to endorse solutions of their own making rather than those that are directed from above.

Once new solutions to problems are developed, a *fifth phase*—experimentation and testing—follows. In this phase, the solutions suggested in phase 4 are tested for credibility on a small scale before they are introduced on a company-wide basis. In addition, the method previously used to generate solutions (interaction and shared power) is carefully evaluated. Further, rather than implementing major changes at the top, numerous small changes are introduced at all organizational levels on an experimental basis. In turn, reinforcement from positive results marks the beginning of the last stage of the model.

The *final phase* of the model is an outgrowth of the acceptance and internalization of change as previously experienced. As the change is found to be successful, and as participant support grows, it is introduced on a much larger scale, ultimately being absorbed into all parts of an organization. This sixth phase is thus one of reinforcement from positive results, leading in due course to an acceptance of new practices. Greiner suggests that, aside from the change itself, the most significant outcome of this phase is generally a greater acceptance at all organizational levels of the use of *shared power* as an approach for introducing change.

In evaluating the above scheme for viewing the change process, it should be realized that all models, inevitably, are oversimplifications of reality. No model is capable of fully explaining the process of change or its results. Moreover, given the situational nature of change, it is impossible to formulate a standard recipe that will apply in all cases.[42]

[42]R. C. Shirley, "A Model for Analysis of Organizational Change," *MSU Business Topics* 22, no. 3 (1974): 67.

Additional Aspects of Successful Change

In reflecting upon the discussions of the change process and basic strategies for introducing change, one should realize that there are several additional aspects to successful change. Margulies and Wallace, drawing on an in-depth analysis of techniques and applications of organizational change, offer several guiding propositions in this area.[43] Among them is the proposition that planned change efforts are much more likely to be successful if initiated and supported by the top management of an organization. A second proposition is that change will flow most smoothly when those who will be affected are brought into the process at the earliest possible stage. These guidelines are, of course, completely consistent with the earlier discussion of participative approaches for overcoming resistance to change.

A third proposition is that successful changes require time and repeated effort. That is, before becoming successfully incorporated as an ongoing part of organizational life, a change effort (as the fifth phase of Greiner's model suggests) will typically require repeated reinforcement over some period of time.

Although not specified by Margulies and Wallace, a fourth and essential aspect of successful change is the careful monitoring of a change effort to secure accurate feedback concerning intended outcomes. Commenting specifically on this point, Kotter and Schlesinger caution: "No matter how good a job one does of initially selecting a change strategy and tactics, something unexpected will eventually occur during implementation. Only by carefully monitoring the process can one identify the unexpected in a timely fashion and react to it intelligently."[44]

Assessing Organizational Change

Before concluding our discussion, it would seem appropriate to comment, if only briefly, on the assessment and evaluation of change. As Brager and Holloway recognize, "Determining the extent to which . . . [an] implemented change achieves its purposes, or has the potential for achieving them, is a central evaluation issue."[45] If properly undertaken, the systematic assessment of change can serve to provide the feedback required to determine the success or failure of a change strategy.

Although the importance of such a determination can hardly be questioned, available evidence suggests that careful assessments of organizational change efforts are relatively rare. Kimberly and Nielsen have offered several reasons for this seeming incongruity.[46] One is that the criteria for success are typically multiple and

---

[43]N. Margulies and J. Wallace, *Organizational Change: Techniques and Applications* (Glenview, Ill.: Scott, Foresman, 1973), pp. 154–157.

[44]Kotter and Schlesinger, "Choosing Strategies," p. 113.

[45]Brager and Holloway, *Changing Human Service,* p. 227.

[46]J. R. Kimberly and W. R. Nielsen, "Assessing Organizational Change Strategies," *North-Holland/TIMS Studies in the Management Sciences* 5 (1977): 143–155.

generally vague. As a consequence, to borrow a colorful phrase, "dozens of methodological monsters raise their heads when one tries to measure change precisely."[47] While it is true that there are numerous approaches for measuring and monitoring change, complex technical problems (beyond the intended scope of our present discussion) still remain.[48]

A *second* reason for the lack of systematic assessments of change programs is that, even when feasible, efforts at assessment may be opposed because successes and failures are equally likely to be highlighted. *Third,* assessments of change can be expensive and time consuming, especially if viewed from a short- rather than a long-run perspective. *Finally,* a fourth factor is that simply specifying, let alone explaining, whatever results have in fact been produced is not an easy task. It is doubtful whether many organizations possess the professional expertise required to undertake systematic assessments.

On balance, despite the recognized importance of assessing organizational change—or the lack of it—evidence suggests that efforts at evaluation are far from widespread. The development of a more complete understanding and, in turn, a more general acceptance of organizational change is directly dependent upon the ability not only to generate valid and reliable information about the outcomes of change efforts but to establish clear criteria against which the resulting effects can be evaluated. Both needs are among the most pressing in the analysis of organizational change.[49]

Summary

As initially suggested, change is a universal and continual aspect of all organizations. A complex and multidimensional process, it is an integral part of organizational functioning. The purpose of this chapter has been to explore the organizational change process and the problems associated with it. In doing so, we identified two overarching objectives: (1) changes in the way an organization adapts to its external environment, and (2) changes in the behavioral patterns of its employees. With respect to the former, it was pointed out that organizations are continually faced with the necessity of adapting to the changing contingencies and constraints inherent in their surrounding environments. With respect to the latter, it was noted that, regardless of other factors, an organization's ability to cope with its environment will not be im-

---

[47]B. A. Benedict et al., "The Clinical-Experimental Approach to Assessing Change Efforts," *Journal of Applied Behavioral Science* 3 (1967): 347–380.

[48]See, for example, N. Bond, "Auditing Change: The Technology of Measuring Change," in *Work and Nonwork in the Year 2001,* ed. M. D. Dunnette (Monterey, Calif.: Brooks/Cole, 1973), pp. 178–206; C. W. Harris, ed., *Problems in Measuring Change* (Madison: University of Wisconsin Press, 1963).

[49]J. M. Nicholas, "Evaluation Research in Organizational Change Interventions: Considerations and Some Suggestions," *Journal of Applied Behavioral Science* 15 (1979): 23–40; D. Gowler and K. Legge, "The Evaluation of Planned Organizational Change: The Necessary Art of the Possible?" *Journal of Enterprise Management* 1 (1978): 201–212.

proved unless its members behave differently in their relationships to one another and to their jobs.

Following a discussion of the above issues, it was recognized that, despite the universality and inevitability of change, it rarely occurs in a smooth and balanced fashion. To the contrary, resistance to change is a frequent and natural occurrence. In this regard, it described four of the most common causes for resistance to change: (1) parochial self-interest, (2) misunderstandings and lack of trust, (3) different assessments of the costs and benefits resulting from a proposed change, and (4) low tolerance for change on the part of organization members.

Building on the above discussion, a variety of approaches for dealing with resistance to change were introduced. Summarized in table form, along with their advantages and disadvantages, they included (1) education and communication, (2) participation and involvement, (3) facilitation and support, (4) negotiation and agreement, (5) manipulation and cooptation, and (6) explicit and implicit coercion.

Next, two methods for introducing change were presented. These were labeled the *what* and the *how* approaches. The former focused on the content of *what* is being changed (the variables), and the latter focused on the process of *how* change is initiated and implemented. As an example of the *what* approach, Leavitt's view of organizations as complex systems composed of four interacting variables (task, people, technology, and structure) was discussed. As an example of the *how* approach, Greiner's *power distribution continuum* and seven major methods for introducing change were presented.

Attention was then turned to a consideration of a model of the change process. Greiner's six-phase model, which stresses the importance of *shared power* and the *developmental nature of change,* was explained. Following a lengthy discussion of all aspects of this model, it was observed that models are inevitably an oversimplification of reality. Similarly, it was noted that, given the situational nature of change, it is impossible to formulate a standard recipe that will apply in all cases.

Finally, after identifying some additional aspects of change, the importance of properly assessing organizational change was discussed.

Review and Discussion Questions

1. Discuss the two overarching objectives of organizational change.
2. Identify and explain several reasons why people resist change.
3. The text identifies six specific methods for dealing with resistance to change. Comment on these six methods, being sure to specify the situations in which each is commonly used and the respective advantages and disadvantages of each.
4. Comment on Leavitt's analysis of the *what* method for introducing organizational change. Identify and explain the four variables he discusses.
5. Explain the three major positions noted on Greiner's power distribution continuum. Comment on the various approaches to introducing change that Greiner associates with each position.

6. Greiner has presented evidence that suggests the existence of six phases in virtually all successful change efforts. Discuss each of these phases.
7. Comment on the four guiding propositions presented in the text for successfully introducing organizational change.
8. Even though the importance of determining the success of organizational change is widely recognized, there seems to be little actual assessment of the effects of this change. Comment on various reasons for this lack of assessment.

References

Barnes, L. B. "Organizational Change and Field Experiment Methods." In *Methods of Organizational Research,* edited by V. H. Vroom. Pittsburgh: University of Pittsburgh Press, 1967.

Bartlett, A. C., and Kayser, T. A., eds. *Changing Organizational Behavior.* Englewood Cliffs, N.J.: Prentice-Hall, 1973.

Bavelas, A. "Some Problems of Organizational Change." *Journal of Social Issues* 4, no. 3 (1948): 48–52.

Benedict, B. A., Calder, P. H., Callahan, D. M., Hornstein, H. A., and Miles, M. B. "The Clinical-Experimental Approach to Assessing Change Efforts." *Journal of Applied Behavioral Science* 3 (1967): 347–380.

Bond, N. "Auditing Change: The Technology of Measuring Change." In *Work and Nonwork in the Year 2001,* edited by M. D. Dunnette. Monterey, Calif.: Brooks/Cole, 1973.

Brager, G. A. "Institutional Change: Perimeters of the Possible." *Social Work* 12, no. 1 (1967): 59–69.

Brager, G. A., and Holloway, S. *Changing Human Service Organizations: Politics and Practice.* New York: Free Press, 1978.

Brager, G. A., and Specht, H. *Community Organizing.* New York: Columbia University Press, 1973.

Cadwallader, M. L. "The Cybernetic Analysis of Change in Complex Social Systems." *American Journal of Sociology* 65 (1959): 154–157.

Coch, L., and French, J. R. P. "Overcoming Resistance to Change." *Human Relations* 1 (1948): 512–532.

Gowler, D., and Legge, K. "The Evaluation of Planned Organizational Change: The Necessary Art of the Possible?" *Journal of Enterprise Management* 1 (1978): 201–212.

Greiner, L. E. "Patterns of Organization Change." *Harvard Business Review* 45, no. 3 (1967): 119–130.

Greiner, L. E., and Barnes, L. B. "Organization Change and Development." In *Organizational Change and Development,* edited by G. W. Dalton, P. R. Lawrence, and L. E. Greiner. Homewood, Ill: Richard D. Irwin, 1970.

Harris, C. W., ed. *Problems in Measuring Change.* Madison: University of Wisconsin Press, 1963.

Kimberly, J. R., and Nielsen, W. R. "Assessing Organizational Change Strategies." *North-Holland/TIMS Studies in the Management Sciences* 5 (1977): 143–155.

Kotter, J. P., and Schlesinger, L. A. "Choosing Strategies for Change." *Harvard Business Review* 57, no. 2 (1979): 106–114.

Lawrence, P. R. "How to Deal with Resistance to Change." *Harvard Business Review* 47, no. 1 (1969): 4–12, 166–176.

Leavitt, H. J. "Applied Organization Change in Industry: Structural, Technical, and Human Approaches." In *New Perspectives in Organization Research,* edited by W. W. Cooper, H. J. Leavitt, and M. W. Shelly. New York: John Wiley & Sons, 1964.

Leavitt, H. J. "Applied Organizational Change in Industry: Structural, Technological, and Humanistic Approaches." In *Handbook of Organizations,* edited by J. G. March. Chicago: Rand McNally, 1965.

Mann, F. C. "Studying and Creating Change: A Means to Understanding Social Organization." In *Research in Industrial Human Relations,* edited by C. M. Arensberg et al. New York: Harper & Bros., 1957.

March, J. G., and Simon, H. A. *Organizations.* New York: John Wiley & Sons, 1958.

Margulies, N., and Wallace, J. *Organizational Change: Techniques and Applications.* Glenview, Ill.: Scott, Foresman, 1973.

McMurry, R. N. "The Problem of Resistance to Change in Industry." *Journal of Applied Psychology* 31 (1947): 589–593.

Nicholas, J. M. "Evaluation Research in Organizational Change Interventions: Considerations and Some Suggestions." *Journal of Applied Behavioral Science* 15 (1979): 23–40.

Patti, R. J. "Organizational Resistance and Change: The View from Below." *Social Service Review* 48 (1974): 367–383.

Patti, R. J., and Resnick, H. "Changing the Agency from Within." *Social Work* 17, no. 4 (1972): 48–57.

Porter, L. W., Lawler, E. E., and Hackman, J. R. *Behavior in Organizations.* New York: McGraw-Hill, 1975.

Selznick, P. *TVA and the Grass Roots: A Study in the Sociology of Formal Organization.* Berkeley, Calif.: University of California Press, 1949.

Shirley, R. C. "A Model for Analysis of Organizational Change." *MSU Business Topics* 22, no. 3 (1974): 60–68.

Student, K. R. "Managing Change: A Psychologist's Perspective." *Business Horizons* 21, no. 6 (1978): 28–33.

Warren, R. L. "Types of Purposive Social Change at the Community Level." In *Readings in Community Organization Practice,* edited by R. H. Kramer and H. Specht. Englewood Cliffs, N.J.: Prentice-Hall, 1969.

Zander, A. "Resistance to Change—Its Analysis and Prevention." *Advanced Management* 15, no. 1 (1950): 9–11.

Organization Theory
in Perspective

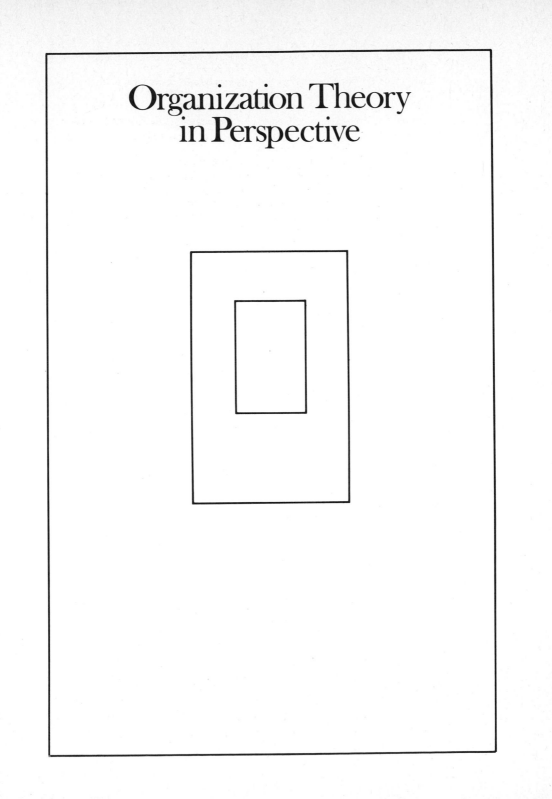

Organization Theory in Perspective

Epilogue

This book has been about organizations. As the dominant institution of our time, they occupy a central position in modern society. Their far-reaching influence is felt in virtually every facet of our daily lives. Indeed, as noted in Chapter 1, their pervasiveness is clearly responsible for several major trends affecting the very structure of our world.

As such, organizations are incredibly complex. They are molded by increasingly fluid and disordered environmental forces that continually threaten their rationally ordered structures and stated goals. How well they adapt to this turbulence will ultimately determine their survival.

It has been the point of view of this book that an appreciation of the basic knowledge upon which our understanding of organization is grounded will greatly assist in developing the perspective necessary for meeting the demands of today's organizational world. While we agree with Lupton that organization theorists "are a long way from the time when they will be able to tell the manager exactly how to match his organization structure to technology, size and competitive position,"[1] we have attempted to explain and integrate the major findings upon which current organization theory and analysis are based, in the belief that this will improve the understanding, prediction, and practice of management.

In hoping for such benefits, we readily acknowledge that the field of organization theory (and indeed the social sciences as a whole) is in a relatively primitive state when compared to the natural sciences. This admission, however, does not negate the fact that over the last two decades numerous solid research findings have been produced. Organization theory has thus steadily moved from the realm of folklore into the world of science.

The Importance of Theory

Although substantial progress has been made in understanding organizations, there remains much room for improvement, particularly with regard to theory.[2] To date, no comprehensive theory of organization structure or design has been developed.

---

[1]T. Lupton, *Management and the Social Sciences,* 2nd ed. (Middlesex, England: Penguin, 1971), p. 126.
[2]W. R. Scott, "Organizational Structure," *Annual Review of Sociology* 1 (1975): 1–20.

The question, of course, is what constitutes sound theory. As indicated in Chapter 2, our ability to differentiate between phenomena of various kinds depends on the adequacy of the theory we employ. While there have been numerous pleas to solidify the underlying foundation upon which organization theory is based, "this is a task," as Stogdill has cautioned, "in which quite moderate aspirations can be easily frustrated."[3] Indeed, as organization theory has evolved, there has been an ever-increasing awareness of the complexity of the phenomena under study. Consequently, it has long been realized that if and when an integrated theory of organization is generated, it assuredly "will not say everything everyone knows [or even wants to know] about every empirical organization."[4]

The Role of Social Values

That organization theory should be free of social values is taken by most organization theorists to be self-evident. Referred to by Albrow as the "original sin of social research," the values of organization scientists have, however, been shown to have a potentially serious (although often unconscious) impact on organization research.[5] All too often a researcher's profession of faith in value freedom and the technical and conceptual sophistication of his or her work have been taken as sufficient safeguards against partiality. Yet published research is by no means value free. For instance, in this book we have for the most part taken what might be termed a "neo-Weberian" or perhaps "institutional" approach to the study of organizations. This perspective has been developed, however, with the almost total exclusion of ethnomethodological, phenomenological, and Marxian views of organization theory. More dialectical in orientation, these approaches seriously question the theoretical and methodological orthodoxies of more positivistic views.[6]

In commenting on this bias, Roberts, Hulin, and Rousseau suggest that most organization scientists pretend that they are apolitical in their research and that values have little influence on what or whom they study. Roberts and her associates, however, contend that the situation is otherwise. They argue that organization researchers (including themselves) "make certain assumptions about the role of organizations in society," generally assuming "that organizations are a legitimate source of influence over our everyday lives." As an example, they note that very little research has

---

[3]R. M. Stogdill, "Dimensions of Organization Theory," in *Approaches to Organizational Design*, ed. J. D. Thompson (Pittsburgh: University of Pittsburgh Press, 1966), p. 50.

[4]W. F. Moore and R. C. Snyder, "The Conference on Theory of Organization," *Social Science Research Council Items* 6, no. 4 (1952): 43.

[5]M. Albrow, "The Study of Organisations—Objectivity or Bias?" in *Penguin Social Sciences Survey 1968*, ed. J. Gould (Middlesex, England: Penguin, 1968), p. 148.

[6]J. K. Benson, "Organizations: A Dialectical View," *Administrative Science Quarterly* 22 (1977): 1–21; J. K. Benson, "Innovation and Crisis in Organizational Analysis," *Sociological Quarterly* 18 (1977): 3–16; G. Burrell and G. Morgan, *Sociological Paradigms and Organisational Analysis* (London: Heineman Educational Books, 1979), pp. 260–278, 365–392.

been done "to support or even address the notion that organizations with assets greater than $1 million ought to be abolished."[7]

In short, it can be concluded only that there are very few safeguards, other than informed awareness, that can guarantee immunity from such bias.

Organizational Domination

It has been repeatedly acknowledged that organizations have become a dominant force in our society. The extent and order of this domination have raised serious questions concerning people's relationships to organizations. It has been argued that modern organizations have taken on a moral force, "shaping and changing American values to suit their entailments."[8] According to Hart and Scott, the cause of this transformation in values is the *organizational imperative*—the emerging belief that *"whatever is good for man can only be achieved through modern organization, therefore, all behavior must enhance the health of such modern organizations."*[9]

Given this imperative, Hart and Scott question the power of contemporary organizations. They contend that "American values have undergone a massive change" as "the needs of organization overwhelm all other considerations, whether those of family, religion, art, science, law, or the individual."[10] In what is perhaps the heart of their argument, they express both ire and dismay over the fact that, although the new values that have been created are suitable for the efficient operation of organizations, they are painfully inadequate for human beings.

As is true in so many other areas of organization theory, one does not have to search far for an alternative, or even an opposite, view. Rosengren, for example, has presented what he has termed the *nutcracker theory of modern organizations.*[11] Rather than organizations imposing values and goals on the general public, Rosengren insists that modern organizations are becoming increasingly subject to the expectations of both their members and the public with which they are interdependent. Factors he sees as contributing to this situation include the increased emphasis on both the rights of citizens and the participatory democracy that have emerged over the last two decades. As a result, it is Rosengren's belief that organizations are becoming increasingly regarded by many elements of society as "general resources

---

[7]H. K. Roberts, C. L. Hulin, and D. M. Rousseau, *Developing an Interdisciplinary Science of Organizations* (San Francisco: Jossey-Bass, 1978), p. 145.

[8]W. G. Scott, "Organicism: The Moral Anesthetic of Management," *Academy of Management Review* 4 (1979): 21.

[9]D. K. Hart and W. G. Scott, "The Organizational Imperative," *Administration & Society* 7 (1975): 261; see also D. K. Hart and W. G. Scott, *Organizational America* (Boston: Houghton Mifflin, 1979), pp. 32–49.

[10]Hart and Scott, "Organizational Imperative," pp. 259–260.

[11]W. R. Rosengren, "A 'Nutcracker' Theory of Modern Organizations: A Conflict View," *Sociological Focus* 8 (1975): 272–282.

which may legitimately be reoriented—by force if necessary—to serve the goals and purposes of multiple external publics."[12]

Taking a middle ground between the positions of Hart and Scott and of Rosengren, Thompson characterized such contentions as "agitated chatter." Denying both that " 'people' are at the mercy of 'organizations' " and that "complex organizations are unwilling to change to meet new conditions and new needs," Thompson asserted that both complaints are "simply wrong." He wrote, "When we get right down to fundamentals, organizations are *not 'them' in distinction to 'us.'* Complex organizations are you and me and the guy down the street. Just as *we* are the family, the community, and the nation, *we* are . . . complex organizations."[13]

Future Trends in Organizational Activities

The preceding discussion leads directly to one final consideration—the direction of future trends in organizational activities. The dynamic nature of our society makes it imperative to pay greater attention to the organizational future. In an early and influential essay, Bennis predicted the future would belong to fluid, organic-adaptive structures and styles.[14] More recent writers, believing that social, economic, and technological changes are likely to accelerate, have argued similarly. Extending their arguments further, however, they contend that organizations should be structured to accommodate rapid change and at the same time to extract benefits from it.[15]

Thus, Wildavsky writes of an ideal *self-evaluating organization* that would "continuously monitor its own activities so as to determine whether it was meeting its goals or even whether these goals should continue to prevail."[16] Similarly, White writes of the *dialectical organization,* "a type of organization which is structured so as to attempt constantly to discover and respond to its own inconsistencies, internal contradictions, and irrationalities."[17] Both ideas are basically identical to the more well-developed concept of *self-designing organizations* introduced by Hedberg, Nystrom, and Starbuck.[18]

Self-designing organizations—"organizations that continually appraise and revise their behaviors and that invent their futures as well as survive them"—are

---

[12]Ibid., p. 277.

[13]J. D. Thompson, "Society's Frontiers for Organizing Activities," *Public Administration Review* 33 (1973): 328.

[14]W. Bennis, "Beyond Bureaucracy," *TRANS-action* 2 (1965): 31–35.

[15]B. L. T. Hedberg, P. C. Nystrom, and W. H. Starbuck, "Designing Organizations to Match Tomorrow," *North-Holland/TIMS Studies in the Management Sciences* 5 (1977): 171–181.

[16]A. Wildavsky, "The Self-evaluating Organization," *Public Administration Review* 32 (1972): 509.

[17]O. White, "Psychic Energy and Organizational Change," *Sage Professional Paper in Administrative and Policy Studies* 1, no. 03–007, 1973, p. 30.

[18]B. L. T. Hedberg, P. C. Nystrom, and W. H. Starbuck, "Camping on Seesaws: Prescriptions for a Self-designing Organization," *Administrative Science Quarterly* 21 (1976): 41–65.

structured to maintain maximum long-term viability.[19] Given that the main requirement for self-design is an unwavering commitment to impermanence, organizations that are incapable of self-design and therefore vulnerable to the pressures of social, economic, and technological changes are easily identifiable. As described by Weick:

They value forecasts more than improvisation, they dwell on constraints rather than opportunities, they borrow solutions rather than invent them, they defend past actions rather than devise new ones, they cultivate permanence rather than impermanence, they value serenity more highly than argument, they rely on accounting systems as their sole means to assess performance rather than use more diverse measures, they remove doubt rather than encourage it, they search for final solutions rather than continuously experimenting, and they discourage contradictions rather than seek them.[20]

As should be clear, self-designing organizations are purposefully dynamic, incorporating a certain amount of inconsistency and much heterogeneity. Although they are intended to evaluate and correct their own defects, it has been suggested that self-designing organizations nevertheless encounter at least three types of problems.[21] *First,* they require efficient information systems that transmit timely information about important problems, so that they will have enough time to explore future options and to invent solutions as they develop. *Second,* they need the means with which to resist inertia and to explore alternative futures. Rapid change necessitates an increase in both risk-taking activities and experimentation by organizations that seek to endure. Such behavior doubtlessly increases organizational death rates but also enhances the viability of surviving organizations. *Third,* they require an exceptional degree of flexibility on the part of individual members. New attitudes toward work and new job systems are needed, and most interpersonal relationships are temporary. Furthermore, given the fluxional nature of self-design programs, both job assignments and hierarchical statuses and prerogatives change frequently. While little is yet known about existing in self-designing organizations, as one would suspect, "there are real reasons for wondering how satisfying such jobs can be."[22]

In evaluating the concept of self-designing organizations, it should be realized that no one can say for certain what the future will bring, let alone design organizations that, as Hedberg, Nystrom, and Starbuck hope, will "match the challenges of tomorrow."[23] Nevertheless, organizations that are capable of redesigning themselves to invent new solutions as they develop certainly seem to hold unlimited promise for the unknown future.

---

[19]Hedberg, Nystrom, and Starbuck, "Designing Organizations," p. 171.
[20]K. E. Weick, "Organization Design: Organizations as Self-designing Systems," *Organizational Dynamics* 2, no. 6 (1977): 37.
[21]Hedberg, Nystrom, and Starbuck, "Designing Organizations," pp. 175–179.
[22]Ibid., p. 178.
[23]Ibid., p. 179.

A Final Remark

As should be clear from each of the foregoing chapters, and especially as stressed in our first chapter and in this, our last, organization theory is an emerging discipline. No optimum, perfect, universal, or ultimate solutions have been offered. Instead, we have seen that organizations are not fixed and determinate entities but dynamic systems continually interacting with the larger world of which they are a part. Much has been learned; much more remains to be learned. Herein lies the challenge of the coming years.

Review and Discussion Questions

1. Comment on the role of social values in the field of organization theory.
2. Hart and Scott, Rosengren, and Thompson present differing opinions concerning the issue of organizational domination. Discuss their differing views.
3. Comment on the direction of future trends in organizational activities. Be sure to include in your comments a discussion of "self-designing" organizations and the problems that it is predicted will be associated with such systems.

References

Albrow, M. "The Study of Organisations—Objectivity or Bias?" In *Penguin Social Sciences Survey 1968,* edited by J. Gould. Middlesex, England: Penguin, 1968.

Bennis, W. "Beyond Bureaucracy." *TRANS-action* 2 (1965): 31–35.

Benson, J. K. (a) "Organizations: A Dialectical View." *Administrative Science Quarterly* 22 (1977): 1–21.

Benson, J. K. (b) "Innovation and Crisis in Organizational Analysis." *Sociological Quarterly* 18 (1977): 3–16.

Burrell, G., and Morgan, G. *Sociological Paradigms and Organisational Analysis.* London: Heineman Educational Books, 1979.

Hart, D. K., and Scott, W. G. "The Organizational Imperative." *Administration & Society* 7 (1975): 259–285.

Hedberg, B. L. T., Nystrom, P. C., and Starbuck, W. H. "Camping on Seesaws: Prescriptions for a Self-designing Organization." *Administrative Science Quarterly* 21 (1976): 41–65.

Hedberg, B. L. T., Nystrom, P. C., and Starbuck, W. H. "Designing Organizations to Match Tomorrow." *North-Holland/TIMS Studies in the Management Sciences* 5 (1977): 171–181.

Lupton, T. *Management and the Social Sciences.* 2nd ed. Middlesex, England: Penguin, 1971.

Moore, W. E., and Snyder, R. C. "The Conference on Theory of Organization." *Social Science Research Council Items* 6, no. 4 (1952): 41–45.

Roberts, H. K., Hulin, C. L., and Rousseau, D. M. *Developing an Interdisciplinary Science of Organizations.* San Francisco: Jossey-Bass, 1978.

Rosengren, W. R. "A 'Nutcracker' Theory of Modern Organizations: A Conflict View." *Sociological Focus* 8 (1975): 272–282.

Scott, W. G. "Organicism: The Moral Anesthetic of Management." *Academy of Management Review* 4 (1979): 21–28.

Scott, W. G., and Hart, D. K. *Organizational America.* Boston: Houghton Mifflin, 1979.

Scott, W. R. "Organizational Structure." *Annual Review of Sociology* 1 (1975): 1–20.

Stogdill, R. M. "Dimensions of Organization Theory." In *Approaches to Organizational Design,* edited by J. D. Thompson. Pittsburgh: University of Pittsburgh Press, 1966.

Thompson, J. D. "Society's Frontiers for Organizing Activities." *Public Administration Review* 33 (1973): 327–335.

Weick, K. E. "Organization Design: Organizations as Self-designing Systems." *Organizational Dynamics* 2, no. 6 (1977): 31–46.

White, O. "Psychic Energy and Organizational Change." *Sage Professional Paper in Administrative and Policy Studies* 1, no. 03–007 (1973).

Wildavsky, A. "The Self-evaluating Organization." *Public Administration Review* 32 (1972): 509–520.

Name Index

Adams, J. S., 148n
Aiken, M., 241, 262n
Akers, R., 35, 194–195, 202
Albanese, R., 214n
Albrow, M., 316
Aldag, R. J., 142
Aldrich, H. E., 131–132, 145, 148n, 188,
  232, 233n, 244
Allen, F. R., 9n
Anderson, C. R., 144
Anderson, T. R., 190–193, 197, 202
Ansoff, H. I., 54n, 55n, 67n
Apilado, V. P., 181n
Arensberg, C. M., 293n
Argyris, C., 197n, 265n
Aronson, E., 97n
Arps, G. F., 281n
Atherton, R. M., 117n
Atkin, R., 120n
Azumi, K., 230n

Backer, T. E., 27n
Backoff, R. W., 197n
Barnard, C. I., 82–83, 105
Barnes, L. B., 33, 294–295, 302n, 303n,
  304n, 305n
Bartlett, A. C., 296n
Bass, B. M., 268n
Bauer, R. A., 157n
Bavelas, A., 293n
Bedeian, A. G., 24n, 43n, 64n, 66n, 142n
Belilove, J. R., 282n
Bell, G. D., 240
Beller, R., 274
Bendix, R., 190, 202
Benedict, B. A., 309n
Bennis, W., 318
Benson, J. K., 316n

Berg, S. V, 154n
Berrien, F. K., 4n, 110n
Betterton, H., 192, 197, 202
Beyer, J. M., 188
Billings, R. S., 234, 250
Bittel, L. R., 43n
Bjorkman, M., 281n
Blau, P. M., 49, 78, 94, 99, 147, 156n,
  167, 186, 187, 188, 190, 192, 197, 202,
  211n, 243, 249, 277
Blowers, T. A., 195, 197, 205
Bobbitt, H. R., 145n
Bohlen, J. M., 203
Boland, M., 197, 204
Boland, W., 197, 204
Bond, N., 309n
Bouchard, T. J., 28n, 32n
Bowers, R., 152n
Brager, G. A., 297n, 299n, 300, 301, 308
Brandenburg, R. G., 54n, 55n, 67n
Breaugh, J. A., 234
Bright, J. R., 275n
Brodie, M. B., 48n
Brooks, K., 279n
Broom, L., 82n
Bryman, A., 189, 197n, 204
Burns, T., 135–137, 141
Burrell, G., 316n
Butler, A. G., 69n

Cadwallader, M. L., 293
Calder, B. J., 43n
Callicoat, J., 279n
Cameron, K., 112, 118n, 120n
Cammann, C., 118n
Campbell, D. T., 25n, 268n
Campbell, F. L., 35, 194–195, 202
Campbell, J. P., 107n, 111, 112, 115n

Caplow, T. E., 3, 8, 53n, 106n, 158
Carter, E. E., 83n
Carzo, R. C., 64n, 65n, 87
Cesta, J. R., 181n
Champion, D., 192, 197, 202
Chandler, A. D., 167, 169, 174
Chandler, M. K., 69n
Charns, M. P., 226n
Child, J., 44, 144–145, 186, 189, 192, 196–197, 203, 244, 245
Cicero, J. P., 67n
Clark, J. P., 118–119, 284n
Clement, D. A., 281n
Coch, L., 293n
Cochran, T. C., 44n
Comstock, D. E., 215n, 250
Cooper, C. L., 13n, 15n
Cooper, W. W., 23n, 302n
Corwin, R. G., 16
Cottrell, L. S., 82n
Cressy, D., 78
Crombie, A. D., 52n, 127, 221
Cummings, L. L., 34, 143, 148n
Cyert, R. M., 83–86, 97, 144, 269n
Czepiel, J. A., 283

Daft, R. L., 189n
Dahle, T. L., 274n
Dale, E., 182n
Dalton, G. W., 219n, 294n
Dalton, M., 26–27, 263
Dance, F. E. X., 264n
Darran, D. C., 142
Darrow, J. W., 282n
Davis, K., 263, 265n
Davis, L. F., 214n, 229n
Davis, S. M., 54n, 69
Dearborn, D. C., 264n
Delbecq, A. L., 215, 234, 248
Denton, P., 95–96
De Pool, S. I., 157n
Dewar, R., 188
Dexter, L. A., 157n
Dill, W. R., 128
Donaldson, L., 229n
Donnelly, J. H., 139
Dornbusch, S. M., 79n
Dowling, W. F., 178n
Downey, H. K., 142n
Drucker, P. F., 16, 81n
Dubin, R., 214n
Duncan, R. B., 132–133, 134n, 144
Dunne, E. J., 69n
Dunnette, M. D., 28n, 110n, 128n, 309n
Dutton, J. M., 157, 158n

Easton, A., 66n
Edelfelt, R. A., 16
Edwards, J. A., 268n

Eilon, S., 229n
Eldridge, J. E. T., 52n, 127, 221
Emery, F. E., 147n
Erikson, K. T., 28n
Etzioni, A., 32n, 78, 97n, 98, 108
Evan, W. M., 147
Evers, F. T., 203

Falcione, R. L., 266n
Farace, R. V., 278n
Fayol, H., 47–48, 67
Fenn, D. H., 279n
Fennema, M., 155n
Festinger, L., 33n
Filley, A. C., 66n, 67n, 141n
Finch, H. H., 49n
Fisher, C. D., 281n
Ford, J. D., 145n, 196n, 214n
Frandsen, K. S., 281n
Freeman, J. H., 94, 179, 189n, 193, 195–196, 203, 245
French, J. R. P., 293n
Friedlander, F., 119n
Friedman, P., 154n
Fries, C. C., 272n
Fromkin, H. L., 261n
Frost, P. J., 248
Fry, L. W., 252n
Fullan, M., 242

Galbraith, J. R., 154, 155n
Gannon, J., 48n
Gemmill, G. R., 69n
Georgopoulos, B. S., 110, 111, 278
Gerth, H. H., 49n
Ghorpade, J., 109n
Gibson, J. L., 139n
Gilchrist, T. C., 275
Gillespie, D. F., 186, 211n
Gilmour, P., 6n
Glaser, F. M., 27n
Glassman, R. B., 99n
Glen, F., 53n
Glisson, C. A., 235n
Goldhaber, G. M., 279n
Goldman, P., 204
Goodman, P. S., 83n, 109n, 112n, 115, 118n, 120
Gould, J., 316n
Gouldner, A. W., 28, 51, 82n
Gowler, D., 309n
Green, T. B., 117n
Greiner, L. E., 174–178, 294–295, 303–307
Greller, M. M., 281n
Grimes, A. J., 215, 245
Gross, B. M., 81n, 98, 179
Gross, E., 77
Grunig, J. E., 282n, 284–285

Guetzkow, H., 152n, 268n
Gulick, L. H., 46
Gullahorn, J. T., 271n
Gullett, C. R., 53n, 167n
Gusfield, J. S., 95

Haas, J. E., 186, 187, 196, 204
Habbe, S., 278n
Haberstroh, C. J., 29, 31–32
Hackman, J. R., 5, 79n, 211–212, 235, 293
Haire, M., 194
Hage, J., 188, 230n, 241, 262n
Hall, F. S., 82n
Hall, R. H., 118–119, 141, 149n, 187, 196, 204, 284n
Hamner, W. C., 23, 34n
Haney, W. V., 281n
Hannan, M. T., 94, 179, 195, 203
Hare, A. P., 261–262, 270n
Harper, R. G., 273n
Harris, C. W., 309n
Hart, D. K., 317
Harvey, E., 220, 221, 240
Havens, A. E., 97n
Hawley, A. H., 197, 204
Haworth, L., 82n
Hay, G. A., 154n
Hays, S., 13
Hazlett, C. B., 234
Hedberg, B. L. T., 318–319
Hellriegel, D., 142n
Hendershot, G. E., 195, 204
Henderson, A. M., 48n
Herbst, P. G., 183, 184n, 185n, 191
Herden, R. P., 110n
Herker, D., 148n
Herold, D. M., 281n
Heydebrand, W. V., 192n
Hicks, H. G., 53n, 167n
Hickson, D. J., 66n, 186, 214n, 215, 221, 230–233, 241, 246
Hills, F. S., 83n
Hinings, C. R., 186, 189, 197n, 204
Hirsch, P. M., 128n, 154n, 157n
Hitt, M. A., 116n
Hofer, C. W., 98n
Holdaway, E., 195, 197, 205, 233n
Holloway, S., 299n, 300n, 301, 308
Hopfe, M. W., 142n
Hopkins, T. K., 32n, 33n
House, R. J., 33n, 66n, 67n, 141n
Hrebiniak, L. G., 215n, 246
Hsia, H. J., 274n
Huber, G. P., 34, 143, 148n
Hulin, C. L., 17n, 316–317
Hunt, J. W., 112n
Hunt, R., 221n

Ilgen, D. R., 281n
Indik, B. P., 4n, 190, 197, 205, 270n, 278
Inkson, J. H. K., 242
Inzerilli, G., 233n, 234–235
Ivancevich, J. M., 139n, 150n, 156n

Jablin, F. M., 265n
Jackson, J. H., 90n
Jacobs, D., 151n
James, T. F., 187, 195, 204, 205
Janger, A. R., 69n
Jelinek, M., 218
Jenkins, J. C., 96
Johnson, N. J., 187, 196, 204
Jones, R. E., 196, 205

Kahn, R. L., 48n, 62, 113, 118, 157n, 256, 260
Kanungo, R. N., 52n
Kasarda, J. D., 189n, 192, 197, 206
Kast, F. E., 10n, 130, 131n, 222n
Katz, D., 33n, 48n, 62, 113, 118, 157n, 256, 260
Kaufman, F., 282n
Kayser, T. A., 296n
Kefalas, A., 143–144
Keller, R. T., 247
Kelley, D., 154n
Kerr, S., 66n, 67n, 141n
Khandwalla, P. N., 247
Kilmann, R. H., 43n, 66n, 110n
Kimberly, J. R., 194n, 197, 308
Kipnis, O., 152, 153n
Kirste, K. K., 268n
Klatzky, S. R., 192, 197, 202
Klaw, S., 46n
Klein, S. M., 215, 245
Klimoski, R. S., 234
Kmetz, J. L., 233n
Knight, K., 69n
Kochan, T. A., 284–285
Koenig, R., 234
Kolodny, H. F., 69n
Korman, A. K., 264n, 272n
Kotter, J. P., 295n, 297, 298n, 308
Kover, A. J., 55
Kramer, R. M., 299n
Kranzberg, M., 13n, 15n, 16n
Kronenfeld, J. E., 189n

Landsberger, H., 262
Lansbury, R. D., 6n
Lanzetta, J. T., 275n
Latsis, S. J., 86n
Lawler, E. E., 5, 79n, 118n, 211–212, 235, 262, 293
Lawrence, P. R., 29, 30–31, 69, 137–142, 158, 219n, 226n, 294n, 295n

Porter, L. W., 5, 79n, 211–212, 234, 261, 262, 263, 285n, 293
Porter, M. E., 151, 153n
Prais, S. J., 6n
Pred, A. R., 45n
Price, J. L., 54, 111
Pugh, D. S., 66n, 186, 187, 188, 197, 214n, 215, 221, 230–233, 242
Pursell, C. W., 13n, 16n

Queen, A. S., 28n

Rae, J. B., 13n
Rainey, H. G., 197n
Raphael, E., 189, 206
Ray, D. F., 117n
Raymond, R. C., 275n
Read, W. H., 261n
Reddin, W. J., 107
Reed, H., 267n
Reiley, Alan C., 46
Reimann, B. C., 66n, 108, 192, 206, 215n, 233n, 234–235, 246, 252
Reitz, H. J., 271
Resnick, H., 299n
Riggs, F. W., 148n
Roberts, K. H., 17n, 256n, 257n, 285n, 316–317
Robinson, R., 97–98
Roby, T. B., 275n
Rogers, D. L., 119n
Rosengren, W. R., 317–318
Rosenzweig, J. E., 10n, 130, 131n, 222n
Rothstein, D. A., 276n
Rousseau, D. M., 17n, 215n, 218, 252, 316–317
Rowland, K. M., 43n
Roy, R. H., 8–9, 212, 213n
Ruben, B. D., 265n, 278n
Rubenstein, A. H., 29, 31–32
Rudman, R., 16n, 212n
Rushing, W. A., 120, 191, 193n, 196, 197, 207, 241
Ryterband, E. C., 268n

Salancik, G. R., 83n, 143n, 145n
Sathe, V., 214n
Schendel, D. E., 98n
Schijf, H., 155n
Schlesinger, L. A., 295n, 297, 298n, 308
Schmidt, S. M., 284–285
Schmidt, W. H., 169, 170n, 171n
Schneck, R., 234
Schneider, H. C., 142n
Schoderbeck, P. P., 143–144
Schoenherr, R., 197, 202, 243
Schoorman, D., 120n
Scott, B. R., 167, 169, 172–174

Scott, J. F., 24n
Scott, W. G., 25n, 276n, 317
Scott, W. R., 28n, 49, 79n, 83n, 112n, 118, 119, 147, 156n, 167, 215n, 250, 277, 283, 315
Seashore, S. E., 109n, 278
Selznick, P., 5–6, 35, 51, 54, 70, 152, 301
Sethi, N. S., 130
Sexton, W. P., 52
Shaw, M. E., 270n
Shelly, M. W., 275, 302n
Shepard, H. A., 271n
Shepard, J. M., 214n
Sherwood, J. J., 261n
Shils, E. A., 49n
Shirley, R. C., 307
Siegerdt, G., 279n
Sills, D. L., 85n, 94
Silverman, D., 129–130
Simon, H. A., 17n, 82n, 84n, 85, 86–88, 93n, 98n, 264n, 268, 296
Slevin, D. P., 43n, 66n
Slocum, J. W., 142n
Smith, M. R., 190n
Snow, C. C., 142, 143, 144, 159
Snyder, R. C., 316n
Sosbauer, J. C., 282n
Specht, H., 297n, 299n
Speckman, R. E., 282n
Stagner, R., 83
Stahl, M. J., 69n
Stalker, G. M., 135–137, 141
Stanfield, G. G., 233–234
Starbuck, W. H., 128, 129n, 143, 157, 158n, 168, 220, 269n, 318–319
Starr, C., 16n, 212n
Staw, B. M., 143n, 148n
Steers, R. M., 79n, 106, 112, 113, 116n, 118, 119–120, 131n, 136n, 275
Stewart, J. P., 278n
Stinchcombe, A. L., 129–130, 179
Stogdill, R. M., 316
Storey, R. G., 142
Strauss, G. A., 262
Student, K. R., 297
Stymne, B., 262n
Sullivan, M. A., 28n
Sussman, L., 266n
Szilagyi, A. D., Jr., 150n, 156n

Tannenbaum, A. S., 110, 111
Tausky, R., 8n
Taylor, F. W., 45–46
Taylor, J. A., 278n
Taylor, J. C., 214n, 229n
Taylor, M. S., 281n
Terkel, S., 97–98
Terreberry, S., 147n

Terrien, F. W., 189, 207
Thain, D. H., 171–172, 173n
Thamhain, H. J., 69n
Thayer, L., 264n
Thompson, J. D., 24n, 84n, 86, 129n,
    145n, 147n, 148, 151n, 155, 156n,
    216–219, 220, 316n, 318
Thompson, V. A., 50, 53
Thorndike, R. L., 112
Tosi, H. L., 142n, 197, 207
Towne, H. R., 45
Triandis, H. C., 267
Trice, H. M., 188
Trist, E. L., 147
Tsouderos, J. E., 194, 207
Turner, C., 186

Urwick, L. F., 45, 46

Van de Ven, A. A., 66n, 215, 234, 248,
    249
Van Fleet, D. D., 64n, 66n
Van Lohuizen, J. R., 157n
Van Ness, E. H., 128n
Vardaman, G. T., 273n
Vardaman, P. B., 273n
Vroom, V. H., 33n, 302n

Wallace, J., 308
Wallace, M. J., Jr., 150n, 156n
Wallroth, C., 89–94
Warkov, S., 190–193, 197, 202
Warner, W. K., 78, 97n, 109n, 118n
Warren, R. D., 203
Warren, R. L., 299n, 301n

Warriner, C. K., 79
Weaver, C. H., 272n
Webb, R. J., 107n, 120
Webber, R. A., 264n
Weber, M., 48–52
Weick, K. E., 34, 143, 319
Weitzel, W., 107, 108n
Wexley, K. M., 281n
White, O., 318
White, P. E., 128n
Whitehead, J. L., 266n
Whittington, G., 179n
Whyte, W. F., 26n, 230
Wiens, A. N., 273
Wigand, R., 283n
Wildavsky, A., 318
Wilemon, D. C., 67n
Wilkinson, I., 152, 153n
Winer, M., 273n
Woodward, J., 66n, 215, 219–220, 221,
    222–230, 231, 240
Wren, D. A., 46n, 49
Wright, M., 272n

Yankelovich, D., 279n
Yanouzas, J. N., 64n, 65n, 87
Yuchtman, E., 109n
Yukl, G. A., 281n

Zald, M. N., 78, 95–96
Zander, A., 300
Zelditch, M., 32n, 33n
Zelikoff, S. B., 15n
Zwerman, W., 242

Subject Index

Absenteeism,
  and information overload, 276
  and measurement of organizational
    effectiveness, 114
Accidents, and measurement of
  organizational effectiveness, 114
Achievement, and measurement of
  organizational effectiveness, 115
Adaptability. *See* Flexibility
Administrative intensity, 189–198,
  202–207, 223, 226
Administrative personnel. *See also*
    Design, organizational
  and communication with subordinates.
    See Vertical communication
  minority group members as, 82
  subgroups of, 191–193, 196–197
Administrative theory, of Fayol, 47–48. *See
    also* Organization theory
Administrator, in Weber's theory, 49–50.
    See also Managerial effectiveness;
    Managerial skills
Age of organization, and managerial
    effectiveness, 174–175
Area departmentalization, 55, 62, 63. *See
    also* Spatial dispersion
Assembly line, 216. *See also* Mass
    production
Aston studies, 230–233
Authority,
  concentration of, 232
  delegation of,
    and internal conflict, 51, 54
    and organizational change, 303–305,
      306
    and organizational development, 177,
      178
    and system of production, 226

hierarchy of, in organization charts, 53.
    See also Hierarchical structure;
    Scalar chain of authority
  legal, as basis of organization, 49,
    129–130
Automobile industry, and technological
    advance, 13, 15
Autonomy,
  crisis of, 175, 177, 178
  in decision making, and strategies of
    organizational interdependence,
    156

Bargaining,
  as cooperative strategy, 151–152, 156,
    159
  as process of organizational goal
    formation, 83–85
Benefits of organizational operation. *See*
    Output
Bias,
  in organizational communication,
    264–281
  of researchers, 316–317
  of subjects in survey research, 29,
    31–32, 118–119, 214
Bifurcation of interests, 51, 54, 98
Boundaries, organizational, 4
Boundary spanners, and
    interorganizational relations, 148,
    150, 282
Bounded rationality, 87–88
Buffering, and environmental uncertainty,
    146, 159
Bureaucracy,
  characteristics of, 49–50
  criticisms of, 50–52
  definition of, 48–49

Costs of organizational operation. *See* Input

Credibility, and organizational communication, 266–267. *See also* Trust

Crises, in development of organization, 169–171, 174–178

Criteria for measuring organizational effectiveness, 105–120

Culture,
change in, and technological advance, 15
as element of organizational environment, 131

Decentralization. *See also* Design, organizational
and communication, 276–277
and goal displacement, 98–99
and organizational development, 172, 178

Decision making. *See also* Managerial effectiveness
and decentralization, 276–277
and organizational change, 301, 306
and organizational growth, 192. *See also* Design, organizational
and perceived uncertainty, 133–135, 144–145, 156, 158. *See also* Uncertainty, environmental

Decline, organizational, 179–182

Delegation of authority. *See* Authority, delegation of

Demographic factors, as element of organizational environment, 131–132

Departmentalization. *See also* Differentiation, structural; Specialization
definition of, 53
as means of relating organization to environment, 138, 140, 144
patterns of, 54–62
and size of organization, 231

Dependence, 147–157, 232

Derived goals, 81, 82

Design, organizational, 4, 43–70
and communication, 256, 258–263, 268, 272, 276–277
and environmental differences, 136–145, 158
goals as rationale for, 80
and organizational change, 302–308
and organizational size, 181–198
and stage of organizational development, 171–174, 178
and technology, 211–236, 240–252

Development,
organizational, 232. *See also* Growth, organizational; Life cycle of organizations
of products and services,
and measurement of organizational effectiveness, 115, 116
and system of production, 227–228

Diagonal communication, 259, 263–264

Dialectical organization, 318

Differentiation, structural, 186–188, 190. *See also* Departmentalization; Division of labor; Specialization
and communication, 277
and environment, 138–139
of separate integrating unit, 183

Directorships, interlocking, 154–155

Distance, physical, and communication, 270–271. *See also* Spatial dispersion

Diversification,
and horizontal communication, 262
and organizational development, 171, 172, 178

Division of labor. *See also* Specialization
in administration, 191–193
general theory of, 52–53
as indication of organizational complexity, 187
as principle developed by Fayol, 47
staff personnel as example of, 67

Domain, organizational, 128–129, 132

Downward flow of communication, 256, 258–261

Du Pont, and product departmentalization, 55

Dynamic dimension of environment, technology, etc. *See* Stability-instability

Economic factors, as element of organizational environment, 131

Economic shifts,
and higher education, 13
and technological advance, 15

Economic theory, classical, and organizational decision making, 86–88

Economies of scale, 145, 168. *See also* Size, organizational
in administration, 190

Education,
as element of organizational environment, 131
higher, 10, 13, 14
and organizational change, 298, 299

Geographical diversification. *See* Area
    departmentalization; Spatial
    dispersion
Goal consensus, and measurement of
    organizational effectiveness,
    115
Goal displacement, 97–99
Goal diversion, 95–96
Goal model of organizational
    effectiveness, 105–109, 111, 112,
    116
Goals,
    organizational, 3, 4, 49, 77–100
        and organizational growth, 168
        internalization of, and measurement of
            organizational effectiveness, 115
        and task environment, 128
        personal, and organizational change,
            295–296
Goal setting,
    and measurement of organizational
        effectiveness, 115
    and task environment, 128
Goal succession, 94–95, 99
Goal transformation, 95–99
Government regulation, 9, 154, 157
Group. *See also* Work Group
    decision making and problem solving by,
        303, 304
    structure of, and environment, 34–35
Growth, organizational. *See also* Size,
    organizational
    and administrative intensity, 198
    and measurement of organizational
        effectiveness, 114, 116
    models of, 169–178
    motives for, 168
    rate of, and managerial effectiveness,
        174–175

Hierarchical structure. *See also* Design,
    organizational; Scalar chain of
    authority
    and flow of communication, 256,
        258–263, 268, 272
    growth of (vertical differentiation), 186
    as indication of organizational
        complexity, 187
    in mechanistic organizational systems,
        136–137
    and organizational change, 303–307
    as shown in organization charts, 53
Homogeneity-heterogeneity, as dimension
    of organizational environment, 131
Horizontal communication, 259, 261–262,
    280, 284
Horizontal differentiation, 186

Human resources, value of, and
    measurement of organizational
    effectiveness, 115

Identity, organizational, 6
Income, median family, 13
Inducements, in coalition bargaining over
    organizational goals, 84–85
Industrialization, and growth of
    organizations, 13, 15, 44–45
Inexperience, managerial, as cause of
    business failure, 179, 181, 182
Influence,
    interorganizational, tactics of, 152, 153
    shared, and measurement of
        organizational effectiveness, 115
Information,
    flow of. *See* Communication
    lack of, and uncertainty in decision
        making, 29–31, 34, 35, 133–135,
        138. *See also* Uncertainty,
        environmental
Information management, as measure of
    organizational effectiveness, 115
Information overload, 275–277
Initiative, as factor in organizational
    effectiveness, 107, 108
Input, 4–5. *See also* Effectiveness,
    organizational
    and complexity of systems, 183, 184
    and environmental uncertainty, 145–147
    and technology, 211–212, 218
Input-output ratio, 109
Instability (of environment). *See*
    Stability-instability
Integrating unit, separate, and increase in
    organizational size, 183
Integration, organizational. *See also*
    Coordination
    and flow of communication, 260
    as means of relating organization to
        environment, 138–141
    and measurement of organizational
        effectiveness, 116
    vertical, 218
    of work flow, 230–233
Intensive technology, 217, 218–219. *See
    also* Technology
Interdependence,
    of organizations, 147–157, 232
    technological, 216–219
Interest groups. *See* Coalitions
Interlocking directorships, 154–155
Internal validity, of research results, 25, 27
Interorganizational relations, 147–157
    and communication, 281–285
Interpersonal communication. *See*
    Communication

Interpersonal skills, managerial, and measurement of organizational effectiveness, 115
Interviews,
    as general research strategy, 28–32
    in research on technology and structure, 214
    strengths and weaknesses of, 28–31, 37
Inventories, and buffering strategy, 146

"Job counts," 231
Job-order production, 219–220, 223–229, 231
Job satisfaction, and measurement of organizational effectiveness, 114
Job structure. See also Design, organizational
    effect of technology on, 212
    and size of organization (horizontal differentiation), 186

Labor,
    and bargaining with management, 151–152
    division of. See Division of labor
    interests of, in scientific management theory, 46
Laboratory experiments, in organization research, 32–35, 37
Labor force,
    education of, 10, 13, 14
    trends in, 6–8
    women in, 10, 12
Labor unions, as large organizations, 9
Language, meaning of, and organizational communication, 271–272
Large batch production. See Mass production
Large-scale organizations, 6–9, 145, 197. See also Size, organizational
Lateral communication, 259, 261–262, 280, 284
Law, as element of organizational environment, 131
Leadership, crisis of, 175, 177. See also Managerial effectiveness
Legal authority, as basis of organization, 49
Life cycle of organizations, 118, 169–181
Limited rationality, 87–88
Line personnel, 66, 178, 226, 232
    and diagonal communication, 263–264
Longitudinal measurement,
    of administrative intensity, 194–196
    of organizational effectiveness, 117–118
Long-linked technology, 216, 217, 218, 219

Loose coupling of organization, and goal displacement, 98–99

"Macro" study of organizations, 17–18
Management,
    and labor,
        bargaining process between, 151–152
        communication between, 272
    levels of, and technological complexity, 223, 224, 226. See also Hierarchical structure
    principles of (Fayol), 47–48. See also Organization theory
    scientific, theory of, 45–46
    systems of,
        and environmental differences, 135–137
        and system of production, 226
    theory of. See Organization theory
    women in, 10
Manager. See also Administrative intensity; Administrative personnel; Design, organizational; Effectiveness, organizational
    owner as, 169, 171, 172
    and perceived environmental uncertainty. See Uncertainty, environmental
    professional, and stage of organizational development, 171, 175
    project, in matrix organization, 69
Managerial effectiveness, 107. See also Effectiveness, organizational
    lack of, and business failure, 179, 181, 182
    and stages of organizational development, 169–171, 174–178
Managerial skills,
    and measurement of organizational effectiveness, 115
    required in different systems of production, 226–227
Manipulation, and organizational change, 298, 300–301
Manufacturing cycle, task functions of, 227–228
Manufacturing firms, as distinguished from service organizations, 234–235
Manufacturing, growth of, 13, 15, 44–45
March of Dimes Campaign, 94
Marketing, and system of production, 227–228
Markets, and organizational domain, 128, 129
Mass production,
    development of, 44
    of Ford cars, 13

Perception. *See also* Bias
  environmental. *See* Uncertainty,
    environmental
  selective, 264
Perceptual approach, in studying
    technology and structure, 214, 234
Perceptual slant, as limitation of survey
    research, 29, 31, 118–119, 214
Performance of organization, goals as
    standards of, 80, 108
Permanence, relative, as characteristic of
    organizations, 4
Personnel. *See also* Employees
  administrative. *See* Administrative
    personnel
  line and staff, 66–67, 178, 196
Perspectives, varying, and measurement
    of organizational effectiveness,
    118–119. *See also* Bias
Planning,
  as factor of organizational effectiveness,
    107, 108
  and measurement of organizational
    effectiveness, 115
Politics,
  as element of organizational
    environment, 131
  and technological advance, 15
Population,
  and organizational environment,
    131–132
  samples of, in survey research, 32
  trends in, 9–10
Power,
  distribution of, and organizational
    change, 303–305. *See also*
    Hierarchical structure
  as motive for organizational growth, 168
Price and wage policies, determined by
    large organizations, 9
Prices, lower, as result of technological
    advance, 15
Private organizations, 188, 197
Process production, 219–220, 223–229,
    231
Product departmentalization, 54, 55, 60–61
Product diversification, 171, 172
Product goals of organizations, 81
Production continuity, 230–233
Production, types of, 219–220, 223–231.
    See also Output
Productivity,
  as factor in organizational effectiveness,
    107, 108
  and measurement of organizational
    effectiveness, 110, 112, 114, 116
  as result of technological advance, 15,
    212

Products, and organizational domain, 128,
    129
Professionals,
  as administrative subgroup, 191–193,
    223
  and technological advance, 15–16
Profits,
  in classical economic theory, 86–88
  and competition, 151
  and measurement of organizational
    effectiveness, 112, 114, 116
  as motive for organizational growth, 168
Program management, 67–69
Project manager, in matrix organization, 69
Psychological change, and technological
    advance, 15
Public organizations, 188, 197

Quality, and measurement of
    organizational effectiveness, 114
Quantification,
  in case studies, 27
  in survey research, 28
Questionnaires,
  as general research strategy, 28–32
  in research on technology and structure,
    214

Rationality, and organizational decision
    making, 86–88
Rationing, and environmental uncertainty,
    147, 159
Raw materials. *See* Input
Readiness, and measurement of
    organizational effectiveness, 115
Red tape, crisis of, 177, 178
Regulation, government, 9, 154, 157
Reliability of data,
  as issue in survey research, 29, 31–32,
    118–119, 214
  managerial, as factor in organizational
    effectiveness, 107, 108
Research and development. *See*
    Development
Research, organization,
  and life cycle of organizations, 118
  methods of, 23–37
Resource acquisition, as measure of
    organizational effectiveness, 116
Resource allocation, and environmental
    uncertainty, 147. *See also*
    Effectiveness, organizational
Resources,
  human, and measurement of
    organizational effectiveness, 115
  and nature of environment, 129, 131,
    132

336   Subject Index

and organizational effectiveness. *See* Effectiveness, organizational

Revolutionary stages of organizational development (Grenier), 174–177

Role and norm congruence, and measurement of organizational effectiveness, 115

Role-set, and interorganizational relations, 147–148

Rule of mutual exclusiveness, 111, 116

Rural population, trends in, 9, 11, 13

Sales, 227–228

Satisfaction, and measurement of organizational effectiveness, 116

"Satisficing" criteria, in decision making, 87

Scalar chain of authority,
in current theory, 62
as principle developed by Fayol, 48
in Weber's theory, 49

Science, and technological advance, 16. *See also* Technology

Scientific management, 45–52

Secondary sources, in study of organizations, 35–36

Self-designing organization, 318–319

Self-employment, trend away from, 6–8

Self-evaluating organization, 318

Self-interest,
of constituent groups in organization, 118–119
personal, and organizational change, 295–296

Semantics, as factor in organizational communication, 271–272

Sensitivity training, 305

Service organizations, 234–235

Services, and organizational domain, 128, 129

Shared power, 303, 304, 306–307

Shareholders, 83, 84, 85

Side payments, in bargaining over organizational goals, 84–85

Similarity, perceived, and organizational communication, 267

Simplicity-complexity,
of organizational design, 183, 184
of organizational environment, 132–135
of technology, 221, 222n

Size, organizational,
and administrative intensity, 189–198, 202–207
and communication, 270
and complexity, 181–189
and managerial effectiveness, 174–175
and structure, 181–198, 231, 232

Small batch production, 219–220, 223–229, 231

Small organizations, 1, 231. *See also* Size, organizational

Smoothing, and environmental uncertainty, 146, 159

Social change, and technological advance, 15

Social systems, organizations as, 4–5, 105, 127, 138, 214, 293

Social values, and organization research, 316–317

Societal goals of organizations, 81, 82

Society, stage of development of, and organizational environment, 129–130

Sociological factors, as element of organizational environment, 131

Span of control,
in current theory, 64–66
as principle developed by Fayol, 47
and technological complexity, 223, 231, 235

Spatial dispersion. *See also* Area departmentalization
as factor in communication, 270–271
as indication of organizational complexity, 171, 187

Specialization. *See also* Departmentalization; Division of labor
of employees in mechanistic organizational system, 135–137
and horizontal communication, 262
and organizational size, 186
and stage of organizational development, 171, 172

Stability,
and measurement of organizational effectiveness, 115
as motive for organizational growth, 168

Stability-instability,
and differing managerial systems, 135
and organizational design, 137–144
of organizational environment, 132–135
of technology, 222n

Staff personnel, 66–67, 178, 196. *See also* Administrative personnel
and diagonal communication, 263–264

Stages of organizational development, 118, 169–181

Static environment. *See* Stability-instability

Statistical analysis. *See* Quantification

Status, and organizational communication, 267–268, 277

Stockholders, and organizational goals, 83, 84, 85

Stockpiling, and buffering strategy, 146

Strain, absence of, and measurement of organizational effectiveness, 116
Strategic choices (of managers), 114–145, 158. *See also* Decision making
Structure of organizations. *See* Design, organizational
Subenvironments of organization, and organizational design, 138–139
Subjectivity, of topic, and accuracy of communication, 260. *See also* Bias
Success, business, and technological complexity, 223, 226, 227, 229
Sunk costs, and resistance to change, 296
Superior-subordinate communication. *See* Vertical communication
Supervision, first-line, span of control in, 223, 225
Supervisory personnel. *See* Administrative personnel
Support,
  as factor of organizational effectiveness, 107, 108
  and organizational change, 298, 300
Survival,
  and measurement of organizational effectiveness, 116
  of organizations in future, 318–319
System goals of organization, 81, 82
System of production, as means of classifying organizations, 219–220
System resource model of organizational effectiveness, 105, 109–111

Target system, and organizational change, 299, 301
Task, as element in organizational change, 302–303
Task environment, 128, 129, 132, 178
Task scope, and departmentalization, 188
Technical diffuseness-specificity, as basis of typology of technology, 221
Technological imperative, 214
Technological interdependence, 216–219
Technology,
  core, 145–146, 196, 215, 216
  definition of, 211–212
  effects of, 212, 214
  evolution of, 213
  as factor in communication, 271–277
  as factor in organizational change, 302–303
  as factor in organizational environment, 131, 137–139, 145
  and growth of organizations, 13, 15–16, 44
  intensive, 218–219
  long-linked, 216, 217, 218, 219
  mediating, 216–217, 218

and organizational design, 188, 193, 196, 214–236, 240–252
typologies of, 215–221
Tennessee Valley Authority (TVA), 35, 51, 152
Theory of organizational choice. *See* Decision making
Theory of organizations. *See* Organization theory
Time, as factor in measurement of organizational attributes. *See* Longitudinal measurement
Townsend Organization, 95, 99
Trade-offs, in minimizing environmental uncertainty, 155–156
Training and development, and measurement of organizational effectiveness, 115, 116
Trust,
  as factor in upward flow of communication, 261, 265–266
  lack of, and resistance to change, 296–297
Turbulence. *See* Environmental turbulence; Stability-instability
Turnover, employee,
  and information overload, 276
  and measurement of organizational effectiveness, 114, 116

Uncertainty, environmental,
  means of minimizing, 145–159, 218
  and organizational design, 34–35, 137–142, 198
  as perceived by managers, 29–31, 133–135, 143–145
Uniformity-nonuniformity, as dimension of technology, 221
Unilateral power, 303, 304, 306
Unions, labor,
  and bargaining with management, 151–152
  as large organizations, 9
Unit production, 219–220, 223–229, 231
Unity of command,
  in current theory, 62, 64
  as principle developed by Fayol, 47
Univariate effectiveness models, 112–115
Universality of criteria, and measurement of organizational effectiveness, 120
Unrationalized categorization of variables, 233–234
Upward flow of communication, 256, 258–261
Urban population, increase in, 9, 11, 13, 15
Utility, in classical economic theory, 86–88